COMHAIRLE CHONTAE ÁTHA CLIATH THEAS
SOUTH DUBLIN COUNTY LIBRARIES

SOUTH DUBLIN BOOKSTORE
TO RENEW ANY ITEM TEL: 459 7834

Items should be returned on or before the last date below. Fines, as displayed in the Library, will be charged on overdue items.

D1437128

With Great Truth and Respect

The author and his wife with Mrs Indira Gandhi
on their departure from India, 1965

PAUL GORE–BOOTH

With Great Truth and Respect

CONSTABLE

LONDON

First published in Great Britain 1974
by Constable and Company Limited
10 Orange Street London WC2H 7EG
Copyright © 1974 by Paul Gore-Booth

ISBN 0 09 459150 4

Set in Monotype Bembo
Printed in Great Britain by
The Anchor Press Ltd, and bound by
Wm. Brendon & Son Ltd, both of Tiptree, Essex

TO
PATRICIA MARY

Contents

Illustrations

Author's Note

When the Secretary of State writes a formal despatch to an Ambassador abroad, he uses at the end the phrase 'with great truth and respect'. The language may seem archaic, but it goes to the root of diplomacy. A soundly conducted diplomacy demands truth in observation and comment, and mutual respect between the Secretary of State and those who serve him. That is why I have chosen *With Great Truth and Respect* as the title of this book.

G-B.

Preface

Even since the days when, in the hands of George Bernard Shaw, the Preface as an institution bloomed, and in the opinion of some became overblown, the custom has gone the other way. Often there will be a dedication, followed by a few acknowledgements, and the reader is then plunged in at the deep end.

Since this is a book about the life of a diplomat and the conduct of diplomacy, I thought that the reader might welcome a little more help. Diplomacy is not necessarily a mysterious process. It is thought to be so because matters of great importance have, for reasons of discretion, practicality and mutual confidence, to be discussed in private by unknown people, and while this is happening Foreign Offices and Embassies present a surface which may look anything from defensive to vacuous. In fact, behind this surface, a lot of ordinary but varied human beings are trying to make international relations work.

I have found it helpful to keep in mind the classic distinction between diplomacy and foreign policy. Foreign policy is what you do; diplomacy is how you do it. Of course the two get mixed up especially when a diplomat is advising on policy or a member of the Government normally engaged in policy decision takes over a diplomatic operation which seems to merit top level or summit discussion. But generally speaking the task of a government is to decide and the task of a diplomat at any level is to try to make the decisions work.

This book can be called, traditionally, a memoir or an auto-biography. But it could also be called, in the modern style, diplomacy by case history. It tells how one person arrived in diplomacy and how he fared over thirty-five years of it. Each such case history is unique and cannot be repeated. But I have ventured some generalizations as I go, and I hope these may help to dispel mystery and to explain why and how things were done and whether they were done well or badly.

Such explanations can be given in textbook form, and this should be attempted from time to time. But I just do not feel able to compete in economy and readability with the late Harold Nicolson's delightful and ever-young *Diplomacy*, written in 1939 and still indispensable reading. Therefore I have tried to write down what happened to me over the years and what it felt like. In this way the ups and downs of diplomatic life can perhaps be brought into a more understandable relationship with the experiences of others.

My main tools have been memory and thought. I have never kept a diary. Being, as the reader will infer, a combination of the industrious and the gregarious, I have always felt too tired by midnight to sit down and talk to myself about the events of the day. In any case, thank goodness, I have had since 1940 a wife to talk and listen to about them. And by next morning the idea of recording yesterday's events has become too cold-blooded. There were other things to do. This is no doubt frailty, but it was soothingly rationalized for me one day by an esteemed Civil Service colleague who said rather fiercely, 'Quite right; you start by running the diary and it ends by running you.' I will settle for that.

Naturally I have, with much help, checked up conscientiously on facts and figures. This very process of checking up has shown that the selectiveness of memory is not a bad sorting machine. What one remembers as important does not vary greatly from what, in looking back, turns out to have been important in fact.

I wrote this book because I wanted to. But I think there is a deeper aspect to this. Everyone has a past. And if that past has been varied and eventful, it can try to encroach on the present and interfere with the future. One should not, and indeed cannot, exorcize it; but one can at least write it down and thus seek to keep it in its place. If, in writing it down, one can share pleasure and interest with others, the impulse and the effort will have been worth while.

Moreover, to remember and record what one can of experiences and feelings makes a small contribution to history. When a historian has assembled all the letters and other reports that exist about a particular event or period he will still lack something – the things that people thought and felt and did not write down. There are many of these, floating round for a limited time and then dissolving in forgotten mist. If anyone can capture a few of these private feelings or collective moods, they add just a little that can be accepted with all caution into the corpus of historical knowledge.*

So one day in August 1970 on a terrace above the small town of Cavareno in the Dolomites, an orchard in front, the campanile below with red roofs nestling around it, and the green rolling valley and the blue mountains beyond, I began. I had wondered whether, if I wrote autobiographically, it should be in the ambassadorial-historical narrative style – 'His Excellency kindly lent me his steam-yacht' – or in the introspective-sociological manner – 'The foreign policy of a country is a projected reflex of its currently prevailing ethos.' It seemed best to let the book decide, and it did.

Taking out something of an insurance policy, I must make it clear that this is not a 'History of our Times'. It cannot be, since for the greater part of an official lifetime, a member of the Diplomatic Service is engaged on particular and concentrated work. For instance, when in 1948 I was concentrating on the execution of British Marshall Plan policy, I could pay no more attention than any radio listener and newspaper reader to details of the collapse of the Nationalists in China. I have, however, sought to put in a few landmarks to show what was happening on a world scale when my own work was specialized.

There is a particular difficulty about people. The writer of a classical novel has the privilege of economizing the number of his or her characters and dealing with their experiences and feelings in depth as they move round a limited chessboard. A diplomatic lifetime has no such tidiness. People make their exits and their

* This thought had been with me vaguely for some years when it suddenly crystallized in this form, thanks to a talk with Professor Bernard Lewis of London University at, I am glad to record, a diplomatic party.

entrances with great variety and no symmetry. In fictional terms we move not in the world of Miss Elizabeth Bennet and Mr Darcy, but of Mr Pickwick, perhaps, and Dr Zhivago. So I owe one immense apology to the many people who have meant a great deal to both of us and for whom there is simply no room on this stage except as anonymous members of a most admired and distinguished chorus.

Finally there is the language. Diplomatic English is mainly good English. It is clear and coherent – it has to be – and most writers of dispatches achieve a good flowing style. But diplomats speak with the voice of government and responsibility and, since their crystal balls are fallible, they have to be careful about absolute statements. Therefore diplomatic English is full of very proper phrases like 'on the whole', 'by and large' and 'other things being equal'. For the general reader these sacred phrases would be intolerable. The battle against them has been long and unrelenting. I hope that, if it has not been won, it may at least have been drawn.

Acknowledgements

Many people expressed to me, both before and after retirement, the hope that I would 'write something'. I am grateful for their encouragement and hope that the general reaction will not be 'This is not at all what I meant.'

For help in making the undertaking possible, I should like to thank first of all my successor, Sir Denis Greenhill, under whose authority I have been able to check up facts. I have had particular help from the Foreign and Commonwealth Library staff under the direction of Mr Bernard Cheesman, the Librarian; I owe special thanks to Mr R. R. Mellor at Cornwall House and those who work with him. I should also mention Mr Clifton Child, who as Librarian of the Foreign Office before the merger between the Commonwealth and Foreign Offices consistently encouraged me to attempt this enterprise.

Among those who have looked at parts of the texts are Sir John Wheeler-Bennett (pre-war Germany), the Earl of Bradford (Austria), Sir Percival Griffiths (India) and Professor Sir Isaiah Berlin. I am most indebted to them all and do not hold any of them responsible for any errors or misjudgements. There has been no absence of criticism inside the family and this has been a stimulating corrective throughout.

I have also enjoyed splendid help on the actual job especially from my secretary, Dr Harriet Harvey-Wood. Mrs Wendy Campbell and Mrs Henrietta Gatehouse have done endless typing, and Miss Sue Humphrys and Miss Jenny de Gex did what can only be called crash research on the more tedious published items so essential for accuracy. I am also indebted to Mrs Edward Norman Butler who on several occasions gave us the freedom of her cottage in Berkshire so that work could proceed without interruption, and to Lady Normanbrook who lent me her late husband's study for a time for the same purpose. My best thanks are due to all of them.

Boyhood and School

1909-1928

Doncaster

I was born at Doncaster, Yorkshire, on 3 February 1909. My father, Mordaunt Gore-Booth, was the younger son of Sir Henry and Lady Gore-Booth of Lissadell, Sligo, Ireland. The Gore ancestry is easily traceable back to Alderman Gerard Gore of the City of London who, in the 1580s, settled in Dublin. The Gores multiplied in Ireland in the seventeenth century and, when the present Earl of Arran inherited the title, he was able to ring me up and say 'Please understand that I am now the head of your family.' This reassurance was of course welcome; it has not had any noticeable practical effect but it shows, as do other variations on the Gore theme, that the family spread itself against an Irish background.

My own part of the family at an early stage moved to County Sligo where they set a tradition of burning down the family home regularly once a century. My uncle Josslyn broke the tradition in the 1920s by turning the fire extinguisher on some blazing mattresses just in time. It is noteworthy that the Irish never had any part in these burnings, for the family, while remaining Protestant, were good neighbours with the Catholic community. My great-grandfather financed an emigrant ship in the 1848 famine and it was never held against him that it sank in a storm outside Sligo Bay.

The Booth half of the family moved to Dublin from Lancashire in the seventeenth century and established themselves there in the legal profession, Sir Robert Booth becoming Chief Justice (in Ireland). Lettice Booth, the heiress of the Booth family, married Nathaniel Gore of Ardtarman, County Sligo, in 1711, bringing her name into the family. It took some generations to decide whether the Booth or the Gore should come first.

My great-grandfather, Sir Robert Gore-Booth, went on the Victorian Grand Tour and strained the family fortunes by buying mediocre Italian pictures at high prices. My grandfather, Sir Henry, married in 1867 Miss Georgina Hill from Tickhill, Yorkshire. She must in her youth have been incredibly beautiful and lively. Even as an old lady she was unforgettable. As an eagerly awaited guest once a year in Yorkshire, she performed exactly as a stage grandmother should. She would sit in an arm-chair, ensconced in the *Daily Mail*, and if my father dared to pontificate, she would interject with 'Stupid!' 'Bumptious!' 'Important!' or 'the *Daily Mail* says . . .'

Sir Henry was also an original. Besides being a rough sportsman in the Irish tradition, he was a very keen explorer and made several expeditions to the Arctic Circle. It was said that when things got too lively at Lissadell, 'the Dom' went off to the Arctic, taking his butler, Kilgallen, with him. It was not surprising that Sir Henry and his wife produced two geniuses, Constance Markievicz and Eva Gore-Booth. Constance, a great beauty in search of a cause, found it in Irish Nationalism and earned herself a permanent place among the heroes and heroines of Irish history. Eva, quiet and visionary but no less radical, settled in Manchester, devoting her life partly to social work but even more to poetry, religion and philosophy, much of it against a background of Irish legend. She is probably best remembered for that small Irish jewel of a classic, 'The Little Waves of Breffny'. But I would hope that, if a taste comes round again for the deeper meanings of Ireland, her many other works will earn the understanding and appreciation they deserve.

My father, much the youngest of this family, had mixed feelings about his background. He loved the informal, outdoor, sailing, fishing and rough shooting life of western Ireland and the company of Irish people. But he had a more methodical, business-like strain to him and a strong feeling of British patriotism. He was sent to school at Marlborough which he liked, and Balliol College, Oxford, which he enjoyed hugely. Like an orthodox younger son of the times he tried first for the navy and then for the army; both rejected him on physical grounds. Eventually through a friend he was introduced to Vickers-Maxim in Sheffield. In 1904, as near as I can tell, he started work in the engineering drawing office at the River Don works, Brightside.

Yorkshire was the home of my mother's family, the Scholfields. Originally from Lancashire, they came to Yorkshire as farmers in the eighteenth century and settled at Sandhall near Howden in the East Riding. If you were to take a boat down the Yorkshire Ouse from York past Boothferry, under the big swing-bridge carrying the main line from Doncaster to Hull, the fertile land on your left opposite Goole Harbour would be the Scholfield estate. Surrounded on three sides by the Ouse, Sandhall is rather isolated, and happiness there depended on a good family life.

This, fortunately, my mother's generation had. My grandfather, Robert Stanley Scholfield, had married my second beautiful grandmother, Ada Elizabeth Paget. She was closely connected with the Beckett family, a member of which, Sir Edmund, was the founder of Beckett's Bank in Doncaster. (Banking, as is well known, being a purely sentimental business, I kept my current account there until 1966.) I have an enlarged photograph of Sir Edmund: he looks as tough – and trustworthy – as the most eminent of Victorians.

My mother, the second child and older daughter, had the kind of private upbringing which was the only one possible for a girl at that time in those surroundings. She had good teachers for the piano and violin, and Mademoiselle and Fraülein came in turn from France and Germany. So you could never fault her over a French or German irregular verb, and her French accent provoked from a puzzled waiter in Antwerp the enquiry '*Madame vient du sud?*' She played the piano excellently but, alas, never played the violin again after marriage as my father hated the noise.

My mother had four brothers, three of whom fought in World War I and by some miracle survived. The two middle brothers, Alwyn and Ralph, have meant a great deal in my life. Ralph was from 1935–38 First Reader of the Mother Church of the Christian Science movement in Boston and has always been a most valued adviser and friend. Alwyn, who kept the

National Records of India in Calcutta from 1911–18 and then, after a short period as Librarian at Trinity College, Cambridge, was Cambridge University Librarian from 1922–47, was a constant companion and benefactor of the family. He intervened in my life in a dramatic way at a decisive moment. Had he not done so, lots of things would not have happened and this book would not have been written.

We now have to bring my father from Sheffield to Sandhall, a distance of a mere forty-six miles. He was a very early motorist and with another pioneer and mutual friend, F. J. Dundas, used to visit Sandhall, where he met and became engaged to Evelyn Mary Scholfield. They were married at St James's, Piccadilly, on 31 January 1906, spent a miserable honeymoon in snow and illness in Kent and thereafter lived to celebrate their golden wedding.

Both my parents had to give up things, particularly my mother who, for all my father's formal education, had the more substantial intellectual background. My father, for his part, made concessions to some almost Puritan ideas from the Scholfields' background. But the two of them lived together until my father's death in 1958 as the most perfect companions, finding extraordinary sufficiency in each other's presence. Their mutual bonds included common high standards of conduct and integrity, and a quick sympathy between my father's sense of fun and my mother's rather sharper sense of humour.

I must allow one more member of an older generation to make a curtsey. I am proud to say that I had a great-great-aunt Augusta. She was Mrs Beckett-Dennison, a formidable lady who lived just down the road towards the Doncaster racecourse and invited children to play in the shrubbery. She also took regular carriage exercise. On one such occasion she came to something very novel at that time, a road being tarred. Observing the empty tar barrels, she turned to a companion and said, 'Deah, what a lot of beer those men drink.'

My first memory is not of Doncaster but a vivid picture of a nursery party at Lissadell which we visited in, I think, 1912. The next one is a picture of my baby sister, born in 1911. I have a distinct memory of her fiddling with a preposterously ostentatious button on a small boy's suit.   She died a few months later. My parents were disconsolate and since no other sisters arrived, I grew up in colossal ignorance of the ways of the other sex. But it was a great joy to everybody when my brother Colum was born in June 1913.

A more coherent early recollection is of a military parade outside our house in Hall Gate signalling the outbreak of the First World War. I asked Carrie, the nursemaid, what a war was. She replied, 'It's when two armies meet.' I thought this must be very polite and glamorous. Later I became intensely interested in the whole performance, and acquired a stereotyped view of the French, the Germans and the Belgians, and a vast curiosity about the Russians who wore rather jaunty-looking military caps, advanced and retreated in great sweeps and were forever trying to take a fort with the impossible name of Przemysl.

Maltby

My uncle Edward Scholfield, my mother's elder brother, owned a small property eight miles west of Doncaster, on which stood a fair-sized house called Maltby Hall. It was larger than 37 Hall Gate, was bordered by country on two sides and offered my father a much less tiresome daily journey to Sheffield. So we moved the eight miles, through the colliery village of Edlington and the ancient hamlet of Braithwell, to the ridge overlooking the church and old village of Maltby.

The move was a great success. We stayed at Maltby until 1926, and I think those eleven years were the most contented of my father's life. He had become the manager of the (steel) tyre mill at Vickers. The work was responsible, practical and congenial.

Family life worked by the clock. At 8.40 each day the old Raleigh car (succeeded by a ten-horsepower Wolseley two-seater) passed by the door on its way to Sheffield. At 5.20 the same noise announced my father's return. His office was in a tall room with large windows looking across a works railtrack to the 'shop'. My father stepped across more than once a day, with a careful glance in each direction for the shunting engine, to have a look round, chat with those on the job and help with small practical problems. The shop was old, as were the machines for stamping and pressing. Every tyre on process was wheeled round lovingly on a 'barrer' by highly skilled Toms and Bills and a special character called 'Mr 'ookey'. My father boasted that he never had industrial trouble. I cannot prove this. But when the time came to go, the men in the shop clubbed together and bought him a resplendent leather suitcase, explaining 'It's a reaight 'un; it were t'best i' t'shop.'

My mother was also content at Maltby because my father was content, and she liked the country. But there were times of loneliness when the garden, the children (who had a 'nana') and the rather sparse company were insufficient. There was some voluntary activity; she became Assistant Commissioner of Girl Guides and worked in a baby clinic with Maltby wives. But there was a friendly gulf between people and People and even People were busy with country pursuits or voluntary work. As she learned to drive a twin Wolseley 10 and as the two children began to make more sense and my school friends began to come and stay in the holidays, this period passed.

Meantime, amid intervals of wartime cooking, which my mother did admirably and hated violently, a decision was taken about education. My father took me down south in the spring of 1918 to put me in a preparatory school in Surrey.

Life with its Sunday Eton collars and its overpowering emphasis on formal religion was terribly intimidating after Maltby. In my second term I was in a form instructed by a ferocious clergyman whose chief weapon of discipline was a sharp cuff on the ear. The boys naturally detested this. One day we read in elementary Latin a fable about a tyrant who was carried off by a wild beast, and in a ghastly moment I heard a voice saying 'I wish it had been you, sir.' It was my voice and since until then I had been desperately 'good' and rather priggish, I simply could not believe my ears. They soon received several cuffs.

Later I became seriously ill in the 1918–19 influenza epidemic, and my mother arrived with butter and other rarities from

Sandhall. Seeing a small boy walking with bare feet in a stone passage, she mentioned to authority that this might not be a good thing. To her astonishment authority replied to the effect that if she wanted to take her son away, she could. So she did.

The next preparatory school was St Michael's, Uckfield. It was a complete contrast. Instead of being enclosed and suburban, it was on high ground with a wind blowing and a splendid view of Chanctonbury Ring. The headmaster was the Reverend H. H. H. Hockey, who in addition to being a pretty unorthodox clergyman, was a fine cricketer and a gifted amateur actor with a genius for evoking effort and loyalty from small boys. The vogue in those days being for adventure stories, larger boys called him 'Baas'. After a fine rendering of 'Tit Willow' in *The Mikado* at the Tunbridge Wells Theatre, they presented him with a new cricket bat.

I have a happy and grateful recollection of St Michael's where I enjoyed everything except the gymnasium. But even there there was a kindly touch; the gym master put in my report at the end of each term the dogged comment, 'Is improved'. There was no other direction in which to go.

The school was actively Christian in outlook and instruction, and, for reasons connected with its history, the versatile Mr Hockey had arranged that boys could attend Anglican or Christian Science religious services. My father disinterested himself in the choice but my mother, having become interested in Christian Science through other members of her family, arranged for me to join this group. When, nearly fifty years later, I retired from my profession, people referred in farewell speeches to the 'faith' which they felt had sustained me throughout. The faith was indeed Christian Science. The discoverer and founder of this world-wide religion, Mary Baker Eddy, wrote 'Hold thought steadfastly to the enduring, the good and the true, and you will bring these into your experience proportionably to their occupancy of your thoughts.'[1] This profound but practical religion, based firmly on the Christian Bible, has been an unfailing source of protection and inspiration. It has provided the mental and

[1] Mary Baker Eddy, *Science and Health and the Key to the Scriptures*, p. 261.

physical health needed for all the moods of human life from endurance to enjoyment, and I cannot exaggerate my debt to it.

The prime question at St Michael's soon became 'What next?' My father had a loyalty towards Marlborough, whose reputation was and is so consistently high. But the Scholfields were heavily Eton-orientated, and it was decided that, as I was easily top of the school in things other than mathematics, I should try for an Eton scholarship. I have never discovered whether there was a fall-back position, should this complete shot in the dark have failed.

The assault on Eton seemed enormously daunting. The buildings looked immense compared with St Michael's; there were over eleven hundred boys; there was the great prestige of a place encrusted in nearly five hundred years of history. Besides which there were a large number of candidates and rumour had it that several preparatory schools had infallible methods of guessing the answers in advance. I was further shaken at my viva voce exam when Dr Cyril Alington, the headmaster, a handsome and formidable-looking man, fixed me with a piercing look and said 'Where is Jugoslavia and why is it called Jugoslavia?' Fortunately I knew where it was, and I supposed that Slavs lived there. I later discovered that the piercing glance had a good deal of fun behind it.

It was all right. There were eleven places going and I was tenth. St Michael's had a holiday with fireworks and we could all relax. When I eventually competed with the other ten at Eton, I astonished them and myself by coming out second, a place I never lost. But I never got near catching that cheerful, hard-working all-rounder, Robert Willis. As I retired from service, he was Number Two in the Inland Revenue. I think he is still a code number or two ahead.

Eton

Soon after I had acquired the rhythm of things, it became pretty clear to me that I was an all-rounder rather than a scholar. I could do passably well in the staple subjects such as Latin, Greek, French, elementary science and elementary mathematics, and even better in the whole lot thrown together and averaged out in competition. But there was one subject which stood out – history.

It all began at St Michael's, where there was a history master called Leslie Carpenter. He was, I suspect, a difficult man. He had been gassed in the First World War and was sensitive and quick-tempered. But he taught elementary history superbly. He organized British history so that never again could you confound the Grand Remonstrance with the Constitution of Clarendon or mistake Richard II for Richard III. So I came to Eton with the scaffolding of British history. Would someone appear who could build the spirit into history as a whole?

The occasion produced the man. Robert Birley became my history tutor as soon as I had passed the School Certificate in 1925, and the period chosen was the Middle Ages. In company with Robert, I attended the crowning of Charlemagne at Aix, I walked to Canossa with the Emperor Henry IV, I marched with the early Crusaders in formation out of Antioch, I thundered imperially into Italy with Frederick Barbarossa, listened in on the papal thunder of Innocent III and cheered at the glamorous ingenuities of Fredericus Secundus, Stupor Mundi. And when in 1250 Conradin died, and the curtain came down on it all, we just stopped. One cannot live all the time at this grand level. But without Robert Birley I could never have thought of human events on this scale at all. It was my first essay in thinking big.

Birley also filled the odd hours, in which you studied what you liked or what your tutor suggested, with reading Jacobean dramas, notably *The White Devil* and *The Duchess of Malfi*. We explored Chekhov and indeed anything within the hours available that could stimulate the mind and spirit to something beyond just learning.

There were many others to whom I am beholden. A. S. F. Gow, my earlier classical tutor, an austere scholar with a *cassant* sense of humour, taught me the principle that things must not be just right but absolutely right. He did not like people translating the Latin word *pedites* (meaning footsoldiers) as 'footmen', so people did it again and again. Kenneth Wickham, a quiet, kindly master, taught four of us Italian in the language hours. (I avoided

the masters teaching German who had a reputation for ferocity.)
We read pages of *L'Incomparabile Jeeves di P. G. Wodehouse* – what
better introduction to day-to-day speech? And one very special
personality was H. K. Marsden, my housemaster (in Eton language
the Master in College, who looked after the Scholars). A bachelor
of immense height, no diameter and a bushy moustache, he was
the epitome of the rough customer with eventually a kind heart –
eventually, because he had no use for small boys at all. In 1927 I
was favourite for the top History Prize and as such was not looking
forward at all to one of those slow torture 'reading overs', where
the examiner starts with 'A. Moron, two marks out of two hundred'
and gradually ascends the scale with lengthening commentary.
Marsden got his advance information, dashed into the hall,
hissed into my ear 'It's all right' and disappeared. This ranks
very high on my roster of kindly acts.

Life at Eton was, indeed, full of variety. I wanted to be good
at cricket, failed and turned out to my surprise to be good at
football and rugger instead, playing both of them for the school.
I became, through extreme dearth of local military talent, a
cadet officer in the Officers' Training Corps and, through a
certain amount of diligence in searching for elusive speakers,
President of the Political Society. When I appeared at the Society's
Jubilee dinner, the politicians commented unbelievingly '*Et
tu, Brute*'.

The difficulty about an institution like Eton in these days is
that so much of the literature about it has been written either by
misfits or adorers, so that it has been difficult to come by balanced
information or impartial judgement. Eton was in my time and,
as far as I know, remains a pre-university rather than a school in
its way of life. Its special nature derived from the possession by
every boy of an individual room, be it never so scruffy, and
from the greater amount of unorganized time available, particularly in senior years, than in other independent schools.

The school was also remarkable in those times for the degree of
delegation of authority from headmaster to housemasters and
housemasters to senior boys. With a competent housemaster,
assisted by a fair-minded group of boys, this was an ideal training

for responsibility; with an incompetent housemaster and an ill-disciplined group of senior boys, it was *corruptio optimi pessima* in a big way. In general boys of personality, especially if they were athletically prominent, held an outstanding position; strong-minded eccentrics also came out remarkably well. The people who had a poor time were those who wanted to be different but had not developed the strength of personality to enable them to hold their own. The seventy Scholars, living in their own community, worked very hard indeed. As for the rest, this depended largely on the house of which you were a member; you could work hard, but, unlike in these days, you could get by on very little exertion. The whole process was one in which a miscellaneous élite put itself through a genuine levelling process within its own ranks.

The result was a breed of people who made their way in the society of the time by what one can only call an ability to cope. Now society has changed, but Eton has always been a highly political community and the Eton microcosm adapts itself to change, sometimes faster than Eton authority. Adaptation is all the more needed because any surviving privilege (and there is precious little of it) is now outweighed by a widespread social prejudice against Etonians.

Should such a place be 'allowed' to survive? The question arouses all my libertarian instincts. I think that in these days, when purchasing power is infinitely more widespread than it was, an Eton or independent school education should be regarded as a priority like any other, to be weighed against holidays in Spain or a profusion of colour television sets. A place like Eton has both a tradition and a momentum, and if parents, with the consent of the young, put this priority ahead of others, then I do not think they should be prevented from doing so. I am pre-judiced because I enjoyed myself there very much indeed and hated the moment of leaving.

Oxford and Germany
1928-1933

If there had been grave discussions about whether I should go to Eton or elsewhere, there was never any question about the university. My father retained a passionate loyalty to Balliol and no one wished to contest it. But before the time came for me to compete, there was something of a cataclysm in our family life.

Until about 1924 nothing happened to disturb the pleasant routine at Maltby. But the tyre mill was reaching the term of its natural life. There was nowhere in Vickers for my father to go and the firm was in any case undergoing a direction and management crisis. So in 1926 the hard decision was taken to move south. My parents much preferred the north and the country, but they undoubtedly felt that in the south they could be more helpful to my brother and myself, and the blow was softened by an invitation to my father to join a city firm as an industrial adviser.

So, after much searching in outer and inner suburbs, my parents took a four-storey house in Victoria Road, Kensington, an attractive street with individual houses of lighter architecture than Kensington classical. No tennis court, such as I had been able to rig up at Maltby, and no garden as we had understood it. But it was a pleasant house with evening sun shimmering through a birch tree at the gate, and it remained home until in 1941 a landmine made it uninhabitable.

Before we left for London, I did something which helped to preserve a memory of Yorkshire. I was competing for a prize on the Simon Report on the coal industry and wanted to inspect a coal mine. The industry was passing through the economic crisis that led to the 1926 General Strike, and when my father rang up a colliery agent to ask if I could go down a mine, he replied wearily, 'Oh no, not another one.' My father reassured him that a day (unpaid) would do. I went down Rotherham Main. There were rails along the main galleries, but in the side galleries one crouched and bumped one's head. At the end a tall man would be hewing the coal face. He would stand up, wipe his brow, say with a memorable warmth, 'Pleased to meet yer,' and return to his hewing. I won the prize. My competitors had not been down Rotherham Main.

So it was from Victoria Road that I parted from Eton and competed for Balliol. In 1926 I did a trial run (Basil Ava[1] won the top scholarship); in 1927 I competed again and won an open scholarship.

There followed months of relaxation. A kind of leisure half at Eton was followed by a walking tour the length of the Pyrenees with Ranald MacDonald,[2] and the beginnings of German with the family of Baron and Baroness Henikstein in Salzburg. The Baron was a quietly sardonic descendant of an Austrian general who had done as badly as anyone else at the disastrous battle of Sadowa against the Prussians. The Baroness, an Austrian O'Donnell, remained a fanatical Irish Nationalist. In the summer I began my musical education in earnest when my mother joined me in Munich and we saw within a fortnight seven Wagner operas, two Mozart operas and, in between, operettas by Emmerich Kalman and Franz Lehar.

Oxford

The British, as I still keep on discovering, are not naturally gifted at briefing each other. I had visited Balliol with my father but had no idea what Oxford was going to be like, and passed some muddled early days getting people and things sorted out. Who were going to be my friends? Not necessarily the chap

---

[1] Fourth Marquess of Dufferin and Ava, Parliamentary Under-Secretary for colonies, 1937–40, director of the Empire Division, Ministry of Information, 1941–42, killed in action near Ava in Burma in 1945.

[2] Ranald MacDonald subsequently entered the Indian Civil Service and served with distinction on the Lushai Hills during the Japanese invasion.

B

I met because he was next on the alphabetical list or shared tutorials with me. Or what did I do when a pleasantly beefy young man came in and said, 'You're just the sort we'd like to see rowing for the College.' (I opted for Rugby Union.)

More importantly, what degree should I do? My family and I had somehow reached a consensus that I should not seek to know more and more about a particular historical period, but should tackle a course involving philosophy and ancient history. Greats enjoyed considerable prestige and it was possible to take the course in three years rather than four by a short cut avoiding a very tough examination in the higher classics.

There was a powerful counter-attack. Cyril Bailey, the senior classics tutor, sent for me and with authoritative persuasiveness told me what riches I would be missing if I took the short cut. These days, no doubt, someone in my position would at that point have said something rude. In those times, at nineteen, one was not so sure of oneself. But I stuck to my guns and won. By this I gained a year which was to be most useful. It was also good experience in standing up to honest persuasion to do the wrong thing.

So I spent three years on philosophy from Plato to F. H. Bradley, via Descartes, Locke, Berkeley, Hume and Kant, in the pursuit of What Really Is, do Reason and Perception co-operate or contradict, and what, if anything, are Good and Right or Bad and Wrong?

I got tired of hair-splitting about good and bad; what I was really concluding, though I did not know it, was that I would not find a satisfactory ethic unless it were backed by a convincing religion. Lectures were disappointing except for a stately progress round Infinity with Professor Joachim of New College. If you missed so much as a single sub-argument, you had lost the Professor and it was difficult to recapture him. For tutorials, I had an immensely enjoyable time with two lifelong friends, Charles Morris and John Fulton. The difficulty was that they both employed the Socratic method, 'Why do you think so?', 'Is that so in all cases or only in some cases?' Eventually a term with a visiting American professor taught me the rules. He said 'Descartes was right because . . . but he was wrong because . . . '. Then I too began to play to the rules. I would never have become a professional philosopher but, unconsciously, I was at least learning how human reason works – that if you assume this, you can't legitimately deduce that, and I found the metaphysics, the tantalizing pursuit of what really is, immensely exciting.

Other Activities

Tutorials produced memorable characters like my delightful Greek history tutor, Duncan Macgregor, with a perpetual Gold-Flake, a perpetual cough and a perpetual glass of sherry as medicine against the other two. And there was the Roman history tutor, C. G. Stone ('Topes'). He had two desks at diagonally opposite corners of his room, and used the 'Topes tangential' method of instruction which meant that when Caesar crossed the Rubicon, Topes dashed across the room from nor' nor' east to sou' sou' west and resumed on the other bank.

In some ways it was unmethodical and unsystematic. But for people who were really good it produced what they needed. When the time came, I withstood a viva examination for forty-five minutes between a first and second class degree, and the examiners opted for a second. Balliol grumbled kindly, but I think the examiners were right. I had not been a single-minded student – early diligence had been followed by a second year in which the scout on my staircase referred to me as 'a very social gentleman', and a third year of frenzied catching up. And I had sought enjoyment in many and varied activities. I made a bee-line for the Oxford Union, causing someone to laugh at my maiden speech at 11.20 p.m. On one occasion I went in to put myself down to speak and was welcomed with a kindly smile behind some very dark hair and moustaches; the name behind the smile was Michael Stewart whom I was to meet next in surprising circumstances thirty-five years later.

And on three occasions I found myself leading debates, one in partnership with Randolph Churchill and another against

A. W. Pethwick-Lawrence[3] on a tariff reform versus free trade issue. The Churchill debate was awkward: I consulted Randolph Churchill in his rooms in Christ Church, but he was interested in a current game of poker; I borrowed a Hansard and went off and did some homework. As a consequence I made a better speech than he did and felt embarrassed.

From the Union I learned several useful things. The first was not to be scared. One might not be better than anybody else, but there was no need to be worse. Secondly I realized that I could not make a speech adequate to Union standard of that time without two days of preparation. So in my degree year I signed off. But diplomacy having become oratorical in free countries, I have always been thankful that I made this two-year investment.

I spoke in the Union as a Conservative and I have often wondered what would have happened if life had not led me into an apolitical career. In the Conservative dilemmas of the 1930s, would I have got the answers right?

There was also drama, when for four summers I toured the South-west and South for a fortnight in Greek drama with the Balliol Players; and a little music – some lyrics for Lancelot Hankey at the smoking concerts of the Oxford University Dramatic Society. There was rugger, where we won the college cup ties twice, and tennis, in which I captained the Balliol six. Dick Usborne, then my doubles partner, tells me we used to think too much about ball games. I have asked him since what was the alternative – discussion of *les grandes vérités éternelles*? 'Or beer or sex,' he replied.

1931, when I earned my degree in Greats, was a year of economic crisis and therefore not a good one to throw oneself on a crowded employment market. So it was decided *en famille*, Balliol willing, that I should do a fourth year. The idea was to take a second degree in philosophy, politics and economics (P.P.E.). Philosophy would have to be taken as more or less read.

[3] A. W. Pethwick-Lawrence, Labour MP 1923–31, 1939–45. As Lord Pethwick-Lawrence, was Secretary of State for India and Burma in the Attlee government, 1945–47. Co-author of *Mahatma Gandhi*, 1949.

Politics would have to consist of my past historical knowledge plus some modern reading, and I would need a crash course in economics. In the tiny digs in Ship Street, three of us worked to a tough routine, relieved by Mrs Priestley's special cup of tea at '11 pm precise'. As economics tutor I had by great good fortune Maurice Allen, temporarily a member of Balliol Senior Common Room. Atmosphere in his room was created by the chess game that was invariably in progress. One asked, 'Supposing, in a period of variable demand, a grain-growing country is visited by three months of flood, followed by prolonged drought, what is likely to be the effect on the balance of payments?' Maurice would produce a lightning axis plus curve and say, 'Something like this, don't you think?' Confidence in yourself. It was ideal psychological teaching.

In September, the college telegraphed the result to me in Hanover, where I was studying German, 'Congratulations, second.' I had done well in economics, satisfactorily in politics, but again, Balliol and the examiners differed over my philosophy.

The result answered a question and answered it right. An Eton master, J. D. Hills, had offered me his flat, his domestic staff and his excellent historical library for six months if I would do his tutorial work while he took a sabbatical period in Australia. I was much tempted by this generous proposal, but saw myself sliding into schoolmastering which did not seem to be my vocation. So I declined and then wondered whether I had been right. The degree result convinced me that the future lay elsewhere than in the academic world.

Oxford had been of immense value. The 'sitting at the feet of' age had passed, but the Oxford mixture remained a stimulating one, and by blasting one out of any limitation of ideas which might have been imposed by family and boarding school, ensured awareness that the other side of the argument was not merely uneducated or perverse. Balliol produced enduring friendships and added an important Commonwealth dimension to them. There was for instance in my time at Balliol a pleasant, rather quiet Indian student called R. K. Mitra. When I passed through Calcutta in 1953, knowing that the State Home Secretary was called R. K. Mitra, I telephoned, 'Are you perhaps the R. K. Mitra who in 1930 or was it '31 . . .?' A lilting Indian voice replied, 'I do not at all remember the date but come at once for a talk.' Even by Bengali standards, it was a long talk.

Balliol also had a good tradition of welcoming people of character as well as those of brains. In the present highly certificated age, this policy may be difficult to sustain. But though scholastic results are essential, there are other ingredients in university life if your selection procedure is bright enough to spot them.

One of the occasional but special pleasures of life at Oxford was to go down to Eton to visit my brother Colum, especially when the visit meant tea with Colum's 'mess' in Mr Howson's house. This foursome included such entertaining company as Jo Grimond, Charles Mott-Radclyffe and William Douglas-Home.

Colum suffered, as we grew up at Maltby, from the disadvantage of being four and a half years younger than I was but having to play with me. In anything competitive I could always win, and, while I wasn't notably unsporting, I wasn't the kind that gallantly lost on purpose. Later Colum must have been harassed by thoughtless people who said, 'It's so nice that you've joined us; I do hope you'll do as well as your brother.' The unintended sting of that remark was that Colum's aptitudes and talents developed quite differently from and much later than mine. He was not good at games, and he was, to say the least of it, intermittent about study. But, in the true Irish manner, he handled gun and fishing-rod as though he had been born carrying them and for art he had a quite exceptional talent.

We were a classic example of the parental dilemma when there is a real choice about education. Common sense might indicate that, to avoid the difficulties my brother had, a younger brother or sister should quite firmly go to a different school. This is too facile. If the second choice works badly, there will be the lifelong reproach, 'Why wasn't I given the same chance as my brother (or sister)?' There is no set answer to this, and we ourselves had exactly the same problem with our children.

The other thing Colum had was an unlimited personal charm,

again an Irish gift. In some ways this was a great help, but it brought with it some of the drawbacks of an easy-going nature. After school he went up to Balliol, but he made so many friends, male and female, and did so little work that with parental co-operation, he took a year off in 1934 to sail to Australia and back. He went as a member of the crew of the Finnish sailing vessel *Lawhill*, one of the last big sailing ships in the grain trade. It must have been very tough, though he assured me that the only dangerous moment for him personally was up aloft in the English Channel going out. Coming back, he decided not to return to Oxford, took a job for a time on a magazine and was then set up by our parents in a studio on Campden Hill.

He had not painted as assiduously as he might have done in earlier years, and he now began art studies. He developed a quite outstanding sense of colour and of what makes a picture, though in the stern discipline of anatomy he was not so strong. I was the first person to pay him something for a picture – a Scottish landscape lost, alas, in a fire.

We then lost touch for some time, as I went abroad and the war years intervened. He painted quite a lot until war came, and then did service with the army and air force, having in the latter a job in camouflage appropriate to an artist. The charm and the easy-going nature endured; I met later many a person who would have been delighted to marry him. Suffice it to say that after some unhappy episodes, he found home and happiness when, in 1947, he married our cousin, Mary Scholfield, daughter of my mother's elder brother Edward. They had three children. He painted less now, but practised picture restoring with great skill. I once saw him look suspiciously at a blue sky in a classical religious picture; he decided to explore and gently and skilfully revealed two angels which had been painted over.

He and I were very different in habits and did not always agree. But two things always brought us together, an affection and regard for our parents and a habit of laughing at the same things. We had a cryptic family idiom which included some wholly lost adventures by a Mr Sidney Melly and his Irish friend, Mr O'Dour. And we had one particularly happy holiday to-

gether in the thirties when we drove to the south of France
to visit the family with whom he had studied French.

In 1959, at the lamentably early age of forty-six, Colum
died of lung cancer. It came very suddenly, though I would
trace its origins back to the war when, under the strain of ill-
health in wartime conditions, he smoked enough to provoke the
direst consequences. He has left behind some attractive paintings,
particularly landscapes, in oil and water-colour. I would hope
that some day an exhibition of them might be arranged.
Meantime the head and shoulder portrait by his friend Kenneth
Greene which shows him at his best, is a worthy memorial.

Germany

By the summer of 1932, study could not be protracted further.
With the help of the Oxford University Appointments Board, I
went in search of a job. I had no precise idea of what I wanted
to be. I only knew one thing – that I wanted to have something
to do with foreigners. With these terms of reference, I called on
a bank, who decided that I was not nature's banker. A mining
company, operating overseas, decided that they wanted someone
with a knowledge of mine engineering and a day in Rotherham
Main was hardly sufficient. I then made a date to see the editor of
the *Financial News*.

At that moment Uncle Alwyn Scholfield happened to intervene
generously – and with decisive effect. On the morning of my
interview with the editor, a letter arrived from my uncle, saying
that, if I would go and learn German thoroughly, he would
contribute substantially towards the expense. I showed the letter
to the editor and asked him what he would do in my place. He
said the equivalent of 'Don't be silly.' So I went to Germany.
This proved to be literally the choice of a lifetime.

We decided that the choice must be deadly serious, and
selected from a list Professor Dr Rudolf Münch, the well-
recommended head of a *Gymnasium* (high school) in Hanover.
Professor and Frau Münch exemplified the best qualities of
German professional people. The professor was kind, conscientious, immensely thorough, had a sense of fun and a good

knowledge of English grammar on which he had written a book. He had one amiable German weakness about which he liked to be teased. We used to say that, as a Master of Arts, he had mastered all the arts except '*die Kunst des Auslassens*' (the art of leaving things out). Frau Münch was a kindly, welcoming lady from Thuringia. The Münchs had living with them their daughter Thea, and a brother of Frau Münch's, a general who was an expert on '*Fahren*' (meaning driving coaches) and spoke such total Thuringian dialect that I never learned to understand a word he said.

The professor and I worked together on alternate mornings. I joined the Hanover Tennis Club, a short bicycle ride away across the wooded Eilenriede, and we usually talked together in the evening. The result was that at lunch I was invariably tongue-tied; but after an hour and a half's tennis could not stop talking. The literature I read, apart from the obstinate hurdle of newspaper German, was various, including the famous novel by Gustav Freytag *Soll und Haben*, and works by Fontane, Thomas Mann, Artur Schnitzler and others. A dreadful penance was reading an immense book called *Volk ohne Raum* by Hans Grimm which was all about Germans being turned out of East Africa and wandering about a world where all Dutch South Africans were husky and admirable and all British foxy and dislikeable. The book reflected some of the afflictions which had fallen on the family of the Münchs' son-in-law.

In September 1932 I went home briefly to take part in the examination for an All Souls Fellowship. (I say 'take part' and not 'compete' because one did not seriously 'compete' with Isaiah Berlin[4] and Patrick Reilly[5].) But the visit to All Souls had a

[4] Professor Sir Isaiah Berlin, President of Wolfson College, Oxford, served during the Second World War in the British Embassies in Washington and Moscow. Holder of numerous academic distinctions in Britain and the United States and author of, amongst other things, works on Karl Marx and the concept of liberty.

[5] Sir Patrick Reilly, Fellow of All Souls, was Ambassador to the Soviet Union, 1957–60, twice Deputy Under-Secretary in the Foreign Office and Ambassador to France, 1965–68. Since 1969, he has been Chairman of the British and French Bank.

pleasant connection with the future. My neighbour and 'uncle' at dinner was Lord Chelmsford, the reforming Viceroy of 1916–21. It was good, thirty years later, to be able to tell the overwhelmingly Sikh membership of the Chelmsford Club in Delhi that I had met him.

I had by now decided to go on from Hanover to the much larger city of Hamburg and obtained from Balliol an introduction to Professor Mendelssohn-Bartholdy, the head of the External Affairs Institute and, through him, to Professor Emil Wolff, professor of English literature. I joined the Wolffs as a paying guest in October.

Professor Wolff was a quiet man, small in stature, with an immense knowledge of English literature, particularly that of the sixteenth century. Indeed he knew so much in this way that he refused to speak any English at all. Frau Wolff was a handsome, energetic lady, daughter of a former mayor and the family lived in a pleasant house in the Gellertstrasse, near the Outer Alster, a large lake in the middle of the city.

I had decided to study a subject at the Institute and chose German-Polish relations from 1918, in short, the Polish corridor. I bought a second-hand bicycle, unanimously christened 'Siegfried', and pedalled to and fro each day.

I also attended a seminar conducted by Professor Hashagen, professor of history at Hamburg University, on (one guess will suffice for those who knew Germany at the time) 'the causes of the World War'. We had laboriously studied the co-responsibility of the French, the Austrians, the Russians and the British. The professor, a fair-minded man, asked 'Can you suggest any other country which might have had a share in this responsibility?' Dead silence. He tried again. Dead silence. I could bear it no longer and said *'Deutschland'* (Germany). There was a panic rustle in the seminar and the professor asked me why I thought that. Summoning up all my courage I replied, *'Weil es im Auslande den Eindruck gegeben hat, dass es einen Krieg wollte.'* ('Because Germany had given the impression abroad that it wanted a war.') The reaction came, too good to be true: *'Sind Sie je im Auslande gewesen?'* ('Have you ever been abroad?')

We could be gay too. The Wolffs had in their hall a bust
of Beethoven. After an evening party, Frau Wolff's daughter,
another friend and I decided to wrap up Beethoven in an overcoat
and install him in an armchair as a harmless surprise for the maid
in the morning. We had forgotten that a mechanical mouse had
been running round the floor at the party and had got lost.

When the maid came in, she rushed up to the ghastly pale
figure in the arm-chair crying, 'Help! A gentleman has fainted.'
As she clutched the 'gentleman', disturbing the chair, the liberated
mouse shot dramatically out from behind and the curtain descended on pandemonium. In principle I am against practical jokes.
They can so easily go wrong.

Those months spent in Germany were a very short time before
the seizure of power by the Nazis. The political and economic
atmosphere in a German city at that time was one of chronic
hopelessness. There were the established political groupings.
In some ways the worthiest party was still the Social Democratic
Party. But the leaders were divided amongst themselves and
uncertain whether to adopt a purer Marxism or a less doctrinaire
line. Moreover, their unpopularity was increasing as opinion
grew yearly harder against the Versailles Treaty and the Young
Plan for reparations, both identified with them. There was no
Briand to help from France and no hope from elsewhere. In
1932 I attended two Social Democrat rallies in Hanover, a
march past which was brave but rather sloppy and muted, and
a choral concert in the Hanover City Hall, when a massed choir
sang hopefully *'Die Gedanken sind frei'*. (Thoughts are free).

The corresponding Nazi outdoor rally looked much more
impressive. March discipline was good and the marchers as
they goose-stepped looked young and cheerful, if a bit fiercely
so. And I went to an evening meeting in Hanover addressed by
Adolf Hitler, a foretaste of his future showmanship and his
ability to pour heavily effective scorn on his opponents. 'Which
Social Democrat am I supposed to believe, Herr Breitscheid
or Herr Braun?'

But the Social Democrats had gone from office two years
before, and a new expedient had been tried, the appointment

as Chancellor of the leader of a small but respectable party, the Centre, Dr Heinrich Brüning. The name 'Centre' was a good one. But apart from failure to grapple with the growing economic crisis, the Centre, as a Catholic party, was too vulnerable to abuse from Protestant and Social Democrat alike as a '*Pfaffenwirtschaft*' (priestly racket).★ And the supreme irony for German democracy had been that the Social Democrats, by refusing to support Brüning at a critical moment, had driven him into government by decree, the fatal signpost towards future tragedy.

After Brüning, through no fault of his own, had lost the confidence of President Hindenburg, there remained only the expedient of government by authority – a kind of embryo technocracy. But the short-lived governments that succeeded Brüning had neither the doctrine nor the ability to deal with growing political tension and an economy carrying some five million unemployed.

Then there were two desperately complicating factors, the Versailles Treaty and the Jewish community. If all the years and tons of research done on the causes of the First World War were weighed in the balance and allowance made for the sins and failures of everybody else – the Russian generals, the Serbian assassins, the Austrian dilettantes, the committed French and the hesitant British – it is my estimate that the Emperor William II and his second-rate counsellors would still have to bear the major responsibility. None the less, to put into a peace treaty a statement of exclusive German guilt was asking for later trouble. The counter-myth grew that Germany had not only not been guilty and had not therefore deserved to lose, but even that she had not been defeated at all. She had been betrayed.

By whom? The Social Democrats, of course. But other people too had international connections. What about the Jewish community? Anyone who went for the first time to Central Europe and moved about among people of almost any background

---

★ Really untranslatable; perhaps 'crows' nest' would do. One of Dr Adenauer's wisest acts of post-war statesmanship was to recognize this disability and to run his Christian Democrat Party on an interconfessional, Protestant-Catholic basis.

was bound to be struck by the neurosis about Jewish descent. If one met someone new, an immediate unspoken question was, does he or she have Jewish blood? This was, at its most neutral, a guide to someone's probable relatives and business or social connections. But there was a long tradition of anti-semitism in Germany, and should the country need a special scapegoat, the neurosis could become very dangerous. Had not many of the original Soviet revolutionaries, Trotsky, Zinoviev, Kaganovich and some of the less important but well-known figures such as Litvinov been of Jewish origin? (It escaped notice that the post-revolutionary managers of power extruded Jewish revolutionaries from key positions.) Doctrines of identifiably Jewish origin, such as the Vienna school of psychology, with presumed effects on human behaviour, aroused more anxiety. But the fatal ingredient in this explosive confusion was the reaction of German grievance and failure to Jewish success.

If you lived in a German city, you were struck by Jewish influence in all the media of publicity and creation. In the Ullstein publishing house, the *Frankfurter Zeitung*, the work of Weill and Brecht, the Jewish element was the creative and obtrusive one and some of this element was highly destructive of accepted views. In a totally different field, if you could not find what you wanted in your local store in the suburbs of Hanover, where did you go? To Sternheim and Emanuel, of course.

When a community, historically prone to become the victim of unreason, finds itself in a position of success amid failure, its only recourse is probably to go to ground. The Japanese *Zaibatsu* understood this; a really successful Japanese business man was and is rarely obtrusive. The Jewish disposition is not like this. Success insistently proclaimed itself where the public could see it.

One had begun to fear for the Jews in their exposed position, though without the slightest clue of the ghastly things that were to befall. One felt that government in Germany was in a sense coming to an end. In November 1932, a Social Democrat friend, Peter Hasenclever, said, 'A Hitler-*Diktatur* (dictatorship) is inevitable.'

At that moment, on the surface at least, all was not yet over. There was a Nazi setback in a general election. Stormtroopers, huddled at street corners with collecting boxes in a November drizzle suggested some deferment of the '*Diktatur*'. I decided to spend Christmas in Germany and then, in pursuance of my studies, to visit Poland and East Prussia. After a congenial and, in the German Protestant manner, touchingly serious Christmas, I took the night train to Berlin. In the grey snowy winter dawn, it seemed an ugly and formidable city.

From Berlin I went on to the frontier town of Schneidemühl, where I spent the evening with German frontier officials who drank kirsch and poured scorn on the Poles. The train then crossed the famous corridor to the Free City of Danzig (Gdansk) where I was regaled with statistics by the Germans and parties by the Poles. One side complained that the whole countryside was peopled with Germans and pro-Germans, groaning under Polish oppression; the other insisted that this was gross misrepresentation and that in any case Poland must have access to the sea. These arguments are all dead now, but they were felt with passionate intransigence then and there was no will to make the corridor work and no escape from the Teuton-Slav conflict of centuries.

In Königsberg Station ('Look,' they said locally, 'we have a wonderful new station and no trains.') I ran into T. P. Conwell-Evans, a bright, birdlike little Welshman who had sat at the feet of my aunt, Eva Gore-Booth. He had devoted himself to the cause of the League of Nations, about which he wrote a classic book[6] and was searching for means to reintegrate Germany into the comity of nations. In the process he developed a surprisingly close friendship with Herr von Ribbentrop, which later enabled him to help many victims of Nazism out of Germany until finally the goodwill ran out.

At that time, T.P. was charitable to the Nazis to the point of credulity. A rally the evening before, he said, had been 'rather like a religious service'. Even in my state of suspended judgement

---

[6] T.P. Conwell-Evans (with Noel Buxton), *Oppressed Peoples and the League of Nations*, Dent, 1922.

I found this hard to believe. But his attitude showed how the Nazis' advent in a distressed Germany could confuse peace-loving people of high humanitarian purpose.

From Königsberg I went to Poland and visited Torun, Poznan and Lodz. The latter made the most lasting impression on me. I was driven round in a 'one-horse open sleigh', but it was not fun seeing through the snow the terrible conditions in which people lived. Again, as in so much of pre-1939 economics, there seemed no way out. I attended a rally of the German minority group. They were more impressive than the official propagandists and I often thought of them when faced, later on, with British communities with their backs to the wall. But one also remembered that the Poles had allowed the rally to take place. Finally I took the train to Warsaw, where I met Polish officials who were disposed to dismiss the whole argument with Germany as paper argument. For a little longer, they were not wrong. Then I turned homeward, spending the night of 25 February 1933 at an *Evangelisches Hospiz* in Berlin and the next day, sightseeing in the city, I walked around the Reichstag. I left that night. The very next day the Reichstag was burnt down, and history took a new lurch towards 1939.

France and the Diplomatic Examinations

It was now urgent to find regular employment, and at this point I met a friend who was studying for the Diplomatic Service examination and had copies of the previous year's papers. I turned to the German paper and found little difficulty in coping with it. This seemed to point to attempting the examination myself. The daunting problem would be French. My French was of the rusty schoolboy variety; I had a commitment to a tutoring job in April, so this meant learning enough French in May, June and half July to get the 60 per cent for the French written and oral which was the minimum required. The standard was high and the challenge formidable.

Arrangements were made for me to go to Paris as the paying guest of Monsieur and Madame Amédée Britsch. M. Britsch was chief librarian of the Law Faculty at the Sorbonne, and the

family lived in an apartment above the faculty itself. M. Britsch
was a spare, fair-haired man with a pointed beard and ferocious
nationalist views, replenished daily from the *Journal des Débats*.
With him I toiled over Voltaire, Flaubert and other selected
classics and, of course, *dictée*. Mme. Britsch was an excellent
mother, housewife and cook and took infinite trouble with her
family and me. It became a gastronomic slogan that '*Monsieur
Bousse aime les fraises*'; so it became strawberries and cream cheese
with most suppers. I had no objection.

But life in Paris was utterly different from life in Hanover or
Hamburg. The family were always intensely busy – it was a
revelation to see how hard the sons worked at school and university. In the centre of Paris there was no leisurely cycling to a
tennis club. The exchange was against the pound sterling and
one had to mind the bawbees. Moreover, whereas the Germans,
who did not know much English at that time, were anxious to
'sell' their country and their case and cheered on one's stammering
efforts to put German sentences together, the French took the
view that their civilization sold itself and were bored stiff with
you unless you could speak French the way they did. It is also
linguistically true that it is easier to speak bits of German than
bits of French. You can play elementary German *staccato*, but in
French you seem from the beginning to need whole sentences
properly constructed. The difficulty with German comes later
when you try to speak like a German.

So, though it was not easy to refuse the company of hospitable
American and British friends resident in Paris, one simply had to
hold off talking and thinking in English. As a distraction I got
wildly excited with what must have been one of the last of the
Chaliapin seasons of Russian opera and went to *Boris Godunov*,
Prince Igor, *Pique Dame* and *Eugen Onegin*. I watched some
international tennis and was invited to a couple of fashionable
balls. But mostly I stuck to my grind, with the semi-exception
of taking the Britschs' schoolgirl daughter to the cinema on
Thursday afternoons unbeknown to her parents. We always
took a newspaper to hide behind in case the man with a beard
waiting for the bus should turn out to be papa. I learned from

Ginette quite a lot of French and more than I have learned from anyone else about what the French are really like. The postlude is sad. She married a Hungarian, was caught in Budapest in the Russian advance and the German retreat in 1944 and died in prison where a desperate Gestapo had confined her in a last drive against 'foreign agents' before they fled.

By mid-July it was time to go home and brush up all the other neglected subjects. When I presented myself at Burlington House in mid-August, it was like the scholarship exam at Eton all over again. I had been to no recognized tutors or crammers, and nobody knew, least of all myself, whether I was a serious candidate. But at least the written examination, which required you to know a little about a lot rather than a lot about a little, was my kind of examination. It was a tremendous labour lasting some three weeks, with very occasional odd relief as when the German oral examiner began my interview with, '*Was denken Sie an der Sterilisationsfrage?*' (What is your view about sterilization?)

And so, exhausted by everybody and everything, I went off with a Balliol friend, Lewis Masefield, son of the Poet Laureate, as far away as we could both afford which was to the top of Vesuvius (then active) via Rome. On arrival in the Piazza Vittorio Veneto, where Mussolini had his balcony, we were promptly detained by the police as louche-looking characters. We were momentarily scared but rapidly released to lunch on spaghetti and an Italian sweet called a *diplomatico*.

On return to London, no news and again no news until I ceased to search the back pages of *The Times*. So when a future colleague one day rang up at breakfast and said 'Congratulations,' I answered 'What on?' It was all right. German had done well; French had staggered through with 163 out of 250, just enough. My handwriting lost 25 marks for illegibility, a spectre which pursued me over thirty years later to the Permanent Under-Secretary's office where Lord Palmerston's admonition to the young men to write better hangs on the wall.

Much temper is lost over the philosophy of examinations, and new methods are now used for Diplomatic Service entry which, to my mind rightly, lean more to versatility and character than to learning expressed in writing. At the same time my particular exam compelled candidates to do clear, intelligent and intelligible work against an acute pressure of time. And if that isn't a vivid description of crisis diplomacy, I don't know what is.

London

1933-1936

I was assigned to the Amercian Department of the Foreign Office. The number of independent countries in the world was still small and the hard language expertise demanding immediate study abroad was largely handled by the (then separate) Consular Service. For a diplomatic officer, therefore, an assignment to the Foreign Office as a beginning was practically automatic. This was a thoroughly good practice. If there is one thing that saves time and even tears at a post abroad, it is for members of the staff to 'know their client,' the Office. You cannot really know the Office without having worked there. In a mission abroad, you have no power but a good deal of scope for making up your mind and acting freely on small matters. In the Whitehall machine by contrast, almost every recommendation or decision means the concurrence of others but, when agreed, is a direct contribution to the real exercise of power.

In modern conditions it is structurally impossible for everyone to start at home. But I continue to maintain that the future success or failure of members of the Service may depend on their having had an early spell at home, if only for two years out of their first seven or eight.

On 12 October 1933 I called on the Department and was introduced to its members. On asking when I should report for duty, I was told, 'Tomorrow at eleven o'clock sharp, please.' The word 'sharp' may sound a little ironical. Eleven o'clock diplomacy was founded very logically in the idea that you finished your work for the day in the day. First thing in the morning, cipher officers would complete deciphering telegrams, typists copying them and clerks sorting them and other documents for the departments when they came in. Under this system,

anyone from a department coming in at 9.30 would just have
been a nuisance. The corollary was that the people who serviced
the earlier hours would go home at 5.30, while the department
had no grievance if it had to carry on till 7.00 or 8.00. Eleven
o'clock diplomacy disappeared fairly rapidly and died totally
in World War II.

The American Department Third Room, the room in which
all four or five members of the Department other than the Head
and Assistant Head worked, was in Room 103 on the second
floor of the Foreign Office building. It faced north towards No.11
Downing Street and the Horse Guards Parade. It had a good
view but no sunlight from one end of the year to the other.
It contained old-style desks, two-piece telephones and was lit
by what I learned to call 'Ministry of Works pendant fixtures,'
i.e. single lights with no efficient shading or reflection. Since
everyone else worked like that, there was no grievance. Indeed, as
things went, we were quite well off, though it was tiresome that
all our papers were filed one floor away.

Diplomatic officials are not enamoured of working three or
four to a room. But for the kind of work you start doing in a
Foreign Office, there is much to be said for being able to listen
to other people handling (or mishandling) telephone conversations
and dictation. And how else could an ambitious, rather bouncy
but helpful new entrant in a neighbouring department have been
dissuaded from answering the telephone with: 'This is the
Foreign Office: what's your little trouble?'

In 1933, the training I received consisted of two days in the
cipher room learning how to work codes, and two pieces of
advice. One was, 'People here use Christian names a great
deal; but I suggest that as a newcomer, you wait till someone
else does it to you.' The second was, 'If the telephone rings and
says "Bodfish here", it is probably your opposite number who has
just joined the Board of Trade; but be a little careful because it
might be the Deputy Under-Secretary, Sir Percival Bodfish,
on the wrong line.'

Although in these days more systematic training is both needed
and provided, there is one peculiarly national hint to be offered to

administrators. New entrants to the diplomatic services of many countries, notably on the continent of Europe and in America, seem to expect their acceptance to be followed by a further considerable period devoted purely to absorbing knowledge. Today's British entrant, boy or girl, comes in with the feeling that, after fifteen to twenty years of being educated, he or she should *do* something and not simply go on being instructed, even if paid for it. The best procedure is therefore to devote part of the day to learning and the other part to 'doing,' alongside someone who knows already how it should be done.

The Head of the American Department was R. L. Craigie. He was the son of a Scots admiral. When *en poste* in Switzerland he had married the daughter of the American Ambassador, a newspaper owner from the Southern States. The Craigies were both to play a momentous part in my life a few years later. Of medium height, dark-haired, with a dark moustache and always rather formally dressed, he was a shy, serious man who looked at one rather fiercely through heavy, horn-rimmed glasses. I was at first a little scared, but he proved basically a kindly man and thoughtful about his juniors. On one occasion at least he brought me into a negotiation, in which I served no particular purpose, simply in order that I should see what went on.

My first preceptor was Patrick Roberts. Like me he was a scholar at Eton but, unlike me, had gone on to King's College, Cambridge. He was a bachelor, somewhat donnish in manner, but fast-moving and with a good sense of laughter. He would never let sloppy work get by, his favourite intervention taking the form, 'Mr Gore-Booth has clearly not re-read sufficiently carefully Annex VII, paragraph 12, to the Anglo-Bactrian Consular Convention.' He was very good company and an excellent teacher, and I have often wondered what he would in the end have achieved. Sadly, he was killed in a motor accident in Greece in 1937.

With one exception, my main work for two and a half years was concerned with the United States. My first official act was to receive on my desk a white folder docketed (entitled) 'United States Plant Quarantine Regulations'. Round the folder was a neat

piece of red tape. I glared at this thing and wondered what on earth
to do with it. Eventually Anthony Haigh[1] suggested 'Look
underneath.' Sure enough, there were the previous year's regulations, accompanied by a minute saying that a copy should go
to the Ministry of Agriculture. I triumphantly wrote the same,
and my first official contribution to national power and prosperity
had been made.

My chief routine was very much a sign of those times. Once
a week, the Embassy in Washington used to write a master
dispatch on the political and economic situation in the United
States. As it was still the first year of President Franklin Roosevelt's
New Deal, these dispatches were massively interesting and were
considered very important. They were also extremely well
written. They were brought across the Atlantic by Cunard in the
confidential 'bag'. As soon as the bag was opened, it was my job
to help the Registry sort out the material and decide what should
be given priority in handling. The master dispatch was always
one of these items, and when it had been registered for record
and identification purposes and had come down to the Department, it was my task as the most junior official to write or dictate
on to the file any comment I thought might be useful. Since the
dispatches were a week old. I kept a small, temporary press-
cutting file and made a short summary of anything important
that had happened in the meantime. With the pace of New Deal
developments, the note could sometimes be quite substantial,
and this function taught me a great deal about the United States.

The Permanent Under-Secretary, Sir Robert Vansittart, was
much interested personally in these developments and used to
read my comments. This gave me an opportunity, unusual for
someone so junior, to meet him. He was an overwhelmingly
impressive man. He showed a remarkably early and clear perception of the dangers of Nazism, though he over-extended his
hope that Mussolini might be able or willing to stick to the path

[1] Anthony Haigh, after experience in many Embassies abroad, became
Head of the Cultural Relations Department of the Foreign Office, 1952–62, and
chairman of the Administrative Board of the Cultural Fund of the Council of
Europe.

of reason; and I also wish he had resigned from the Office when he had to hand over to Sir Alexander Cadogan, instead of accepting the unrewarding post of Chief Diplomatic Adviser. But Vansittart was the outstanding personality in the Office at the time, and when I left in 1936 for posting abroad, he gave me the kind of mixed commendation and pep talk which lifts you right off your feet. The one thing that would never have occurred to me was that I should end up in his chair. A diminished chair if you will, but one from which I was able to remind a party of French journalists in the closing difficult de Gaulle days that it was in that selfsame room that there had developed much of the earlier work on the Entente Cordiale and Vansittart's vision of what the end of the thirties would bring.

One special subject with which I found myself struggling was liquor smuggling from the high seas into the United States. During the Prohibition period this was a highly profitable adventure. The technique was for small or medium cargo ships to present themselves just outside the American twelve-mile limit of territorial waters and for fast craft to load the liquor on board and make a dash for the shore. The American coastguard had the right to detain such craft within territorial waters and to chase them in 'hot and continuous pursuit' outside the twelve-mile limit. Since many of the cargo ships were British and came from the British West Indies, there were constant disputes involving international, American and British law and colonial administration.

The British object had to be to protect the rights of British vessels and seamen without letting arguments with the Americans reach a pitch of ill-temper which would affect larger issues. We also had a limited target of setting up a system of certificates of origin so that, if ships set off from the Bahamas to Newfoundland laden with liquor and arrived light, at least questions could be asked.

Under Patrick Roberts's careful supervision I could just about manage this. But one Friday Patrick walked in and announced that he was leaving us on Monday to take charge of another department. I was appalled. With a few months of seniority I

would be left with this flamingo-like file, and the prospect of
getting anyone else interested was practically nil. Nor was there
any point in getting Patrick to retain a watching brief; nothing
is as dead as yesterday's expert.

So I struggled on. We got our certificates of origin and then
I was delivered by President Roosevelt getting rid of Prohibition.

In those days there was an arrangement by which, if an
officer decided to spend his leave or a good part of it in the country
on whose affairs he was specializing, he might receive a contribution from public funds towards his visit. The arrangement was
under severe scrutiny because, it was alleged, some smart aleck
had written a report on Hungary in a sleeping-car between
Vienna and Bucharest. But the offer held good in my case, and
from mid-May until late June, 1934, I was on a busman's holiday
in the United States. On return I wrote an amateur but serious-
minded report.

I visited New York and Washington. I called on the Ambassador, Sir Ronald Lindsay, whose craggy form seemed to project
from his deep arm-chair right across the study; and on Arthur
Wiggin, a much loved and respected member of the service
who died in sad circumstances at sea some time later. The sum of
their sensitive wisdom was that I should never if I could avoid it
draw comparisons between things American and things British;
and that if, as would be quite common, Americans should start
running down their own country and ask for my comment, I
should never agree. The second item was immensely valuable.
At the height of the New Deal, Americans who disliked the policy
and felt that it struck at the root of individual freedom and
private enterprise, expressed themselves in terrifyingly abusive
language about the President and his advisers. But, paradoxically,
if a foreigner were rash enough to agree, he was insulting the
Presidency and subverting the Constitution. America is still a
country where people feel deeply and speak strongly, and where
the middle of the road is sparsely trodden.

I am eternally grateful that I was born in an age when people
still travelled in liners (whatever class) and in American long-
distance railroad trains, two of the most civilized forms of

transport ever invented. But I did, between Chicago and Minneapolis, take my first aeroplane flight; nobody warned me what an unpressurized flight does to your ears. At Minneapolis I was entertained and looked after in the way that only Americans know how. On a public holiday I became part of a family outing to one of the lakes which surround the city. On another day a business man, also hitherto unknown, asked me to join him and his family for supper. He cleared his desk and then bent over his safe and brought out a revolver which he slipped into his belt. 'We have to live like that,' he said. Minneapolis had been the scene of some ugly riots arising from unemployment and drought, and one couldn't be sure.

The contents of my report are not significant. But I did learn something about America. I had wondered incredulously whether life was really like life in the movies. About fifty per cent of it was. People really did say 'Gee, that's swell,' a wholly romantic notion in Britain at the time. And a tough American really did tell me in describing an argument with a business competitor in the office of a member of the Administration, 'I knocked the guy flat. The Secretary saw my point.'

But I also saw the other fifty per cent: unknown Middle America at work and play and this was far more important. It has been fashionable, ever since Sinclair Lewis began his brilliant and curiously not totally unkind debunking campaign, to laugh and later jeer at American suburbs and small towns. But American suburbs are, I hate to say it, more attractive and comfortable than their British counterparts and I have never lost my admiration for the good, serious, church-going, community-minded people who inhabit them. They are the America you do not know until you go there. And if their prejudices are strongly held and expressed, and their outlooks sometimes limited by corn and hogs, well, other people have their limitations too. These people are the sheriff and posse of American society, when you really need a sheriff and posse and are not just imagining that you do. One only hopes that they will not be megalopolized out of existence.

During the summer holiday months junior members of the

Department took in each other's washing. I learned a great deal about the afflictions of British bondholders in Latin America who had lost heavily in the great slump. I also became acquainted with one of the oldest active files in the Office, the boundary dispute between British Honduras and Guatemala which started substantially in 1858 when the British Treasury refused to authorize the expenditure of £500,000 for road construction as part of the boundary agreement. It is not yet closed.

At Easter in 1935 I took short leave on my own in Germany, and revisited the Münchs in Hanover. Tragedy had hit them. The General, Frau Münch's brother, had always been immensely scornful about the Nazis. When they took over, seeing no other honourable course, he took his own life.

Little things also showed how life was going. I revisited the tennis club. It had moved from its informal quarters near the slaughter house and had set up in attractive surroundings in the Eilenreide. I had a look at the revised rules posted in the hall. Rule 1 was now 'Aryan descent'. A girl whom I had known came in at that moment. She had been a cheerful type and usually, in the custom of pre-Nazi times, gaily made-up. She looked now as though she had been scrubbed. I took a tram into the city and asked for a ticket to 'Kröpcke', the Eros-type landmark in the city centre. Everyone in the tram looked round in nervous alarm: Kröpcke had been renamed 'Adolf Hitler Platz'.

I have mentioned that Craigie was the son of an admiral. He had maintained a personal interest in naval matters about which he knew a great deal. This meant that the American Department had as a side line the handling of the diplomacy of naval affairs. Two important items came up while I was still there.

First, there was the bitterly controversial Anglo-German Naval Agreement. Concluded in June 1935, it allowed to the growing German Navy an aggregate strength of 35 per cent of the naval strength of the British Commonwealth, with the provision that there might in future be an adjustment to allow Germany to reach 100 per cent in submarines. The argument in favour was that with the rapid German advance in armed strength, there was advantage in having a German signature on a binding instrument of limitation. The European side of the Office felt that no reliance could be placed on such a signature, but in 1935 this pessimistic view was not yet generally accepted. Craigie invited me to attend the opening formal session of the negotiations, and I have a vivid recollection of the pompous entrance, with eloquent pause on the threshold, effected by the head of the German delegation, Herr von Ribbentrop.

In the summer of 1935 Craigie sent for me and said that the Department was going to have to organize a Naval Conference including the United States, Japan, France, Italy and the British Commonwealth to review the whole naval disarmament question. Adrian Holman[2] was coming to be Secretary-General, and he would like me to assist him.

Naval Limitation was regulated by the terms agreed at the Washington Conference of 1922, the principal achievement of which was the famous 5–5–3 ratio of battleships between the United States, the British Commonwealth and Japan. Japanese dissatisfaction with this inequality had been growing for some time, and the Japanese put forward their claim to equality in the phrase which became a household word, the 'common upper limit'. In the matter of smaller warships, the London Naval Disarmament Conference of 1930 had made an attempt to bring about agreement on cruisers, but it had not been possible to induce the French and the Italians to agree. Another effort was to be made.

Adrian Holman and I went over to the Cabinet Office accompanied by our naval team-mate, Lieutenant-Commander Bremner, to find out whether we could obtain any help in organizing the event. There seemed to be no worthwhile information in the Foreign Office. The Cabinet Office said that they 'knew about' conferences, but added that they had neither time nor people to give any practical help. So we went off to invent a conference.

Adrian proved an immensely dynamic Secretary-General. The Ministry of Works produced an excellent building in Matthew Parker Street, confusingly called Clarence House, and spruced

[2] Sir Adrian Holman, British Political Representative in Rumania after the Second World War and Ambassador to Cuba, 1950-54.

it up. To give a nautical effect we borrowed some seascapes from the Maritime Museum at Greenwich. The General Post Office acquired great merit by producing an especially efficient and good-looking team of telephonists, and the weeks went by with the preparation of endless briefs, programmes and invitation lists and the setting up of interpreter and other facilities.

There was one curious way in which the composition of the conference and, therefore, the seating at the table (roughly a three-sided square) reflected the moment of history in which the conference took place. The Statute of Westminster, establishing fully independent status for the Dominions, was only four years old and the British Government were immensely anxious to prove that this independence was real. That meant that the four Dominions (Canada, Australia, New Zealand and South Africa), as well as the Irish Free State, were separately represented whatever the size or the real 'independence' of their navies. The Irish High Commissioner was understood to represent one gunboat. The foreign delegations accepted this with an incredulous patience and courtesy.

Another peculiarity was that, long-distance air travel being in its infancy, the Japanese delegation came by sea, so that an interval of some five weeks passed while diplomacy as it were turned off the switch.

When the Japanese admirals arrived, every kind of persuasion was tried in smaller meetings to persuade them that the 'common upper limit' which they proposed was unacceptable. The Americans held responsibilities in two great oceans, the Commonwealth just about everywhere while the Japanese could not claim responsibilities wider than the Western Pacific. Craigie, in particular, negotiated with limitless resource in suggesting that if a formal note wouldn't do, how would it be to have a protocol or a signed appendix or anything else. But by the end of the year the Japanese had not budged and had referred for further instructions. There was an interval of further suspense, but no change.

Meantime the debates on the smaller ships continued, the Italians talking flexibly, the French toughly. But behind the Conference the atmosphere of the Italo-Abyssinian crisis persisted and, at the end, the Italians received instructions to pull out.

So the Conference failed, and such limitations of naval armaments that existed between the main naval powers disappeared. The failure was in no way the fault of the conduct of the conference and I was present when Mr Eden, who had become Foreign Secretary during the Conference, expressed his congratulations and regrets to the First Lord of the Admiralty, Sir Bolton Eyres Monsell, who had conducted it with great patience and suavity. And the Department had shown, rather breathlessly, that it could organize a conference.

The parties dispersed and we sent a telegram to Captain V. H. Danckwerts, Craigie's very able chief naval colleague who went off to command a flotilla of destroyers. It simply read: 'Job, 33:22' which being elaborated reads, 'His soul is now in hell and his life among the destroyers.'

There is much argument about British foreign policy and diplomacy in the 1930s. Given that memoirs have been written and documents long since published, there is little to add except perhaps to recall how autumn 1933 to spring 1936 felt from below.

The Foreign Office and Foreign Service of the time were seeking to serve a restive and difficult world with a system which was partly modern and partly what had served the country well before 1914. Early in the century men of humane intelligence like Grey and Balfour had time to view the world reflectively and, with the advice of a few experienced people, arrive at mature conclusions. Politically, economically, socially and technically, the post-1918 world did not allow this pace and method to return. Improvements were made, one of the most important being the requirement first instituted in 1919 that members of the service should serve both at home and abroad instead of one or the other; this was an essential aid to mutual understanding between London and posts abroad. A bitter battle with the Treasury over the setting up of an Economic Relations Department in the Foriegn Office was fought and won. What was lacking, as I look back on it, was any conscious policy-forming machinery. Because people were intelligent and, at the top, experienced, policy emerged, but the process was laborious, involving reams of minutes written in the hope that Sir Robert Vansittart would umpire correctly.

This was not greatly different from the diplomacy of other people, and British diplomacy maintained its prestige abroad. At home, it remained a magnet for ability and ambition. As one entered, it was just possible to survive on one's salary, £270 a year. I quote the figure since it is a modern habit to quote ancient figures uncorrected for changes in the price level in order to emphasize modern grievances. In fact, on £270 one managed, living at home; though living independently for the modern diplomat without private means was, given necessary expenses, not easy. Now after two and a half years at home, it was time to go abroad, not as a student or a wanderer, but as a diplomatic officer. I had meantime been asked whether I had any preference for posting: I had worked this one out quite clearly and replied 'Central Europe or Japan.' During the conference Derick Hoyer-Millar, who in those days, as Number Two Private Secretary, handled junior promotions and transfers, told me that the Office wanted me to go to Vienna. Apparently my reaction was pretty deadpan. But of course I was delighted.

Austria
April 1936-December 1937

Denis Allen,[1] with whom I shared a telephone extension in the American Department, had a few days off in April 1936 and we drove together to Vienna. We crossed Germany, avoiding all politics, but visiting the splendid interior of the cathedral at Meissen. We had just time to admire the beauty of Prague and to get, in a restaurant at Tabor, a feel of the spontaneous liveliness of the then truly democratic Republic of Czechoslovakia. In Upper Austria we drove along an untarred main road: as traffic was sparse and local custom strong, men smoothing out the dusty surface stepped back and touched their hats as we passed.

The complexion of political life in the Austria to which I had been posted was Catholic and conservative in a way that needs a little historical explanation.

Austria had passed through an extraordinary series of agonies since 1918. The collapse of the Austro-Hungarian Empire had left it a small country equipped with a large, imperial capital and a people divided bitterly between Marxist socialists in the cities and Catholics and agrarians in the countryside, and the almost exact equality of representation of the two tendencies in Parliament made the country extremely difficult to govern. The Catholic side began to cast about for alternatives to one man one vote democracy, arguing that a state organized on a corporate basis with representation from organizations and professions might achieve the much-needed political stability. Though initially

[1] Sir Denis Allen occupied many important posts in the Diplomatic Service, including Head of Chancery in Washington, Deputy High Commissioner for South East Asia, 1959-62, Ambassador to Turkey, 1963-67, and Deputy Under-Secretary in the Foreign Office, 1968-69.

it would have to be authoritarian it would, it was hoped, be only mildly and acceptably so.

There were two main obstacles to an Austrian corporate state on this model, Austrian socialism and, despite the prohibition placed on Austro-German union by the former allies, a strongly persisting Pan-Germanism. Both were removed dramatically in 1934.

On 12 February when diplomats and other dignitaries were attending a service in St Stephen's Cathedral in Vienna, the lights went out. The electricians had gone on strike. The strike developed rapidly into a bloodthirsty civil war in Vienna, ending in executions and imprisonments. Subsequent allegations of conspiracy by one side and provocation by the other have never been wholly cleared up, but the result was that the socialist party was eliminated as a political force.

In July of the same year, armed men broke into the Federal Chancellery and shot Chancellor Engelbert Dollfuss as he apparently sought to escape through a door which had been bolted. He was allowed no medical help by his assassins and died seven hours later. The background to the murder turned out to be a highly organized, nation-wide Nazi-type plot which the authorities were able to suppress. Fortunately for the Catholic ruling party, Dr Dollfuss had made it clear that Dr Kurt von Schuschnigg would be his political heir and there was therefore no fatal interlude of weakness. A pan-German threat of a sinister kind had been removed.

Thus Austria in 1936 was in a sense politically convalescent. It was conservative in so far as conservative elements supported the Schuschnigg government. But it was forward-looking in the sense that the government had a political and social objective. Dr von Schuschnigg's Austria was to be a 'German' country, but its mission was different from that of the German Reich. It was, he maintained, human, cultural and unique, deriving from the diversity, tolerance and (mainly Catholic) Christianity of the old empire and based on the idea of the corporate state. Austria could fulfil this mission without danger to anyone else and in full co-operation with Germany. It was Dr von Schuschnigg's

Sir Henry and Lady Gore-Booth and Mordaunt, in about 1890

Constance, Mabel and Mordaunt Gore-Booth at Lissadell in the 1880s

hope that, even as Nazi power grew, he could preserve the independence of his country.

If I had had more time for reading before I went to Vienna, I would have understood better the background to this constrained freedom, in which political discussion was not ruled out, but discussion of the fundamental nature of the Austrian state in the making was better avoided. I doubt whether, even now, in the preparation for a new posting, members of the service get enough time to digest the historical background, political, economic and social, of the country in which they will be serving. I suffered from this lack again later. One has to cope with domestic upheavals, possibly a new or rusty language and requests from the post for early arrival; there is too little time to do more than the sketchiest historical reading. And, whatever the teachings of the anti-historical school, history is an important background to intelligent and sensitive diplomacy.

By 1936 the question was no longer what kind of Austria would survive into the future but whether Austria, as an independent state, would survive at all. On the importance of Austrian survival my chief, Sir Walford Selby, had the strongest possible views. He also had a great affection for Austria itself and regarded its independence as something intrinsically good. But he also insisted that the loss of that independence could upset the power balance in Central Europe with ominous consequences for peace. This was exactly what happened.

Sir Walford insisted continuously and sometimes at very great length on this point. But it is difficult to know what the British Government of the time could have 'done'. So long as things remained as they were in 1934 when, after the murder of Dollfuss, Britain, France and Italy pledged joint support for Austrian independence, the diplomatic course was plain: but as soon as Mussolini, with a Nazi competitor in the north, started in Abyssinia on the path of conquest, this co-ordination was no longer easy or natural. British public opinion would have found it hard to reconcile discussion of sanctions against Italy over Abyssinia with close co-ordination over Austria, about whose

C

system of government there were certain reservations. In any case, no British Government of the mid-thirties was going to commit itself to armed support of Austria, even against a by no means heavily armed Germany: it was to be one of the ironies of the period that in 1939 Britain undertook to Poland and Rumania obligations which two years earlier had seemed unthinkable in the case of Austria.

My immediate task, however, was to explore the humbler problem of what a Third Secretary on arrival at his first post actually does. I had arranged with Gerald Newport[2] that he and I would share a flat and he had installed himself in a third floor apartment in the Kolschitzkygasse, belonging to an Austrian diplomat serving abroad. It was quite large and had a lovely view across the city to the Kahlenberg ridge to the west. It was fully furnished, complete with trophies of the chase, a large porcelain stove, a grand piano and a maid who was genuinely buxom and promoted me to the seemingly unattainable rank of *Legationsrat* (Counsellor).

The Embassy offices were in the lower ground floor of the Residence. The Minister entertained on the fine *piano nobile* above and lived above that. The offices were neither very attractive nor very adequate, and the whole set-up has now been changed. The staff included a First Secretary, a Commercial Department of three British officers, a Chancery consisting of two Honorary Attachés and myself as Third Secretary. The Commercial Department were kept busy with enquiries from London about the creditworthiness of Austrian individuals and firms and with helping British commercial visitors. In those days export promotion of the kind now familiar to diplomats was supposed to be done by industry, but commercial and financial advice and reporting was part of the job, since the effect of economic developments on Austrian morale was considered an important element in political calculation.

In the office things were held together largely by the archivist,

[2] Gerald Newport succeeded his father as Earl of Bradford in 1957, was president of the Timber Growers' Association, 1962–64, and chairman of the Forestry Committee of Great Britain, 1964–66.

Mr G. B. Taylor. 'Herr Schneider',* as we spontaneously if not very brilliantly called him, was a real character. He had been in the British North Russian expedition at the end of World War I and always wore a black Astrakhan hat in winter. He smoked Gold Flakes the whole time, so that when he went on leave and I had to do his work, I could not use his desk for a few days until the fumes had dispersed. Herr Schneider had a meticulous knowledge of the rules for registering papers which he used to enunciate in a slow, deferential but determined voice. When he was away, I found several ways of handling files better and quicker. When Herr Schneider returned, he took one look and said 'Ah, but *this* is the way it is done' and we heard no more of the improvements. His wife, who was sweet-tempered and very, very English, did our shorthand and typing. The Taylors lived with a canary in a small but comfortable flat where no window was ever opened. I visited them once in retirement in Bourne-mouth. It was a most affectionate reunion with two people of whom I have a most affectionate memory.

My own job as Third Secretary was that of factotum. I had to deal with all the correspondence other than commercial. This meant anything from highest policy to lunatic fan mail. 'The Office ought to know what really happened in Styria at the week-end; please draft something.' 'An Indian official visitor is not getting paid while taking a cure locally; why not?' 'A lady, who will not give her name, has something very important to communicate but refuses to say what it is. Will you see her, please?' I developed a few specialities, such as pioneer work on behalf of the British Council. What was singularly lacking, by comparison with later posts, was work with opposite numbers at my level in the Austrian Foreign Office. This was because on the Austrian side everything of policy interest was discussed and decided at high levels. Exchanges at junior secretary level would have been unprofitable.

The Legation was particularly well-informed on the local and European political situation, enjoying, as Sir Walford Selby

---

* German for 'tailor'.

has himself explained, the closest relationship with an outstanding British press corps. His operational instruction to me was 'accept everything'. This compelled me to find my way about, officially and socially, by sampling all kinds of people and organizations, whether on my own account or representing the Minister when he could not go himself. It taught me that an interesting-looking occasion might turn out to be deadly dull and an unpromising one highly interesting or amusing. Accepting could also be expensive. Austrians of all classes and occupations lived modestly, and it was extremely usual to accompany invitations with a green document called an '*Erlagschein*'. This was a form of payment to whatever cause the party was in aid of, including meeting the expenses of the party itself.

And I learned very quickly that getting to know people in Vienna had one very special complication. Society was very rigidly divided into *Erste Gesellschaft* (top society), *Zweite Gesell-schaft* (second society) and so on through professional and other strata. If at a party at a particular level of society, someone appeared whose presence did not seem to be justified by his social or official standing, it was quite understood if an Austrian of assured standing ostentatiously ignored the intruder or even chose to walk out. The host and hostess would not escape later censure for having allowed this danger to arise.

Accordingly I made two resolutions. One was on no account to confine my acquaintance to one social level. The other was never to invite to the same gathering any two people whom I had not already seen together at an Austrian party. The second resolution worked very well. There was no 'blamage' as far as I was concerned, and towards the end of my time I was beginning to make a few very cautious modifications.

In addition certain circles were 'out' altogether. I should like to have known some socialists and indeed, through a private introduction, I used to visit a delightful old gentleman previously active in the famous socialist housing projects in Vienna. He had a delicious Austrian accent and spoke in resigned terms of the existing position of the socialists. But this acquaintance was exceptional. The Austrian Government, it was understood, would not have welcomed any extended acquaintance among socialists. And the illegal left-wing literature which we received and studied was violent to a degree in content and language.

The Austrian Nazis for their part were not particularly keen to be seen with us, though I did know one or two families suspected of being friendly to them. These were significant and tiresome limitations, but they were as nothing compared with the total control of contact and acquaintance imposed by post-Second World War Communist countries.

Since priority has to be given to official work, a year and a half is not a long time in which to develop wider contacts even in a welcoming country like Austria and given my knowledge of the language. There was always the agreeable and hospitable ambience of the *Erste Gesellschaft*, with its international connections and outlook. I made friends in the professions and among Jewish people – a community of their own without many bridges to others. I was fortunate enough to make the acquaintance of the historian, Count Egon Corti, the biographer of the ill-starred Empress Elizabeth, wife of the last Emperor but one, Franz Josef II who reigned for no less than sixty-eight years. Visiting the Cortis in their beautiful apartment in central Vienna gave one something of a perspective on the immediate past and a feeling for a dynasty and for a period which had its comforts and delights as well as its tragedies and unsolved problems.

Tennis at the Vienna Park Club was another escape from official life; and there was always the opera. Every night that I had nothing special to do, I went to the fourth gallery. It was the cheapest place. While visibility was a little less good than in the third gallery, the air and the acoustics were better and little individual lights enabled you to follow a performance in the score. I will describe only my most exciting evening. The opera was Richard Strauss's *Electra*, with the name part to be sung by Rose Pauly. No recording from the opera existed and I knew nothing about it. An opera-goer demands too much – a great vocal concert, a great orchestral concert and a great dramatic production all at once. But after about ten minutes, I was suddenly gripped by the feeling that it was all happening. The splendid prayer to Agamemnon, the gorgeously rich orchestral climaxes, the frenzied dancing of Electra and the overwhelming emotion of the recognition scene between Electra and Orestes – the perfect rendering of them all was too much for a crowded house, and at the end the usually rather sceptical Viennese audience stood up and applauded for twenty minutes.

I wrote off to a Director of Covent Garden and said he should book the show at once. A suave reply said 'not quite at once' – but it made it in the end.

Some diplomats were, and a very few still are, inclined to regard visitors as a tiresome interruption of business routine. But if visitors will accept the principle, as they nearly all do, that there is a measure of priority in a Mission's time and that not everybody can have the Head of Mission's ear, then visits become an item of interest, opportunity and pleasure for both sides, and a channel of introduction for the Mission itself to places where it would have no expectation of entrée on its own account. A classic case happened to me in Vienna. I saw in a newspaper a heading 'Sudbahndirektor Maunsell in Wien' (Director of the Southern Railway Maunsell in Vienna). I remembered that my father had a close friend of that name, a brilliant railway engineer who had played a great part in the electrification of the Southern Railway suburban system in London. So I took a chance and called at his hotel, had guessed right and received a tremendous welcome. From this followed contact with the Federal Railways administration and some enjoyable rides on the Austrian Railway system.

I started a visitors' book in 1937 and have kept one ever since. On page one is the signature of the jazz band leader Jack Hylton and his then wife, a Viennese girl with red hair called Fifi. In the Viennese section of the book are also the writers John Lehmann and Stephen Spender, intellectual refugees from Spain where the Republican cause had gone extreme and the insurgents had never been anything but authoritarian.

Visitors also meant emergencies, like a party including an MP who landed in Vienna in a private aircraft on their way to Budapest only to find that they had no Hungarian permit to proceed.

To make things easier it was a public holiday and raining cats and dogs. I eventually routed out a Hungarian colleague whom I didn't know and who spoke German astonishingly badly. We had an interminable discussion at the (closed) Hungarian Legation, but in the end good sense and good will prevailed and the party went on. They later sent a very gracious letter of thanks. Most British visitors are of this calibre and deeply appreciate what is done for them, and this makes the occasional exception something of a shock.

The most distinguished visitor in my time was HRH the Duke of Windsor. He came three times – as Prince of Wales, as King and shortly after abdication. I remember one morning receiving a handwritten letter on a half sheet of hotel paper asking if some small thing could be done, signed 'Edward'. I did a double take, my first reaction being that I didn't know anyone called Edward. Only then did I realize that it was a note scribbled off by HRH.

Not long after the abdication, when the Duke and Duchess of Windsor came back to Austria, Sir Walford and Lady Selby invited me to a small family lunch with them. I was struck by three things, the supreme social skill and confidence of the Duchess, the extraordinary range of knowledge, experience and interest of the Duke and, the intervening doubt, the slight inaccuracy of his information on anything I really knew about myself. It was a rather overpowering little occasion, to be there with someone who had just been the head of four hundred million people and had suddenly become a most distinguished but shy private citizen. I could understand the human sympathy felt by very many at the time. But when the abdication took place and the first news movies flashed out in anticipation the caption 'God save King Albert,' one had an instinct that we had as sovereign the right man for difficult times to come.

Such an amalgam of business, learning and pleasure may appear unsystematic and undirected. This is partly because one cannot tolerably describe the purposeful daily round and common task. It is also because the process of finding one's way around a foreign capital is in its nature untidy and even chancy. One way to appreciate this is to imagine oneself arriving in London or Paris as Third Secretary in the Embassy of Anonima and to wonder how, consistently with office work, domestic problems, a language difference and limited means, one would set out to conquer the city. There is no measurable cost-effectiveness of miscellaneous activity; but no real feel for a country is attainable without it. And so miscellaneous activity goes on in its different forms, depending on the political background and cultural pattern of each capital city. The frustrating posts are those in which government policy or theology imposes a barrier to personal contact.

Vienna was a wonderful background for this apprenticeship. The city knew it needed radical improvements but had no money for them. Too many people had too little to eat and, contrary to belief, the citizens unlike those of Budapest went to bed early. But Vienna was not going to surrender to gloom. Apart from the natural instinct of the people, gloom would not help the essential tourist trade which must have a little romance about it, a little spring, a little wine. So Gerald and I took lessons in waltzing, not just to avoid letting the side down at the Opera Ball but also to be a part of what our hosts felt.

After I left Vienna, I did not come back for over thirty years. When I did come, accompanied by wife and younger daughter, we sought a '*Heuriger*,' a traditional garden restaurant in Grinzing, where people drink new wine to the sound of the Schrammel-Quartett, a small ensemble with violin and harmonica. We found one which had not been commercialized out of the old spirit. After the Schrammel-Quartett had played several numbers like '*Fein, Fein, schmeckt uns der Wein*,' introducing the family to music I had tried to imitate for years, two quiet, modest Viennese ladies came one after another past our table. Having finished a modest glass of wine, each of them said, with gentle dignity, 'We are glad you like and understand our city. Please come again.'

In May 1936 Prince Starhomberg, leader of the *Heimwehr*, a voluntary defence organization which had given stout support to Dollfuss, resigned from the Government. The resignation was inevitable, since the Prince's links with Italy were strong and Italy's attitude to Germany and Austria was beginning to change. But the event was weakening to the Government since the Prince, if no professional politician, had *panache*, an ability to make an exciting public impression which Dr von Schuschnigg's team otherwise lacked.

There followed much diplomatic activity. On 11 July, after confidential negotiations, Dr von Schuschnigg concluded with the German Government an agreement defining the relations between the two countries. The Austrians declared that the internal affairs of Germany were none of their business, and the German Reich stated that it would 'recognise the full sovereignty of the Federal State of Austria and regard the internal political development of Austria, including the question of Austrian National Socialism as an Austrian matter on which (it undertook) to exercise no influence whether direct or indirect.' By signing this agreement Dr von Schuschnigg affirmed his confidence in the unity of his country and the effectiveness of his control.

But as the Italian resolve to defend Austrian independence weakened, Nazi try-ons increased. Herr von Papen, then German Minister in Vienna, tried to obtain ambassadorial status, and thus to outrank all the other diplomatic representatives who ranked as Ministers. The Austrian Government turned this down. Bonfires in the shape of a swastika were regularly lit on the mountains above Innsbruck, to warn Austrians of the inevitable.

At the end of 1937 anxiety persisted. Two recent Government appointments had seemed to show acquiescence to Nazi preference, if not pressure. The initiative lay with Hitler, and everything was possible. The Nazis might march in tomorrow or not at all. If they did march in, they would find supporters, though few people could be sure in advance who they would be.

Such was the atmosphere of hoping against hope when I left at the beginning of December 1937. In February 1938 Hitler decided to lose patience. Chancellor von Schuschnigg was summoned to Berchtesgaden and after intense bullying went back with the minimum assurances he felt Austria could accept. The Legislature accepted them. But the pressure continued and finally on 24 February 1938 Dr von Schuschnigg appealed to his countrymen to affirm by plebiscite their desire for an independent Austria. They would probably have done so by a good majority, so Hitler was 'compelled' to use force and on 11 March Nazi troops entered and occupied Austria.

Japan
1938-1942

Before Pearl Harbour

Sir Walford Selby left Vienna on 15 October 1937 and early in November I received a letter saying that I should pack up with all speed and proceed to Nanking, capital of Nationalist China. This was a total shock. I had at last, after a year and a half in Vienna, got my bearings and felt I was beginning to be of some use. Besides which I was enjoying myself enormously and had no wish to be interrupted.

Less than a week later, a huge bagload of papers arrived from London. They were deposited, no doubt by Herr Schneider with his quiet malice, in a great unsorted heap on my desk. Right at the bottom was a small official envelope which said in effect 'Not Nanking; Tokyo.' So I had at least half the mental readjustment all over again.

This change was not in fact a piece of bureaucratic inefficiency or callousness. A whole complex of changes was in progress, and there were good reasons for making this one. I was very pleased in one way, as it sent me where I had asked to go and moreover, with Craigie, now Sir Robert Craigie, as Ambassador in Japan, there would be less to relearn inside the office. The person who sent me his *Japanese for Beginners* was Con O'Neill.[1]

After Hal Mack, the First Secretary, and his wife had given one of those gay-sad farewell affairs to which one gets so used in diplomatic life, but which are always a little moving, I drove off for home early in the morning in Vienna's first flurry of snow.

[1] The Hon. Sir Con O'Neill, Ambassador to Finland, 1961–63, Ambassador to the European Communities, Brussels, 1963–65, Deputy Under–Secretary in the Foreign Office, 1965–68, in charge of economic affairs, exercising special responsibilities in connection with the European Communities.

The Embassy at Tokyo were, I gathered, in a hurry for me to get there. Posts usually are. They then tend to welcome you with: 'What? You here already?' But in Japan the situation was indeed critical. In my concentration on Central European matters, I had little real idea of events in the Far East and Japan's attitude to Britain. I called on Nigel Ronald,[2] the Under-Secretary concerned with the Far East, and asked whether the Japanese were being difficult. 'Very,' he replied gloomily.

I asked if I might go to Japan via the United States, Canada and the Pacific. My uncle, Ralph Scholfield, was at that time reading at the Mother Church in Boston. As the term is a three-year one, this would be my only chance to hear him. It was a bit more expensive than the P&O route via India but I pointed out that my route would oblige the Embassy by getting me there quicker. It was agreed. I asked whether I got a tropical clothing allowance. A kindly but sad man said 'No.' I went back two days later and he said 'Sorry, I meant "Yes".' So that was all right too.

With all this, the Japanese Embassy to call on (they duly furnished me with some bulky information volumes), friends and relations to see, it was a pretty desperate three weeks. It would have been more so had I realized that I would not be seeing my parents again for nearly five years.

I went off on Christmas Eve, of all days, in a huge empty liner. In a restaurant car between New York and Boston, I received from a fierce American imperative instructions to 'Tell those so-and-sos where they get off' (they had just sunk an American gunboat) 'and keep the United States out of war.'

I duly attended my uncle's reading, which I admired greatly. When a boy, even as a glamorous fast bowler who accounted for many Harrovians in the match of 1903, he had been handicapped by an impediment of speech which he had handled with good humour but some inconvenience. Now his voice hit the back wall of an auditorium for six thousand with a bang and every word was clear.

I crossed Canada by the Canadian Pacific Railway Trans-

[2] Sir Nigel Ronald, Assistant Under-Secretary in the Foreign Office, 1942, and Ambassador to Portugal from 1947 until his retirement in 1954.

Continental. This was a marvellously comfortable ride through miles and miles of prairie covered in snow. I got out at White River Junction, Ontario, to see if it was as cold as people said. It was. After three days we came down the fabulous Kicking Horse Pass, watching trains circle round above and below us, and so into the kinder moist air of Vancouver. Then aboard the CPR's liner *Empress of Asia* for the fortnight's sail across the Pacific.

On this sort of journey you do not get exhausted and you can get something done. I had, by a curious accident, studied some Japanese history at Eton. I now tackled the language and took a daily stint of Rose-Innes's Japanese grammar. There was no question of my studying to become a Japanese language expert, which takes two years' full-time study, but I did make an effort to get somewhere on my own.

When I got to Japan, I immediately asked that wisest of men, Sir George Sansom,[3] what to do. He said, 'Learn as few words as you can manage with, but practise them so that in the end you can use them without thinking.' It was splendid advice, and thanks to it I have never forgotten the minimum that I learned. The difference it made to getting things done was immeasurable, especially as Japanese people find foreign languages difficult. Even in crisis times I took two lessons a week with Colonel T. Isobe, a very persevering retired army officer, whom it was a wonderful pleasure to meet again in 1970 at the age of ninety-one.

When I arrived in Yokohama, we rattled up the bumpy Yokohama-Tokyo road which I was to get to know so well. A faint smell of soya bean became part of the daily environment. It was clear from that journey alone that Japan had in some measure already a war economy.

Everything was as different as could be from Vienna. Austria was a small power being pressed by others. Japan was a large and growing power, putting pressure on China. I knew German;

[3] Sir George Sansom, Consultant Professor at Stanford University. Specialist in Far Eastern studies, economic and historical, and member of the Japanese Academy in 1951. Publications include *Short Cultural History of Japan*, 1931, and *History of Japan*, 3 vols.

I did not know Japanese, and as nationalism was growing there were less and less signs in English.* Despite the politics, Austria had been gay and relaxed; Japan was very serious and Anglo-Japanese relations were beginning to be tense.

Above all things, there was the difference in human approach. In Britain, the United States, Austria and most of Europe, the approach was individual; you asked one person one thing and you usually got an individual reply, right or wrong. In Japan the approach was collective; it was much better to find five people together who would work out an answer; a person on his own was likely to be among the don't knows.

The British Embassy is in a compound on a commanding site overlooking the moat round the Imperial Palace. The moat is a fine sight, but the Palace has always been a modest affair: indeed the Tokyo of 1938, despite a few notable buildings, was a disappointingly featureless city. There were, however, lovely little corners which you discovered when you were seeking your way among capriciously numbered houses.

There had once been some informal but pleasant buildings in the compound but they, like so much, had been destroyed in the earthquake and fire of 1923. When houses were rebuilt in the late twenties, they were designed with a structural flexibility to cushion them against earthquakes, but in other respects they justified the criticism that they must have been designed for somewhere else: they not only lacked certain fundamental requirements for Japanese conditions but offered, as a bonus, a few original inconveniences. One gathered that the then Ambassador had not worried himself overmuch about the details of buildings. The moral, not lost on me, was that unless the head of a post takes personal interest in accommodation matters, the right things will somehow not get done.

The operation in Tokyo was naturally much larger than in Vienna. In place of one Herr Schneider in the Registry, there were three registry officers, and they were hard put to it to keep up. In addition to the Chancery (political officers), there was a special

* English labels did not exist in the National Museum; it was strange to find the same thing in Libya thirty years later.

section, the Japanese Chancery, run by two British officials with expert knowledge of Japanese, assisted by translators. There were full-time instead of part-time service attachés, the Naval and Military Attachés having assistants. There were always three commercial officers from the service, and their work was supplemented by a network of Consulates in the big cities. As elsewhere, however, there was no information work at all.

In the office, work was very intense. Case after case came before us involving misdeeds by Japanese military authorities or personnel at the expense of British enterprises or individuals in China. At the time I arrived, a major demand was being pressed that the banking business of the Chinese Customs should be handed over from the British Hong Kong and Shanghai Bank to the Japanese Yokohama Specie Bank. With the Japanese in control of the China coast, while the British fleet (about whose immediate combat readiness there was some doubt) was required in home waters and the Mediterranean, total resistance was impossible. You had to get the best terms you could in endless and complicated negotiation both in China and Japan.

Embassy business was directed, on behalf of the Ambassador, by the Head of Chancery, Ashley Clarke.[4] He did this with great efficiency and good temper, assisted by Anthony Haigh, my colleague from the American Department in London. The office was understaffed but was, to my sloppy Viennese ideas, in a slightly obsessional state about it all. We worked from 9.00 till 1.00 and again from 2.30 to at least 7.00. When I suggested a cup of tea at 4.00, I was told that there wasn't time. So I had to make my own arrangements to have tea with the typists.

But I think the reality of any internal tension in the Embassy was political. There were two very definite schools of thought about Japanese actions and British reactions. One school, headed by Colonel, later Major-General, F. S. G. Pigott (who, like his father, was a great expert on and lover of Japan), held that the current hostility did not represent the real Japan at all, and that this real Japan would in due course reassert itself, with its natural

[4] Sir H. Ashley Clarke was Chief Clerk (head administrative officer) of the Foreign Office, 1949–53, and Ambassador to Italy, 1953–62.

friendship for Britain, the sister island empire. The Ambassador tended towards this view, partly, I think, because it supported his very proper efforts to keep Britain out of trouble in a time of growing crisis in Europe.

The opposite point of view had a protagonist in the Naval Attaché, Captain Bernard Rawlings.[5] He took a very absolute view that the Japanese were behaving outrageously and that sooner or later they would have to be taught a lesson. Sir George Sansom did not go quite as far as this, but he was much nearer this view than that of General Pigott, and his opinion weighed very much with me.

I must on no account give the impression that disagreements about policy and ensuing tensions meant an unhappy ship as a whole. On the contrary, there were no desperate feuds and, as pressure against Britain grew, cohesion within the Embassy increased.

There were also outside influences affecting the atmosphere. One of the occupational difficulties of diplomacy is that, when two countries with which your own country has important ties fall out with each other, it is very easy for the Ambassadors in the two capitals to get into a kind of private war with each other. Each must make clear to his own government the point of view of the country in which he is serving; but the distinction between 'presenting' that point of view and advocating it is a fine one, and I fear that Sir Robert Craigie in Japan and Sir Archibald Clark-Kerr[6] in China fell somewhat into this trap, which is the easier to fall into if the two people start with differing tastes and temperaments. I had cause to remind myself of this when Morrice James[7] in Karachi and I in Delhi were trying to

[5] Later Vice-Admiral Sir Bernard Rawlings, Second-in-Command in the Far East at the end of the war.

[6] Later Lord Inverchapel, for a time Ambassador in Moscow and subsequently in Washington.

[7] The Rt. Hon. Sir Morrice James was High Commissioner in Pakistan, 1961–66, then Deputy Under-Secretary, Commonwealth Office, 1966–68, when from March until October he was Permanent Under-Secretary. He then became High Commissioner in India, 1968–71, since when he has been High Commissioner in Australia.

interpret the Kashmir dispute. Fortunately we knew each other very well, and it was easy for us, a quarter of a century later, to hop into aeroplanes for note-comparing visits.

We had also to bear in mind in Tokyo that from day to day British public opinion was not in the least interested in the Far East. True, there were important commercial, industrial and financial interests that were involved and vocal, and there was a lively Colonial Office and Conservative interest in Hong Kong. But the British may well rank as having been, in proportion to the extent and importance of their Empire, the most insular imperialists in world history, and when a remote quarrel mainly concerned two foreign countries, the regular appetite for knowledge or participation was very small. Only occasional incidents such as the searching of British women going in and out of the British Concession in Tientsin in 1940 aroused sudden indignation, often accompanied by impracticable demands for redress. This chronic disinterest was very relevant when Japanese intrusions into British interests became much worse, and it was our duty to consider whether we ought to take retaliatory action, despite the vulnerability of our Far Eastern trade and investments. But the circumstances of impending and actual war and the growing realization that it was the American rather than the British role that would be decisive in the Far East, made these dicussions inconclusive.

In Japan there was always quite a lot of contact with opposite numbers in the *Gaimusho* (Japanese Foreign Office). Much of the business concerned China, and, as we guessed then and know now, the army authorities kept the diplomatic representatives at more than one arm's length. But we had to insist on our case and the *Gaimusho* officials welcomed at least this degree of official and personal relationship.

Initially, they also welcomed social contact, particularly those who had had some educational or other experience in Britain. But two years later such contact ceased with a sad letter addressed by a Japanese official to a colleague of mine, in which he said he liked our company very much but as it did him so much harm officially, would we help him by leaving him alone.

Our closest diplomatic relations were with the American Embassy. As events proceeded, it became more and more clear that, while in terms of economics we stood to lose much more than did the Americans in China, the question of whether or not there would be effective resistance to Japanese expansion would depend entirely on the United States. Japan was in many senses primarily an American rather than a British interest. It had been opened up by the American Commodore Perry; the first diplomatic representative of the modern age had been that remarkable American, Townsend Harris; much of the strongest missionary effort in the Far East was American; and the leading English-language daily in Tokyo, the *Japan Advertiser*, was American-owned and edited. It was not always remembered in Britain that the Treaty of Portsmouth, ending the Russo-Japanese War, had been signed in New, not old, England.

The American Ambassador was Mr Joseph Clark Grew who served for ten years from 1931 to 1941. He was tall, grey and handsome, liked Japan and the Japanese, and it is one of those singular ironies of diplomacy that so outstanding an envoy should have started his mission in the sunshine of good relations and ended it in war. A little too much was made at one time of the legend that he 'foresaw' Pearl Harbour. In fact the Peruvian Ambassador, Dr Ricardo Rivera Schreiber, heard a story in April 1941 that the Japanese would enter the war with an attack on Pearl Harbour and the Americans with their usual thoroughness reported this to Washington. But it was one of many stories and the American Embassy of the time would not have claimed to have 'foreseen' Pearl Harbour.

Sir Robert Craigie saw his relationship with Mr Grew in its right proportions: he kept Mr Grew *au courant* with developments on our side, sought his advice frequently and his diplomatic support if ever there seemed a chance that Washington would agree to it. It was appropriate that on the morning of 8 December 1941, when a Japanese party came to our Embassy to announce a state of war, Sir Robert was at the American Embassy having a last session with Mr Grew.

The American Embassy was in any case very strongly staffed,

and included some outstanding members of the US Foreign Service including Charles E. ('Chip') Bohlen, afterwards Counsellor of the State Department and Ambassador in Moscow and Paris.

The French Embassy were talented and excellent company. In 1939 the First Secretary arranged with us that, if and when France had officially declared war with Germany he would telephone to us the single word 'Napoleon'. He did. We couldn't repress a smile but accepted the patriotic intention and didn't reply 'Waterloo'. Alas, the French Embassy in the unhappy events of May-June 1940 went the Vichy way, Gaullists coming from the business community. I have always been grateful to a stout-hearted Gaullist named Humbert whom I met the day after we had engaged the French fleet at Oran. I said to him, 'I'm very sad – what more can I say?'; he replied, 'What else could you have done?'

And there were many other congenial colleagues. The Dutch who, with their Empire in the Netherlands East Indies, were well-informed and helpful (Herman van Roijen, probably the ablest Dutch diplomat of our time – and the standard is very high – was a very hospitable Counsellor at the Netherlands Embassy); and even the Germans and Italians started by being amiable. There was a little time lag between Europe and the Far East, after which they gradually drifted away.

In 1938 the military secrecy network had not yet clamped down and one was able to travel quite widely. I visited the old capital of Kyoto, saw the sights and stayed with John Pilcher in his Japanese house. His nearest neighbour was the celebrated Japanese master potter, Kanjiro Kawai, a personal friend of the English pottery master Bernard Leach. A visit to Mr Kawai was always a delight, with a Japanese tinge of ceremony, and it tested one's spoken Japanese to the limit. On one visit countless persimmons were served and before each persimmon was eaten, Mr Kawai gave a brief lecture, as good as that of any Continental wine connoisseur, on where it came from.

In 1938 also, Henry Sawbridge of the Japanese Secretariat and I went to Korea and after visiting Seoul took a walking tour in the Diamond Mountains, now in North Korea. It is beautiful country. A mountain hut contained Mozart records provided by the Japanese.

Then Ian Morrison (the Ambassador's eccentric private secretary), two American girls and I did a tour in the Izu Peninsula. This is the cul-de-sac of land southwest of Tokyo where the Japanese ostensibly made the first Americans welcome in the hope of sealing them off. It was charming in the persistent winter sunshine, with oranges in full crop and the strawberries coming in from the Shizuoka terraces next door. We stayed in Japanese inns, in those days enjoyably inexpensive, and relaxed from Embassy labours except on one afternoon when we appeared to be off course and were pursued by a Japanese policeman with a sword across a paddy-field. We were unarmed, so we won.

But the expedition to end expeditions was the attack on Mount Fuji, organized in the summer of 1938. There is a Japanese saying that only a fool never climbs Mount Fuji and only a fool climbs it twice. Determined to achieve the sane compromise, I joined the expedition containing notably two American naval students and a solid Swiss called Charlie Hinnen. The plan of attack hardly rivals that of John Hunt of Everest: the idea simply was to drive to 3,000 feet and walk all night up the remaining 9,395 feet, where there is a pumice and lava track all the way, and a tea house every 1,000 feet. None the less, it seemed a good idea on a mountain to attach oneself to a Swiss, so I attached myself to Charlie.

The naval students got there easily first. Charlie and I plodded steadily up, ignoring tea-shops, at the orthodox 1,000 feet per hour, and reached the top at about 6.30 a.m. The top with its booths and flags in summer is a bit of an anti-climax; the real joy was round sunrise, slightly below the top, when one looked down on the whole world without interruption save for a few little flakes of cloud for foreground contrast.

As Fuji is so central to Japanese legend and art, I must pause over two other pictures. One was my first view of the mountain from Lake Hakone. Fuji seemed to be invisible, as I was walking through some reeds. Suddenly it appeared in the shape so favoured by oriental art; you could see the cone and perhaps half way down, but you could not see the base for mist. It looked like a vision suspended in air.

Later we rented a tiny Japanese house at Zushi on the coast. At about five o'clock one morning my wife said, 'Look!' Through the open Japanese *shoji* (sliding door) there were to be seen just four things – the sea, one small pine tree, the full moon and Mount Fuji. That is how many Japanese still like to think of their country; at that moment one was seeing with them something of its true beauty.

When, after six months at a desk, you walk over 9,000 feet straight uphill, the reaction is rather different. On the way down I didn't bother about the path or my companion; I just made a dash for it. I zoomed down through a lot of loose ash, causing one beautifully kimonoed and made-up Japanese lady to fall flat on her face with alarm. I stayed the night on my own at a Japanese inn and next day went straight up to Chuzenji for a fortnight's local leave. I slept, essentially, for three days.

Chuzenji has been described by many people and I need not compete. It consisted of a few furnished houses on the side of a beautiful mountain lake, five hours' drive from Tokyo, where you could sleep, swim or take part in elementary but fiercely contested sailing races. Ashley Clarke had lent me his house with which went gramophone records of the whole of *Die Walküre*. So I just lay there, with the feeling that an oak tree really was growing, in the way Miss Anna Russell used to say, 'in the middle of the drawing-room' until I nearly knew the first act by heart. Such was my physical reaction to Fuji.

For the rest of 1938 and the first part of 1939 it was mainly cases, cases, cases, in the China dossier. Anthony Haigh was transferred and later Ashley Clarke. Since the staff was small and there was no scope for specialization save for the Japanese Chancery, I found myself for a time in charge of these voluminous files and, since urgent enquiries might mean a lengthy organization of paper, I kept an immediate reference volume of my own.

This proved a godsend. We had a visit from Mr John Swire, Chairman of Butterfield and Swire, one of the two leading

British shipping and trading firms in China waters. He was invited to go over with me such cases as he was interested in. The reference volume saved his time and my life. This meant more than it sounds now, because even in those days a British China *taipan* was regarded as a formidable client and it helped all round if an Embassy could show it was on the ball.

But Europe pressed on us more and more and the period of the Munich crisis in September 1938 was particularly oppressive. The weather does not normally reflect the international situation. But in that month it did. Day after day was dark and murky, as we followed Mr Neville Chamberlain's movements and hoped he could pull off something which would maintain national self-respect. I had the experience of maintaining contact with the Czechoslovak Minister, Mr Frantisek Havlicek, so I used to have supper with him from time to time. We would discuss the affairs of his country and Japanese attitudes to them, on which he was very well informed, and then he would go to the piano which he played exceptionally well and lose himself in Mendelssohn's *Rondo capriccioso* or in a sentimental little jewel of a piece called *Poem* by the Czech composer Fibich. He represented so many of the Czech virtues, intelligence, instinct, artistic understanding and sensitiveness, and yet all with a certain brave resignation. I think I wanted him to be angrier with us than he was.

When the result of Munich came, the Ambassador made the best of it and drew our attention to certain points on which something had been saved; but most of us felt only that this was a great defeat. What underlined this for us, no doubt illogically, was the fact that the details of the Munich agreement reached us first from the German Embassy. This was an efficient courtesy by the Germans, but its effect was simply to increase our ill-humour.

It also caused us to take a look at our communications with the Foreign Office on matters of general world interest which had manifestly become too slow. I accordingly prepared a letter for the Ambassador suggesting that in the 1938 state of the world, a system for keeping posts swiftly and confidentially informed of important events and their significance to Britain was overdue. Doubtless other such letters were written at the time, but this letter must have played its part in the establishment before the war of an excellent system of immediate information and guidance which for many years made our Embassies much the best informed of any.

Then came the 1939 summer of the British negotiations with the Soviet Union. There has been something of a campaign to suggest that if the British Government had sent someone more exalted than Sir William Strang[8] to Moscow, things would have been different. From the other end of the world one sometimes sees things more clearly. It was quite clear to us that the Russians were using the British desire for their support to obtain something we could not give – a stab in the back to our new Polish allies in the form of a Soviet military presence on Polish territory. It is arguable that we should not have concluded the Polish alliance, but having concluded it, we had to stick to it in good faith. Subsequent events showed that the Poles were not being quite so unreasonable as they may have seemed at the time.

But it is worth adding that, if the Russians had wanted a high political personality they would have asked for one and got one. The Soviet Government have often shown that they do not subordinate policy to 'face'; to think that they do is to impute to them a characteristic which is Chinese, not Russian.

The hours we worked and the growing ominousness of the international situation made it imperative consciously to seek recreation. For me, this partly consisted in improving the little garden behind my semi-detached residence. I built up some stone steps, covered a disused well with a disused stone vase, and

[8] Sir William Strang (Lord Strang from 1954) was Permanent Under-Secretary in the Foreign Office, German Section, 1947–49, then Permanent Under-Secretary, Foreign Office, 1949–53. He was chairman of the Royal Insitute of International Affairs, 1959–65, and a Deputy Speaker and Deputy Chairman of committees in the House of Lords. Author of several authoritative books on diplomacy, including *The Foreign Office*, 1955, *Home and Abroad*, 1956, *Britain in World Affairs*, 1961, and *The Diplomatic Career*, 1962.

with Colonel Isobe's help, stocked the garden with camellias, gardenias, daphne and azaleas.

At the same time, the increasing Japanese withdrawal from social contact with foreigners 'liberated' a great deal of time which proved a great incentive to the (Anglo-American) Amateur Dramatic Club. My first venture was in a production of some scenes from Shakespeare's *Henry VIII* as a farewell evening for the retiring English professor at Tokyo University. I was offered the part of the executioner but when meticulous research revealed that he had nothing to say, I nervously suggested to Ashley Clarke that I would rather watch from the audience. I graduated to Surrey, one of the angry lords in Act III. But I was on the way up with unstoppable momentum. Ashley was to play Cardinal Wolsey and Vere Redman, the *Daily Mail* correspondent, of exactly the right height and shape, was to play the king. At the last moment the *Daily Mail* could not do without Redman in Manchuria, and I (wrong height, wrong shape) inherited the King.

The next year we did Emlyn Williams's *A Murder has been Arranged*. Mr Williams may not regard this as the greatest of his plays, but it has one moment of terrific theatre. A party on the stage is going to be all right because the wicked cousin, Maurice Mullins, is safely ensconced in Australia. The party is just beginning when enter, l. back, a figure in faultless evening dress (white tie), waving a cigarette and saying blithely: 'I hope you don't mind my smoking. My name is Maurice Mullins' (Curtain.)

In all my attempts at trafficking round a stage, I have never enjoyed anything so much as that entry – the prepared gasp from the stage, the spontaneous gasp from the audience, and the fall of the curtain with no time for anti-climax.

We had a producer of genius, Tommy (T. R. G.) Lyell, an Englishman who taught English at Waseda University. He had a magic with young people, an extraordinary response to the rhythms and sounds of poetry and superb instinct for the theatre, which he could communicate to others. He indulged in numerous minor human frailties, was wonderful company and could be in the same five minutes wildly cynical about one thing and wildly emotional about another. I wanted him very much to write a book about English poetry appreciation. But as a former Anglican priest converted to Catholicism he felt it his duty to write a verse translation of the Psalms. It was good, but the poetry book would have been better.

When the Nazi-Soviet Pact of 23 August 1939 burst on the world, the Japanese were bewildered and furious. Their chosen associate had betrayed them in favour of their greatest enemy, the country they had defeated in war thirty-four years previously, but which now hung over them threateningly in the north and west, and constantly interfered with their fishing. The reaction was still in full spate as war in Europe followed, and a breezy Japanese friend walked into the Embassy and said 'I see you people have bought the *Nichi Nichi*.'* However, Japan did not suddenly veer round to the Allied side; the war was after all in Europe and there could not now be a change of Japanese policy in China. But at least we benefited for the time being from suspended judgement. And the sinking of the German battlecruiser *Graf Spee* off Montevideo in December 1939 helped to maintain the impression that we were not as effete as Nazi propaganda had portrayed us.

It was now urgently necessary to start an Information Service and I was deputed to do this with the aid of Dick Ledward, one of the student interpreters. Apart from trying to organize a somewhat more methodical coverage of news from Britain, we concentrated on two things, the quick production of a short pamphlet on the causes of the war, and the setting up of an informal mixed committee of members of the Embassy staff and of the unofficial British community to discover both what they wanted from us and what they could tell us.

As we debated where to go next, the *Nichi Nichi* carried an item saying that Vere Redman, the *Daily Mail* correspondent who was in London at the time, had been appointed Press and Information Officer at the British Embassy. If there is one thing

*One of the leading national dailies which tended always to favour the Axis against the Allies.

that makes an Ambassador rightly furious, it is to be informed
through the press of changes in his staff. But everybody realized
that the early days of the Ministry of Information were unavoid-
ably chaotic and that we were getting a first-class man who
understood the Japanese and was known, trusted and liked by a
great many of them.

Redman took our unusual committee in his stride. He set
up a small but highly efficient unit, and used the daily operational
tea-party we had instituted to make continuously sure that the
political and information wings of the Embassy never functioned
at cross purposes.

The committee developed as a corporate activity a lunch
held at regular intervals at the (old style) Tokyo Club to exchange
information and views with leaders of the British community.
At first we talked pretty confidentially. Later, when the Japanese
changed the venue for us, we had a correct suspicion that this
was done to help their bugging operations. We became more
careful, but Japanese intelligence always thought there was more
in it than met their eyes.

Another new activity was initiated through an unexpected
visitor to the Embassy. His name was Frank Hawley. He was
a huge north-countryman who had come to Japan to teach
English, had taken completely to the Japanese way of life,
married the daughter of a prominent Japanese railway official and
apparently settled down for life. When the war broke out he
appeared, told us that he regarded all diplomats as living in an
unreal world and asked what could he do to help? Jim Henderson,
who had succeeded Ashley Clarke, took Frank on and after some,
complicated negotiations a British Council operation was
started which enabled us to keep in touch until Pearl Harbour
with a good deal of intelligent Japanese opinion. Henderson
did not have an easy time, since the real world of Frank Hawley
involved a certain casualness, to say the least of it, about Organization and Methods. But it was the start of something enduring and
the vision of someone in London (I think it was Sir John Pratt)
who got the authorization through was a matter for immediate
and lasting gratitude.

As with the Czechs in 1938, I tried to help the Polish Embassy in their distress in 1939 as their world collapsed, refugees poured through and the Polish Ambassador and his wife hit on the ingenious experiment of giving a non-party for Polish relief. But otherwise the phoney war period passed with only one major local flurry, the interception by a British cruiser near the coast of Japan of a Japanese ship bringing some Germans from America on their way to Germany. Japanese reaction was fortunately more violent in words than deeds. But some of us felt increasing worry about what was really happening at home. A chance to find out came in February 1940 when Edmund Hall-Patch,[9] British Financial Commissioner in the Far East, came to visit us direct from home and someone put the leading question 'Is the situation in Britain as bad as it seems?'

Hall-Patch, as I often saw him do later, took a look at the door as though to see whether anyone unauthorized was listening, turned round melodramatically and said, 'My dear, it's far worse.' He told us something of the hesitancies, half-measures and confusions which seemed to dog those early months. It was hard to believe; though I learned later to believe Hall-Patch when he was oracular.

When the full blast of war came in April 1940, we had tremendous pep meetings with our French allies; they were always good and always followed immediately by disaster. Jimmy Cox of Reuters rang me up: 'How are we doing in Belgium?' 'Oh, not too bad.' 'Well, we've just lost Brussels.' Then Dunkirk was shrouded in fog and the German Assistant Military Attaché was rash enough to predict the outcome.

The effect on the Japanese was enormous and from our point of view disastrous. Their Axis had been right after all. Dunkirk

[9] Sir Edmund Hall-Patch became First Assistant, then Deputy Under-Secretary of State, Foreign Office, in charge of economic and financial affairs, 1944–48. In 1948 he was appointed head of the UK delegation to the OEEC and chairman of the Executive Committee. From 1952–54 he was the UK executive director of the International Monetary Fund and the International Bank. On retirement in 1954 he became director (1957–62, chairman) of the Standard Bank.

might be a temporary deliverance, but the *Blitzkrieg* was going
to overwhelm everybody. Pressure in China tightened. There
followed a serious incident in Tientsin. Some Chinese, suspected,
probably rightly, of a successful bomb attempt against the Japanese,
took refuge in the British Concession. The Japanese put the
Concession under siege and demanded the surrender of the
Chinese. We had to give way, and I had the miserable duty of
announcing our surrender at a press conference, the first one I
ever gave. Only the presence of Relman (Pat) Morin, a good
friend from the American Associated Press who understand these
things, made the occasion tolerable.

We lost Jimmy Cox. He was a very tense man who had come
to loathe Japan and the Japanese and did not try to conceal it.
He was detained by the *Kempeitai* (Military Police) on a charge
which was never clear, and his body found after falling from
a third-floor window. It was alleged to be full of injection marks.
We feared murder, but it seemed probable that Jimmy, feeling
himself in a corner, had taken the only way out and the Japanese
had sought to revive him.

But the most serious pressure in the Chinese context was the
Japanese demand that we close the Burma road into China.
We had a special meeting with the Ambassador at which he
asked each of us in turn what we thought. We all, as far as I can
remember, said we saw no alternative to recommending closure
at this juncture in the hope that, if our fortunes improved,
the road could be quietly reopened. This is exactly what happened.

At this point something momentous took place in my private
life. But I must go back a bit in time in order to explain it.

By 1939 I was nearing thirty-one still unmarried. This was in no
sense a policy. It just happened: as I mentioned at the very
beginning, my education in the ways of the other sex began late.
It would however have been impossible to go through Oxford,
to be in and out of London dances (it was far too exhausting to
work at the Foreign Office and be 'in') and then to pass a year
and a half in sentimental Vienna without having had serious
emotional ups and downs. But in this age of frankness, I have

some sympathy with Lord Chandos's regard for an age that was more reticent, and shall not disturb the memory of people who are not now here or the tranquillity of those who are by mentioning any names at all. In 1939 there were no entanglements.

Early in 1938 I had had a serious conversation with a serious young lady of sixteen, born in Kobe, Japan, and just returned from school in Australia, called Miss Patricia Ellerton. We talked earnestly about port towns in South Australia, where she had been at school, and which my brother had visited on his sea voyage. She went to work for the Danish business man and honorary Consul, Mr A. H. Hansen, and I did not see her for a year and a half.

At the outbreak of war, Miss Ellerton came to offer her services to the British Embassy. Since I was doing an unorthodox job in trying to get information work started, she was instructed to give me special help. It soon became apparent that I was going to want Miss Ellerton's company for longer than the duration of the information section. So after anxious thought I tried the idea out on a ski slope at Akakura. The result was that I ended up in a bush 20 feet below her, leaving a rather bewildered Miss Ellerton aged eighteen saying 'No'.

The situation was now very awkward. Miss Ellerton continued to do my work, but there was need, from my point of view, for Highly Confidential Bilateral Negotiations. This was what you just could not have in Tokyo because there were very few foreigners left and no chance of meeting without arousing comment. In the end I discovered a piece of road by the sea near Kamakura where nobody ever seemed to go, and under cover of some driving lessons, negotiations progressed.

Progress was helped, though conclusion delayed, by the absence of Mrs Ellerton in Australia. She was a mainstay, or perhaps I mean *the* mainstay, of the Australian Trade Office in Tokyo. She had been born in Australia and had met my father-in-law in Japan during the First World War. When she returned, negotiations were completed with Mr Ellerton and herself, though my own parents had, inevitably, to be confronted with a *fait accompli*. This was based on two not very good photographs. The better one consisted of Miss Ellerton with motor car; I told her my mother's comment would be, 'That's a nice looking motor car.'

A telegram of blessing came from London and the next step was to tell the Ambassador and obtain his goodwill and that of Lady Craigie. This latter might have proved a step of some delicacy, because Lady Craigie had conducted several unsuccessful campaigns to marry me to other people. But finally, I made an appointment. Just before the hour arrived, a telegram came with news of the battle of Oran, and it would be for me to take it to the Ambassador. I did, and all I can remember about the interview is that I said something like, 'Sir, we've sunk half the French fleet and I want to marry Miss Ellerton.'

The worst was over and the best to come. Lady Craigie at once rallied to the new cause and both she and the Ambassador showed the utmost kindness to Pat and me. They insisted that the wedding reception should be in the residence. We decided to have as short an engagement as possible and were married by the Rev. C. K. Sansbury[10] at St Andrew's Church, Shiba-ku, Tokyo, on Saturday, 21 September, 1940.

We had a splendid congregation of British, American, Japanese and diplomatic friends. We sang Milton's 'Let us with a gladsome mind, Praise the Lord for he is kind . . .', followed by Bunyan's Pilgrim Hymn and ending with Blake's 'Jerusalem'. On the steps of the church the *Japan Advertiser* took the only wedding picture that we possess.

The wedding coincided with the Battle of Britain and Ashley Clarke, now in the Foreign Office, sent a telegram: 'Blitzkrieg unimpressive; thumbs up here'. My parents sent 'Malachi, 3:10'.* Don Brown, our American best man, made a brief

---

[10] The Rev. C. K. Sansbury, Bishop of Singapore and Malaya, 1961–66 and from 1966 general secretary of the British Council of Churches and Assistant Bishop in the Diocese of London.

* 'Bring ye all the tithes into the storehouse, that there may be meat in mine house, and prove me now herewith, saith the Lord of hosts, if I will not open you the windows of heaven, and pour you out a blessing, that there shall not be room enough to receive it.'

speech and I for the first time in my life, very slightly teased the Ambassador.

The honeymoon was practically Don Brown's invention. I had got to know him as News Editor of the *Japan Advertiser*. Finding we had kindred tastes in current affairs, history and music, we had dined together regularly once a fortnight. Don, after much deliberation, asked us whether dollars might not be a useful wedding present, and our acceptance made it possible for us to go to Honolulu. (The alternative, Peking, was too full of Japanese policemen.)

We had a gay trip in SS *President Taft*, as we played deck tennis and danced to 'The Cockeyed Mayor of Kaunakakei' and 'My Wonderful One, Let's Dance.' On arrival we were taken in hand by the Associated Press who had heard from Pat Morin. The correspondent said firmly, 'I am going to show you a number of hotels, and you mayn't choose until I've shown you the lot.' About the second one we saw was the old Halekulani Hotel, quietly spacious, in garden surroundings and facing on to Waikiki Beach. Excitedly we said 'That's it,' but discipline prevailed. In the end we went back to the Halekulani and could not have done better.

Right at the beginning of our stay there occurred one of those guardian angel episodes which make life so worthwhile. The day after we arrived we went to an evening church service. When it was over, we asked a nice-looking young man how to get back to the hotel. His reply was 'You wait a moment. Then you come with me for a banana-split at the drive-in [both new concepts to us] and I'll take you back.' As he left us at the hotel, he hesitated for a moment and then went off. In the morning we found in our pigeon-hole a note. 'Dear Friends, I can use the company car for a week; mine is outside and here is the key. Benton S. Wood.'

So we drove in style round Oahu, much less built up than now, with the car radio (another new experience) going all the time. We felt as if we were for once in, rather than watching, a Hollywood movie.

The other world would not quite go away. A large ship

stood off the shore, visible from the hotel. We asked each other what it was; a soft voice behind us said 'It is American miritary transporto' – not a fifth column but a Japanese-American waiter. One day we drove past Pearl Harbour, on the other side of the anchorage from the ships. I felt that even I could have reached an American battleship with a medium iron. We looked at each other and did not 'foresee' Pearl Harbour, but we did say 'Isn't that a little insecure?'

On the way back, by SS *President Coolidge*, we were playing table tennis in a verandah on a dull day when the deck became unsteadier and unsteadier, the sky grew angrier and we had to stop. As we went to our cabin, members of the crew were putting up special rails and ropes on the stairs. Soon typhoon warnings were sounded and all passengers summoned to the drawing-room. One cabin porthole had already been blown in. We sat on a carpet, the chairs having been roped up in a corner. Suddenly, the carpet took off and bore its occupants from port bow to starboard stern. As the wave passed it heaved us back again. The next wave, rather bigger, did the same, only this time, to our horror, the grand piano cut loose from its moorings and came in pursuit of us. Fortunately the reverse roll came just in time and the piano was quickly lashed down. We remembered all this a year later.

On our return to Tokyo, our first house-guest was my mother-in-law. Many jokes but no damage. The work went on as before. We were elated by Wavell's advance in the desert, concerned by its eventual running out of steam as the Greek crisis loomed. I was even more concerned deep inside by the visit to Europe in April 1941 of Mr Matsuoka, the Japanese Foreign Minister. It seemed to me that if I were Mr Matsuoka, a dynamic and ambitious man known to be fiercely anti-American, I would be trying to organize a combination of Germany, Italy, the Soviet Union and Japan to intimidate the British into making peace and the Americans into not making war. (It was interesting later to learn that Mr Matsuoka's Prime Minister, Prince Konoye, had the same idea.) Fortunately I was too pessimistic. He did indeed have some success in Berlin and Rome, and he also achieved a neutrality

*The author receiving the Japanese delegation
to the Naval Disarmament Conference, London, 1935*

Wedding photograph, 21 September 1940

agreement with the Soviet Union; but he seems also to have tried after all to keep a bridge open to the United States. In any case Hitler attacked the Soviet Union before the nightmare of the Great Combination could be realized.

Meantime we had the magnificent Greek resistance to Italian and then German invasion. At the time Vere Redman was away on business and had bequeathed his weekly magazine to me. I celebrated the Greek resistance with the famous epitaph to the defence of Thermopylae:

> Go tell the Spartans, thou that passest by,
> That here, obedient to their words, we lie.

I also found myself doing a major shipping operation with Mr Athanase Politis, the ebullient Greek Minister. There were some thirteen Greek ships on their way from the west coast of the United States to Japan, bringing much needed iron ore for Japanese industry. The shipowners naturally wanted all the ships to get to Japan and out of the way as quickly as possible. But, as Mr Politis and I begged and shouted over the telegraph, if they did that, the Japanese who were already detaining one Greek ship would probably confiscate the lot, reckoning that, if released, the ships would not come back but, if detained, they might be very useful to Japan. We argued that if the ships came one by one and departures equalled arrivals, then the promise of more iron ore to come would cause the Japanese authorities to let them go. Mr Politis often came charging into the Chancery with news or enquiries, reaching my office before the front door guards had time to ask him his business. But we won a little victory for the Allied merchant marine.

Then came the virtually incredible news of Hitler's attack on Russia.

'The almost impossible has happened,' exuberated the *Weekly Bulletin*. In the *Daily Bulletin* we were able to reproduce at once most of a great speech by Litvinov in London but, owing to the tricks of wireless reception in Tokyo, we got considerably less of a key-note speech by Stalin. (We realized that this breach

D

of Soviet etiquette was a pity.) We all responded to the Church-
illian line – never mind what these people are like; they are our
allies and we must do everything possible for and with them.
In Tokyo the first problem was to get to know them.

The best thing to do on the information side seemed to be
to pay a call on my Soviet opposite number. So I made an
appointment with Mr Sergeiev for three o'clock one very hot
summer afternoon. As it was a formal call and the Russians have
formal instincts, I got my friendly driver Ishida-san to take me. It
was a gradual business getting in. First we had to slow down to a
stop at the gate of the Soviet Chancery to enable the Japanese
policeman to take particulars of the car and the measure of me.
When I got out, I was confronted at the door with an eyehole. I
rang a bell and an eye appeared. It satisfied itself, the door opened
and I was ushered into a reception room. The *décor* was inter-
revolutionary, Russian-Victorian-French.

After five minutes a man brought in a plate of caviare sand-
wiches. Another five minutes and enter a bottle of vodka.
Another five minutes and enter Mr Sergeiev, dark, stocky and
quite young. Now I do not drink alcohol. But I had taken some
advice about vodka. It appeared that you could modify the
effects by ensuring that when it went down it had something
absorbent to fall on. So when the moment came when it would
have damaged the new alliance to have declined, I hurriedly
prepared an infrastructure of caviare sandwich.

Mr Sergeiev and I confirmed our arrangements for the supply
to us of Soviet material, drank all manner of appropriate toasts
and in half an hour finished off the vodka. He then escorted me
out, and as the car stopped again to allow the exit policeman to
verify that the same person came out as had gone in, I thought to
myself that it was just as well that in 1941 a Second Secretary in
Japan could afford a driver.

Pat and I also got to know the *Tass* correspondent and his
wife, Mr and Mrs Samoilov. We went to their house twice for
supper. Neither he nor his obviously talented wife spoke more
than a fragment of English and we had no Russian; so we agreed
that after the coffee we should sing. We led off with 'There is a

Tavern in the Town'; the Samoilovs countered with '*Stenka Rasin*' and so it went on for an hour. As we came downstairs we saw a large motor-bicycle. Summoning all his English, Mr Samoilov said, 'That is the motor-bicycle of Mr Kozlov; it is more dangerous than the Bolshevik propaganda. Ha!'

I also gave a supper for some Russian colleagues at which Chip Bohlen provided a link of knowledge and language. All this took place in the summer of 1941, when I think the personal atmosphere between the Russians and ourselves had a level of spontaneity which I have never met since. I have of course had very pleasant relations with Soviet colleagues. But at that moment the Russians were a bit scared and, moreover, grateful that in their peril they had a real and worthwhile ally. Some even seemed to wonder whether, given August 1939, they really deserved it. When two years afterwards I had some dealings with the Soviet Embassy in Washington, the reserve, the party-line talk and the uncommunicativeness had begun to re-establish themselves. We must in 1941 have caught a brief period between the instructions.

The German invasion of Russia in a sense straightened things out for the Japanese. They were no longer embarrassed by the new friend (Germany) being tied up with the old enemy (Russia). Moreover the old enemy was now tied up with the possible (or even, in the eyes of the Japanese Army, prospective) enemy, Britain. Should Japan then intervene? Hitler would of course have liked an attack on Eastern Siberia. But the Japanese were on the way southward with their Greater East Asia policy and had not much relish for operations in Siberia. They decided to continue southward, relying on the neutrality pact with the Soviet Union to protect the northern flank. Thus not for the last time there was an alliance with Germany but no co-ordination.

Japan's immediate step was to mobilize a million men on 2 July, 1941, and Tokyo became alive with rumbling vehicles and marching men. Then a new silence descended. Where had they gone? One could only suppose westward and southward. A new tension in the local and international atmosphere reflected Washington's obvious unease, and an economic blockade of Japan in aid of China was on the way. I had been in Japan for three and a half years and was due for an extended leave. But there was no possibility of getting home and, with the growing anxiety, it was obviously important for Jim and Karma Henderson, who had a family of three and a baby expected, to be the first to get away. Meantime it had been agreed with London that a small Butterfield and Swire ship, the *Anhui*, should come to Japan as the last chance of evacuating British subjects. Coincidentally Clark-Kerr in China was in difficulty over shortage of staff, and the proposal was made that Pat and I should leave on the *Anhui* for Hong Kong to help the evacuation, and then go for a short assignment to Shanghai. The main Embassy in China was at Chungking but a sizable Shanghai office was needed for dealing with the problems of the British commercial community in Japanese-occupied China.

There was a complication about the evacuation. British subjects included Indians. An active anti-British lobby headed by Mr Rash Behari Bose put pressure on Indians to stay in Japan, both as an anti-British gesture and a sign of confidence in Japan. The Indians who wanted to go were not inspired by any particular feelings for us but simply felt that in the event of trouble, they would be more comfortable in India than in Japan. Mr Bose's people picketed the *Anhui* but of the three hundred and sixty-five people who left, almost exactly half were Indians. Our part was to help in making sure that Indians who came on board suffered no adverse discrimination on any ground. Mr A. G. Hard, the Australian Commercial Counsellor, who was the Chairman of the evacuees' committee on board, was very firm about this too, and as far as I know there was no trouble at all.

It was a strange shipload since, without Indian experience, one could not foresee that the presence on board of representatives of a wide variety of Indian communities meant, spread all over the deck and elsewhere, every kind of cooking apparatus and ingredient to cope with variations in diet and eating custom.

At first all went smoothly. Then one day as I was quietly reading *Our Mutual Friend* on the deck, I became gradually less conscious of the fortunes of Mr Boffin and Mr Wegg as the sky grew grey and the wind more insistent. There was no way for the Captain to know in which direction to steer; the Jesuit weather station at Siccawei outside Shanghai had been silenced as weather was a military secret. So we plunged ahead hoping to avoid the worst of the gathering storm.

At supper time, Pat and I thought we would try to eat early. We had just got inside, when the wind suddenly became much stronger. The door between the dining-room and the deck was sealed up for safety. (A distinguished British citizen of Kobe was thereby confined on deck all night.) We went down and got into our bunks, but we had to hold on and there was no question of sleeping. In the middle of the night water began to stream down to the lower decks and splash around the floor of the cabins. Damp streamed everywhere from straining seams. Children cried and Indian women wailed. At about 5.00 in the morning, as we rolled to and fro, there was a great crash as a mighty wave hit the ship. The *Anhui* heeled over to a frightening angle, and there she stayed. We could hear screams from the cabins all around. Then there was a great shudder and slowly she came back to vertical. It had been a very near thing.

Typhoons do not subside in five minutes, but we were over the worst. A little later, I went up on deck. One of the ship's lifeboats had lodged somewhere up on the bridge; another could not be seen. Lengths of the rail had just disappeared. There was an indescribable confusion of cooking utensils all over the place. Yet in twenty-four hours I was, by invitation of Captain Evans, steering the ship in a dead calm sea, and that evening we had a concert with British choruses and that elusive Indian conjuring trick in which thimbles appear and disappear on and off a row of fingers.

In a day or two we were off from Hong Kong to Shanghai in another ship with a totally contrasting skipper. Captain Evans had been calm and steady. Our new Captain was irascible, drank hard and had a very rude parrot. When, making conversation, I asked him if one used a tug to go alongside at Shanghai. 'Tug,' he roared, letting off a barrage of oaths so eloquent that you could see tugs sinking in rows. We wandered up the fascinating course of the Whangpoo River watching Shanghai appear from all points of the compass. On arrival all tugs avoided us like the plague and the skipper did one of those angry and perfect alongsides.

No doubt Shanghai at that time was full of bad money, drugs, long knives, brothels and other evils. But after wartime Tokyo it was gay and wonderful. It was also an exciting experiment in international living: the International Settlement had an International Council consisting of an American chairman, Chinese, British and other members, and a British Secretary. The city had the special animation of Chinese crowds, it had riches and poverty, dazzle and squalor. But above all it had life. The French Concession had that ineffaceable French 'feel'. The Japanese held Hongkew across the creek, where it was all soldiers and policemen. A little of the feel of Shanghai at that time can still be gained in Hong Kong, but a Government House and a residue of primness hangs about the colony, and of these in Shanghai there was no trace.

The work was odd in the extreme. The office had been run for some time by an overworked Ian le Rougetel,[11] who had been so accustomed to being on his own that he automatically took all the papers that came in and dealt with them as best he could. He was grateful for my arrival but the habit had so grown on him that in order to pull my weight I used to go and plunder his in-tray when he wasn't looking.

With the Japanese in a position to take over the International Settlement whenever they wanted, Ian had done a wise thing in ordering the destruction of any confidential papers that we did not absoluely need. It meant however doing business on the basis:

Inward letter: 'We are grateful for your letter of the 13th but would appreciate some explanation of the point in your paragraph 3 which we do not fully understand.'

Note attached: 'No copy kept.'

[11] Sir John le Rougetel was Ambassador in Persia, 1946-50, and in Belgium, 1950-51. He was then High Commissioner in South Africa, 1951-55.

On 17 October 1941 the Emperor of Japan sent for the previous War Minister, General Tojo, and asked him to form a government. He accepted. There was a bag from Tokyo to Shanghai fairly soon after, in which came a letter to me from John Mason, a young language officer who had married Pat's bridesmaid, Barbara Chapman. It was very brief. It said, 'I think this is it.' This message made us restless, and I put in an application to return to Tokyo. A replacement was arriving in Shanghai and, if the balloon went up, we much preferred to be in our own house among our own people and with our own things.

The only way to go was to start by the fast Japanese ship from Shanghai to Nagasaki in Kyushu, the south island of Japan, take a train from there to Moji, cross the ferry to the Japanese mainland and then take the train to Tokyo. On this train, ran the doctrine, every berth was taken unless Japanese authority could be specially persuaded to release it. Through the good offices of the Japanese Foreign Office we were allotted a compartment on the night of 30 November.

We were asked if we would take eight Foreign Office bags to Tokyo where a great deal of confidential material needed by the British Embassy was overdue. As each bag was a full-size sackful, to be guarded full-time, night and day, we agreed to take two each and hope someone would occasionally help with our own things. The crisis came when at Moji we were confronted with a sign, guarded by policeman with sword, 'Passengers left, baggage right.' In a split second we decided we were baggage and descended unexecuted on the meat-safe lift leading to the hold. Thenceforth the journey was uninterrupted, but we arrived just about dead in mind and body.

As soon as possible I went and had a look at the latest confidential telegrams. In my numb state I read a telegram which said that the Americans had insisted formally that Japan should withdraw from China. No doubt in Tokyo this was not new, but it was new to me. I went to bed and stayed there for a day, conscious that, if I had read the telegram rightly, war in the Far East was not only inevitable but near.

In our absence the Hendersons had been able to leave and

Jim's successor, Douglas Busk,[12] had arrived. I discussed with him the 'destruction' policy in force at Shanghai. We decided to destroy everything which, if the Japanese broke the international rules governing Embassy immunity, would give them any information about the conduct or state of hostilitities, or about British policies elsewhere. We did not, however, destroy the files dealing with Anglo-Japanese matters, notably the 'cases', because if war came it did not seem to matter whether the Japanese authorities read our sentiments about them or not.

Pearl Harbour

We now come to the singularly weird morning of Monday, 8 December 1941. During the weekend there had been a few telegrams from Indo-China indicating southward movements of Japanese ships. On the Monday morning, at 0500 hours Japanese time, Vere Redman came in to take the early morning news watch. Listening had to start at this hour if the Embassy's morning bulletins in English and Japanese were to be up to date and issued in time to be useful. Almost at once Redman got a message which came via Lisbon and Ankara to the effect that the Japanese had attacked Pearl Harbour. But this channel had extended the war several times before and he sought confirmation. It happened (and this has been widely recognized) that this particular morning was one of quite extraordinarily bad wireless reception. He could get nothing, and went on trying.

At about six o'clock the secretary of the Japanese Foreign Minister rang up the Embassy and got through to the duty officer. He said that the Foreign Minister wanted to get in touch with the Ambassador. The duty officer went round to the Residence but was unable to get any response from either the Residence or the servants' quarters, so he went back to the telephone to try to get some more information from the Foreign Ministry before trying again. He got no reply. This was because the call had come neither from the Japanese Foreign Office nor from

[12] Sir Douglas Busk, later Ambassador to Ethiopia, 1952–56, Finland, 1958–60 and Venezuela, 1961–64. Author of *The Craft of Diplomacy*, 1961, a standard work on the subject, and of books on mountaineering and exploration.

the Minister's residence; it had come from the official residence which was normally used only for entertaining.

Eventually the Foreign Minister's secretary got through on another line, and at 7.15 or so Sir Robert went to see Mr Togo.

At about 7.30, I looked into the cipher room to see whether anything new of importance had arrived. There was another telegram from Indo-China which did not need action before breakfast. Suddenly, at eight o'clock Vere Redman came through on the intercom, with a flood of news. Manila had certainly been bombed and probably Pearl Harbour and there was no doubt that a war was on. We decided to go across to the Ambassador at once.

Sir Robert was still with the Foreign Minister, so we gave all the information we had to Lady Craigie. It seemed urgent to spread the news in the compound, which Redman undertook, while I got hold of the Embassy Constable, Mr Molineux, and he and I started to ring as fast as we could all the members of the staff living outside the compound who had telephones. Our message was that this was the news, and we suggested that they and their families come into the compound quickly; we reckoned that they would be better off there without their effects than outside trying to get in. The telephone was cut at 8.20 and the long wait endured by the Consul, R. L. Cowley, who was next and last on the list, showed how right we had been.

The Ambassador returned and heard the news with utter consternation. The Minister had simply told him that talks with the Americans had finally broken down, and the two of them had then had some talk on what everybody should do next. Sir Robert tried at once to get back to the Foreign Minister again, but Mr Togo eluded all such efforts. I think myself that the news was so terrible and the Minister's consciousness of having failed to communicate it to Sir Robert so embarrassing that, as a Japanese, he simply was not going to face the agony of a further talk. There was also a technical point which emerges at the next stage.

During all this commotion, I ran into Ned Crocker of the

American Embassy who had come over early to check information with us and had not heard the news. We warmly invited him to spend the next few months with us, but advised him that he had better race home.

Meanwhile distress signals came from another quarter. As Vere Redman had been on duty, Mrs Redman was alone at home. A message came through that military police had entered the house and were demanding the surrender of her husband. This was entirely contrary to international law as Redman was a member of the Embassy staff, but these niceties did not interest the military police.

Various people at this point had to decide rapidly what to do next. We had had no declaration of war, which gave us some freedom of action, but we had also no telephone and it was only a matter of a short time before we should be under total siege. The Ambassador decided to have one last session with the American Ambassador while this was still possible. The Counsellor, Bill Houston-Boswall, went down to the Ministry to try to get the pressure off Mrs Redman, and the senior Japanese language expert, Wilfred Cunningham, went on a similar errand. The otherwise unoccupied manpower got down to burning the remaining confidential papers; it is pleasant to recall that no effort was made to interfere with them.

While the Ambassador and Counsellor were still out on these missions, and the Cowleys were trying vainly to get in, Mr Saburo Ohta, the counsellor in the Ministry of Foreign Affairs handling relations with Britain, arrived with a group of Japanese and asked to see the Ambassador. He had in the end to be content with a trio consisting of Douglas Busk, Henry Sawbridge (Cunningham's deputy) and myself. He said he had come to read us a document and to search the Embassy for our radio transmitter. We said we would hear the document but that he could on no account search the Embassy.

The document turned out to be a series of accusations against Britain ending with the statement that a state of war existed.

We all looked at each other and then I took it on myself

to speak.[13] I had had many dealings with Mr Ohta. I had liked him and admired his versatility and the quality of his work. So it was perhaps right that the comment should come from me. I said that what he had just read showed that all that was worst in the Japan of the day had come to the top and taken charge of the country. It was perhaps as well that it would now be destroyed in war. We hoped to live to see the day when a better, peaceful Japan would emerge.

It is practically never given to a diplomat, even in a country where things are obviously going wrong, to speak his full mind. Now there was nothing to be lost, and it was a satisfaction to get these few, nervous words off my chest. I then asked Mr Ohta to let us have the paper to telegraph the text home as our last official act. To our astonishment he said he could not do this.

There was then something of a pause, broken by Henry Sawbridge offering to go through the document taking down what was necessary in English or Japanese. This was done. Then came the awkward question of the search for a transmitter. Mr Ohta said he had no discretion in the matter at all. He must go ahead. We said we had not any either. Moreover, there wasn't a transmitter. The object was now rather desperately to waste time until the Ambassador returned.

When the Ambassador did return, an absurd compromise was reached by which Mr Ohta and party searched the compound everywhere except for respecting the immunity of the Chancery strong room and the Ambassador's residence where the transmitter, had it existed, might just as well have been.

It had been a grotesque morning – the radio black-out, the behaviour of Mr Togo, the initial failure of various people in the Embassy to coincide, and the general retrieval of our arrangements later. It made one feel that some supernatural jinx had been at work. Not that, if everything had been more rational, history would have been different. But the whole approach to war by the Japanese military element, who had long had the whip hand, was in itself so strange, secretive, fanatical and

[13] See also Douglas Busk, *The Craft of Diplomacy*, p. 17

destructive that it was not surprising that the atmosphere itself
should be confused by the events of which it was the scene.

The reason that Mr Ohta did not give us the document was
because he had not got a copy. Thus, had Mr Togo told Sir
Robert the truth, he might have been in the position of a Foreign
Minister informing an Ambassador that a state of war existed
without, apparently, being able to hand him a formal declaration
of war. The drafting of the paper read to us by Mr Ohta had
started on the Sunday morning, twenty-four hours before,
when he had been ordered, to his vexation, not to go for his
Sunday morning's golf, but to come to the Ministry. Who said
what to whom in the Japanese hierarchy during those twenty-four
hours, or when the Emperor, who had been briefed about
Pearl Harbour, relinquished any opposition to what was proposed,
may never accurately be known. But it seems as if, up to the end,
the Japanese did not want to present us with a formal declaration
of war, or indeed a formal document of any kind.

Such great and tragic events can hardly be said to have happy
endings. But there was one small thing which happened in
Burma in 1954 that gave me great pleasure. Mr Ohta was
appointed Japanese Ambassador to Rangoon. I happened to be
away when he arrived. When I returned I found a charming
note from him in which he said he looked forward to 'renewing
our old friendship'. That from the person who has in effect
declared war on you shows that there is a sense of proportion
somewhere.

Once the scurrying round and the early organizing were over,
we all wanted to think over the immediate past. The Ambassador
would in any case have to write a final report, even if it could
not be read in London for months. We had a long and thoughtful
discussion with him on whether we could have done anything
differently or better to dissuade Japan from entering the war.
After all, judged austerely by results, Sir Robert's mission had been
a failure, and he continued to feel that, if he had been given a
little more freedom of action, a little more encouragement and
certainly more information both about American proceedings
and about events in Indo-China, he might have been able to do

something. I did not agree. I had felt for some considerable time that the Japanese had embarked on a course which they could not reverse; we had all done our best to warn and dissuade them, and there had been nothing in this respect on which the Ambassador should reproach himself. (Some time later, on a visit to Washington, Julian Ridsdale,[14] who had been a military language officer in Japan, reminded me that I had said in the summer of 1940 that we should have to fight the Japanese.) Later knowledge has shown that American proceedings were not always logical or calm: there were, as there were bound to be, lurches forward and periods of quiescence or apparent withdrawal. But I still stick to my belief that no diplomacy by us and no policy conceivable for a British Government of the time could have prevented those who had the real power in Japan from going forward when the only road to peace would have been to go back.

It was a little sad that Sir Robert Craigie was not invited to do another comparable job. True, there were at the time very few posts available at that level and some of them were being held for good wartime reasons by people with political background. Moreover Craigie may have overstated to the British Government the possibilities of improving the situation by diplomatic action and governments do not like to be misled. None the less, it had been a brave effort, and I have myself great cause for gratitude to a chief from whom I learned so much. I am glad that, later in life, I had the chance of meeting him several times quite apart from official life and learning what a friendly and rather uncomplicated man he really was.

Internment, 8 December 1941–31 July 1942
From being busy cogs in a busy machine, we had all become within an hour or two people of absolute leisure, and absolute leisure in confinement in a hostile country has its special problems. Ours were of course as nothing in the massive chronicle of prison camps and internments of the 1940s, and, when we were

[14] Julian Ridsdale, Conservative MP for Harwich since 1954, was president of the British Japanese Parliamentary Group in 1964.

later welcomed home with the headline 'Mercy Ship Arrives,' we felt something of a fraud.

We had to organize ourselves to accommodate a community of ninety in a compound where thirty had been living before. This meant organizing the organizers, and Douglas Busk being the most resourceful of people was appointed by the Ambassador to deal with allocations, although he had been in Japan only a week. Our house which had contained just ourselves became a somewhat crowded community of seven, including one small boy, with a new baby expected. There were a few rearrangements later to avert the inevitable clashes of personality but no crises developed. Wilfred Cunningham took charge of relations with those Japanese authorities with whom we retained direct contact, such as the police and the suppliers of goods and services. A roster of Japanese-speaking 'gate-watchers' was appointed to deal with any problem arising at the compound entrance. And the most important post of rationing officer was handed not to an official but to Mrs Mason, mother of John Mason, the language student who had written to me in Shanghai. Mrs Mason was a formidable lady of immense energy and efficiency who had already been supervising allied ladies doing sewing and other work for prisoners of war in Europe. Though rather terrifying, she was scrupulously fair; and since no kind of favouritism or chiselling could elude her, nobody tried. Never has an OBE been more deservedly earned.

The Ambassador dealt personally with relations with the Protecting Power, which was first Argentina, and later, for reasons of administrative convenience (for Señor Villa did us very well), Switzerland. The function of the Protecting Power was to look after British people and property in Japan as far as possible and to be our channel for business with the Japanese Government. The most important objective from our point of view was to get out as soon as possible. We had the right, under international law, to be exchanged, on the basis that if you have to stay in a country on public duty until war breaks out, you have in return the right to be allowed to go when it starts provided that the other country's representatives are accorded the same right. It took eight months to arrange and effect. Of course we grumbled and got impatient; but there were complications we were not to know about. The whole business of organizing safe-conduct ships in both directions in conditions of grim war at sea was difficult enough. Then there was the detailed negotiation necessary to extend repatriation not just to officials but, as was eventually agreed, to as many private people as the ships chosen could accommodate. Some of us said that we would like to go via Siberia rather than wait for a ship. This was turned down because use of overland routes, as we learned later, would have enabled the Japanese to reinforce understaffed missions in Europe by sending evacuees via Sweden to Germany.

The Japanese security authorities had convinced themselves that Vere Redman was an intelligence agent, the distinction between 'Information' and 'Intelligence' being unknown to them, and demanded that he be handed over to them. This was wholly contrary to international law, but the Japanese Foreign Office and the Protecting Power were powerless. Since pure capitulation might have been interpreted as consent and used as a pretext for further misdeeds, we could not just give in. So it was arranged that the Japanese police would have to come into the Residence and forcibly break down a door to remove their prisoner.

Redman was diabetic and on a strict regime of diet and injections. When he was taken away few people, including his heroic French wife Madeleine, expected to see him again. But the story did end happily. Vere's captors, after first letting him collapse by withholding his insulin in an effort to force him to talk, realized that dead he would be no use to them. He survived his eight months' solitary, was evacuated with the rest of us, played a notable part in information work in India in the war, and returned to Japan later to become something of a legend as the foreigner with the most personal friends among the Japanese.

Meanwhile, the most urgent task in the compound was to counter boredom with activity. We organized classes in Japanese, Russian, French and Spanish, given by members of the Embassy staff. Instruction in shorthand and typing was available, and

Mrs Cunningham taught *ikebana* (Japanese flower arrangement). There were rudimentary air raid precautions to be observed. Colonel Himatsinhji, our Indian Military Attaché and brother of the Jam Saheb of Nawanager, took responsibility for keeping the compound tidy, and later we set up a garden squad. Ffree Simpson, the newest arrived Secretary, and I completed an inventory of British business and personal property in Japan. We had had all the replies to a questionnaire we had sent out as a precaution some months earlier, and enforced leisure gave us the time to sort them out.

Just before Japan's entry into war, a ship had arrived at Kobe from Singapore bringing emergency food supplies for the Embassy, and the Ministry of Foreign Affairs achieved a useful success in getting these supplies to us. They contained a good quantity of sugar. We rationed ourselves carefully and made our Christmas puddings with carrots so that, profiting from a bumper orange crop, the ladies were able to make three-quarters of a ton of marmalade mainly for allied prisoners of war held by the Japanese. When we finally left, our Embassy community emerged rather undernourished, but given the degree of undernourishment of the Japanese people themselves, there could be no grievance.

Recreations included much music, from which our household profited greatly by having one of the two pianos in the compound. There was squash in the winter, tennis in the spring and summer and lessons in Scottish dancing given in the squash court by Mrs Macrae, the wife of the Commercial Counsellor.

Morale remained a pressing problem nevertheless. All the news was bad – the loss of the battleships off Malaya (which we could hardly believe), the fall of Singapore and the Netherlands East Indies, the failure of the 1941–42 offensive in the Libyan desert and the Cripps-Gandhi negotiations in India, the appalling losses of merchant ships in early 1942. All this was gleefully catalogued in the Japanese press. We had lots of mimeograph paper, but on the world situation we could only produce a thin daily sheet from Japanese press or medium wave radio sources. Short wave listening was prohibited. We had a middlebrow

Weekly Review which I edited and Bridget Busk illustrated, and a more literary magazine produced by Charles Johnston.[15] The magazines, by producing, for instance, articles on each other's occupations and interests outside official work, helped us a little towards more intimacy and mutual understanding.

But the most vital of our morale-boosting activities was a secret from most of us, organized by Douglas Busk. Under the cover of genuine judo lessons given by our high-ranking, black belt, 32 degree judo expert, F. H. Leggett, he saw to the construction of a short wave wireless receiving set, tuned in to what became our old friend 'Radio Station KGEI, San Francisco Bay'. What was thus picked up could never be reproduced in writing or identified in conversation, and it would have been dangerous to listen in every night. But the very few in the know used a kind of 'I wonder if . . .' technique to infiltrate among us the more cheerful sides to the news and suggest honest doubts about the totality of Axis successes. These items, together with an actual improvement in allied fortunes after the Midway naval battle in June 1942, kept us going.

We celebrated Pat's twenty-first birthday with a nightclub party at our house which was illuminated briefly with the sign 'PAZZI's'. And the most exciting moment of all was the Doolittle air raid on April 18th. There were a few bangs and other confused noises, so assuming a stupidly conscientious diligence, I put on my tin hat and gas mask and scrambled on to the roof, remaining deaf as long as I could to orders from a Japanese policeman to come down. I could not see much, but it was exciting to feel that Japan could even then be reached by American bombers, and the effect on the Japanese around us was clearly disquieting.

Pat and I enjoyed one special privilege. The Australian Trade Office had become a Legation. My mother-in-law had remained

[15] Sir Charles Johnston was Ambassador to Jordan in 1956, Governor and Commander in Chief in Aden, 1960–63, Deputy Under-Secretary of State, Foreign Office, 1963–65, when he became High Commissioner in Australia until retirement in 1971. Author of *The View from Steamer Point*, on his experiences in Aden, and *Mo and Other Originals*.

with the office and my father-in-law, who spoke Japanese faultlessly, had joined it also. Accordingly they were both interned in the Australian Legation.

One day a friendly policeman sidled up to Pat and said, 'I think good idea if Oku-san (Madam) have injection.' Pat looked baffled. 'Mrs Erraton-san-wa having injection . . .' with a big wink. Suddenly we saw that we needed injections very badly and next day were driven to a hospital where we had half an hour's non-injection with my parents-in-law. Later we had a similarly pleasant non-appointment with a dentist.

At last, after eight months, it was time to go. The Americans and Canadians left at the beginning of July. At the end of the month it was our turn together with our European allies.

It is interesting to think back on the mood in which we left Japan, for relief was curiously mixed with regret. Those who only knew the Japanese of the Siam Railway or the worst of the prison camps can be excused for feeling unforgiving. Indeed some Japanese shared their sense of outrage, for when one complained at the Japanese Foreign Office of this or that piece of hooliganism or brutality by Japanese troops, the reply could be, in all seriousness, 'But Japanese don't *do* such things.' But they did. And a few of the foreigners living in Japan either took their cue from that fact or for other reasons hated the place and never wanted to go there again. But the great majority of foreigners, even those who might have been subjected to ill-treatment under interrogation, refused to be turned against the Japan they had known. There was something about the beauty of the country, and the way of life of this unique, serious people that made those who had lived there feel they could forgive much and that, when the current aggressive madness had been purged, they would like to come back. That is why my parents-in-law returned there after the war, and Mrs Ellerton lived on there till the age of eighty-three. That, I think, is what I meant in my little farewell speech to Mr Ohta.

London

1942

Japanese courtesy broke down on the day we left. We were suddenly told that there would be no help for anyone in carrying baggage. So we carried that of older people as well as our own and got on to the ship somehow. The *Tatsuta Maru* was curtained so that we could see nothing in Yokohama Harbour. But who cared? We were off.

We called at Shanghai, Saigon and Singapore to pick up some more British, Australian and European citizens. En route to Lourenço Marques in Portuguese East Africa, we had to work out with M. Hausheer, the Swiss representative, and the evacuee families where everyone wanted to go, conscious that many answers would depend on messages received on arrival and the sheer existence or non-existence of onward transport. There was also relief and welfare work to be done.

In Lourenço Marques we performed a solemn ceremony in which, while we walked off gangway A, Japanese came on board via gangway B. Lourenço Marques was, obviously, paradise, with its bougainvillaeas, its sunshine and its freedom from captivity. With help from Dermot McDermot,[1] I ran a sort of tourist office in a warehouse, in which we tried to help people towards their destinations. We were all a little neurotic, and neuroses came out in many passengers as a conviction that despite, or perhaps because of, eight months of total absence, they were needed at once in some key job in some improbable place. One man insisted on making his own arrangements. With ingenuity and pressure, he got on to a vessel going direct to

[1] Sir Dermot MacDermot was Ambassador in Indonesia, 1956–59, Assistant Under-Secretary, Foreign Office, 1959–61, and Ambassador to Thailand, 1961–65.

New York, only to be torpedoed off Brazil. Happily he survived. It was better to let things take their course and go with a safe-conduct ship to Britain or Australia.

Besides freedom the other joy was news from home. Pat and I had heard some months before through the Protecting Power that we were to go to Washington. On enquiry this was now confirmed but we were instructed to come home for briefing first. I am sure someone had thought about my parents too.

A second ship had come with people from China, and there was a second great allocation exercise. We parted sadly from my parents-in-law who were bound for Australia, wondering when we should meet again (the reunion was twelve years later in Burma), and set off for Cape Town and Liverpool, our lights shining to advertise our guaranteed safe-conduct. We travelled in a small rather crazy ship called *El Nil*, belonging to the Egyptian Merchant Marine but with British officers.

There was, as always in war, sadness too. My parents-in-law sent us a telegram telling us that Pat's older brother David had been killed. After service in the RAAF in North Africa, he was on the point of ending his period as a fighter pilot when he volunteered to try and rescue an American flyer stranded off the north of Australia. The beach proved treacherous and David's plane overturned. I missed a great deal through never having met him.

Then came the arrival at Liverpool. After eight months of enemy versions of Britain's plight, it was wonderfully heartening to see ship after ship steaming up the Mersey with war supplies. As a party, we had developed a habit of making our own organiza-tional arrangements, and were half prepared to do so again, but from the moment Mr Molyneux of the Home Office and his team arrived on board, we gratefully subsided and did what we were told. We were transported off to a comfortable house in the suburbs for the night and a train took us to London in the morning. At Euston, my father was waiting with a bunch of anemones for Pat. We went straight to our temporary home, the Crofton Hotel in Queen's Gate, and, joined by my mother, took a quiet meal at a little restaurant in the Gloucester Road called the House of Peter. That was how we met again after almost five years, and that is how my parents met their daughter-in-law.

We were impatient to know what had really happened to my parents in 1941 and since. On 10 May 1941 there had been perhaps the biggest raid of the war on London. The next letter from my parents had been sent from elsewhere but, in accordance with censorship rules, gave no explanation of the change. What had happened was that, on the night of the raid, my father had been coming up from the basement when a landmine exploded opposite. The grandfather clock came downstairs to meet him. The house had not been ruined, but had been rendered unsafe for habitation.

Meantime my father had grown furious with impatience at the failure of any authority anywhere to fit him into the war effort. He had finally written a fulminating letter in Irish prose to a Scots friend who was a director of Vickers. This fetched a Celtic response, and my father joined the Iron and Steel Control. His knowledge of people and habits in the North of England steel industry made his work highly valuable.

We were in Britain for six weeks from mid-October 1942 to the beginning of December. There was an air raid alarm at the moment we arrived in London but after that there were no further alarms for the whole time we were there. The entire German air force was evidently concentrated on Russia or in North Africa where the Allied landing was made on 7 November. The Allied bomber forces were becoming more aggressive, and as part of my indoctrination for Washingon I went to the English Electric Company works at Old Trafford to see Lancaster bombers being built. Then I was taken to Syerston Aerodrome in Notting-hamshire to see them being used in a raid on Northern Italy. I was still there when they came back. It was, thankfully, a night on which none of our aircraft was missing.

But my main indoctrination was in the feel of Britain at that time. It struck me at a random moment as I was standing in the hall of Waterloo Station, how very noticeable it was that every-body moving to and fro carried about him or her a feeling of purpose. It might have been a very little purpose, like getting home before black-out, or a very big one like planning the winning of a campaign. But there was something to be done and something to be won. There was something to be defeated too – not so much bad people as a gruesomely bad thing. There was a quietly exhilarating feeling among the losses, the gashes and the ruins, a memorable experience both for itself and because a latter-day touch of it is something which we as a nation badly need now – without a war.

In my official briefing I had a long talk with Gladwyn Jebb, who had been put in charge of the Foreign Office post-war planning operation. I was delighted both by the progress of this thinking and also by the modern-looking set-up which Jebb had created. He told me that I would be expected to work in Washington under the supervision of Redvers Opie, a former don at Magdalen College, Oxford, who was in close contact with the corresponding side of the State Department headed by Leo Pasvolsky. The hope was that, just as we had achieved the closest co-operation with the Americans in wartime operations, we could start studies and perhaps produce papers together on aspects of post-war policy. Naturally I was very pleased with the assignment.

Tony Rumbold[2] arrived back from Washington and briefed me for an hour very fast at the top of his voice in a typical wartime smoke-filled room at the Dorchester Hotel. Even those rooms, where too many people had to shout in order to say too much in too small a space during too short a time, have their nostalgias.

On 2 December we set off for Greenock to catch Transport D 2.

[2] Sir H. Anthony C. Rumbold was British Minister in Paris, 1960–63, Ambassador to Thailand and the UK representative on the Council of SEATO, 1965–67, and Ambassador to Austria from 1967 until his retirement in 1960.

United States
December 1942-1945

Embassy

D 2 turned out to be the *Queen Elizabeth* in a semi-finished state.
So it was metal and austerity in the cabins but wonderful in the
dining-room where all that mattered was unlimited rolls, butter
and jam. As there were only a few thousand people on board,
mainly Americans and Canadians going on leave or invalided
home and British going for training, there was no need for shift
sleeping and shift eating as on the eastward sailings. But if you
wanted to read a book and felt that a deck seat in December was
uninviting, you had to hang around the big lounge near someone
who had reached last-page-minus-ten of his book, or near a poker
game that looked like finishing, and be the first to dive into the
vacated place.

A civilian gang sorted itself out consisting of William Haley,
then editor of *The Manchester Guardian*, Christopher Chancellor,
editor of Reuters, Lord Bearsted, Professor T. North Whitehead
from the American Department of the Foreign Office, and ourselves. When we were mooring in Halifax after our zigzag
crossing, however, we found ourselves hard put to it to discover
how to get off. The air rang continuously with 'Canadian Army
gangway 3, platform 2,' and 'RAF Training Group for USA
gangway 1,' and so on, but the civilians were nobody's business.

We finally found a very young, very long-haired (old style,
behind the ears) officer, who said helpfully, 'You'd better have
a document.' We explained that we hadn't one of that kind.
'Then we must produce one,' he replied. So with his help we
drafted and typed a splendid document implying that the war
would take a serious turn for the worse if we did not get to
Washington at once. He stamped it – twice for good measure.

'Onward transport?' we asked. He agreed that we needed it.
The Professor leaped into the breach. 'I'll go and see,' he said
bravely, snatched the document and disappeared. After a time
he reappeared looking like my favourite-but-one Shakespearian
stage direction 'enter Artemidorus reading a paper'. He was
festooned with great streams of paper attached to each other,
taking us on a tour round Nova Scotia, over the ferry from Digby
to St John, New Brunswick, another strip of paper for sleeping
accommodation and so on to Montreal. It was a splendid performance. The caravan could roll, baggage and all; we cheered
the young officer and later presented the Professor with an
American 'red cap' (railroad porter's official headgear) as a
reward for his services. After an all-day saunter through the
landscape in the warmth of the train, with snow on the ground
outside and a bright sun in the sky, we crossed the strait and at
St John fell into our train berths. My next memory is of waking
up and looking snugly and lazily out of bed on to the snow-
bound woods of Quebec through which the train wound its
unhurried way. And so, equally unhurriedly, to a wonderful
North American breakfast. Luxury may pall in excess but a
sudden dash of it does wonders for the body and cannot do much
harm to the soul.

Next day our American train groaned its way slowly into
the Union Station, Washington. There were William and Iris
Hayter[1] to meet us and William pointed to the view of the
Capitol neatly framed in the archway of the station.

It was important to get settled as soon as possible as Pat was
now expecting a first child. We were lucky. We found a house in
Garfield Street which was roomy and convenient. It had been
occupied by a Russian major and was in the scruffiest condition,
but there was no house *en face*, just the road and the green space
below the cathedral. And in the long distances of Washington it

---

[1] Sir William Hayter, Minister at the British Embassy in Paris in 1949,
Ambassador to the Soviet Union in 1953, and, on retirement from the Diplomatic Service in 1958, after a short period as Deputy Under-Secretary of
State, became Warden of New College, Oxford. Author of *The Diplomacy of
the Great Powers, 1961.*

was only twelve minutes' walk to the Embassy. No one in Washington ever walked, but you never knew. We employed a black maid, Violet, laconic to a degree: her one phrase down the telephone was 'Everythin's O.K.' – and it was.

And so to work. On my desk I found a welcoming note from John Russell[1], who had been my successor in Vienna. I presented myself to the Chancery and the State Department, and found there a number of friends from Tokyo. But it was less easy to discover what exactly to do. I can best begin an explanation by photographing the war situation and the Anglo-American relationship in Washington when we arrived at the end of 1942. As we can see in retrospect, the Midway battle of 5–6 June 1942 meant that, on any sensible reckoning, the war could no longer be lost in the Pacific. Further, the Russian defence of Stalingrad and the Allied landings in North Africa had ensured ultimate victory in Europe. History becomes telescoped, and it is hard to remember now that the Allies still faced two and a half years of grim step by step warfare in four continents, with accompanying political strains and without any of that general feeling of assurance that hindsight can give.

Meantime a year and a half of growing United States–United Kingdom co-operation and a year's full alliance had brought about by 1943 an integration of effort of truly astonishing proportions between two completely independent countries. Except for operations in the Pacific, where Admiral King and General MacArthur preferred to keep foreigners, so to speak, in the waiting-room, the conduct of military operations was controlled, subject to final Government decision, by the Combined (American and British) Chiefs of Staff. On the production supply and transport side, the Combined Boards occupied a similar position of authority. The British position in these combined operations, however, was vulnerable. True, we had obviously special contributions to make ranging from skill and experience in contemporary war to real estate and its contents all round the

[1] Sir John Russell, Ambassador to Ethiopia, 1962–66, Brazil, 1966–69, Spain since 1969.

world; but in the matter of finance and production, current and, even more, future, the Americans were infinitely the stronger, and if we were to keep our end up, needed to take special measures to do so.

This could partly be achieved by the personal relationship which lasted until nearly the end, between President Roosevelt and Prime Minister Churchill. But you cannot delegate a personal relationship into all the channels of production and negotiation. Something more was needed. Hence it came about that there assembled in Washington such a concentration of British industrial and financial talent as can never before have lived for so long in a foreign capital. Nearly all the heads of the British Missions in Washington were or became after the war chairmen of major British companies; for instance, Sir Clive Baillieu, head of the Raw Materials Mission, Chairman of Dunlop, Sir Robert Sinclair, as British representative on the combined Production & Resources Board, later Chairman of Imperial Tobacco, R.H. ('Bob') Brand, Chairman of Lazards, and so on.

Naturally this constellation of stars was not achieved or maintained without mistakes and frictions. But, again by 1943, there was an efficient British Supply Council, with a Government Minister as Chairman and a strong Secretariat, headed by Derick Hoyer-Millar, to ensure self-consistency in our effort. Over this whole aggregation, civil and military, stood the supreme but gently exercised authority of the Ambassador, Lord Halifax.

The question in which I was involved in the smallest possible way was whether anything remotely corresponding to this degree of combined working could be evolved on the diplomatic and, in my case, post-war planning side. There is one big difference which distinguishes diplomacy from military or production and distribution operations. On the military side, you either landed in Sicily or you didn't; on the transport side, a ship needed above all a quick turn-round and you had to decide, against a deadline, whether the stores with which it would be loaded went to Britain or North Africa. Big decisions in this field involved tremendous strains, but in the end the answer had to be yes or no and could not be 'perhaps'. But on the diplomatic side there are many intangibles. We and the Americans were not running the whole world; we had allies who had views about their current treatment and their future prospects. There were differences of view between the Americans and ourselves, notably on French leadership and on the future of colonies. And there was often the option of putting off a decision until things might look easier. There was also at Foreign Secretary level in 1943 no real parallel to the relationship between Roosevelt and Churchill. Eden was conscious of post-war problems but Cordell Hull, the American Secretary of State, while formally his opposite number, did not cover the same range of business as that covered by Eden, and the two could not work in a personal way together.

As for post-war perspectives, there were important differences of approach between the three major allies. It was only the Russians who, even with their backs to the wall, fought the war throughout with an eye on their post-war national and ideological objectives. Their immediate, exclusive use of their power in Rumania and Bulgaria in 1944 showed this clearly. The British from 1940 onwards had an intermittent eye on post-war problems, particularly those concerning the Commonwealth, such as colonial development and the future of India; only in the later phases did Churchill try to translate into policy some of his justified anxieties about the future of Europe. But the Americans, or at least the American Administration as a whole, scarcely thought in these terms at all. Their object was to go hell-bent for victory with all the stupendous war-winning momentum which the United States developed. The peace could be dealt with as it came. This outlook had its advantages, notably the saving of lives, and one must not formalize the comparison too much. Plenty of people in North America thought about the future and the American contribution to the United Nations Charter was immensely important. But the White House did not act primarily in terms of post-war problems and when post-war considerations did arise in planning military or political strategy, they were not decisive. In his last days, when he was no longer at the height of his powers, the President appeared to improvise some views, but these did not reflect an accurate and sensitive insight into the political and ideological world in which we were going to live.

This was the more awkward because of the way in which, in external affairs at least, the power of the Presidency works, a feature of presidential government to which the British, accustomed to Cabinet government, had constantly to adjust themselves. An expert team would come from Britain, with a full brief, carefully studied, everybody speaking in a different tone but with one voice. There would be a first meeting with the Americans who would be unrehearsed and divided, some even arguing for the British case. The British team would imagine that this was a cinch, a pushover, and expect early agreement. There would then be a hush while the Americans side did its homework and found in the British proposal an insufficient regard to the American national interest. A revised proposal might then go to the White House. At the next meeting the British would say they had a couple of minor amendments, whereupon the Americans would look sad and say that a revised American version had been prepared which had the White House assent and they were therefore not authorized to alter a comma. Then the high-level tussle would begin. But if on the other hand there was no reference to the White House or no reply, the debate could go on inconclusively and indefinitely.

I have not drawn this picture with a view to criticizing either side. It was simply that two different methods ran into each other and we learned from experience. The British were ready, at least orally, to chance their arm a bit and see whether something could not be distilled out of combined thinking, the Americans were not accustomed to doing it that way. And if on the lines of my principal brief we achieved more or less nothing, it was not for want of trying or of good personal relations. Redvers Opie had a close personal relationship with Pasvolsky and although he shared with Pasvolsky a preference for keeping his own counsel, he constantly tried to prise something out of the American machine. I had excellent relations with Harley S. Notter, who was Pasvolsky's deputy on the political side and Leroy D. Stinebower on the economic side. Like the whole of the State Department of that day, they made one warmly welcome even when one just dropped in without an appointment. But nothing definite emerged and a glimpse of what may have been happening can be read in Dean Acheson's book – in short, questions were often lost in a proliferation of committees.[2]

My own work on post-war problems in the end developed in quite a different way. But meantime, as in Tokyo, I did other jobs when they needed manpower rather than expertise. Occasionally I sat in on a military intelligence committee. This has always made me wish I had had more to do with the services. British service people are exceptionally good to work with. Contrary to some current popular superstitions, they are pleasant people as working colleagues and masters of their particular crafts.

I was inveigled into membership of an inter-allied information committee in New York. It was regarded by our own Information Services with deep suspicion as taking money (however little) which could better be spent on purely British operations, but it did in fact do some modestly useful work and several of its members later occupied senior posts in the United Nations. The organization itself was killed in 1945 by the Russians who objected to it as representing '*émigré* groups'.

This commitment was useful in keeping me in touch with people in New York. In particular it brought me an introduction to a leading New York lawyer, Mr John Foster Dulles. I shall have later to be critical of Mr Dulles on certain points, and I should like therefore to record here that he was quite extra-ordinarily courteous and patient with visitors like myself, who had no particular claim on him, and one always got something out of meetings with him.

I had also an assignment to deal with exchanges of civilians and the treatment of prisoners of war. Another evacuation from Japan took place, but difficulties of organization and communication and the growing shortage of ships made more efforts impossible. We did much detailed work on the treatment of prisoners and others in former Italian territories, working as a team with our American opposite numbers; but events moved capriciously,

[2] Dean Acheson, *Present at the Creation*, p. 65.

as will happen in war, and it was difficult to keep pace with them.

However, this work brought me one permanent friendship which I have valued very deeply. My opposite number on the American side was very often Lieutenant-Colonel Murray C. Bernays. Had you tried to deduce Colonel Bernays from the name, you would have gone very wrong: his real name was unpronounceable, he came from a Russian Jewish family, and his first recollection, he told me, was of shots being fired as he and his family fled from Russia across the German frontier before 1914. He had become a highly successful lawyer in New York, had a handsome presence, a splendid head of grey hair and was an immensely hard worker with a perpetual twinkle in his eye alert for the amusing or ridiculous.

One day we drafted together a difficult telegram to London. 'The first paragraph,' said the Colonel gravely, handing the file to me, 'will be drafted in Piccadilly English.' 'The second,' I rejoined, on completing my paragraph, 'will be in Broadway "American."' 'Park Avenue, if you please,' snapped the Colonel.

Bernays later played an important part in handling American material for the Nuremberg trials and retired as a full Colonel. Friendships like these are among the treasured rewards of diplomacy.

In 1943 there were for us two special beginnings. On 13 May 1943 we gave an official cocktail party. A GI guest as he left, looked at Pat and said, 'If that girl doesn't have twins, I'll eat my hat.' The next day things began, three weeks early. Arriving in wartime Washington with family well on the way, we had no chance of hospital space, so we hurriedly explained the situation to a patient house-guest who tactfully withdrew. At 4.00 a.m. on 15 May a boy arrived. At that point Pat observed to the doctor, 'I don't think we've finished,' and we hadn't. The GI could keep his hat.

At breakfast time we still hadn't, and I had to go to the office. So we issued an agreed communiqué through Lady Halifax that we had had a son. General satisfaction. I returned about noon to find a second son had just arrived. We agreed that a second communiqué was required: 'For one son, read two.'

So I rang Lady Halifax again, and her cry of astonishment led her gathering lunch party to wonder what the emergency could be. She was quoted afterwards as saying 'Pat always does the right thing.'

Thus the family began. The twins had been a total surprise. There was no trace of twins in either family, and, as Pat had been very well throughout, the doctor had left her very much to herself. Later we asked the Department of the Interior whether David Alwyn and Christopher Hugh might have a claim to American citizenship. The Department replied that they were diplomatic children and no concern of theirs. But the boys are Washington-ians all the same, which is a long way from either Kobe or Doncaster.

Conferences

On January 1st, 1942, the representatives of twenty-six nations signed at Washington the Declaration of the United Nations. In this they pledged support for the principles of the Atlantic Charter of August 1941, they bound themselves to an all-out war effort, and they undertook to make no separate armistice or peace. In a sense, therefore, the United Nations 'existed' from that date.

President Roosevelt conceived the idea that the United Nations, while carrying out these pledges, should also show themselves as engaged together in peaceful, forward-looking activity even before the war ceased. He therefore proposed that there should take place in May 1943 a Conference on Food and Agriculture to be held at Hot Springs, Virginia.

The first reaction from at least some of the Allies, including the pragmatic British, was that they were busy fighting for their lives and conferences could wait. But there was no question of refusing and, in retrospect, I feel that the President's instinct was right. At any rate, the United Kingdom produced an immensely distinguished delegation, led by Mr Richard Law, MP,[3] then

[3] Richard Law, Lord Coleraine, Parliamentary Under-Secretary and subsequently Minister of State in the Foreign Office, 1941–45. On the return

Minister of State in the Foreign Office, and containing among others Sir John Maud,[4] who had done so much at the Ministry of Food to shape wartime rationing policy, economists of the calibre of Professor Lionel Robbins[5] and Robert Hall,[6] and leading agricultural experts. The Conference was purely re-commendatory, but a useful start was made on the road to setting up United Nations Specialized Agencies, and specifically the Food and Agriculture Organization.

For me, the Conference was a second beginning within a few days of the beginning of family life. It set off a whole series of attendances at international conferences on post-war subjects which occurred repeatedly until immediately after the end of the war and never entirely ceased thereafter. A change was taking place in the style of diplomacy, and the nature of my assignment to Washington put me right in the middle of it. The Hot Springs Conference was also, for me, an object lesson in how a large national delegation to an international conference should be run. For quiet and friendly efficiency, I have never seen anything to

of the Conservatives to power in 1951, he did not come back to office, but during the fifties and early sixties was outstandingly active as chairman of social service groups, retaining his connection with the United States as chairman, for nine years, of the Marshall Scholarships Committee.

[4] Lord Redcliffe-Maud, during the war Second Secretary of the Ministry of Food, then Permanent Under-Secretary of the Ministry of Education and subsequently of the Ministry of Fuel and Power, 1945–58. Later High Commissioner to South Africa and Ambassador when South Africa left the Commonwealth. Became Master of University college, Oxford, in 1963. Among a great number of public services he was chairman of the Royal Commission on Local Government, 1968–69.

[5] Lord Robbins economist; a governor of the London School of Economics, 1961–70; 1961–64, chairman of the Committee on Higher Education. A trustee of the National and Tate galleries and of the Royal Opera House, Covent Garden. Member of numerous foreign universities. Author of many authoritative works on economics, including *The Theory of Economic Policy*, 1952, and *The Economist in the Twentieth Century*, 1954.

[6] Lord Roberthall, after the war for many years Economic Adviser to the British government and also chairman of the OEEC group of economic experts, 1955–61, President of Hertford College, Oxford, 1964–67.

beat the performance of Bill Hasler[7] and John Wall.[8] And the pleasant political personality of Richard Law showed what the right political touch can do in an international governmental gathering on an important technical subject.

The next conference I attended was that held at Atlantic City in New Jersey in November for the purpose of setting up UNRRA, the United Nations Relief and Rehabilitation Association. There was the first ripple of trouble with the Russians: at Hot Springs the Soviet delegate, Mr Krutikov, known as 'Mr Inskrutikov', had exposed no surface.

I was not involved in the highly successful and productive Financial Conference at Bretton Woods in 1944 but very much involved in the Chicago Conference on Civil Aviation in October/November of that year. This was not the worst conference I have ever attended; we shall come to that later. But it was, from beginning to end, one of the oddest.

As part of my terms of reference, I had been handling civil aviation matters in the Embassy. I had therefore made preparations to go, but was suddenly informed that a senior colleague who knew nothing about the question would go as diplomatic adviser instead. With a wisdom which still rather surprises me, I made no protest. In fact Pat and I simply took a weekend bus trip to Gettysburg.

It was mostly pretty rainy. But, recalling the Robert Birley technique, we marched up and down with General James Longstreet wondering whether there was anything more to be done by the Confederates to force the Federal position. We stood (having no horse) on the Ridge with General Meade, impassively watching over the unbroken resistance of the Federals. We saw ourselves in the Peach Orchard as Colonel Pickett got the last ounce of valour out of his regiment in the final, unavailing

[7] W.G. Bill Hasler, an outstanding civil servant, who was tragically drowned with his wife off Devon in 1946.

[8] Sir John Wall has been chairman of International Computers since 1968. Before that he was a director of Cunard, 1966–68, Managing Director of EMI, 1960–66, Director of other large industrial concerns, and from 1971 a governor of the Administrative Staff College.

E

Confederate charge. Gettysburg is not only the shrine of those who died there and of Abraham Lincoln's immortal Address. It is also one of the great physically preserved battlefields of the world. There are not so many which tell their own story, but in this it ranks with Syracuse in Sicily which has all the poignancy of Thucydides, and Kohima in Nagaland where nature as well as art shows where the Japanese advance on India was stopped. The Americans have done a magnificent work of preserving Gettysburg, and it is one of the most moving places to visit in the whole of the United States. This is the more true if you pay it the compliment of first finding out what happened there and why.

On return to Washington I found a laconic message. 'Please go to Chicago after all.'

It was clear that the leading roles in the Conference were going to be taken by the United States and ourselves, and that we were going to disagree. The issue was how post-war international civil aviation was to be organized. The Americans held a simple, free-for-all view: the world was going to need as soon as possible international air transport services of an extent and capacity never dreamed of before, so the fewest possible restrictions should be placed on their development. This policy suited them, since the United States was the only country which would be able to provide quickly the needed aircraft; and other countries, notably the Latin Americans who were not interested in manufacturing aircraft or, for some time to come, in operating national air services, supported this line.

The British, with support from France, Australia and New Zealand, felt that it would be fairer and more acceptable to have a system of regulating frequencies of service which, even if it made development in the short run a little slower, would give countries less immediately able to organize civil aviation industries and services a chance to protect their longer term interests. In particular, these countries argued, there should be a code of 'escalation' which relates increases of service frequencies to the ratio of passengers carried to seats offered.

In such a situation, it was important, if the conference were not to present a spectacle of allies at loggerheads, that the leaders of the American and British delegations should have a good personal understanding. There were difficulties here. The British leader, Lord Swinton, was a fine, fighting, non-highbrow Conservative political leader, with a remarkable political record. He suffered however from the limitation of having no conversation other than business or political reminiscence. Mr Adolf A. Berle Jr the leader of the American delegation, in contrast, was an extremely able New York radical lawyer, an intellectual who did not repudiate the title and bore a streak of intolerance in his make-up. Both leaders tried strenuously to make the Conference work but the instinctive harmony that sometimes develops between leaders was simply not there.

The situation was also not helped by conditions in both delegations. The American delegation contained outstanding people in the civil aviation world, notably the expert with the scholarly manner, Dr Edward Warner, later to become Director-General of the International Civil Aviation Organization. But it also contained, for good political reasons, the famous Mayor Fiorello La Guardia of New York, a national figure who had done much for New York and for aviation, but whose warm heart and ambitious mind were matched with little discipline. When the American delegation began to feel that the Conference had done what it could and should quietly come to a close we had agreed, Mayor La Guardia rose in public session and made an impassioned speech saying that the eyes of the peoples of the world were upon us and we must not fail: the Conference must go on. The conference cheered and did so. Even for those in the British delegation who knew America, this was a bit hard to take; for those who did not, it rated as unabashed perfidy.

Conditions in the British delegation were not much better. The two leading advisers, Sir Arthur Street, the Permanent Under-Secretary of the Ministry of Aviation, and Mr George Cribbett, the leading expert on International Air Transport, informed us that they were too busy to attend delegation meetings. Now if there is one rule which is unbreakable in international conferences and observed by any serious delegation, it is that a complete delegation must meet regularly, preferably daily, for a mutual exchange of news and views. If Lord Swinton had had more international conference experience or if I had had more rank at the time, this nonsense would have been stopped. As it was, the delegation met from day to day in the absence of the top aviation policy experts. Equally, what we might have picked up in moving round in the highly political atmosphere of the Conference did not easily reach the senior expert advisers.

It became indeed progressively clearer that our doctrine, in particular the idea of escalation, would not be approved by the Conference. So Lord Swinton finally appealed to London to be allowed to drop it. Lord Beaverbrook, the Minister for Aircraft Production, telephoned from London; Lord Swinton swore that he replied, 'Max, go to hell: it's three o'clock in the morning here,' and rang off, so a telegram followed making several points, one of which was, 'You may abandon escalation.' We whooped with delight and rushed down, announced this decision and were suddenly as popular as any sinner that repenteth. Two hours later a 'chaser' telegram arrived saying 'In my previous telegram, before "abandon" insert "not".' Too late. A British delegation does not go back on its word.

In the end the conference was outwardly a failure and essentially a great success. Much had been learned about the various 'freedoms of the air' and their application while behind all the sound and fury anonymous people were going carefully over all the technical ground that needed to be covered in future agreements. Out of this emerged the whole basis of the regulation of international civil aviation in its technical and safety aspects.

In the middle of this tension came the news of the British military intervention in Greece. The British delegation shared the universal censure in the United States of the British action, the lone voice of Walter Graebner in *Time* expressing the contrary doctrine which a few years later pretty well any American would have held.

In the summer of 1944, a start had been made on the enterprise on which so many people had placed their hopes, the formation of a United Nations Organization. It was agreed that it was not possible to think in terms of a revival of the League of Nations: despite the idealism devoted to the League, the name spelt failure, and moreover, one of the boldest acts of the League, the expulsion of the Soviet Union when the Russians invaded Finland in 1939, made it unthinkable that the Soviet Government would agree to renew international co-operation under that banner. The Americans, too, had the unhappy memory of the Senate's rejection of the League in 1919, so the United Nations was based from the beginning on a realistic understanding that an international political organization intended to be universal had to be assured from the start of full American and Soviet membership and that, within reason, other intending members would have to pay a price for this assurance.

I had, in the early summer of 1944, attended a non-governmental conference at Lake Couchiching, north of Toronto, at which some of these problems were discussed by a mixed group of academics and people in government. Great stress was laid on democratic institutions and the rights of smaller nations; but there was also some realization that effective international executive power would be needed. This led the discussion not in the direction of a strong executive committee such as the Security Council, which might lead to discrimination between great and small nations, but to the idea of investing very great powers in a top international official. The conference was thinking mainly in security and peace-keeping terms, so this official became known as the 'Commander-in-Chief'. Feeling instinctively that the thinking at the conference would not accord with the British Government's ideas, I continued to help the drafters of the report on condition that my name would not be connected with it.

The basic argument in 1944–45 was not between the Russians and the Western Allies, though there were crises in that field too. It was between the big powers and the rest. The former insisted on exercising a great measure of authority in an organization in which they were going to have to bear the major responsibility, whether for keeping the peace or paying the bills. The rest contested very strongly any departure from the principle of one country one vote.

The first formal steps in the new enterprise were the big power talks at the Washington mansion of Dumbarton Oaks in August 1944 with Mr Cordell Hull, the American Secretary of State, as host. When Lord Halifax, the leader of the British delegation, stepped out of his plane, accompanied by Sir Alexander Cadogan (the latter complete in a Washington August with light over-coat and rolled umbrella), and again when Mr Gromyko made his first appearance, one was acutely aware that on the initial efforts of this small group so much of the future depended.

It may, and indeed did, seem strange that the Chinese were not there, for during the war the Americans had, for immediate political and military reasons, promoted them, de facto, to Great Power status. The gesture of course made much more sense in terms of the long range future than in terms of China's capacity or performance in the Second World War, and for the immediate purpose of founding the United Nations, China presented a considerable problem. Relations between the Kuo-mintang Government and the Communists were bad, so the Russians were not likely to commit themselves to the former. It was necessary to try to arrive with the Russians at a text to which the Chinese would agree without difficulty, since any counter-proposal of any significance from the Chinese was likely to cause delays which could endanger the summoning of a United Nations Conference.

The atmosphere of these talks was by and large good, and the surroundings and hospitality offered by the Americans materially assisted. Mr Gromyko's deputy, Mr A. A. Sobolev, proved to be exceptionally good to deal with and, while naturally not abandon-ing any important positions, had a manner and a technique which helped progress. In the end the Chinese, no doubt under strong American pressure, accepted in all important respects what had been drafted and the talks concluded successfully. The main tasks of the Dumbarton Oaks powers now shifted elsewhere, as the draft was expounded to third countries.

I had been only a minor back row 'element' in these pro-

ceedings and soon after became involved in the Civil Aviation
Conference already described. But through the winter 1944–45,
despite the German offensive in the Ardennes and uncertainty
about the duration of Japanese resistance, informal discussion
was turning more and more to the future, to post-war Germany
and Japan, and the prospects for India and for the colonies of
European powers. Through personal friendships and some
introductions from Colonel Himatsinhji, I seemed to become
easily involved in argument about the Indian future.

The normal American view was the doctrinal one, inherited
from the American Revolution, that we ought to get out of
everywhere and the sooner the better. (At that stage, those
who remembered the American Indians found it wise to be
silent.) The British were constantly tempted to give the wrong
reply – that people were better off under British rule than they
would be if independent. There was a story that an Indian
Nationalist spokesman used to take round on tour in America a
tame British friend to give the wrong answers which he would
then annihilate. I spent quite a lot of exasperated time urging my
fellow-countrymen that the difference between good government, or fairly good government, and self-government is not
one of degree, but one of essence. Sooner or later self-government
would come. The only valid and effective reply to American
criticism at the time was to say, as did those American service
people who returned from British war fronts, that we had been
and were fighting for our lives, that the war was now going pretty
well under the present management, and for heaven's sake, do not
root up everything, including responsibility, until after the end of
armed conflict.

It was in this context that I first met Ralph Bunche, who was
working in the post-war section of the State Department.
The first time he came to our house, we were talking idly about
Washington life and I asked him where he had lunch. 'In the
State Department – where else?' was his reply. That was sufficient
comment on the race situation in the District of Columbia at the
time. We visited the Bunches and they visited us. One is not
at all surprised that he should have risen to such heights in the

United Nations. With great vision and humanity he always tried to prove that America could not only produce people of stature from his race but could also give them opportunity to serve. Later, despite bouts of ill-health he carried a killing load in the UN. I called on him in 1968. When we had discussed international affairs, I asked him about the racial situation in the United States. He said something very sad. 'I am afraid it is near civil war.'

With Christmas 1944 and the New Year over, I was suddenly told that I was to be a member of the British delegation to the Conference to be held in San Francisco in April to draft the United Nations Charter and that I should return to London at the end of February to study the documents and take part in briefing meetings. This meant that the family would not fore-gather again until the Conference was over.

In London I stayed again at the Crofton Hotel with my parents, and once more I was fortunate in that the worst of the buzz-bomb raids was over. I spent a lot of the time at the Foreign Office briefing meetings, advising on American public and congressional opinion, at that time still unpredictable. Before we left we had the shock of Mr Roosevelt's death; for a day or two it was hard to imagine that anyone else could be President.

One thing I did which seems to me in retrospect to have been brash and inconsiderate, but which was in the circumstances rather well received. I had become accustomed in Washington to certain standards of office organization and work, including adequate secretarial help – thanks no doubt to the higher American standards with which the Embassy had to compete, and to the business people in our wartime organization. My own perform-ance (I do not mean volume of output) had been greatly im-proved by these standards.

The nuts and bolts (as opposed to personnel) organization in the Foreign Office on the other hand had always been pretty sketchy, and now it looked deplorable. So, ignoring the fact that the office was full of tired people who had by sheer guts ground their understaffed way through the worst of the war, I settled down with the only typewriter available, my mother's favourite pre-1914 Corona, and wrote a complaint. I said I had been trying to get things done and was constantly confronted with telephones which no one answered, high officials fussing round with boxes and keys, insufficient copies of everything and general frustration to one's minor efforts in an important cause.

I ought no doubt to have received a curt 'There's a war on' type of reply. Instead I got a bouquet from James Crombie, borrowed from the Treasury to be Head of Administration, who commented, 'Mr Gore-Booth has said with more courage and clarity what I have been trying to say for a long time.' I do not say that my ill-typed efforts achieved anything direct, but the episode gave me an incentive to persist when I came back later, at a time when administration was gradually becoming more professional and responsive.

When the time came to leave for San Francisco, I was allocated to a plane carrying the Deputy Prime Minister, Mr Attlee, and the Parliamentary Secretary of the Ministry of Home Security, Miss Ellen Wilkinson. We gathered in black-out conditions late in the evening of 18 April and set off via the Azores and Montreal in an austerity Constellation with late-war hard seats for all.

I had always wanted to read Tolstoy's *War and Peace* and had never found time. This seemed to me to be the right moment in history to try and the length of the journey might get me so far that I should be compelled to finish. Mr Attlee, whose requirements were modest and definite, did not interrupt. But half way across the Atlantic Miss Wilkinson interrupted a ball in St Petersburg with a torrent of protest. The flight, she complained, was uncomfortable, the food was awful and why wasn't I, as being in charge of the party on behalf of the Foreign Office, doing something about it? It had not occurred to me that I was 'in charge'; if I was, nobody had told me. And there seemed to be a number of authoritative persons about, quite apart from the RAF whose plane it was. However, there was objectively much in what Miss Wilkinson had said, so I cautiously approached the RAF. They were very sympathetic, thought the food was pretty bad themselves and would do their best. There was no trouble after Montreal, and in San Francisco I finished *War and Peace*.

Meantime, with the prospect of a long family separation I had made a date to meet Pat in Montreal. I had ordered some flowers to greet her on her arrival. I am not quite sure what happened, but when I walked into the room it was like a gold-medal rose stand at the Chelsea Flower Show. Never have so many roses collected on every table, shelf, console, window ledge and whatnot in a First Secretary's hotel bedroom. It was a splendid reunion.

On arrival at San Francisco we found that the Americans had put an immense amount of work into the organization of the conference. In addition to supplying, through the State of California and city authorities, the accommodation for the conference sessions and the delegations, they produced the entire secretariat, including the normal facilities for interpretation and the production and distribution of documents. The secretariat was in the charge of Alger Hiss, then Assistant Under-Secretary in the State Deparment. In view of his later tragedy, it is right to say that he handled his task with tact, fairness and efficiency.

The United States Administration had appointed the Secretary of State, Edward R. Stettinius Jr, to lead the delegation, and, heeding the warning of 1919, when President Wilson had omitted to include a Republican in the American delegation, they included both the Democratic Chairman of the Senate Foreign Relations Committee, Senator Tom Connally of Texas, and the Minority Leader of that Committee, Senator Arthur Vandenberg of Michigan.

The British Government took the view that its delegation must be of the highest possible standing and effectiveness. War had not ended in Europe and there could be no question of Mr Churchill leaving London, but Mr Attlee, as Deputy Prime Minister, led the delegation, accompanied by the Foreign Secretary, Mr Anthony Eden, and the Commonwealth Secretary, Lord Cranborne.[9] The Ambassador, Lord Halifax, joined the

[9] Lord Cranborne, son and heir of the Fifth Marquess of Salisbury. MP for Bournemouth West, 1950-54.

delegation in San Francisco. Junior Ministers were appointed from all political parties and allocated to the various Commissions which the Conference set up to study the draft Charter. The chief official advisers and negotiators were Gladwyn Jebb and Professor C. K. Webster,[10] but there were also top officials to deal with economic, social, labour and colonial matters; a legal team was headed by the chief Foreign Office legal adviser, Sir William Malkin and his colleague, G. G. Fitzmaurice; public relations were in the hands of Francis Williams, Mr Attlee's public relations adviser; and, not least, the nuts and bolts had been taken really seriously and a high-powered delegation secretariat was established. On later return to London I played some part in converting it into the permanent Conference Department of the Foreign Office.

At the opening ceremony on April 25th we were welcomed with the genuineness which always characterized President Truman. But there was initally a curious absence of emotion, until the Philippine orator to end orators, General Romulo, began his speech with 'Let this be the last battlefield.' And the Conference woke up when Mr Eden, who had rewritten his official draft, concluded bravely, 'Let us do it quickly and let us do it now.'

I had been instructed to advise our Ministers allocated to Commission 1. This commission had to deal with the preamble of the Charter and the articles covering purposes and principles, membership, the secretariat, miscellaneous provisions and amendments of the charter.[11] The pioneers, like Gladwyn Jebb and Charles Webster, had to deal with the nub of the Charter, the Assembly and the Security Council, and high level experts looked after economic, social, colonial and judicial matters. Behind the generalities allocated to Commission 1 lurked principles of some importance. Article 1, for instance, conceals a

---

[10] Sir Charles Kingsley Webster, historian and biographer, Stevenson Professor of International History at the LSE, 1932–53. President of the British Academy, 1950–54. Member of the UK delegation to UN conferences. Author of numerous works, including *Palmerston's Foreign Policy* and *Art and Practice of Diplomacy*.

[11] Chapters I, II, XV, XVI, and XVIII.

lively debate on whether you maintain international peace and security in accordance with 'justice' or 'the principles of justice'. I was instructed to argue for 'the principles' because who knows what 'justice' really is? To my astonishment I converted the New Zealand spokesman to an Anglo-Soviet point of view and 'principles' it is.

Article 2(vii), providing for non-interference in matters of a country's internal jurisdiction, was very important to both the United States and the Soviet Union; it is an essential provision though it always lies on the edge of controversy when there is international criticism of the internal affairs of a member state. Article 99 is one of the most important of the Charter, since it gives the Secretary-General the right to 'bring to the Security Council any matter which in his opinion may threaten the maintenance of international peace and security'. In other words, there can be no silent conspiracy by the big powers on the Security Council as a whole to keep a matter undiscussed if the Secretary-General has, at the psychological moment, the judgement and courage to insist on discussion.

The Commission divided into two Committees, and ploughed through the draft texts sentence by sentence, line by line, sometimes word by word. The Ministers I was advising were Miss Ellen Wilkinson, now gastronomically pacified, and Mr William Mabane, Parliamentary Under-Secretary for the Ministry of Food. Both Ministers were experienced and highly articulate parliamentarians. Their instinct was to bring Westminster into the International Council Chamber, to interrupt boring speakers with awkward questions and to harass incompetent chairmen into decisive action. I hated having to advise them at intervals that the pace of an international drafting conference has often to be the pace of its slowest member and that, if the delegate of the Republic of Hydropotamia had not quite understood the question and simply had to get a set speech off his chest, international courtesy compelled one to let him do so without limit of time.

On 13 May a time-bomb burst in the British delegation. A General Election was announced in Britain. The delegation reduced itself on the political level almost overnight into Lord

Halifax and Lord Cranborne, and I suddenly became the UK spokesman on purposes, principles and miscellaneous provisions. This was an alarming moment, even though my instructions were explicit, the Committees were very agreeable in their personal relationships and it would have been hard to go badly wrong.

But occasionally quick thinking was needed. One of the curiosities of Commission 1 was that given its miscellaneous remit, illustrious people came in specially to address us on their particular subjects. At one such session, Mrs Eleanor Roosevelt came to propose that the organization be called 'The United Nations'. This evoked great enthusiasm, except among some European lawyers who thought that you ought not to call an organization by a name that was not organizational. In any case, they asked, would you say 'The United Nations is' or 'The United Nations are'? The French made jokes on the initials of the UN (*Nations Unies*) in French. When the Dutch delegate rose and asked what I thought, I put forward a motion to the effect that we accept Mrs Roosevelt's proposal subject to a committee of jurists being satisfied that the term 'United Nations' presented no legal difficulty. It was accepted and the question did not arise again.

There were other memorable sessions. One was when Field-Marshal Smuts, in his animated and heavily South African speech, introduced the preamble to the Charter, which he had drafted himself. The other was immediately after the announcement of victory in Europe, when Mr Hambro of Norway and Mr Jan Masaryk of Czechoslavakia bade a breathless farewell before returning in haste to their liberated countries.

When we came to Chapter XVIII, Amendments, we were on very delicate ground, because the draft Charter provided that any amendment would require first a two-thirds majority in the General Assembly and then ratification by two-thirds of the members, including all the permanent members of the Security Council. Nothing less restrictive would have obtained the assent of the Soviet Union or, possibly, the United States, and since these acceptances were the key to the Conference, the views of the United Kingdom had to be firmly and authoritatively stated. In the absence of a Minister, they were presented by

Colonel Denis Capel-Dunn of the Cabinet Office who had been working on the Charter since the beginning. I should like to have known this thoughtful and interesting man better. But when the conference was over he, together with Sir William Malkin, our senior legal adviser, and several members of the staff of the delegation, set off for home in an aircraft which was never heard of again.

The Commission contained a number of people who later became prominent in public life, such as the very able Ecuadorean delegate, Señor Galo Plaza.[12] Lester Pearson, later Prime Minister of Canada, though not a regular member of the Commission, attended several meetings. But in a way the most interesting colleague for me was Semyon Tsarapkin[13] of the Soviet Union. He was a man with a determined jaw and an obstinacy in defending every comma which, if he had been in the Crimean War, would have doubled the length of the siege of Sevastopol. He was a pleasant colleague, though, and we occasionally took a drink together and discussed the situation a little awkwardly in our only common language, Japanese.

Other distinguished people were present in San Francisco who made their voices heard outside. Prominent among these was Mrs Vijayalakshmi Pandit, sister of Pandit Jawarharlal Nehru, who led a kind of anti-official Indian delegation in the lobbies. She was later to become President of the General Assembly of the organization which the official Indian delegates were helping to build.

The Charter was signed in June and came into force on 24 October 1945 having by then been ratified, as required by Article 110(iii), by the permanent members of the Security Council (China, France, the Soviet Union, United Kingdom and United States) and a majority of the other signatory states. It has proved a document of encouraging endurance. It may go

[12] Señor Galo Plaza, Ecuadorian Ambassador to the USA, 1944-45; President of the Republic of Ecuador, 1948-52; Member of UN observer groups and committees in the Lebanon, the Congo; Cyprus (Mediator 1964-65), Secretary-General of the Organization of American States, 1968.

[13] Semyon Tsarapkin was Soviet Ambassador to Bonn, 1966-71, and head of the Soviet delegation at the disarmament talks in Geneva, 1961-66.

too far in protecting the position of the big powers; yet the realistic logic of this is difficult to dispute, and the British can draw some national comfort from the fact that under Article 108, so long as the Charter is the operative world instrument, we cannot be deprived of our veto without our consent. Some of the purposes and principles make rather sad reading now: in how many countries are social progress and better standards of life being promoted 'in larger freedom'? But it is a good basis for world business all the same.

The atmosphere of San Francisco was wonderful. The Golden Gate and the entrance to the bay are breathtakingly spectacular, and the climate was just right for hard work intermingled with spontaneous enjoyment. Doors of institutions and private homes seemed permanently open to us all. If a vote had been taken there and then, without reference to mundane matters like distance from the rest of the world, San Francisco would have been chosen unanimously for the future headquarters.

The achievement of the Charter in this atmosphere has led to a legend that we were all in a state of chronic political euphoria and thought we had solved all the problems of the world. I hope I have said enough to show that the Conference as such was deadly serious and in no sense disregarded the realities of world power. It had been sobered up right at the beginning by the news that sixteen representatives of the Polish Government had accepted a Soviet invitation to lunch and been flung into prison on arrival. Yet those attending the Conference strove to maintain the general hope that, although the Russians had been difficult allies, the joint victory in the war and the achievement of a Charter of peace and security would enable them to relax and help bring about a new kind of world community. This did not happen, and to that extent our hope was mistaken. But it was always a sober hope and not a wishful illusion and it was worth maintaining as long as it could last.

With the Conference ended, I reported briefly at Washington, and then went straight off to Northport, Long Island, where we had rented a small house for the summer. The boys, who had been lively but unintelligible when I last saw them five months before, were bubbling with words, and I was advised in a long and eager stream that this was a table and that a telephone. It was a wonderful fortnight's rest and recreation.

But other people were going on leave and I had to return to Washington where I suddenly found myself acting Head of Chancery. Any Embassy has an officer of First Secretary or Counsellor rank with the title of Head of Chancery. In a big Embassy like Washington he is a kind of universal joint between all sections of Embassy activity and to a considerable extent between these sections and the Head of Mission, so he has to deal with a number of people senior in rank and experience to himself. He will also need to speak in the name of the Ambassador without any suggestion that he is seeking to limit the right of direct access to the head of the post. If he can manage this with tact, much can be smoothed out at high middle level which, if everybody stood on protocol, would waste the Head of Mission's time with laborious detail. It follows that the good functioning of the Embassy machine depends greatly on the performance of this universal joint.

It was an exceptionally heavy August. There was the aftermath of the dropping of the atomic bombs, and the cynical Russian declaration of war on Japan only a few days before the end of Japanese resistance, There was VJ day. There was the appearance on my desk of a small piece of mimeograph paper perfunctorily announcing the end of Lend-Lease – an unhappy decision by President Truman on literal-minded advice which disregarded the serious economic implications of a decision taken without discussion with allied governments. One hot day, I was beginning to find the job too much for me. I went home, had a long rest and thought out a better way of organizing my work, and never, had any further trouble. I owed this recovery to many things, more especially to the impeccable work of two people. George Middleton was one.[14] The other was Donald Maclean.

As the month went on, we all hung on one great expectation,

[14] Sir George Middleton was Deputy High Commissioner in India, 1953–56, Ambassador to the Lebanon, 1956–58, to Argentina, 1961–64, to the UAR, 1964–66.

the essential ratification by the United States Senate of the
United Nations Charter. Over and above participation in the
San Francisco Conference, I had a particular personal involvement since in Washington I had been close, on a strictly non-
interference basis, to the work done by Senator Joseph H. Ball
of Minnesota and three colleagues to convince Senators generally
that there should be no repetition of the American post-First
World War retirement into isolation. Mindful of the possible
danger, the Administration left nothing to chance. Having
assured the support of the leadership by including Senators
Connally and Vandenberg as active members of the delegation at
San Francisco, they mounted after the Conference a publicity
campaign in which even the normally reticent Leo Pasvolsky
took part. The Senate vote eventually came on a grey, warm
August afternoon and the majority was the triumphant one of
91–2. 1920 had been decisively reversed.

I happened to be in the office when the news came through.
I knew that the right congratulations would be addressed to
the Administration. But it seemed to me to be such an impressive
result that someone ought to express congratulations also to
Senator Connally, as Chairman of the Senate Foreign Relations
Committee, especially as we had worked so closely with him at
San Francisco. I consulted a colleague who took a rather 't'aint
necessary' attitude. This decided me to go and do something
myself. So I drove round to the Senator's house in Rock Creek
Park. A small car was there and underneath it, the Senator. He
was scrabbling for a bag of peaches he had brought to present
to Mrs Connally in celebration of the occasion. So I joined the
Senator under the car and we retrieved the scattered fruit. We
then went in and found Mrs Connally playing the piano as she
waited for her husband.

It was a perfect domestic moment and I naturally withdrew
quickly after an exchange of expressions of pleasure and con-
gratulation. But I can recall no occasion on which an instinctive
action proved so timely and so happy.

At the end of August I was instructed to come home to help
with preparations for the first meeting of the General Assembly of

the United Nations which, thanks to a generous suggestion by the United States Secretary of State, Edward Stettinius, was to be held in London. This in fact meant transfer home. I had no regrets about returning to battered London. But we were also sad as we had accustomed ourselves to the pleasant if breathless rhythm of Washington. The transfer incidentally meant a second journey with a baby on the way.

A retrospect of Washington at that time brings first to mind the quality and drive of the American war effort, an unforgettable combination of organization and bravery, though not without moments of humour. An American general was ordered to fly from Washington to St Louis to attend a lecture by a professor of whom he had never heard. After much grumbling, he complied. His office exerted his air priority at the expense of a passenger of lower rating. The general arrived, only to be told that the lecture had been cancelled as the professor had not arrived. 'Why the hell not?' 'He was thrown off the plane by some general or other.'

I must devote one more word to the Ambassador and Lady Halifax. There could not be a day to day relationship of the kind one had at a smaller post, for the whole operation was so large that Lord and Lady Halifax reigned over it like two kindly deities. The beginning had been difficult. In Sir Ronald Lindsay's time, the British had had to keep their heads down and their mouths shut, lest they be suspected of dragging America into unwanted foreign entanglements. In Lord Lothian's crucial year, 1939–40, it had been necessary to begin to tell the American public something, but not too much and not the wrong thing. Lord Lothian did this with an unfailing instinct until his untimely death. Lord Halifax came with the stigma of 'appeasement' and his reception was mixed. But he was not only an ex-Viceroy and a Fellow of All Souls; he was also a Yorkshire farmer and capable of an earthiness unexpected by his detractors. He travelled inexhaustibly in all the states usually accompanied and expertly advised by Angus McDonnell[15] and Archie Gordon, both of

[15] Angus McDonnell, Lord Halifax's cousin who lived many years in America and is accurately described by Lord Birkenhead, Lord Halifax's biographer, as the Ambassador's 'bear-leader'.

whom combined expertise with humour. Lord Halifax's great
public relations triumph was when, on having eggs thrown at
him, he remarked how nice it must be to have some eggs to
throw.

There are so many more people who could be mentioned, but
I will only mention one, Isaiah Berlin. Isaiah wrote every week
a summary of the week's events which was then telegraphed
to London. It was usually very long but so good that everyone
with access to it simply had to read it. I suggested that, prior to
drafting, he might like to hold a meeting of a few people
interested in the specifically American side of the work in case
others had ideas which could help him. These sessions were an
informative delight. They led to the reflection that you can pass
three virtuous years in Washington as a diplomat working with
US Government departments without really 'getting' the United
States at all. Americanology or United Statesmanship is a dimension of its own, and I was fortunate to have been thrown into it.
Immersion does not affect your critical capacity; if anything it
heightens it. But it also enabled me later to keep a sense of proportion about American affairs at a time when the British,
obsessed with their own frustrations, and subconsciously jealous
of the assumption by the Americans of world leadership exercised
in a non-British style, became too easy victims of any insinuation
to the American detriment. There was plenty to nag about. But
if one knew how things happened in the United States, the
results could be understood whether one approved of them or
not and it was possible both publicly and privately to keep one's
head.

London

1945-1949

United Nations

The Labour triumph in the 1945 General Election provoked an immediate reaction in America which can only be called stupefaction. People could not understand how the British could be so ungrateful as to reject Winston Churchill to whose leadership they had owed their deliverance. Additional alarm was caused by the logical if misleading assumption that, as the Chairman of the Labour Party for the year happened to be Professor Harold Laski, the country would be run strictly in accordance with his teachings. However, the appearance of Mr Attlee and Mr Bevin at the Potsdam Conference accompanied by the same professional advisers who had advised Mr Churchill, was felt to be odd but reassuring. And Richard Miles from the British Embassy reassured the National Press Club in Washington with the quip, 'Right or Left, my country.'

At home, people understood exactly what they had done when they cheered Mr Churchill and voted for Mr Attlee. The failures of the 1930s governments had not been forgotten, failures that ran far deeper than Mr Neville Chamberlain's diplomacy; and there had been a certain lack of inspiration in Mr Churchill's public references to post-war policy. There was an instinctive feeling for the big things that would have to be done to prevent the recurrence, through uncontrolled economic forces, of industrial depression and mass unemployment, and for the help and protection which in the future must be given to the individual, vulnerable citizen.

On the Foreign Office side there was the instant knowledge that, with Ernest Bevin as Secretary of State, the voice of Foreign Affairs in the Cabinet would be powerful and authoritative.

What we did not know was the degree to which Bevin in his long trade union career had acquainted himself with facts and tendencies in the outside world. We were in for a highly favourable surprise.

Comparisons may be odious, but in my diplomatic lifetime, no Foreign Secretary engaged the loyalty and affection of the whole Diplomatic Service as Ernest Bevin did. It is difficult to explain this affection in cold print. Contrary to much invention, the Diplomatic Service could not care less about the social antecedents of its political master. What the Service does understand is reciprocal loyalty. It accepts that you serve the Secretary of State and not the temporary incumbent of the post. But if that incumbent, in addition to his political ability and standing, openly stands up for those who serve him, there can be a co-ordination of heart and head which is both rare and invaluable. And if, in addition to being powerful and likeable personally (and in his earlier days, Bevin may have been less likeable than he became), the Secretary of State comes to power at a moment which enables him both to demonstrate power and vision and to stand up for his team in public, the Service will do anything for him.

Bevin is not the only Secretary of State who had the legitimate interests of his servants at heart. The reforms carried out by Eden in 1943 are evidence of this. But the importance of showing it openly has not always been understood. It in no way presupposes an uncritical attitude; Bevin could be suspicious, and could show himself severe if he thought he had been let down. But general mutual confidence made individual censure more acceptable and drew from members of the Service that little extra effort and feeling which they did not know they had in them. The only sadness is that Bevin's physical strength could not quite last his full time when the best of him was still so badly needed.

I returned to London in September on that most civilized of aircraft, the old Boeing Clipper (a flying-boat). Against an Atlantic headwind its ground speed was, less than 100 mph, but it had a bed for each passenger which made up for everything.

On arriving in the Foreign Office, I found a much changed situation on the United Nations front. Gladwyn Jebb had gone over to Church House to take charge of the United Nations Preparatory Commission, and with him had gone David Owen who had been the economic and social prop of the department. Professor Webster was still with us, and there was new vigorous political leadership in Philip Noel-Baker, Minister of State in the Foreign Office, with his many years of League of Nations experience, and the able assistance of Hector McNeill. Nigel Ronald was supervising Under-Secretary but had other cares, including ill-health. Jack Ward, the Head of the department of which I was to be assistant head, had more than enough on his hands with a Big Three Foreign Ministers' Conference in London, the whole apparatus of peace-making and the politics of atomic energy.

There seemed to me to be a danger of lack of coherence in our United Nations affairs. Accordingly at a meeting to discuss future plans, I suggested that I should become secretary of the United Kingdom delegation to the Preparatory Commission and the first General Assembly. This being approved, I added that if I were to do this, I should need a secretary. This was considered, by some, incorrect procedure, but in no other way could I have got the secretary I needed.

Matters having been settled, I had to return to America to fetch the family back. We travelled from Philadelphia in the Danish grain ship *Jutlandia*, an agreeable journey despite the frightening number of places where small boys could easily walk overboard. Meantime my parents had found a house, No.11 The Vale, Chelsea. We had agreed that, in the immediate post-war circumstances, we would start together, and this house seemed to have room for all, so we went over to see it without delay, liked it despite its war-soiled look, but were alarmed by the appearance of requisition notices on the doors of adjoining houses. It seemed best to establish occupation so my father and I took a rug each and spent the next night aching and shivering on a bare floor. Next day we moved in with some bits of furniture and the requisition notice went up on the door. We did not budge, but I sent a note to Mr Noel-Baker's office to the effect that, if the UK delegation were to have a secretary, he had better live somewhere and could the Minister possibly help? Evidently he did, because we were not interfered with and in due course our 'community' reached eight people. So we did not feel our action had been anti-social.

Basic procedure in the Foreign Office had not changed greatly since I had worked there in 1936. But the war had brought about overdue change in method. This applied particularly to work being done in consultation with other Government departments. Pre-war, there had indeed been meetings and committees, but a great deal of consultation had been done through rather solemn letters beginning, 'With reference to . . . , I am directed by Secretary Sir John Simon to inform you, etc., etc.'* Now much more was done orally. Letters, when necessary, began 'Dear Joe'; there might be a risk of less precision, but there was certainly less delay. Committees were of course numerous and long but given good chairmanship and accurate minutes, were much quicker and more satisfactory than letters.

As secretary of the delegation to the United Nations Preparatory Commission, it was my job to have and be aware of every single paper distributed from Church House. This was because some one person had to be sure that everything being said and done was mutually consistent. And there were also items of immediate importance in which I had to take substantial part. One was the question of a permanent location for the United Nations. The Preparatory Commission was invited to make a recommendation to the first General Assembly. The British and other Western Europeans, while resigned to the demise of the League of Nations, thought that work should begin again in Geneva under the new title. Buildings were there, the site was in a neutral country, easy to reach from Europe and the Middle East and from the East coast of the Americas.

As against this, many of the Latin Americans preferred the

---

* The most famous one, real or apocryphal, was attributed to Philip Guedalla, the historian, and began, 'With reference to . . . , I am directed by the Army Council to hint . . .'

United States as nearer to them, more closely allied to them politically and in a less disturbed continent. The Americans expressed no opinion. One could feel through one's skin what they wanted, but their spokesman, Adlai Stevenson, if a bit winsome, was strictly and correctly neutral. The decision therefore rested with the Soviet Union and its East European followers. The Russians, it is interesting to recall, plumped firmly for the United States. No doubt the memory of expulsion from Geneva still burned. But it is also possible that, at a time when Mr James F. Byrnes, who had succeeded Mr Stettinius as Secretary of State, was giving an impression of following a late Rooseveltian line of playing off the Russians against the British, the Russians may already have begun thinking in 'two super-power' terms.*

Even this Russian decision did not conclude the argument. Under the rules of procedure, the proposition had to receive a two-thirds majority. In a close contest with the prospect of more than one ballot, this requirement always evokes tactical manoeuvring since the ultimate decision may be affected by the choice of resolution to be voted on first. After an exciting debate and a preliminary deadlock, a sufficient majority voted for the United States.

Later there was strong competition between the American cities. We liked the Bostonians but felt that the Philadelphians made the best offer. But when the Rockefeller offer of a gift of the New York site came in, there was no resisting it, though the Arabs stood out for San Francisco against the strongly Jewish environment of New York.

It is somewhat pointless to argue whether it would have been 'better' if the United Nations had settled elsewhere. There is no solution which would have combined all advantages. New York has enabled the United Nations to grow up in a real, modern world and thereby to escape the dangers of living at any rate physically in a sheltered world of its own. The disadvantage for Europe and, to my mind, for the United Nations too, has been the time lag of five hours between New York and

---

* This was the period of the pungent and unfair epigram: 'The State Department fiddles while Byrnes roams.'

Greenwich mean time. Much UN history is made at night, and the time lag has meant that last night's news could not and still cannot catch the European morning papers. Nor has even live television helped decisively since few are going to watch UN history at, say, 4.00 a.m. Consequently the European public has had little chance to know at first hand the United Nations as a functioning body, nor see the appalling difficulties faced by delegations such as ours in tense periods of cold war or anti-colonial emotion.

The Preparatory Commission concluded its work in good time for the first session of the United Nations Assembly to open in the Central Hall, Westminster, on 10 January 1946. Given that the war had ended less than six months before, it was a thoroughly brave show. It owed much to the devoted energy of Philip Noel-Baker, and to the skilful handling of the Commission by its Colombian Chairman, Dr Zuleta Angel. But particular credit belongs to Gladwyn Jebb, who brought to the Preparatory Commission not only the imagination and energy of mind which had already served the British Government so well but also a quality which the British do not always understand, *panache*. There are things other than justice which need to be seen to be done, and work of historic meaning should be carried out in such a way as to show that those who do it understand its significance. The translation in London of the Charter into a living organism did have a feeling of occasion and distinction about it, and for this the United Nations owes a perpetual debt to Gladwyn and his team.

In diplomatic life something always happens in the midst of something else. So it was that on the morning of 6 January 1946 I was at 11 The Vale and heard my mother trying to telephone me at the office. A daughter had arrived. 6 January being Twelfth Night, we wanted to prove that there was something in a name. But both Viola and Olivia seemed to us to have their difficulties. We decided all the same not to forsake Shakespeare, and Celia duly became an actress.

In my period of United Nations work, I attended three sessions of the General Assembly, two in 1946 (technically two parts of

the first General Assembly) and one in 1947. There was a sharp
dividing line both generally and for me personally between
the 1946 and 1947 Assemblies. In 1946 there had not yet begun
the rush to independence of large parts of the world till then
governed by others. What were to become the separate countries
of India and Pakistan, for instance, were represented largely by
future Indians and Pakistanis, but these representatives were still
under British authority, however lightly exercised. In August 1947
India and Pakistan gained independence and the 1947 Assembly
had quite a different tone with members of the Indian National
Congress like Mrs Pandit and Krishna Menon speaking and
voting for the first time as independent Indians.

The 1946 Assembly in London had to concern itself greatly
with elections and organizational affairs. There was strong
Soviet pressure on the Assembly to elect Mr Trygve Lie of
Norway as President; there was a gasp of surprise when it was
announced that we had elected M. Spaak of Belgium. But this
resulted in Mr Lie being elected to the more enduring important
role of Secretary-General. There were more inklings on the
coming cold war as the Soviet Union pressed for the World Federation of Trade Unions, the Communist organized international
body, to be sole representative of Trade Unions with official
status at the United Nations, and as the affable Mr Manuilsky
who represented the Ukraine in San Francisco became tigerish
in London in his attacks on the West. But on the whole the
United Nations did not need to feel displeased by its beginnings
and further organizational work during the year offered prospects
of a useful second Assembly in New York.

For this Assembly I had a changed capacity. We appointed
a most efficient pair of Secretaries in Howard Smith[1] and Claude
Berkeley,[2] and I went to New York as Assistant Political Adviser
to the delegation. Gladwyn Jebb, who had returned from United
Nations to British Government service, was Political Adviser,
but so much of Mr Bevin's time in New York was taken up with

[1] Howard Smith, Ambassador to Czechoslovakia, 1968–71. UK representative in Northern Ireland, 1971.

[2] Claude Berkeley later joined the staff of UNESCO.

difficult peace negotiations with Mr Molotov for which Gladwyn's help was required that I found myself giving far more political advice to the delegation than I had bargained for. This activity cannot be described in any minute to minute way: it was a matter of being ready to answer questions and put forward ideas on policy or tactics at any moment, day or night. It meant a desperately long day, since after the day's journeys to Lake Success lasting an hour at least and protracted committee meetings, telegrams had to be composed or at least vetted and despatched in the middle of the night. The only way I found of getting any relaxation at all was to be extravagant and have 'room service' breakfast (paid for by myself and not by any special allowance) and to budget for half an hour's total relaxation before dressing and going to the daily delegation meeting.

Quite apart from policy or tactical advice, there was the diplomatic task of helping out the delegation with its own internal relationships. These were in no sense bad. But a delegation to the UN Assembly lives pretty intensively with itself over anything up to three months, and 1946 was the first occasion on which professional diplomats found themselves working in New York with and for the 1945 generation of Labour Members of Parliament to whom these diplomatic activities were new and could be surprising. My San Francisco credentials were a useful ingredient in helping the two elements in the delegation to understand each other.

One of the most exciting episodes of the second Assembly was the debate on nuclear energy which also seemed to me to be one of the significant 'might-have-beens' of the period. The Americans presented the Baruch Plan for the future international manufacture and control of nuclear weapons. The sponsor of the idea, Mr Bernard Baruch, was a kind of eminence or, as the Japanese used to put it, *Genro* or elder statesman who created a style of advising by sitting on a park bench in Washington recognizably engaged in thought. The Administration were somewhat divided in their attitude towards the Plan, but it went to the Security Council in June 1947 with US Government consent and was rejected by the Soviet veto. A proposal for internationalization came up again at the UN Assembly in the autumn.

The idea as such had particular appeal in Britain and notably to the Labour Party. On the other hand it seemed clear that Mr Molotov, the Soviet Foreign Minister, would not be able to accept it. So with the agreement of the delegation, Sir Hartley Shawcross decided to take any risk that might be involved and to challenge the Russians at least to give the idea a trial on the basis that if they did, so would we. It was an exciting scene, Sir Hartley with a red tie and a red handkerchief looking like a young knight charging into battle while the older professionals sat worrying in the stands. Mr Molotov could produce no convincing reply and deadlock was rapidly emerging when Dr Wellington Koo for Nationalist China made an emollient speech saying we must all go away and think about it and on this note the debate ended.

When the debate was over, it was essential to report at once to Mr Bevin. He might well have disapproved of Sir Hartley taking the risks he had, in which case there would have been some explaining to do from our group to Mr Bevin and Mr Bevin to London. Mr Bevin sat, looking to one's tired eyes like an enormous frog, behind a brittle Waldorf-Astoria occasional table. I wondered whether a crash of a fist would make this its last occasion. But Sir Hartley put forward an excellent presentation and Mr Bevin said briefly, 'I approve.'

Of course the idea had been a splendid one but its acceptance would have meant international manufacture on an American model with American preponderance, at a time when the Soviet Government must already have decided to devote the country's new-found power and technical advances to catching up with the Americans in this field at whatever cost. There was some relief at Dr Wellington Koo's intervention and one Commonwealth adviser, pale with anxiety, said to me 'You must never do that again.' It had been unorthodox, but it was still the nearest we ever came to international manufacture and control.

In 1947 Jack Ward, the Head of the Department, was posted abroad. His successor, considerably senior to me, had had no experience of United Nations affairs (which were, after all, still a very new subject), and all enquiries at departmental level tended to come to me. This was more than I could cope with and it was embarrassing personally for both of us. Authority solved this problem neatly by splitting the Department into two, United Nations Political, in charge of the new arrival, and United Nations Economic and Social of which I became the Head. Later we were joined by the Refugees Department. Obviously the UN Political Department was the senior department and mine was very much the junior. But it was a department of my own, and it had the special reward of leading, through such organizations as the National Council for Social Services and a number of women's organizations, to a more knowledgeable contact with life in Britain than can be the case with a department wholly concentrating on diplomatic work.

This change in organization also caused a change in my competence at the second General Assembly, my last such assignment. This time I had the task of advising and assisting Christopher Mayhew, then Parliamentary Under-Secretary in the Foreign Office, in Committee 2, Economic Affairs. This did not preclude my putting in a little wing-forward work in the Assembly and its corridors.

It was already becoming apparent that, contrary to some hopes at San Francisco, the Economic and Social Council was not going either to run world economic affairs or co-ordinate the Specialized Agencies. International financial decisions would be taken in the International Bank and Fund, commercial policy matters were gravitating towards the Havana Conference, which gave birth to the General Agreement on Trade and Tariffs. Specialized Agencies, such as the Food and Agriculture Organization, did not have the same membership, country for country, with the United Nations and were adopting their own rules and claiming their own spheres of influence. Even the regional Economic Commissions would later show a life in the regions which the Economic and Social Council at the centre would find it difficult to emulate or control. Thus the Economic Committee of the General Assembly was already tending to become a useful review of reviews but not much more.

In 1947, however, the Eastern Europeans decided to use the Committee's general debate for an onslaught on the Marshall Plan. It was not difficult to repel, given the negative position into which these countries had put themselves or been forced to put themselves a few months previously. But we did enjoy a little international debunking diplomacy which is, if not over-done, both essential and enjoyable. When news reached us of the impending attack, I sent for the text of the reasons why the Polish Government had declined the original American invitation. The Polish case was argued by Dr Oskar Lange, who had made rather too much of a public virtue of renouncing American citizenship to become Polish again. As I had rather expected, Dr Lange gave in the Committee in October a series of reasons for refusal wholly different from those which his Government had given us all in July. Mayhew was therefore able to say how strange it was that the Polish Government had thought up a whole set of other reasons which would have been the ones they would have used had they thought of them at the time. Very occasionally, the exposure of another Government's humbug is an end in itself.

The new Indian delegation was much in evidence, making an obvious and entirely proper effort to work closely with the Nationalist Chinese. The purpose was clearly to form the core of a bloc to give Continental Asia east of the Middle East a greater say in the Assembly. Apart from this, the Indian delegation was much concerned with two things, the treatment of Indians in South Africa, on which Mrs Pandit made a most effective intervention, and the colonies. On the latter the chief Indian spokesman was Maharaj Singh, a friend of my father's at Balliol. He talked such extreme nonsense that I thought I could tackle him. The following conversation ensued.

G-B: 'Maharaj Singh, you know quite well that half of what you say is nonsense.'

Maharaj Singh: 'I am very tired.'

G-B: 'But do you all the same have to talk all that nonsense, when you know it is nonsense?'

Maharaj Singh: 'I am very, very tired.'

In Indian terms, Maharaj Singh, a member of what you might call the minor nobility, had decided in full conscience to throw in his lot with Indian Nationalism. (His sister Rajkumari Amrit Kaur was a convinced Nationalist and friend and follower of Mahatma Gandhi, while always retaining a strong personal affection for Britain.) The choice had its price for someone who knew the British case, but that price had loyally to be paid. I think I understood this instinctively and therefore laid off.

A bizarre success ensued from my first dealings ever with Krishna Menon. The latter appeared everywhere and it was not surprising that he should have appeared in our Committee when it discussed a Byelorussian motion to apply an economic boycott to Spain. It was a purely cold war exercise – one could hardly suppose that things were getting hot in Minsk. I thought I would have a word with Krishna Menon and told him off stage that, while I knew what his instincts would be, he should realize that if the motion was passed and implemented, the main effect would be to throw a lot of innocent Spanish iron ore workers out of a job. Krishna Menon's response was characteristic. He made a violent speech attacking Britain at every point but ending abruptly, 'Nevertheless, I shall not vote for the motion.' The vote was very close, so this was important.

I did not get involved in the major political items like the Dutch-Indonesian dispute and the Israel-Arab dispute, except for making a formal protest in Committee about the Israeli execution of two British soldiers. When the *New York Times* found this part of the news unfit to print, I thought of the Arab plea for San Francisco as UN headquarters.

Since 1947, I have from time to time revisited the General Assembly, but I have never again sat through a whole session. Lasting for at least three months, a regular session is a grinding task. Four consecutive sessions, if one may count in the San Francisco Conference, are about what one can manage, though brave tough colleagues have done much more. But it is a wonderful education in the world and its ways. It gave me, for instance, an insight into Latin America which I should never have acquired otherwise without being posted there. Similarly Arab psychology can only really be studied in Arab countries, but for someone fated never to serve there, this glimpse of Arab thinking was an outstanding future help. In these early days one also saw sadly the inevitable advance of bloc voting. It started with the Latin Americans and the Communists. By 1946 the Arab-Asians were beginning and the Africans have come since. The Western Europeans went on for years, to their great credit, talking independently and individually until they too had to close their ranks in such self-defence as was possible.

As a functioning organization, the United Nations was never quite so good again as it was in the Sperry Gyroscope factory on Long Island, hurriedly and optimistically renamed Lake Success. At Lake Success, the offices and committee rooms were spread out laterally and there was always plenty of chance of meeting a friend from another delegation or from the Secretariat with whom one could sort out in five minutes some minor point waiting in the back of one's mind. You can still do this in the Delegates' Lounge on the East River, but Secretariat business is done vertically in a high building and you cannot hog a luxury express elevator for five minutes.

No one who has a chance of serving in New York should miss it. And if the oratorical behaviour of people in public does not quite come up to the common sense they may be prepared to talk in private, this is a price for the necessary attempt at an open forum of the world. It is also a warning that in one way the UN Assembly is the voice of the world and in another it is not. The dangers of overrating and underrating the Assembly are about equal. There are aspects and episodes which the historians of the United Nations will wish had not happened, particularly the whole history of the opportunity, lost by dogma and demagogy, of making the United Nations a helpful forum for peaceful transition from empire to independence. But two things outweigh the shortcomings. First there is the development, inherited from the League of Nations, of the habit of living and working internationally. Second, there is the continued existence after a quarter of a century of a place to which Presidents, Prime Ministers and Foreign Ministers feel they have to go to make and defend their international case and to meet each other in the process. This may seem modest but its universality might have been useful in 1939 and even if it may appear fanciful, it is worth reflecting what it might have meant in 1914.

European Recovery

On 23 January 1947 it began to snow in London. At the beginning of March, the two-month-old snow was still frozen stiff on the pavements. The previous mild winter had hinted at a slow but not too painful convalescence of war-torn Europe. 1947 revealed shatteringly the weakness of the surviving economic structure.

Out of these afflictions came the finest piece of American policy and diplomacy of the period, the Marshall Plan. The basic concept of self-help and mutual aid with American backing was simple; but let it not be forgotten that it involved the Truman Administration not only in diplomacy vis-à-vis Europe, but also in tough negotiation with a sceptical American Congress.

The immediate impact in London was exciting. After the initial flurry of discovering against the time lag what General Marshall had actually said, Mr Bevin 'grabbed the Plan with both hands' and launched with his French colleague, M. Georges Bidault, a massive investigation of Europe's immediate capacities and needs. This investigation, carried out by the Committee of European Economic Co-operation, presided over by Sir Oliver Franks, in turn led directly to the setting up of the Organization for European Economic Co-operation and the distribution of American aid to Europe.

Right at the beginning there arose a crucial political point. In the Foreign Office it was hoped that the Americans would invite Russian participation and that the Russians would turn the invitation down. This was not in the least cynical. It would have been wrong to fail to invite the Soviet Union and the rest of Eastern Europe, and the Americans did not make this mistake. But we had now much experience of Soviet non-co-operation and obstruction over Berlin and other matters, and a feeling,

F

which proved correct, that the worst of the cold war was still to come; and that, if the idea launched by General Marshall were to work and, above all, work quickly enough to meet an immediate, desperate need, it must be operated by like-minded people with no objective other than general economic recovery.

The Russians rejected participation. They obliged the Poles to refuse also, and the Czechs to withdraw their prompt acceptance. To Western Europe, including the neutrals, the winter, which had brought disaster, ultimately brought in its wake bigger and quicker economic reinforcement than would ever have come otherwise. The merit of the American initiative lay not simply in its boldness and its imagination, but also in the essential doctrine that Europe must tell the United States what it needed and what it would and could do for itself, and the United States would then see what it would contribute towards completing the recovery.

In the fluidity which prevailed in Whitehall as government settled itself down after the war, one person who came to the Foreign Office was Edmund Hall-Patch, whose visit to Japan in 1940 has been described earlier. He was, at the beginning of 1948, Deputy Under-Secretary in charge of Economic Affairs. He sent for me and explained that we were approaching the second stage of the Marshall Plan. The Franks Committee studying the needs of Europe was reporting shortly and it had been decided that the Foreign Office must set up a special department to deal with subsequent work, notably the drafting of a convention. He would like me to be the first head of that department.

The work of the United Nations (Economic and Social) Department had been mainly one of reconciling views and co-ordinating action between different government departments so that our delegations to the various United Nations bodies might be fully briefed on policies and tactics. This process taught me a great deal about the courtesies and conventions of interdepartmental business and how to get things done when more than one Ministry is concerned. But the international organizations with which we were dealing were still very much at the stage of laying down general principles and setting up new, subsidiary bodies. In the European Recovery Department, by contrast, the subject matter was the quite different and brutal one of what have we got, what do we want in order to keep going and how can we get it.

Work of this kind is not susceptible to the conventional foreign policy comment that, say, the French or the Italians wouldn't like what we were proposing. If you tried that, there would be half a dozen people on your Committee who could tell you why what we were proposing was so much to our advantage that the French, the Italians and everybody else would have to put up with it. In this company one could do no good arguing one's own corner until one had learned enough to see problems from other departments' economic, technical and some-times Ministerial-political corners. Only then could one argue respectably and reasonably convincingly on their ground as well as one's own.* On that basis Foreign Office comment was always welcome.

One conclusion relevant to later events follows this argument. It will be deducible from what I have said that one's Home Civil Service colleagues dealt with their affairs in a highly professional manner. Their profession is to know their subject, to argue their case and to handle their work in such a manner that the Minister concerned can present what is needed clearly and in full substance to his colleagues in the Cabinet, to Parliament and the public. The civil servants then have to execute what is decided, which often means considerable organization of people and things. This is public administration as understood and practised in Whitehall. It is a science and an art combined in a profession. The whole activity is intricate and expert and to refer to it, as was done twenty years later in the unhappy first chapter of the otherwise highly constructive Fulton Report, as being based on 'amateur philosophy' is misconceived, misplaced and misleading.

I speak as severely as this partly because, if I did not, I should be

---

* The best Ministerial-political comment I ever heard from a Civil Service colleague was a remark made deadpan in the jargon of the time: 'But if we do that, my Minister will no longer be politically viable.'

lacking in the courage to say publicly now what I said privately then. I say it here, because I shall come back to administrative questions later and I do not want any later comment to be associated with my strong condemnation of that particular expression. The Duncan Report of 1969 on British Representation abroad was not caught in a similar trap. It spoke of diplomats as 'professional generalists', a neat and just phrase. The Fulton Report could have referred in a similar neutral manner to the 'role of the all-rounder in the Civil Service' and thus have provided the basis for a scientific as opposed to emotional discussion. As it was, the issue was falsified. And I say this with such authority as I possess as having worked probably far longer and more closely with home civil servants without being one than pretty well anyone who has declared himself on this issue.*

In 1948 I dived in at the deep end, but fortunately under the careful supervison of Eric Berthoud. Eric had been in the oil industry before the war and therefore understood industrial problems as an industrialist sees them. But he was also, as an official, accurate and conscientious. He had been the Foreign Office representative on the so-called 'London Committee' handling Marshall Plan problems from the beginning. We went to Paris together in April 1948 for the drafting and signature of the Convention setting up the Organization for European Economic Co-operation. Once again I found myself, as at San Francisco, on the job of drafting sentence by sentence and word by word.

The atmosphere at the Paris meetings still reflected the initiative of Mr Bevin and M. Bidault. The pace was being set by Britain and France, the outstanding personality on the French side being M. Robert Marjolin, then Secretary-General of the newly formed O.E.E.C. He combined intense seriousness about the project with a certain natural gaiety of personality which kept things moving at a great pace. But there were already slight signs that the two countries might one day turn in different directions. There was always a suspicion that the British might recede from their current enthusiasm and go back into a traditional

---

* If the two civil servants who endorsed the Report are quoted against me, I must simply observe that they were in an impossible position.

reticence. It was therefore satisfactory, in our drafting sessions, for Eric and myself to be able to make one rather important contribution which allayed any such fears for the moment.

Article 13 of the Convention reads in part as follows:

'In order to achieve its aim as set out in Article 11 the Organization may:

(a) take decisions for implementation by Members . . .'

The original draft limited itself in a routine way to 'recommendations'. It occurred to us that if the official representatives of the sixteen countries were engaged, under instructions from their Governments, in an urgent practical co-operative exercise, they ought to be empowered to take decisions and not merely make recommendations. If this were written into the Article, the Convention would both be, and look, stronger and more serious. The drafting session was a bit surprised to note the quarter from which this suggestion came. But it had a Gallic logic about it which ensured acceptance. And it had a useful influence twelve years later.

The Convention was signed on 16 April 1948. Signature was both accompanied and followed by a mass of negotiations and organizational adjustments. Among sixteen countries working by a system of unanimity, even an urgent common purpose does not solve problems of detail overnight, particularly if they involve sensitive national interests. There were chairmanships to be allocated, and committee memberships to be chosen when committees were not committees of the whole. A notable case was membership of the Executive Committee of seven, the chairmanship of which was held by Britain. Hall-Patch was given this important assignment and moved to Paris. Meantime numerous technical committees, already practically in existence, were geared into the new machine and the whole organization, delegations and secretariat, concentrated on one immediate end, the distribution of the first instalment, $ 1,000 million, of American aid.

By midsummer of 1948, the urgency and complexity of this work had exposed a weakness in our delegation. The pressure on Hall-Patch, Hugh Ellis-Rees and John Coulson in the delegation was such that, except for the work actually conducted in committee, the delegation ceased to have any time for its own external relations. One result of this was the growth of the belief that in some way the British were dragging their feet. There was always something of a pull between the view, represented by the French, that the centre of gravity and activity should be the secretariat and the opposing view, espoused by the British, that the chief responsibility lay with delegations: and it did not of course help that the Secretary-General was French and the Chairman of the Executive Committee British. In Paris there was a natural tendency for French officially inspired comment to capture public opinion (the French media had their scepticisms on domestic affairs but, unlike the British, tended not to apply them to external policies); and the Americans, not always recognizing this and by tradition preferring personalities to committees, tended to accept local Paris criticism of what were alleged to be British policies. I was therefore asked to join Hall-Patch's team temporarily as a kind of mobile fifth wheel with the job of being in contact with everything relevant, official and unofficial, but involved in nothing.

Being bad at prolonged hotel life, I found, after much enquiry, an apartment on the Avenue d'Iéna consisting of a salon with grand piano and a sizable bedroom and bathroom; the loo was down the passage in neighbouring territory. Paris still suffered from food shortages, notably of milk, and I began each day with an inspiring breakfast of black coffee and the writings of Stendhal. The rest of the day was a continuous series of dialogues with all delegations, the secretariat and the press. In the evenings there might be official engagements. If there were not, I would look in on Hall-Patch at 7.45. He never accepted dinner engagements other than the most important official ones 'in case something should turn up'. So nearly always, Hall-Patch being a connoisseur of French food, I enjoyed his company and made the acquaintance of yet another French restaurant which knew how to adapt shortages to the demands of the customer.

One friendship, sadly cut short, was with an intelligent and deeply impressive Swede, who did more than anyone at the time to bring the Swedes back into Europe. It needed doing because the Swedes, being the only North European country untouched by the Second World War, had collectively withdrawn into a shyness about Europe, particularly vis-à-vis the Norwegians and Danes, who had not come in by choice but had gained glory by staying in till the end. His name was Dag Hammarskjöld, and when he came to be spoken of as a possible successor to Trygve Lie as Secretary-General of the United Nations, one could only say, 'Why did no one think of that before?'

All this, against a background of Paris in the autumn, was an exhilarating experience, which Pat came and shared for a few weeks. Eventually the pace slowed down and in December I came back to my own department.

I returned to the routine of committees on agreements, committees on purchasing programmes under chronic foreign exchange shortage conditions, committees on those shortages themselves, with one break to lead the United Kingdom delegation to a meeting in Geneva of the United Nations Economic Commission for Europe. Given Eastern Europe's position on the Marshall Plan, this was a courteous political gavotte and not a serious economic debate.

It was at about this period that people in the Foreign Office and other Whitehall departments began to recall to themselves that despite economic emergency, it was about time to ease off from working as though there were still a war on. Over six years of war, a habit of continuous all-out work had developed, and it continued almost unconsciously for several years after 1945. When, in 1947–49 our family lived in Wimbledon, with garden and view, I counted myself lucky to catch the 7.32 train home. We began at last to realize that this was not sensible and that the long road to peace and prosperity would have to be travelled in more sober conditions.

The outlook for the success of the Marshall Plan was set fair. Full recovery would be a long climb as I realized when on a brief education visit to the Rhineland I saw Cologne by night as a city of neon lights amid the ruins. The prospects of a Europe more closely united and the problems this would offer to the

British were still not clear; we were still a year away from the Schumann Plan for an Iron and Steel Community. In this atmosphere, Pat and I took a light-hearted trip to France and Italy in a tiny Ford Prefect (to save petrol) with our old friends Mr and Mrs William Stringer, of the *Christian Science Monitor*. We returned feeling that the prospects for Europe were not at all bad.

United States
1949–1953

Public Relations
Early in 1949, George Middleton, the head of the Personnel
Department, visited me on his rounds. He asked me what, in
my opinion, was the best thing for me to do next. I said I had been
talking almost exclusively English for six years and suggested that,
as a Foreign Service officer, I ought to go somewhere they
talked something else. George nodded. Six months later he came
back and said, 'We're sending you back to Washington as head of
British Information Services.'

He explained that, with the previous Director-General,
W. P. N. Edwards, coming back to the Federation of British
Industries in London, it had been decided to give the job of
Director-General to a member of the Diplomatic Service. I
had been chosen. The choice seemed to me surprising. I knew
something about the United States. I had had spasmodic experience of information work in Japan and Paris and I had made
a number of good friends in the newspaper world in Tokyo,
Washington and London. But even so, I knew that I should
frequently be asked how it came about that I had started my
public relations career at the top, and should have to reply, 'You
have to begin somewhere.'

Bill Edwards called at my office at ten o'clock one morning.
We then talked concentratedly for five hours. I don't think I
ever talked shop without stopping tête-à-tête for five hours
before or since. I emerged exhausted. But by the end Bill had
given me all that could be conveyed from one man to another
about BIS, USA, and I was enormously grateful.

In the isolationist thirties in the United States, when the
British were well advised to keep their heads down and their

mouths shut, the only British agency other than the Embassy and
Consulates for providing official information was a small office
in New York called the British Library of Information. The
Library had a remarkable knowledge of Britain and feel for the
United States. But its watchword had to be 'Don't speak unless
spoken to, and then only softly.'

In the Second World War, once the ice had been broken partly
through the passage of events and the patience of Lord Lothian
as British Ambassador, this policy became wholly inadequate
and the character of British information work was able to change
completely. There were many controversies, but eventually, by
the time I got to Washington in December 1942 for my first
period there, an enduring pattern had been set.

In the United States there is a major physical difficulty about
government information work on any scale. American policy
is made in Washington; any suspicion of policy being made in
New York died in 1932 with the end of the Republican era of the
1920s and the beginning of the Franklin Roosevelt New Deal.
British policy vis-à-vis the United States Government and the
rest of the world was conveyed to and discussed with the Americans either through the American Embassy in London or by the
British Embassy in Washington. The man who knew all that
could be known outside London about British policy was the
British Ambassador.

But, although Washington had graduated from being a small
town, it was still not a major publishing centre. The news
agencies, the radio and television networks and the publishing
business all had their headquarters in New York, some 240 miles
or four hours' train journey away.

The British Government had met the problem by placing the
Director-General in Washington with immediate access to the
Ambassador, and the 'factory' as one might call it, under the
Deputy Director-General in New York. During the second half
of the war, the Director-General was Sir Harold Butler, former
Director-General of the International Labour Office. Sir Harold
did not have a great flair for information work, but he was a
large, dignified, highly-respected figure, puffing away like all

recognizable Englishmen at his pipe. He was at the right 'level' in the high-powered Washington wartime community The factory, providing answers to any question about Britain and issuing releases, photographs, texts and films as well as maintaining the best in personal contacts and library services, was under the capable and inspirational charge of Aubrey Morgan, a Welshman of splendid efficiency and fire. It was to be my great good fortune that, when I was appointed to Washington in 1949, Aubrey was already installed as personal special assistant to the Ambassador, Sir Oliver Franks.

These were good foundations. But for me at the London end things did not begin too auspiciously When the appointment was announced at the beginning of August 1949, we had some neutral headlines ('Briton gets post here' – *New York Herald Tribune*) and the *Sligo Champion*, bless its Irish heart, announced 'Sligo Diplomat's Appointment'. The *Evening News* had some doubts: 'The most successful information officers in the States have been those capable of mixing with American Journalists on social terms. Mr Gore-Booth, a brilliant scholar in his time at Balliol and a most successful diplomat, is charming but shy and reserved. It will be interesting to see how the experiment works.' The *Evening Standard* had no such suspended judgement: 'I am one of those who believe this [British Information Services] a total waste of our dwindling dollars, that the information service is utterly unnecessary. But if the Government insist on squandering the money, they should see that men of experience get these appointments. . . .'

We crossed the Atlantic in October in the *Queen Elizabeth*, a somewhat different vessel from the D 2 of 1942. On board were two eminent Canadians, Graham Spry, the writer and Agent-General in London for Saskatchewan, and Lord Beaverbrook, owner of, among other things, the *Evening Standard*. Graham, a good and loyal friend, had been much upset by the *Evening Standard* comment and proposed to express his disapproval to Lord Beaverbrook. I presently received a message that 'there would be no further personal attacks on Mr Gore-Browne'. This near-miss seemed to be less satisfactory than nothing at all. So I decided to talk to Lord Beaverbrook. An opportunity came naturally . He was utterly charming and said I must understand that he knew all about information work; had he not been Minister of Information in 1918? Certainly he understood the problems and he wished me well. I do not suppose that anything had been achieved. But if I had travelled across the Atlantic in the same ship as Lord Beaverbrook, and had not met him, I should have kicked myself for negligence or timidity ever after.

After a quick visit to the BIS office in New York, Pat, three children and I travelled down to Washington and moved into an old house in an oak forest which we later left for a charming one two hundred yards from our wartime residence.

I walked into my new office and felt like Ogden Nash's man,

'I sit in an office at 244 Madison Avenue
And say to myself you have a responsible job, havenue?'

It was on the first floor of the temporary building rushed up during the war and apparently made of cardboard. The story was that there was no elevator for the four floors because the vibration would have caused the building to collapse. But it was pleasantly designed and I had no complaints.

My room was long and narrow and was carpeted and furnished in brown throughout. At one end was a television set and at the other the Director-General. I looked out eastwards on to some straggly trees. After a few months I moved to the opposite room, carpeted in grey and facing west – hotter but better. The television set was behind me so that I could turn it on and off, a radical improvement. Above my desk was a graphic and simplified map of American travel and transport routes. It was to prove a constant guide, philosopher and friend.

Bill Edwards' briefing had shown that the organization was experienced and professional in outlook and performance. The task was to make a good organization even better and to carry the professional public relations officers with me.

Certain adjustments were needed. The first was that, while our press contacts throughout were extremely good and very important, our radio and television contacts were less consistent. Things were all right in New York where our Major C. Berkeley ('Bill') Ormerod had a genius for knowing everybody. Being outside the administrative stream and acting as the public relations officer of a public relations organization he could devote all his time to the very numerous people whom he liked and who liked him and whose photographs covered the entire walls of his office. But it was necessary to have good radio and television contacts elsewhere, notably in the national capital.

It is important to understand that in America there was and still is a much greater access to the air than in Britain. Even a medium-sized town would have at that time four or five radio stations and, since then, a similar variety of television stations. While therefore, it is much more difficult to reach the whole listening or viewing public than it is in Britain with its mono-poly or semi-monopoly conditions, it is infinitely easier to get on the air somehow and reach some people somewhere. But this requires constant and ubiquitous relationships between information officers and station managers.

Another needed development was the re-balancing of our information posts. We had for instance a well-staffed post in Boston, but nobody at all in Atlanta which my map showed clearly to be the centre of converging communication throughout the south-eastern states. In Los Angles we needed not so much more people as rather more senior people with louder voices. It was not easy to regulate these things, as, in the main, we were not drawing on the Diplomatic Service but on British people visiting or resident in the United States. But by patient seeking we were able to find people with some journalistic or public relations experience or people with natural gifts and appropriate ambitions. (It is nice to remember that in my time we gave BBC's Robin Day and Geoffrey Johnson Smith MP their first jobs.) But the process of getting the balance right took all of three years. In government one cannot bash on desks and say 'You're fired.' It is better thus, but it takes longer.

One other change was urgently necessary. In Washington we had another press and public relations genius. His name was Charlie (Charles H.) Campbell. With an upright carriage, a bald head and a greying, quasi-walrus moustache, Charlie looked for all the world like a stage British colonel of a bygone age. But he had in fact lived in New Orleans and edited the *New Orleans News-Item*, and behind the olde Englyshe façade and the *bonhomie* was an immensely shrewd public relations mind.

The Embassy was about a quarter of an hour's drive from the Press Building where the vast majority of American newspapers had their offices. But I found Charlie located neither in the Press Building nor in the Embassy. I gave him full authority to get out of this halfway house and into the Press Building as fast as he could. If he couldn't nobody could. So in due course he did.

In those years what Britain thought and did was of immense interest not necessarily in the Middle West or California but certainly in the Eastern States and sometimes nationally. Interest meant an answer to all questions in five minutes or less – not in a day and a half. We were well equipped to respond. But, as I emphasized later in some notes for the Drogheda Committee,* the very best you can do must depend on understandable and reasonably successful policies at home. It was not difficult, for instance, to defend a policy on which there was disagreement with the Americans, such as British recognition in December 1949 of the Communist regime in Peking as the legitimate Government of China, because the reason for recognition was logical and intelligible. It was very difficult indeed to expound and defend British policies over the Iranian oil crisis in 1951 when British moves were very hard to follow or (after I had left) the Suez crisis of 1956, when a clear British policy did not exist or at least did not emerge. Our work was beset with uncertainties due to differences in national characters and habits. To take one instance, the Americans have a great tradition of personal accessibility and never could understand why a junior British Minister should find that he 'had no time' to see at short notice a travelling representative of an American publication circulating in an area many times the size of Britain. Since those days the British have

* A Committee set up in 1952 to enquire into the overseas Information Service, under the chairmanship of Lord Drogheda (Cmd 9138, HMSO).

become more accessible, the Americans more understanding.

As often as not, the job would be not so much the peddling of a British line as the supplementation of American thinking with a quick British reaction or reflection, with or without knowledge of what the British Government was in fact going to do or say. Such a reaction would normally be 'background', not directly quotable but usable if useful. On this basis, Nigel Gaydon as Press Officer in the Embassy spoke pretty well daily with Reuters, the Associated Press, the United Press, the *New York Times* and the *Washington Post*. Charlie Campbell dealt with the rest, and both dealt fluently with the constant enquiries of British correspondents resident or visiting. Howard Smith dealt with economic publications. All this activity had to be continuously shared with the New York office, since a skilled American or British correspondent would be the first to spot any inconsistency.

In handling initially as an amateur an organization containing highly able professionals, I took the situation gently and accepted all advice until I felt firmly enough established and well enough informed to demur or to go further or faster than the accepted form. But there was one convention which I used privately to enjoy. With the leading public relations professionals status was very important. If, therefore, one of our staff outside Washington took me as head of the organization to visit an important local personality, I would be at best 'our director from Washington' or 'our man from uptown'. I never quibbled and accepted the implication of this introduction that, wherever a public relations officer is working, he is to the local people 'head of the organization'. This tactic was valid round the United States. I only broke my own rule of tolerance once. When I called on Field Marshal Montgomery in London and he heard what I was doing, he said briskly, 'So you're one of Bill Ormerod's "boys".' I replied sharply, 'No, he's one of my boys.' Better get the record straight in Britain anyway. But it was a nice Oscar for Bill.

Besides inheriting a good organization, I had the further advantage that my immediate boss in London was Mrs Mary Agnes (Molly) Hamilton. This remarkable lady had been a

Labour MP from 1929–31, but had lost her seat in the Conservative and National landslide in 1931. During the fourteen years of Labour wilderness, she had written, among other things, biographies of Ramsay MacDonald and Arthur Henderson. In the war she joined the Ministry of Information, where she worked in the American division of the Ministry. In 1945 came a moment of decision and Molly decided wrong. She felt that Labour would not win the election and that she would not win back her old seat. Had she decided right, she would certainly have been or become a Cabinet Minister in the Attlee Government. As it was, she moved from the Ministry of Information to the American Information Department of the Foreign Office of which she was the head when I went to America.

She was a person of extraordinary compassion, alertness and humour, with none of that personal rancour which sometimes distorts otherwise genuine compassion today. It was a delight to be at the other end of the line, and I carried out a continuous chatty personal correspondence with her of the kind you can only carry on if you know the other side responds even when it doesn't answer. She did answer when I sent her a cutting explaining how I had tried to explain Socialism, British style, at the very conservative University of Rochester, New York. She wrote, 'It warms the cockles of my heart.'

In those early weeks in which, because one does not yet know too many people, one has a time for reflection, I worked out my own role. I was obviously responsible to the Ambassador for the efficiency and welfare of the organization and the channel of communication between him and it. This meant living in Washington, commuting to New York at least once a month (less would have been negligent and more would have seemed fussy). Initially there would be a good deal of travel to check up on our posts round the country.* Under this head I flew almost at

* In 1949 there were information posts at Boston, Detroit, Chicago, Seattle, San Francisco, Los Angeles, Houston. Roughly speaking the Chicago and West Coast offices contained two officers, the rest one. The Chicago area was immense, but by the end of my time Stafford and Hélène Barff seemed to know everybody in it.

once to Chicago and Los Angeles to deal with staff decisions.

It was also clearly going to be my job to take over actual operations when they assumed political importance – for instance, a visit by the Prime Minister. I had time to study the craft before these began. Meantime, having been engaged in United Nations work for some years and subsequently in European economic problems with a topical politico-economic background, I could help in relations with columnists and 'think-piece' writers and broadcasters without interfering with the daily contacts handled by Gaydon and Campbell. It was of course important that the Ambassador himself should see the leading people from time to time.

It was wonderfully rewarding for me to deal with such outstanding people as Walter Lippman (known in our office by the Sherlockian title of 'the Illustrious Client'), Elmer Davis, Marquis Childs, Joseph C. Harsch and many others. We were still in the heyday of the independent radio commentator, and the work of such men as these from Washington and the incomparable Edward R. Murrow from New York gave the American public a wider and more serious sophistication on world affairs than I have ever seen elsewhere. I think we had it better than our successors. There are now less newspapers in the United States and the television approach to news analysis is much more distorted towards the visual than that of the radio giants who had more time to analyse and who, if they needed a visual image, had to create it by their words. There were unregenerate characters too, but that is half of what the game is about.

American Opinion
The background of opinion in America about Britain in which I started operating was not a very happy one. Articulate American opinion about Britain was by no means flattering. It was generally assumed that Britain was old-fashioned and inefficient and that this inefficiency proceeded directly from four years of Socialist Government. Unfortunately there had been some injudicious talk in Britain exaggerating the degree of genuine and total British economic recovery, and when this was followed by the

1949 devaluation of the pound sterling, the worst American apprehensions seemed only too well founded. There was a particularly strong medical lobby preaching the gospel of opposition to 'socialized medicine'.

There was also something a little deeper. Dean Acheson writes: 'Of course a unique relation existed between Britain and America – our common language and history ensured that. But unique did not mean affectionate.'[1]

I believe this judgement to be at once nearly right and entirely wrong. There is enormous affection between the two countries, in the sense that thousands of individual Americans have the greatest affection for Britain, even those who, like the famous Colonel McCormick of the *Chicago Tribune*, were our most bitter political opponents. But the many people who felt a personal and a political attachment were always a little too scared of the people who did not – a nervous projection of American history up to 1940. Moreover there was an almost morbid fear of up-setting third countries by appearing too friendly with Britain. The consequence in some rather crucial years between the end of the war and the mid-fifties was a curious aridity of the heart as opposed to head of this side of American affairs. For the first time in two hundred years a tired and battered Britain could have done with an occasional pat on the shoulder from Britain's closest wartime associate which had so outgrown the British in wealth and power. But it always seemed that one mustn't upset the French, ruffle the Italians or the Irish, discourage the Japanese or appear to the Russians to be ganging up. So the warmth which existed never really came out in published as opposed to personal and professional attitudes, and I cannot avoid the feeling that this failure of sensitivity or courage contributed to coolnesses later.

Operations and Challenges

The first public argument I ran into was over British recognition of the Chinese Communist regime. Shortly after this happened, I was invited by a good friend, Ernest K. Lindley of *Newsweek*,

[1] *Present at the Creation*, p. 387.

to do a television programme with him; it was my first ever and took the form of a dialogue in front of eight Middle Western Methodist Ministers, each of whom held on to a rubber bulb, all the bulbs being connected by a pipe to an indicator. When those in favour of British policy were invited to register by pressing on their bulbs, it turned out that the team registered pretty solid support for me. We then discussed; Ernest, normally a quiet man, developed a tigerish aggressive manner. I held on and at the end the Ministers were invited to re-register. I hadn't lost a Minister.

I never recorded how many television interviews I did in America – it must have been hundreds. I do know that, in the next three and a half years, I made more than two hundred and fifty public speeches – peanuts for a politician but a mouthful for a diplomat. I did some of these tours alone. But for all the big ones Pat and I travelled by car together, fulfilling both joint and separate programmes. We each drove for an hour and a half alternately, sticking to this rule strictly so that neither of us arrived exhausted for the evening's engagements. In 1950 came the first public relations tour, 5,555 miles round the southern States. Speeches everywhere to Rotary, Kiwanis and Lions, and to groups interested specifically in international affairs, an almost clandestine visit in Georgia to a black university, more Rotarians in Houston, Texas ('You were there last weekend? Boy, you should see it now'), more speeches via Dallas to San Antonio, back through Oklahoma City, assisting in judging a beauty competition at the University of Arkansas, then the cotton festival at Memphis, Tennessee, and back through miles and miles of Virginia as the spring weather collapsed in rain.

We learned a few things the hard way. We had a dinner date at Atlanta, Georgia, made months before. We drove from Chattanooga, Tennessee, by the route of Sherman's Civil War invasion of the south. I insisted on a look at General Joseph M. Johnston's defensive position on Mt Kenesaw. We arrived at a club in Atlanta at 7.45 p.m. 'Sorry, they've all gone home. Thought you weren't comin'.' Moral: remember that Americans eat early and like frequent confirmation that you are actually coming.

On the return journey we had a lunch date at Chattanooga with the Public Relations Officer of the Tennessee Valley authority to meet a local editor. We took it easy that day and arrived at the PRO's office at 11.40. Atmosphere like an impending hurricane. 'It's all washed up.' I looked at the PRO's clock. It said 12.40. Without noticing it, we had crossed a time-line. 'Out of the nettle danger' we plucked a sympathetic interview from the editor's lady gossip writer. We never got the time wrong again.

Our next long tour, in the fall of 1950, took us to Notre Dame University, South Bend, Indiana, a traditional home of strong anti-British isolationist sentiment. We had a warm, academic reception and an interesting and instructive session with faculty and students. We went on to Chicago, Illinois, where we were the guests of Governor Adlai Stevenson, our good friend from London UN days and not yet a presidential candidate. After watching in fur coats and ear muffs a tough football game in which North Western University unexpectedly slaughtered the highly favoured 'Illies' (University of Illinois), we flew with Stevenson in his plane to be his guests at Springfield, the state capital. To stay with this lonely, thoughtful, sensitive man in the executive mansion of Abraham Lincoln was a most moving experience and a denial for all time of the myth that Americans have no history. That history may not be long, but it is exciting, turbulent, intensely personal, full of heroes, villains, idealists and time-servers, unlimited in its aspirations, dramatic in its violence and its cycles of corruption and reform. Stevenson did his best as Democratic Governor of a normally strongly Republican state to be worthy of the memory of his Republican predecessor of one hundred years before, the greatest democrat of all time. This had made him a bitterly controversial personality. Naturally gay, he was not quite the tough character to laugh this off; the laugh was sometimes a little hesitant. The later presidential campaigns were brave, eloquent, humorous and humane. But the campaign was a shade inefficient and in the end I wondered, as did many other admirers, whether this uniquely gifted man would have been a good president.

And so it went on, sometimes a long tour, like the 1942 drive right across the country and back, sometimes a few places at a time. Once, after addressing a service club at Columbus, Ohio, I was approached by a slightly bleary citizen with at least one and a half days' dark beard. 'Say, I'm from the *Ohio State Journal*. I go to a lot of these things and you won't mind my saying I slept through most of yours. Have you some notes or something?' I had, and he published the lot. Who shall say that one doesn't get fair play in the Middle West?

We were wonderfully fortunate to be able to 'do America' in that way. I do not see how else one can get the feel of the country as a whole. I have sympathy for the prisoners of Washington, journalistic and diplomatic, who have to try to get it all from there.

Shortly before I left America in 1953, an English newspaper (not, this time, the *Daily Express*) informed its readers that the British information effort in the United States lacked drive. Someone at a dinner party in Vermont had not known the exact extent of the British defence effort. Just imagine. One felt a little wistful.

But it is time to stop driving and return to Washington for another major feature of the work – 'occasions'. The first arose when Queen Mary and various friends had made a handwoven carpet which, it was hoped, would be sold in North America to earn dollars for the export drive. The initial suggestion was that the enterprise should receive 'discreet publicity'. This is my non-favourite expression in public relations. In America in 1950 you either went for publicity or you didn't. I suggested that a carefully chosen member of the Embassy staff should fly the Atlantic on the carpet. This proved difficult to arrange, but we stepped up the publicity and got a good showing from the display of the carpet at the Smithsonian Institute in Washington. Even better, the episode ended in the purchase of the carpet by the Daughters of the British Empire in Canada.

The lesson was that, if you were going to do a public relations job in America, you had to do it all out or not at all. 'All out' in terms of the BIS budget was not much (some research revealed that, whereas the British Government in the early fifties spent about 680,000 dollars a year on advertising itself in the US, Messrs Proctor and Gamble spent 125 million dollars). One did not need to despair, but one did have to choose carefully. A television network expert told me that when during the war we tried to sell a British Cabinet Minister for a few minutes to a network, the reply was 'What's he got to say that's worth 10,000 dollars?'

Japanese Peace Conference

In 1951 the Conference to sign the peace treaty with Japan was to be held in San Francisco. The date, September, fell in my two-year interval leave period. But given the importance of the event and certain particular complications it was clearly my job to be there.

One problem was that until a late date it was not known whether the Russians would attend or ignore the conference, or what line they would take if they did attend. Further, Ernest Bevin had finally reached the end of his physical powers, and had had to stand down. The new Foreign Secretary, Herbert Morrison, had had little experience in international governmental affairs. There was an uncomfortable feeling, long before there was any direct experience, that the choice, if politically inevitable, might not be a good one. As I learned later, Morrison had in fact consulted Molly Hamilton as an old friend on whether he should accept. 'Certainly not,' Molly had replied, 'it's not your style.' Morrison had been indignant and rejected the advice. But something occurred right away which confirmed Molly Hamilton's wisdom.

The Conference was to be chaired by the American Secretary of State, Dean Acheson, who did it brilliantly. The United States' case was to be presented by John Foster Dulles, who was most ambitious, and most likely, to become United States Secretary of State if the Republicans won the 1952 election. The British were co-sponsors of the conference. We had earned this position both by our losses and sufferings in the Far East War and the 'Defeat into Victory' campaign in Burma, and by the very great contribution which a British team, under the leadership of Sir Gerald Fitzmaurice, Foreign Office Legal Adviser, had made to the draft treaty. But the Conference was being held in the United States and the United States had borne the brunt of the Pacific War. If therefore we were to hold our own as co-sponsors diplomatically and public relations-wise, we needed our top team there all the time.

On the day fixed for the opening of the conference, Mr Morrison had arranged to be on holiday in Norway. He had been through a tough session in Parliament in a Labour Government elected in 1950 with a majority of only six. He had seen Mr Bevin exhausted by the strain of foreign affairs. He decided not to give up a well-earned holiday, but to arrive a few days late at San Francisco. These were good reasons for his decision. But it showed a wrong instinct; foreign affairs were, as Molly Hamilton had said, 'not his style.'

We all did our best, Kenneth Younger at the Ministerial level, the officials in discussion and the public relations officers outside, and Mr Morrison went at it with a will when he arrived. But you cannot keep pace with your more powerful allies on this basis, and it showed. Good advice is usually available to a Minister; he needs a good instinct and good luck as well.

My chief memory of the conference was my impression of John Foster Dulles. He gave an outstanding exposition of the treaty, explaining the positive side and also strongly criticizing the rigid Soviet attitude about the Kurile Islands and Southern Saghalin, still claimed by the Japanese as their territory. But there was one omission, the omission of any reference at all to the co-operation between the American and British delegations which had produced the text. This discourtesy towards the junior partner did not intrinsically matter. But it was a sign that, if the Republicans won the 1952 election and Mr Dulles became Secretary of State, we were in for trouble.

I have a different estimate of Mr Dulles from the one which is facilely popular. I believe that he was essentially a 'good' man in the absolute sense. He is much scoffed at for possessing and professing 'cold war' anti-Communist views; but who, now, can confidently reproach him for wishing that the smaller Eastern

European countries should have something called 'liberty'? What was wrong was something quite different. His choice of word and method was from time to time unfortunate because, though active politically he was not a professional politician. This meant that when he became Secretary of State, his judgement of when he must follow apparent public and congressional opinion in America and when he should challenge it was faulty. This led periodically to loss of confidence by America's allies in the United States Administration.

Washington Occasions

Sometimes in public relations one has an occasion totally *manquée* for reasons which have nothing to do with the idea or the planning of the operation. In 1950, largely through the initiative of Sir Percy Spender, External Affairs Minister of Australia, the Commonwealth had produced the Colombo Plan. The title was a neat if over-ambitious way of describing a framework within which, to start with, bilateral mutual aid and technical assistance would flow between the Commonwealth countries. In 1950 it was a considerable novelty. It came in the wake of the Marshall Plan, but it had its own originality of inception and execution. It was a Commonwealth initiative. It dealt less with the repair of wartime devastation than with future mutual aid between structurally developed and under-developed countries (as they were then called) or between under-developed countries themselves. We thought it would appeal in the United States. We decided to make, with other Commonwealth missions in the United States, a big effort to publicize it. Press releases, photographs, background material – the whole lot were organized. D-Day was set for 1 July 1951. On 30 June (D-Day minus one) came the first reports of General MacArthur's forces being hurled back from the Yalu River on the boundary of Korea and China. The U.S. media occupied themselves with nothing else and the initiative of the Colombo Plan passed silently by.

Sometimes press contact developed into diplomatic action. One of the outstandingly industrious and penetrating correspondents in Washington for years has been J. B. (Scotty) Reston of the *New York Times*. One day in 1950 Scotty came to see me in speculative mood. The atomic energy relationship between the two countries had gone wrong. Perhaps, suggested Scotty, we might be nearing the time when the two governments could have a go at improving them?

Such a suggestion from this quarter was obviously a serious one, however unofficial. Naturally I commended it to the Embassy. Maybe we were on the edge of something positive. Within ten days came a warning telegram. The Fuchs atomic spy case was about to break. So any idea of progress based on American confidence in British atomic security had to be, for the time being, abandoned.

One lives with, but does not brood over, the consequences of hopes gone wrong. It is more profitable as well as more cheerful to look back on occasions which meant learning public relations not so much by acquiring as by anticipating experience. One of these was the visit in February 1951 of Princess Elizabeth and Prince Philip. This was also a Commonwealth occasion, and, since the senior Commonwealth representative in Washington was not the British Ambassador but the Canadian Ambassador, Mr Hume Wrong, everything had to be done in the closest consultation with him and his staff – particularly my PR colleague Paul Malone. Mr Wrong gave the formal dinner for President Truman but we, as having the larger Residence, gave the reception for between 1,500 and 2,000 people.

One very serious organizational problem was how to satisfy the writers and photographers without spoiling the party at a time when Prince Philip was having a running battle with the press. For the writers, we built a long low stage across the end of the Embassy ballroom, so that all the guests filed slowly past the writers on their way to shake hands with the royal visitors. Each gossip writer could have a word with his or her favourite client. The stage being raised, the writer also had a good view of the actual handshake.

The photographers presented a more difficult problem. Clearly there could not be flash bulbs throughout, and, in a horrifying denial of precedent, photographic agencies and newspapers would have to represent each other. Photographers are notoriously individualistic and temperamental and the doctrine of a few photographers for a short time would be enormously difficult to sell. It was decided that some four photographers could photograph during a quarter of an hour about half an hour after the party had begun. If it had not been for Charlie Campbell, we could never have sold this proposal. But by that time in his career, Charlie had only to say 'no', and everybody was delighted at what would have been scandalous mistreatment at the hands of anybody else. The arrangements went without a hitch, and photographs of General Omar Bradley who paraded at the right moment were much admired.

This is all mechanics, maybe. But for want of proper mechanics, the politics can go sour. In much of diplomacy, things that go well do not necessarily do identifiable good. But things that go wrong do obtrusive harm, and as the Ambassador insisted, this was a battle which was won or lost before it began.

Churchill's Visits

The biggest responsibility came at the beginning of 1952. The Conservatives had won the General Election in the autumn of 1951 and it was the natural wish of the Prime Minister, Mr Winston Churchill, to visit Washington as soon as convenient. There was every reason to make the visit as soon as possible. President Truman was beginning his last year of office and there were a number of important questions of mutual interest needing top level attention. The visit was therefore made immediately after the New Year.

Mr Churchill came firmly by sea, accompanied by Mrs Churchill, by Mr Anthony Eden as Foreign Secretary and the usual retinue. The reception party did the normal chilling routine of clambering into a US customs cutter in New York harbour before dawn to the accompaniment of an icy air-stream from all directions. One wondered temporarily why one had been born.

Then came the eagerly-gulped hot coffee on board the ship, followed, after the Ambassador had done the courtesies, by introduction into the presence. On this occasion the public relations situation was complicated. Since Mr Eden had a somewhat different programme from the Prime Minister, the Foreign Office head of News Department, that wise veteran William Ridsdale ('Rids') was specifically handling his needs and movements. I was to deal with the Prime Minister's requirements in both the United States and Canada. When both statesmen were to appear together, there was an exemplary Alphonse and Gaston act between Rids and myself which usually handed the privilege to me. The first item was a formal press conference, and nerve was severely tested when, on arrival at the elevator in the warehouse where the press conference took place, Mr Churchill refused utterly to wait for Mr Eden, dashed on to the 'stage' and, with a hint of mischief, launched the conference alone. Nothing could be done about this, but the situation of affection tempered with tension between the two was revealed again later when I brought back from the State Department a jointly-drafted communiqué which spoke of the President and his advisers conferring with the Prime Minister and his advisers. This was in British terms a serious constitutional impropriety. It caused some fraying of nerves and a rapid translation of half the sentence into English.

There were top level meetings on 7 and 8 January. An immense array of subjects was discussed which included Korea, NATO (including the command structure), the Middle East, atomic co-operation and international trade; but for the PR man they gave rise to an acute version of a familiar difficulty. It was a golden rule, and no doubt so remains, that when a most important event is taking place and correspondents are going to write about it whether they know anything true and useful or not, it is better that there should be some guidance, however thin, than none at all. We agreed on this occasion that I should see the British correspondents and my American colleague the Americans. At the end of the first of the sessions, the principals agreed on a sentence which was to be all that was to be said. As we prepared to go out, Mr Churchill waved a threatening finger at the two press officers saying loudly 'The sentence, and nothing but the sentence.'* And so we walked out into the January air to entertain what was called in the cliché the world's press élite for half an hour with – one sentence. All one could do, while plugging the sentence, was to improvise on subjects which obviously had been discussed (deducible from the *dramatis personae* of the meeting), avoid ones the discussion of which was better not revealed, and hope not to get fired. The correspondents, many of them old friends, received me with a gratitude legitimately tinged with friendly irony. Next morning I studied the American press and the BBC's invaluable summary of the British press with the utmost apprehension. The correspondents had reported and I was not fired.

The expedition then betook itself to Ottawa. As no meeting of the Prime Ministers was scheduled immediately I was apprehensive about possible misleading press speculation and decided to hold what might be termed a pre-emptive press conference, that is, to try to help the media with what little can be said in advance. But any press officer, especially an ad hoc one as I was, who tries this technique may well have to do it on his own initiative. High authority tends not to understand what you are doing; if you get it right, high authority will not know; if you get it wrong you may achieve disaster. On this occasion the conference was very useful, highest authority never heard of it, but authority somewhere in the middle felt it to be its duty to disapprove. A small and by no means unexpected price for a necessary tactic.

There was a splendid moment when a rather confused private conversation at a public dinner between Mr Churchill and Mr St Laurent, the Prime Minister of Canada, got on to the broadcasting circuit; and another laugh when the aircraft manifest contained an entry, 'Sir Harold Parker, Ministry of Defence, no publicity,' which the press had no difficulty in interpreting as: 'General Templar on board.' (He was in fact appointed to the Command in Malaya from Ottawa.) It is difficult to convey the

---

* I have not attempted to translate into print Mr Churchill's cadences and pronunciations, but everyone who is familiar with them at first or second hand is encouraged to use his own version.

atmosphere of flurries punctured by intervals of calm and vice versa, all in an atmosphere of welcoming Canadian warmth, topped by the British with cigars and brandy and against the undulations of snow and partial thaw without.

When a VIP visit of these proportions is over, one's hope is for at least twenty-four hours' sleep. But this time it did not quite work that way. Mr Churchill and his party left on 5 February. At 6.30 in the morning on 6 February the telephone rang. 'This is NBC. Did you know King George has died?' (Note, not the King of England, nor King George of England, but an implication of 'our' or at least 'the' King George.) The NBC network wanted to know whether the Ambassador would like to make a statement. So off we go again. I found the Ambassador and Charlie Campbell at the Embassy Residence amid an atmosphere of sombre haste. The Duke of Windsor came through on the telephone. In the midst of it all Charlie and I drafted a statement and I rushed down to the studio to deliver it on the TV.

But the pace is not always like this and there were times for reflection and innovation. During one of these we produced a basic brief entitled 'Sixteen Stinking Questions' which contained a non-shirking answer to questions on the sixteen most difficult subjects of constant interest (China, 'colonialism', the Iran crisis, the Common Market and other more ephemeral points). I invented a pamphlet called 'Britain in Brief' which had to fit into the average wallet and to be no more than twenty-four pages long. It was a tremendous boon because it contained what was needed and could not get lost. Later the printing was transferred to London to save foreign exchange, which was sensible, and the pamphlet was somewhat enlarged, which frustrated its main purpose. We worked constantly on the quality of our best publication, *Economic Affairs*, most ably edited in New York by Chaim Raphael. And we achieved something of a breakthrough in television with British documentary films still in their prime. This was promptly undone when the Conservative Government of 1951 abolished the Crown Film Unit. We found time for enjoyment with children and friends; there was an interesting square grand piano in the house and we kept the little garden reasonably attractive. One hobby was a little more specialized, my membership which I greatly enjoyed of the Washington Civil War Round Table. This was a group of savants who met from time to time to hear learned papers on why Stonewall Jackson failed to be his aggressive self at the seven days battle and why Jeb Stuart failed to collect for the South the necessary intelligence before the battle of Gettysburg. I had the temerity to read a paper on British policy in 1862 dealing among other things with the effect of Queen Victoria's summer vacation in Gotha on the recognition or otherwise by the British Government of the Southern Confederacy.

On Boxing Day 1952, I went over in the afternoon to the office to catch up quietly on a few items. The United Press came on the line. 'Is it true that Churchill is coming in the New Year?' I did not know and checked up with Nigel Gaydon. He had been asked the same question by the Associated Press and did not know either. But we sensed that it must be true and grumbled about not being advised.

Not only this, but there was no guarantee that on arrival the Prime Minister would tell the press anything about the timing which in terms of American politics seemed extremely odd. Mr Truman was still President but he was on the way out and his party had been defeated in the presidential elections; what was the point of visiting him? Mr Eisenhower had been elected but not yet inaugurated. He was, therefore, technically, not yet President and what was Mr Churchill doing getting at him in advance of his taking office?

So there was much defiance in the Washington air and some resentful counter-blasting from the British end. Accordingly it was most important that Mr Churchill should give a press conference immediately on arrival to dissipate these discontents. My job, with the help of the new Ambassador, Sir Roger Makins, was to persuade Mr Churchill to perform.

Again we went through the chilling dawn routine. Mr Churchill, when he appeared, made it clear that he did not enjoy early mornings in general or this one in particular.

'I have got nothing whatever to say,' he declared.

'No, dear,' commented Mrs Churchill, 'and you'll go out and say it exactly like that.'

A bearish growl followed, and apparently reluctant consent.

And then Mr Churchill gave a press conference of consummate artistry. He threw a compliment to the Captain of the *Queen Mary*, and a modest one to the people of Britain, and picked up, with real or assumed surprise, a coincidence – he had landed the previous year on exactly the same day. From this he plunged light-heartedly into the point of controversy.

'I was going on a short holiday to Jamaica, hoping to get a little sunshine and warmth and, naturally, I looked in here to pay my respects to your President and to see again General Eisenhower. There is nothing extraordinary in our meeting. I suppose General Eisenhower and I have met at least a hundred times to deal with business of one kind and another – some quite important business. But even if this was a hundred and first time, it does not follow that it should go wrong any more than any of the other meetings. And then I am looking forward to seeing Mr Truman whom I have worked with for months at the end of the war and who I went to Fulton with – you remember Fulton – I got into trouble for being a little in front of the weather . . . .'

After which, no trouble. The visit became personal and relaxed.

After calls on the incoming and retiring Presidents, Mr Churchill prepared to leave Washington for his family holiday in Jamaica. All of us who had played some part on the visit were invited to say an individual good-bye on board the aircraft. Mr Churchill was sitting in the centre of an otherwise empty plane. He asked me whether he was likely to have any more press encounters. Recalling the prelude to his visit, I replied that he might conceivably be attacked again. With familiar and splendid inflection he replied, 'If we are attacked, we shall defend ourselves.'

Coronation Special

The last operation in the United States, in which Pat and I shared completely, or at least complementarily, was the press and television coverage of the Queen's coronation. The occasion turned into an hilarious mixture of triumph and disaster.

We were, as it happened, particularly well prepared for this event. In addition to the material supplied officially, Pat had been home in April to see the boys and came back in mid-May well supplied with literature including texts of the Westminster Abbey service. We had also been briefed by Mrs Doris Langley Moore, an outstanding specialist in historical and ceremonial costumes.

In late May, a voice rang up from the National Broadcasting Company, New York, and asked would I help them with the Dave Garroway early morning show on the NBC television network. (It was entitled, interestingly, *Today*.) Of course I would. In the meantime the Columbia Broadcasting System had asked Pat to help them. This was highly gratifying. There was at that time no satellite television and it was necessary, if the coronation was to be covered live, for live radio transmission to be interleaved with still pictures and live commentary from New York. If the New York studios were going to get both the actual proceedings and the historical interpretation right, well-informed British help would be needed and British Information Services were the people to provide it. Apart from anything else, the choice of moments in which to interrupt the local commentators with the actual music and words from London depended both on a knowledge of the Westminster Abbey service and on an ability to persuade the director to switch at the right moment.

Apart from the technical difficulty, there was a difficulty of policy. As on the technical side, so on the policy side we were ages removed from present-day habits. Those in charge of these things at Buckingham Palace were delighted that American television should carry the event in the best possible way, but, it was insisted, there must be no advertising. In the United States at that time the equation no advertising=no television was absolute. But BIS must insist

On the basis of this impossible brief, we reached an unwritten agreement with the networks that there would be no network, i.e. universal, advertising. This meant, of course, that, if local stations did not feel financially able to carry the programmes

Lord Halifax (with author, right)
addressing San Francisco Conference, June 1945

Lord Salisbury (then Lord Cranborne) at San Francisco Conference with the author behind him

without advertising revenue, they would look after their own interests, and no power on earth including Britain could stop them.

On 1 June, Pat and I went to New York. The NBC voice who had invited me having gone ill, we had dinner with Frank Blair, the well-known newscaster. We were just sitting down when the thrilling news came through of the conquest of Everest by Sir John Hunt and his team. We had a rather dizzy dinner in the aura of this coronation present to the Queen and retired early.

We had to get up at 4.00 and be in our respective studios at 5.00. Pat's programme went off with the greatest smoothness and aplomb. We in NBC could watch 'the competition' on a near-silent T.V. set in the corner of our studio and there was no doubt about its attractiveness and appeal.

In Radio City we had a somewhat more rugged time. I arrived by 5.00 and found a mass of unshaven people drinking coffee from plastic mugs and groaning about life. The programme started at 7.00 and just as we were installing ourselves in the studio, a character faded in and said, 'Is there anyone here who knows anything about the coronation?' I said, rather meekly, the equivalent of 'Me, sir.' 'Oh, that's swell,' said the character and faded out.

Gradually we got sorted out, including Mr Garroway's pet monkey at the end of the studio. I worked out with Dave as best I could a possible selection of moments in the service at which local interruption could let up. So we began, things working astonishingly smoothly. A moment of triumph came when I nudged Dave and said, 'Think you'd better get London now,' and the organ broke in on the split second into the splendid prelude to Handel's *Zadok the Priest*. Thus we continued until, quite casually, Dave said 'I think I'll go and talk it over with the monkey.' I was a bit horrified, but with earphones, microphone and all, also a bit immobile. I was just able to say, 'I don't think that's a good idea. But if you must, for God's sake turn off Westminster Abbey.' Dave's sense of local appropriateness was impervious to bureaucratic advice, and off he went to discuss

G

with the subsequently famous Mr J. Fred Muggs the question of coronations in the monkey kingdom.

The programme continued fluently after its fashion, ending with a foursome in which the veteran commentator, H.V. Kaltenborn, joined Dave, Frank Blair and myself and asked some fairly rude questions designed to get sharp answers. At the end of it all, Top Brass in a stiff white collar came down, congratulated us all and, like others, disappeared from my life.

For the rest of the day, while jet aircraft raced across the Atlantic with television films, the honorary British advisers to the competing networks attended this, that and the other gay function, trained back to Washington and attended a happy Coronation Ball at the Mayflower Hotel. The weather had been, unlike London, dry and mild and we sank to sleep at 3.00 in the morning.

We then, deservedly as we thought, took a couple of days off. We were interrupted by a message from Nigel Gaydon, 'Trouble brewing.' Various hells were breaking loose. Protests were coming from home about the advertisements; the service had been interrupted by soap, cigarettes, breakfast food and washing machines; hadn't it been understood, etc., etc. The *Daily Express*, having no particular story available, were interviewing a Mr J. Fred Muggs who had apparently butted with all four feet into the coronation. It wasn't difficult to answer the advertisement messages; dams were things over which water had flowed. But Mr Muggs would not lie down until there had been public discussion, a question in Parliament and the expression by various Hon. Members of strong views, including an appreciation of the difficult position in which Mr Muggs had been placed. The Ambassador was tolerant and in the middle of it all came a delightful letter from Mr Garroway, unconscious of these great events, ending: 'Peace, Dave.'

Later, when I was in Rangoon, a report came in that Mr Muggs was on a world tour during which he would be visiting Burma. I said that if that happened, the British Ambassador would be lost, touring in up-country jungle. Mr Muggs passed by at an early hour in the morning and went straight on. He died in California not long after. He was commemorated indirectly by Mr Christopher Mayhew who wrote an article about a commentator by name J. Frederick Muggeridge. I wonder who that was.

After these events, my next duty was to have been the handling of Mr Churchill's public relations on a visit in HMS *Vanguard* to Bermuda to meet President Eisenhower. I flew to London to join *Vanguard*, but Mr Churchill had had a slight stroke and the visit never took place. Before returning home, I had written tactfully to ask the Personnel Department whether, having been in Washington for approaching four years, we should take our summer holidays in America or at home, since either decision would involve major family logistics. I was, in fact, expecting, without any evidence, to be transferred, possibly to be Number Two at a big post. Indeed I believe this had been contemplated. But my breath was completely taken away when the Permanent Under-Secretary, Sir William Strang, said, 'We are sending you to be Ambassador in Rangoon.' I was astonished. Getting a post of my own at the age of forty-four was not unprecedented but it was very early. And I was privately conscious of having met precisely one Burmese in my life. (He turned out to be an Arakanese, which is the equivalent of saying that the only Englishman I ever met was a Welshman.) Naturally I was overwhelmed and delighted and dashed back to Washington to an equally astonished Pat. From then on we were committed to a policy of, as it were, taking the pictures off the wall while telling nobody why, until the Burmese Government had agreed to my appointment.

We avoided the difficulty in part by going to say an unavowed farewell to kind friends in Maine with whom we and the children had spent a delectable summer holiday the year before. I also made a visit to Mr Eden in Rhode Island. He had just come out of the Leahy clinic and looked thin and frail. He was a charming host for an afternoon and evening, and under the frail appearance maintained a strong determination not to let his illness cause him to be pushed aside from world politics into a shadowy Deputy Prime Ministership.

When my transfer could finally be divulged, we had a quietly hectic fortnight evacuatinq – guiet, because early August is a dead time in Washington. A farewell lunch with the Ambassador introduced us to Hugh Gaitskell. There was already talk of a Labour Government to succeed the Conservatives in the mid-fifties and there was some speculation about who would be the next Labour Foreign Secretary. Gaitskell made the wise remark that more often in life than you suspected, position depended on 'availability'. In later years, when engaged on helping to fill difficult diplomatic posts, I thought again and again of Gaitskell's remark. On reflection, it had also a tragic twist.

In America at mid-century there was an air of cheerful expansiveness in which it was invigorating to live. No doubt there were scandals and squabbles. But, as I suggested to a small farewell Press Club lunch, America was the one country in the world where any accomplishment seemed possible.

There were a few shadows. Denis Brogan warned the readers of *Harper's Magazine* of December 1952 of what he called 'The Illusion of American Omnipotence.' The Republican Administration did not pay much heed, and it is widely forgotten that Brogan was so prescient so early. In Anglo-American relations there was something of a turning point. The permanent criticism problem crossed the Atlantic. In an unsigned article in *New Republic* a writer termed Mr Kingsley Martin, the editor of the *New Statesman*, the Colonel McCormick of Fleet Street. The determination over many years in the United States to criticize Britain at all costs had transformed itself into a similar but opposite phenomenon in Britain with Kingsley as the archetype. One would like to claim the progress in America as part of the work of British Information Services, but I fear this goes too far. We did our best. But major forces in world history had propelled the United States somewhat reluctantly into the position of World Power Number One and the penalty of that position is chronic abuse and jealousy from others.

Prejudice apart, there was at that time one good reason for uneasiness abroad about the United States. One day I happened to be in a corridor of the Senate Office Building after a talk with a Senator about a visit to his state. A friend who was a liberal radio commentator came by and we both said, 'What are you doing here?' He was going to a hearing of the McCarthy Committee and invited me to come too. I said I had no pass; he replied, 'OK I have; I'll show while you fumble.' It worked.

The experience was unforgettable; this was not so much for anything anyone said, but for the scenario. Raised high above the floor level, in a sort of semi-circle, was a line of Senators and aides. At two points there were strong arc lights directed at the witness (I almost called him 'prisoner'), a middle level government official. He sat at floor level below at a table with a microphone, desperately alone. His sole comfort came from an occasional murmur of support from the spectators behind him. It was a truly frightening spectacle and Americans are still wondering how they ever let it happen.

I had been lucky to get this job in 1949. Britain had become a junior partner in our most important alliance, but we were still, in terms of assumed if no longer real physical power, in the same league as the United States. Therefore what we said was, for better or worse, of real interest to Americans beyond those directly involved. We had a very good organization with which to say it, and I was extremely grateful to my two chiefs, Oliver Franks and Roger Makins, for the free hand they gave us in what we did.

Public relations is a state of mind. In terms of press information and current events this state of mind shows itself in the attitude with which each morning one listens, say, to the CBS or NBC, the BBC or All India Radio and reads *The New York Times, The Times* or *The Times of India.* The diplomat will look at the essence, may know what is missing and, if the item is of interest, will discuss it 'in due course' with an opposite number in the Foreign Ministry of the host country. Quite possibly he will wait or ask for instructions before doing so. The Information Officer asks himself at once, 'How are people going to take this?' – referring of course to his clients, the local media and public who will be imperfectly informed and interested in isolated points and not in thorough analysis, and will not be prepared to wait. In the United States one had to be constantly conscious that an immediate reaction to an enquiry was best and that waiting-time might extend up to five minutes. In diplomacy comparable urgency can arise but it is the exception. Accordingly when people with tidy, chart-guided minds recommend that the (diplomatic) Chancery of a big Embassy can 'take over' information work, they are asking that someone shall combine two contradictory psychologies and routines, which is usually too much for one busy person. It can be managed up to a point, but in an emergency the conflicting priorities will arise at the same moment.

I have been told that diplomatic officers on the whole do not like to be, as they feel, 'side-tracked' into public relations work. Maybe. But anyone who arrives at or near the top without having done a stint in this business lacks a practical and important dimension of personal experience and, therefore, professional judgement.

Was all this advising, organizing, rushing around giving forgettable speeches and ephemeral interviews worth while? This kind of work, to be of any consistency and thoroughness in a big country enjoying freedom of speech, is not just a matter of personal flair and energy. It needs an infrastructure to organize and disseminate information and to build up receptivity where it is needed. The field is infinite, the law of diminishing returns applies but the decision where it begins to bite is pretty arbitrary. In my time perhaps the most effective single piece of public relations we did was a short letter, published by *Time* magazine, on the British defence effort. It contained two sentences and one figure and it bounced around far and wide. But who can tell how much know-how and how much effort went into the production of the right letter saying the right thing in the right way at the right moment? What one can say is that the process of building up this capacity is a long one and it takes efforts by many people over much time to put a government information service abroad on a basis of both interest and credibility. If no one believes you, the whole machine can go home. The greatest strength of BIS in the United States was that people believed and rightly believed what it said.

It was not surprising that my parting with BIS was rather an emotional one. I have enjoyed ever since revisiting the offices in

New York and Washington. Nothing has 'gone wrong', but BIS came inevitably under the axe as crisis followed crisis in our balance of payments and the thoughts and deeds of British statesmen (unlike the British monarchy) became of less interest to the ordinary American. Subsequent New York official homes have not compared with the swashbuckling vitality of the forty-fourth floor of the Rockefeller Center. But that operation set a standard which is still remembered and emulated. In 1953 it was described by the Drogheda Committee in the following words:

'We were very favourably impressed by the British Information Services in the United States of America which are a model (although of course on a larger scale than is needed in most countries) of what can be done in the information field in a highly developed country. The Headquarters office in Washington and the operational centre in New York struck us as being on the whole adequately staffed and equipped, but we agree with the Foreign Office that an additional officer in New York to handle television is needed since this is becoming such an important outlet for our films. The only other requirement in the United States of America is to strengthen the organization outside Washington and New York in order that there should be an adequate coverage in this vast country.'

I have no comment to add.

Burma

1953–1956

In October 1953 I set off by air for Burma. Pat and Celia were to follow by sea. Ultimately this proved inconvenient and they followed by Comet 1, then at the height of its glory. I retain that pit-of-the-stomach recollection that out of our family of six, four are Comet 1 survivors.

I had permission to stop off at Karachi, then the capital of Pakistan, and learned much from the High Commissioner, Sir Gilbert Laithwaite, formerly Private Secretary to the Viceroy of (united) India and later Permanent Under-Secretary of the Commonwealth Relations Office. In Delhi Sir Alexander and Lady Clutterbuck made me most welcome in a house in which, as could not possibly have occured to me at the time, we were one day to live. Nor could it have occurred to me that when that was decided Sir Alexander would be my departmental chief at home. By happy chance my visit coincided with the first showing in Delhi, attended by Mr Nehru, of John Hunt's film on the conquest of Everest. At the Ministry of External Affairs I was received very cordially but came away with a feeling of Indian unwillingness to become nationally involved in the affairs of countries further east.

During these brief halts India seemed so established and Pakistan so pioneering. The Pakistanis were manifestly striving to prove that, in the task which they had set themselves, they had it in them to catch up.

The Union of Burma Airways Dakota from Calcutta stopped at Akyab in Arakan of Second World War fame. The British community of four had heard a few hours before that I was coming and rushed down to the airport to welcome me to Burma.

Then on to Rangoon where I was welcomed by Rod Sarell.[1] Our Chargé d'Affaires, and his wife Pam; Bob Acly, Minister at the American Embassy, was kind enough to be there too. After some very simple formality, Rod and Pam and I adjourned to the Embassy Residence for a drink. I suggested on arrival that the two toads forming a welcome committee on the staircase might be ushered out. We then settled down to talk about the new assignment.

If there is one thing I am certain of, it is that no moment in a diplomatic lifetime is quite so exciting as taking up one's first post as head of a diplomatic mission. Be it never so humble, it is the first place on your journey where you can say, in President Truman's phrase, 'The buck stops here.' This is not entirely true; plenty of bucks are transmitted by telephone, telegraph, mail and bag to headquarters. But on the spot there is no one from home, no Cabinet Minister, no Under-Secretary and no diplomatic colleague of senior rank looking over your shoulder, and no appeal beyond you. Anyone who does not get a modest thrill out of this moment is lacking in some ingredient of human nature. But the thrill had better be modest.

One advantage I did enjoy in going to Rangoon was that I had had time to read most of the few good books then available about Burma. When, as a British diplomat, you serve in a country which has been under British rule, you will find ambivalent attitudes. Local memories and the local celebrations will be coloured with anything from resistance to resentment. On the other hand, there will still be a pleasant familiarity with British ways and for a little longer sympathetic personal relationships from the past. You are expected to know 'my friend, Colonel Smith, who lives at Newcastle'; the choice between not knowing him or looking as though he were a special friend is not easy. In Burma a few governors, as in India more viceroys, were well remembered or recorded in history. And depending on national tastes, this or that British bequest might be approved, whether a golf course in Burma, a cricket ground in India or a system of justice in both.

[1] Sir Roderick Sarell, Ambassador to Turkey since 1969; before that, Ambassador to Libya, 1964–69.

But in Burma there were also certain special disabilities. The British had established their final authority in Burma late, in 1885 to be exact. Thus the period of their tenure of power before twentieth-century Asian nationalism broke surface was too short for that kind of understanding to develop which made co-operation and sympathy between intelligent and sensitive Indians and many British officials quite natural.

There was also one political decision which had altered history and altered it adversely. King Mindon Min reigned in Mandalay for twenty-five years (1853 to 1878), during which time he had handled foreigners with the same skill which has enabled the neighbouring Thais to keep them at bay. Towards the end of his life, however, he had failed to take any decision about the succession which it was his right and indeed his duty to do. The result was that he was succeeded by his son Thibaw, who was dominated by his wife and middle Queen, Supayalat. The regime was bloodthirsty and xenophobic. The (British) Chamber of Commerce in Rangoon was up in arms. So, for reasons which would not be looked at twice today but were considered expedient and indeed honourable in the imperial age, the British, already in occupation of half the country, advanced to Mandalay, deposed King Thibaw and annexed the rest of it to the Indian Empire. The reason was that there was indeed no suitable heir to the Burmese throne. But the decision ignored the total difference in racial origin and national temperament between the Burmese and any Indian race. In particular Burmese do not, except for certain Burmese ladies, share the Indian aptitude for finance and commerce. Given freedom of movement in the Indian Empire, there was a great influx of Indians who became business men and, fatally, powerful money-lenders to whom Burmese farmers tended to mortgage themselves beyond their ability ever to repay. This created a divided society in Burma, particularly in Rangoon.

For over forty British years Burma was a peaceful and beautiful end of the line. Natural land frontiers made a large military establishment unnecessary, and economic development followed the traditional line of producing those things such as teak, rice, metals and oil as afforded a respectable profit to private enterprise.

There developed also a meritorious judiciary, an adequate administration and the beginnings of politics. In the thirties, Burmese nationalism, responding to Indian example, began to boil over, and when in 1942 the Japanese overran Burma they were hailed as liberators. On the Japanese advance being finally checked at Kohima and Imphal in 1944, the Burmese resistance leadership began to question whether they were resisting the right enemy. There followed the famous meeting in May 1945 between the British commander, General Slim, and the Burmese nationalist leader, Aung San.

From all that I have read of Aung San and learned about him from his family and others, I have little doubt that, had he survived into the independence period, he would have emerged as a statesman of world stature. From being narrowly and violently anti-colonialist, he had developed a feeling for affairs which was quite extraordinary in one whose background had contained only pre-war Burma and some resistance training in Japan.

On the liberation of Burma from Japanese occupation, the lieutenant-governorship was temporarily in the capable hands of Major-General Sir Hubert Rance. But during the period of Japanese occupation a Government of Burma had been kept in being in Simla under Sir Reginald Dorman Smith, the Governor at the time of the evacuation in 1942, and the post-war British Government felt it right to send him back to carry out the plans which the exiled administration had been preparing. The decision was psychologically wrong, and could only mean, in Burmese eyes, a return to irrelevant pre-war thinking.

In some desperation the British Government, in consultation with Lord Mountbatten, sent back Sir Hubert Rance. He had been universally popular and had shown an ability to understand how Burmese national consciousness was developing. Some hope was entertained not only of a better relationship but also of Burmese membership of the Commonwealth. But the Burmese did not hit, as did the ingenious Indians, upon the brilliant expedient of a Republic within the Commonwealth. And once they had openly opted for total separation, it would not have been politically possible to turn back. Aung San himself understood what had been missed but there was nothing to be done.

This was regrettable, but there was a far worse disaster to follow. Rance and Aung San developed an extraordinary mutual understanding which could have translated itself into the wider context of Anglo-Burmese relationship after independence. But this was not to be. On 19 July 1947 Aung San and seven of his colleagues were mown down with machine-guns in the Assembly building in Rangoon by assassins organized by a political rival.

Progress towards independence was not interrupted and Burma became independent with U Nu, the former Speaker of the Assembly, as Prime Minister. The transition was peaceful and the relationship with Britain friendly, but the future looked and proved to be full of risks and trials.

Events such as these were important elements in the attitude of the Burmese towards their former rulers, the British, and of the psychology with which any British Ambassador had to deal. It meant an extraordinary combination of intimacy and sensitivity. During my period in Burma, the political and personal relationship remained happy, despite efforts by the hostilely minded, abetted by disciples of anti-colonialist orthodoxy, to bring about separation. Much of the pleasant atmosphere which accompanied our time in Burma is attributable to the Burmese character itself. The Burmese, when not living under fear of indigenous or foreign authority, are naturally and sometimes breathtakingly frank, direct and gay. (The first words ever addressed to me by the wife of a Burmese Cabinet Minister were, 'Is your wife going to feed her baby herself?') Somewhere deep down may lie a violent streak. But there is an instinctive preference for good cheer and for non-involvement in dogma or deep intellectual exercise. If the world will leave Burma alone, Burma can be one of the happiest places in the world.

The Embassy Residence in Rangoon is the former residence of the General Manager of the Irawaddy Flotilla Company who in British days ran the river transport. One might have expected that the frugal Scotsmen who ran this company would have built either a Victorian palace or a granite fortress. Instead they produced, from a simple design, a two-storey house with an arcade verandah round three sides and, on the ground floor, excellent rooms for entertaining. On the first floor was a set of bedrooms and bathrooms of total geometric simplicity, three rooms left (east) and three right (west), all with verandahs. On my first night I went to sleep with the windows open, assuming that November was late enough for this. It was, but long before dawn I was woken up by the peeping of pipes and the clash of cymbals. It was one of the famous Burmese *Pwes* in the open and it went on all night. I wondered at about 6.00 a.m. whether this happened every night. At about 7.00, a procession of four people entered the room, each in a different Burmese or Indian national costume, and emptied four buckets of tepid water into my bath. I privately decided that this way of living was too nineteenth century for me.

My first two problems, even before I presented my credentials, were so much a relic of the British past that I could not quite believe them. The British captain of the Rangoon Golf Club had had a row with a prominent if rather difficult senior Burmese member. On the swimming front, the Kokine Road Swimming Club was remaining obstinately Caucasian and refusing to admit anyone even partially Asian. In the end both golfing warriors became good friends of ours, and this led to a cease-fire. The Swimming Club for its part elected one day in a mixture of conspiracy and absent-mindedness a Eurasian office worker and the battle was over. It was extraordinary how these things, typical of a minority, died so hard, and it was part of the British Ambassador's business to hasten the interment without being too obvious in his intervention. And it is right to add that the people who urged me to do this were two prominent members of the British community.

The President, Dr Ba U, was kind enough to arrange for the earliest possible presentation of credentials, partly in order that I might attend the official dinner for Vice-President Richard Nixon.* In Burma, as in India, I was invited to present my

* The Vice-President had made a mark in Burma by stepping out of his car as an anti-Nixon demonstration approached and saying 'I am Mr Nixon. What can I do for you?' The crowd giggled nervously.

entire diplomatic staff numbering seventeen (plus two consular staff). This is a nerve-racking affair, when you have only just learned the names and identities of your staff yourself. I can only advise that, if you are ever in this position and forget the name of your Military Adviser, you should mumble 'Colonel Bogey' and move rapidly on. The President won't know.

The first serious business with the Burmese Government was something of a shock. Since independence the Burmese Armed Services had been aided with training and advice by a British Services Mission, and at the end of 1953 the agreement establishing and setting the conditions of service for the Mission came up for renewal. About the time I arrived, the Embassy received a long memorandum setting out terms for renewal, which I was instructed to present to the Burmese Government.

I was rather appalled at the length and complexity of this document. The Burmese governmental machine was small and not very sophisticated, and this essay would surely be a bit much for it to digest. With the aid of the Mission, we simplified a few details. But there was no alternative to presenting the document pretty well as it stood. The Permanent Under-Secretary, U Tun Shein, received it with a rather bleak look.

After a week or two's silence, the Burmese simply announced that they did not propose to renew the agreement at all and the Mission would terminate. No explanation was given, though the Prime Minister, U Nu, told me that there was no question of ill-feeling.

Quite soon after, we all of us came to the view that, if there had been a renewal, relations between the Mission and the Burmese Services would very likely have gone slowly, but with increasing ill-temper, downhill. While some of the Burmese higher command were well disposed to the British connection, others were not and in the post-1945 climate there was not much point in seeking to retain or restore a position which, while honourable to both sides, was vulnerable to nationalist pressures.

There were other events of a more positive nature. Burma was entering the period when one of the main motifs of co-operation with foreign countries was the industrial joint venture.

The foreign interest concerned and the Burmese Government would take shares in a joint enterprise, the proportionate shareholding being different in different cases. A new agreement had been concluded between the Burmah Oil Company and the Burmese Government, and an expedition went off to the oilfield at Chauk, some 400 miles away, to celebrate the occasion.

As part of the expedition we also visited Pagan, describable briefly as the Burmese Angkor. It is a flat piece of ground bordering the Irawaddy River, on which there are the remains of, it is said, 4,999 pagodas, dating mostly between AD 1000 and 1300. Thanks to the dry climate, and, in the case of the best-known temples, to work of preservation and restoration, the main temples are in good condition, and the whole area is a wonderful and beautiful sight, with an air of Buddhist peace pervading it. There is a tranquil westward view over the river to high, waterless hills on the other bank. As we stood there in the sunset by a small pagoda, U Nu said to Pat and myself, 'This atmosphere means that you and I have met each other here before.' I have often wondered whether this feeling had anything to do with Pagan never being developed in his time as a foreign exchange-earning tourist attraction.

There was, as it happened, a major Buddhist event in 1954, the two thousand five hundredth anniversary of the founding of Buddhism. Despite grumbling from financial experts, U Nu had caused an artificial cave to be erected on the outskirts of Rangoon for the celebration. There was a great concourse of visitors and I advised the British Government that they should send a greeting. The question was how to deliver it. The anniversary authorities thought it should be read at the opening ceremony and it was left to me to decide how to dress. It was clearly inappropriate to appear in full tropical uniform, including a sword and a helmet looking like a 1914 Prussian *Pickelhaube*. On the other hand, one must be suitably ceremonious. I therefore attended and sat on the floor in the uniform coat (white tails with brass buttons), no scabbard or sword, one medal and no shoes or socks. In due course I got up and read my message to the presiding Buddhist eminences. The combination of ceremonious and informal seemed just right, and it is now too late for the Order of St Michael and St George to declare this variation inadmissible.

British trade with Burma was not doing too badly. Our exports to Burma were running at about £22 million a year and we had just concluded one or two highly useful contracts. But some of the stories of inertia in British industry were worrying. We had lost a contract for some railway rolling stock at least partly because the company concerned, having had genuine difficulty about strained capacity, had told the Burmese that the finished stock would have to stand in a siding while awaiting shipment, for which the Burmese would have to pay rent. The Burmese went to Japan. Some British articles were absolute winners, like the Land Rover, but the Rover Company, which could have flooded the world, preferred to remain small, and the service from Britain was miserable.

On the Burmese side there were the first signs of the run on Burmese foreign exchange reserves which was later to have far-reaching effects. But the appointment as Minister of Trade Development of U Raschid, a most able Indian Muslim who had opted for Burmese nationality, was a sign that the problem was not being ignored.

The political weather remained fair. We had an enjoyable visit from Mr Berkeley Gage,[2] our newly appointed Ambassador to Thailand. Burmese relations with the Thais had been anything from prickly to unfriendly ever since the year 1767 when the Burmese invaded Thailand and sacked the ancient Siamese city of Ayuthia. Reconciliation had lagged and there had been even at the end of 1953 an incident in which Burmese aircraft appeared to have been in action over Thai territory. There was a strong suspicion in Burma that the Thais were harbouring what were called in the local jargon 'Kuomintang remnants', and the Communist Chinese were clearly putting pressure on the Burmese to tidy this situation up.

I took Berkeley to the President, the Prime Minister and

[2] Sir Berkeley Gage was Ambassador in Bangkok, 1954–57, and Ambassador to Peru, 1958–63. Chairman of the Latin America Committee of the British National Export Council, 1964–66.

the Minister of Defence, U Ba Swe, and found an attitude very much what one could have expected under U Nu's leadership. Certainly the Burmese wanted reconciliation; there was nothing to quarrel about any more. Berkeley Gage found a cautious but not wholly unreceptive mood on the other side. We cannot claim a great part in a reconciliation, which would have come about anyway, given U Nu's intentions, but perhaps we had given a useful little nudge.

Thus in 1954 the atmosphere was friendly and the objectives modest. It was not surprising that Burma should have declined an invitation, handed in by me to U Ba Swe, to join SEATO. It was gratifying but to be expected that Burma should join the Colombo Plan. It looked as though Burma would develop quietly and positively with the joint ventures, with American and United Nations aid and technical advice, Indian sympathy and Japanese reparations.

But there were some disquieting signs on the horizon. The collapse at Dien Bien Phu of the French effort in Indo-China meant probable future tension in that area. Hitherto the Communist powers had taken comparatively little direct interest in Burma. They were of course represented diplomatically and the (Communist) Chinese Ambassador was the doyen of the diplomatic corps – an inconvenient arrangement since the Americans and others did not recognize him. The frequently asked but unanswered question was whether, and if so when and how, the Chinese neighbours would take notice?

They did so, very emphatically, when the Chinese Foreign Minister, Chou En-lai, landed in Rangoon in June 1954 on his way home from the Geneva Conference on South-East Asia. It was not so much that anything decisive was done on that occasion, but that the visitor impressed himself on the Burmese as a very powerful man of great charm, surrounded by what seemed to be an army of identical small men wearing horn-rimmed glasses and identical uniforms. When in the evening a Chinese opera was performed in the open air, there seemed to be an endless sea of Chinese faces all around as a reminder of the size of the Chinese community and the latent power of the northern neighbour.

Diplomatic life in U Nu's Burma however did not consist solely of political argument or commercial promotion. In fact this period in my diplomatic life contained more time off and cheerful enjoyment than any other. I acquired in Burma a habit of taking half an hour's sleep after lunch, a habit very useful later in India, but occasionally a little embarrassing if it resurrected itself in Whitehall. In Rangoon, there was much social life but the pace needed to be a little slow: the climate is relaxing and even in cool weather a temperature under 70 degrees F is deeply resented. Sound health and equable temper are infinitely better than overstrain and slow recovery.

In this relatively calm atmosphere of 1954 there occurred a great diplomatic event, the birth of the younger daughter of the wife of the British Ambassador. This took place at the nursing home in the Prome Road maintained by the British community. Everything went with the utmost smoothness until the actual conveyance to me over the old Burmese telephone system, surviving from British times. It was like this.

Voice: Your wife has gurgle gurgle.
Me: What?
Voice: Your wife gurgle gurgle.
Me: Yes?
Voice: Your wife has had gurgle gurgle.

The rest may be improvised. Joanna, being born on a Thursday, had to receive an honorary Burmese name beginning with 'M' and she has remained, in Burmese eyes, 'Myint Myint' ever since (the 'T' is as mute as the 'P' in Psmith).

Travel within Burma was important for knowledge and perspective. It was also very erratic. Northern Burma from a line Mandalay–Maymyo–Lashio was accessible and very safe. But within the 400 miles between that line and Rangoon the country was infested with various hostiles, Red Flag Communists, White Flag Communists, Karens or simply dacoits. You could only reach the north by flying over them. Only just as we left Burma in 1956 were the first diplomatic cars allowed to drive up to Taunggyi in the Shan State.

So one hopped over insurgency to peace. Mostly we used the Union of Burma's gallant fleet of Dakotas. Once a Burmese hostess whom we knew said, 'Do you mind if you don't get stewardess service this time? It's my third trip today.' We didn't and she fell asleep on the floor. At other times we flew around showing the flag in an elderly Anson aircraft of the RAF which we shared with three other posts. It was a godsend but it was terrifyingly slow off the ground. Once I wanted to give a stranded nun a ride back to Rangoon. The Air Attaché looked sad. I picked up the signal and as the plane was still bumbling along the ground 50 yards from the end of the runway, I breathed a prayer of thanks for the sacrifice of Sister Charity.

A memorable tour was one taken as guests of the Defence Minister, U Ba Swe, and his delightful wife, Daw Nu Nu, on the Burma Navy ship *Mayu*. The Minister was taking a trip to the southern parts of Tavoy, Mergui and Victoria Point. Several diplomats were invited but we were the only couple whose acceptances survived against other demands. The moral is that it is no good being so short-staffed that you can never get away from your desk.

We saw some very beautiful scenery, took part in a Burmese wedding, visited a Government tin mine, and met, in addition to many Burmese, a few compatriots who had struggled on in the area, keeping plantations going or awaiting the time when private tin mining could be safely resumed. Since the way from our cabin on the ship to our bathroom was through the cabin occupied by the Minister and his wife, we established a singularly relaxed family relationship with them.

Another memorable trip was the ascent of Mount Popa. This mountain, in central Burma, is especially sacred, and U Nu invited Pat and me to come up with him and dedicate a new pagoda. We drove up part of the way, leaving three thousand feet to be done on foot. As we walked past U Nu's tent in the early morning, he put his head out and, seeing my old hat, rucksack and shorts, exclaimed,'Ah, I see you are professional mountaineer.'

We went up the military way, fifty minutes' tramp, ten minutes' breather. U Nu wore his party out by walking very slowly and

never stopping at all. He arrived at the top with his cheerful
smile under an Italian straw hat. We went for a short time serious
as the pagoda was dedicated, and we then adjourned to watch
the famous Burmese dancer, Shwe Man Yee (Golden Smile from
Mandalay), who had come up too. Half-way down we were
entertained by a man playing with three cobras. One got impatient and headed swiftly for a terrified audience but happily
stopped and showed itself off when almost within striking
distance. The snake charmer, when asked why a colleague of
his had been fatally bitten, replied tersely, 'Snakes and alcohol
don't mix.'

So there was gaiety and humanity mixed in with the pressures
of the world outside. The most basic experience was the annual
water festival each April. During these four days, it is not so
much your right as your duty to spray or drench anyone within
reach. There is a religious tradition of purification in the background, and indeed as a gentle ceremony it is very attractive.
But mostly it has become an excuse for drenching oneself and
others at a time of year when everyone is tired of hotter and
hotter weather and longs for the monsoon. Thus it came about
that for the first and only time in my life it was my pleasure and
also my duty to throw the wife of a Chief of Police into a pond.

There were local personalities whose company one could
enjoy without that pressure of business which impedes leisurely
contact in bigger and busier countries. I have spoken already a
good deal of U Nu. He was somewhat older than most of his
Government and this and his devout Buddhism made him sound
like a solemn character. This was by no means so. He had a unique
smile compounded of saintliness and gaiety; he also had a certain
political shrewdness which he used in day-to-day business and
which made him for that period the undisputed leader of his
country. As time went on, he became subject to the criticism
that he was too prone to listen to the advice of the last person who
spoke to him. None the less he remained and remains someone
for whom one can only feel regard and affection.

The cohesion of the state depended entirely on the ability
of U Nu and his two chief lieutenants, U Ba Swe and U Kyaw

Nyein, to work together. U Ba Swe was the party organizer; U Kyaw Nyein the student with the enquiring mind who, in his capacity as Minister of Industries, would jump into his jeep before breakfast to pay a quick visit to the German-designed steel mill and see how it was getting on. With U Nu carrying all that was needed of political charisma, the position seemed impregnable.

A special friend was Daw Khin Kyi, the widow of the murdered Aung San. A quiet lady of few words but of great depth and strength of character, she reappeared later in our lives as Burmese Ambassador in Delhi.

And for two people, the future was to hold big things. U Thant was serving first as Secretary in the Information Ministry and then as a special adviser to U Nu. His quietly helpful personality and his good understanding of English and the British caused him to be much missed when he left Rangoon to be Burmese representative at the United Nations. I do not think anyone would have guessed what would happen later. The head of the Armed Forces was General Ne Win. He had been one of Aung San's associates and had received training in Japan. The army being for historical reasons very much the senior service in Burma, the General had naturally become the Commander-in-Chief. He played a somewhat elusive part in Burmese public life, alternating between bursts of energy and an enjoyment of golf, racing and family life. As the story will show, he had an instinct for power and political manoeuvre unusual among Burmese in public life and much of the history of Burma over the period is a history of how he used these skills.

The British community numbering some three hundred had excellent leadership though there were some who did not belong to the present age. Apart from our business friends, there was a unique man, Professor Gordon Luce, a gymnastics teacher from Manchester who had become the greatest living expert on the languages and past civilization of Burma. He had married the sister of the Burmese professor of English at the University of Rangoon, and he and his wife, in the midst of their scholarship, ran a home for waifs and strays brought to them off the street by the authorities. We spent many an enchanted evening with the

Luces, eating Burmese food and watching the boys dance Burmese free-style to Schubert records.

There were also our visitors from Britain and elsewhere. Thanks to the international air services, Rangoon for the first time in Burma's history found itself on a world travel route. So it was that in 1954 a strong Labour party delegation, headed by Mr Aneurin Bevan, visited us on the way home from China.

I gave a large buffet lunch, which included the Chinese Ambassador and the Soviet Chargé d'Affaires. I sat Sam Watson, the Durham miners' leader, next to the Soviet Chargé. He leaned across and said in his best North Country, 'Do you believe all that boonk put out by your Government?' The Soviet colleague managed.

The delegation had been so overwhelmed by China that they seemed scarcely to realize that they were in an independent country. (An honourable exception was Dr Summerskill who went determinedly to investigate the exploitation of women; on the whole Burmese women through the ages have stood up for themselves pretty well.) But Mr Bevan later in the day gave, before a small, select audience, an unforgettable lecture. His theme was that no people should again go through a classical industrial revolution experience with its callousness and cruelties. But if this were to be avoided perhaps there would be a necessity for some degree of repression of personal freedom which might turn out to be less cruel than what the early industrial workers had experienced. I do not know whether the audience got this sophisticated message; I certainly did, and I noted that it was wholly contrary to the outlook of the British Government at the time. Visiting members of Her Majesty's Opposition do better, in normal circumstances, not to confuse the country's external image. But in the circumstances and given the brilliance of the exposition, I decided not to feel too aggrieved.

In Burma, as elsewhere, visitors meant pleasure and opportunity. The problem was to connect with, say, Burmese Ministers who on the whole did not make appointments. I had a telegram one day from the British Governor of Malaya asking us to help a young member of the not yet independent Malayan Government coming to Burma to buy rice. We promptly asked him to stay. On a strict reckoning of political status, he did not rate a call on the Burmese Prime Minister (U Ba Swe at the time), but I felt he ought to see the Prime Minister somehow. Fortunately the final of the national billiards championship was about to take place and there was to be an opening stroke by the Prime Minister who was an addict. U Ba Swe opened with an unbelievable fluke, which he turned into a break of fifteen and the introduction could not have taken place in more auspicious circumstances. Such were the ingenuities necessary if visitors were to be suitably looked after.

1955 was wholly different from 1954. In 1954 U Nu had stayed at home and there had been few official visitors. In 1955, we started with a visit from Marshal Tito and the visiting in and out never seemed to stop. U Nu paid a series of visits to the neutral world, to Eastern Europe, to the West and to China. In his absences the economy deteriorated, and with it the opportunities for British trade and the prospects for British interests.

Before U Nu's touring got under way, we had one two-hour visit which involved an awkward piece of what one might call internal diplomacy. I had been attending at Singapore a conference of ambassadors, governors and service chiefs. This conference held annually was always a useful and distinguished briefing session; on this occasion it had been attended for one day by Mr Anthony Eden, the Foreign Secretary. Mr Eden's next major halt was at New Delhi, but he had decided to stop in Rangoon for an hour to talk with U Nu. There was much argument about the degree of formality to be observed, Mr Eden being anxious to meet informally and not keep Mr Nehru waiting at the Delhi end, U Nu being anxious not to give Mr Eden a reception unworthy of his country.

Mr Eden's son, Simon, had been lost over Burma in the war. The aircraft had been found, but the remains being unidentifiable, the crew had been buried collectively at Htaukkyan, the Commonwealth War Graves Cemetery sixteen miles north of Rangoon along a road regarded as a security risk. Initially Mr Eden had felt that he could not visit the cemetery. Ten minutes before the plane was due to land in Rangoon, he sent for me and said he had changed his mind. Could the programme be rearranged?

It is not easy for a very junior ambassador to say a direct 'no' to his Secretary of State. But it was clear to me that a change of this magnitude without notice would upset whatever arrangements U Nu had made, besides upsetting U Nu himself. I therefore took a deep breath and said I thought the change, however desirable, could not be managed. Mr Eden accepted this unwelcome advice unhappily.

Five minutes later he sent for me again. Could a visit to the cemetery be added after the appointment already arranged with U Nu? I said I would do my best.

As soon as we disembarked, I tugged the head of Chancery, Keith Oakeshott, by the sleeve and told him what was needed. The main party went into the airport lounge where U Nu had invited his entire Cabinet to lunch. Each of us sat in an individual wicker chair with an individual small table on which was set a Burmese dish. U Nu had won his point about the worthy reception, and Mr Eden briefed the Burmese Government in session on the tense situation between the Chinese Communists and Nationalists confronting each other in the crisis of Quemoy and Matsu.

At the end of an hour I was able to tell the Foreign Secretary that an entire procession of officials and security guards had been gathered together to take him and Mrs Eden to Htaukkyan. An hour later still, the party left for Delhi with their missions accomplished, leaving the British Ambassador limply thankful that he had given the right advice and that his boss had taken it.

U Nu's western tour included a visit to Britain. We adjusted our home leave programme so as to accompany him. He began his visit at Glasgow which had long-standing trade connections with Burma. At the beginning of the long summer of 1955 Glasgow was tactfully the warmest place in the United Kingdom. The visit was, I think, a happy one and all friends of Burma did their best. U Nu made an excursion to Pitlochry. As we passed a large monument, U Nu asked what it was. It was a memorial, we explained, to William Wallace, the Scottish patriot. 'Ought I to lay a wreath?' said U Nu with a suitable twinkle.

There were talks with Ministers and officials, but when U Nu returned to Burma, there were suggestions in the Burmese press that, while he had been accorded proper dignity and hospitality in other countries, he had been slighted in Britain. There had, in fact, been no such intention and U Nu had no complaint himself. But it is a constant cross which the Foreign Office has to bear that the British are the least demonstrative of all people in the matter of receiving foreign dignitaries. There are physical reasons; the journey to London Airport is long and inconvenient for busy people – whereas, for instance, Washington National Airport is ten minutes' drive from the White House. And the British press uniquely ignores visiting heads of state unless they are very important or very eccentric. It is all part of British insularity and is something for which we pay a foreign policy price.

During the summer of 1955 I took David and Christopher to the House of Commons where we heard the Prime Minister, by then Mr Eden, announce that the Soviet head of state, Mr A. N. Bulganin, and the Secretary of the Soviet Communist Party, Mr N. Kruschev, had accepted an invitation to visit Britain. This was very well received. Meantime, in the autumn Messrs Bulganin and Kruschev set off on a tour of Asia, including India and Burma. I obtained permission to arrive back in Burma towards the end of their visit, anticipating correctly that there was no point in being there earlier to listen to a series of rudely anti-British speeches without a right of reply. But to have missed the visit altogether would have been an obvious discourtesy to both Russians and Burmese.

When I did arrive, there occurred an incident which belongs for me to the narrow escapes department. The Russians were hosts to a large supper party in the garden of the President's house. A high table had been arranged and the Russians had seated at it, not the senior ambassadors as strict protocol would have demanded, but the ambassadors of the countries included in their leaders' tour. This departure from protocol was accepted by the Burmese and nobody objected.

What went wrong was that, having made this exceptional arrangement, the Russian hosts paid not the slightest attention to the remaining ambassadors who were given neither welcome nor guidance but left to fend for themselves. This is contrary to the common sense rule that if you are going to disregard protocol, you must take special care that those whom you demote are properly and indeed rather specially looked after.

The discourtesy was too much for my Ceylon colleague, Mr A. E. Goonesinha, a former labour leader and a gentleman of character. He seized the Thai Ambassador with one arm and the Pakistan Ambassador with the other and walked out. At that moment I was talking with Burmese friends in another corner of the garden and missed the incident. I claim no credit for avoiding involvement, and had I been with Mr Goonesinha, I should probably have felt bound, on grounds of Commonwealth solidarity, to accompany him. Then, against the background of the Eden announcement, we should have had the cliché head-lines, 'British envoy snubs Soviet leaders.' 'No sooner had the British Ambassador returned to Burma than . . .'

The Soviet appearance at this level at this point of time had an immediate and overwhelming effect on the Burmese. Through the year 1955 the Burmese economic situation had been worsening. Negative measures to prevent further drains on foreign exchange had been taken in some desperation earlier in the year. But rescuers were not at hand. The Indians were becoming more nearly self-sufficient in rice, at any rate temporarily, and were neither buying from Burma nor offering a loan. The Americans, far from being able or disposed to help, were insisting, by Congressional demand, on making further mass-produced high-quality rice available as aid, to the detriment of Burma's sales prospects. Nor had the Burmese had time to do anything effective to improve quality or efficiency in rice production or to offer a more popular price. In Britain the possibility of a small loan was discussed, but resources were scarce and the kind of loan we could have afforded could not have done anything decisive.

Therefore when Mr Kruschev at the end of his tour gave the impression that the Soviet Union would take all Burma's surplus rice, he was playing an unbeatable card.

In the end during a visit by Mr Mikoyan early in 1956, the amount accepted was 500,000 tons in a barter agreement by which the Burmese would be paid not in cash but in Eastern European manufactured goods. The western Ambassadors protested very strongly at measures which at one stroke eliminated Burma as a market for manufacturers which the Burmese, as consumers, preferred. Possibly we took too righteous a line; the Burmese had come, no doubt partly through their own fault, to a position where there was no other relief. This kind of aid with strings was, in fact, better than nothing, since it enabled Burma to continue old lines of production at a time when the creation of new forms of employment would have needed more capital than Burma could have raised.

The Government produced a list of goods which importers seeking for licences would have to import mainly or exclusively from East European barter countries. These included electrical goods (100%), hardware (80%) and machinery (70%). Importors were also invited to apply for licences for cars, cycles and buses, which were to come 100% from barter countries. The Burmese Government implicitly reserved the right for government orders to be placed anywhere, and figures for other goods were more liberal. But British exports were seriously hit. Commercial diplomatic pressure brought about a few alleviations, but the effect in the end was to reduce British exports to Burma from some £22 million in 1953 to £17 million in 1956. Given that so much of the Embassy's work had been devoted to helping and encouraging British trade, this was immensely disappointing. It was some consolation that the Burmese Government insisted that there had been no change in their external non-aligned policy. But with a Soviet-financed hotel and technical institute in the offing, with a number of puzzled satellite diplomats arriving in a, to them, very strange country, obviously the Soviet presence would henceforth be of an entirely new importance.

If there was little that we could do on the economic and commercial front, we were at least continously active on the personal and political. At the beginning of 1956 we had a visit of some weeks from Sir Hubert Rance, the last British Governor, and Lady Rance. When independence comes to a country, the future relationship with the former rulers depends very much on the handling of the transfer of power. The tact and understanding shown by Rance, a performance likely to be underestimated by historians, was not lost on the Burmese of that generation who received him with particular warmth. Then followed a visit by Lord and Lady Mountbatten. Lord Mountbatten was coming to receive the highest Burmese award. From the beginning there was one tiresomeness after another. The Pakistanis had just chosen 23 March for their national day celebration; this meant that the Pakistan High Commissioner's official reception was by then bound to coincide with our reception for the Mountbattens. Then General Ne Win, the Burmese Chief of Staff, announced that he was not going to be present in Rangoon at the time (with no indication where else he was going to be). So arrangements were handed over to the Burma Navy, who, under Commodore Than Pe, rose perfectly to the occasion. I sent my (Burmese-speaking) Counsellor, Peter Murray, to Madras to give the party a verbal briefing and then, fearing that our standards might not correspond to the visitors' probable expectations, spent the only involuntarily sleepless night in thirty-five years.

This, it proved, had been unnecessary, and the highly organized programme went with great fluency and momentum. The Embassy also profited by an impressive briefing on defence matters, and it seemed to me that the Burmese, through General Ne Win's attitude, had thrown away an excellent chance of a similar briefing, which they could have had without political or military commitment. The General, who remained perfectly friendly thereafter, had acted no doubt from a complex set of motives: lacking Aung San's self-assurance, naturally suspicious of foreigners and perhaps feeling a sense of professional inadequacy to the occasion, he may, I suspect, have decided to avoid at all costs the danger of giving either nationally or individually any impression of lower status. Thus he stayed away from a national welcome to a friend of Burma and an occasion on which he would, as head of the defence services, have met Lord Mountbatten as an equal.

Before the summer of 1956 and Pat's return to London to look after family matters, we made one more trip, this time north to Myitkyina (the Wingate-Stilwell country) and thence along the Chinese border to Lashio. We stayed a night at the hospital at Nam Khan run by that eccentric anti-authoritarian American surgeon, Dr Gordon Segrave. He was something of a smaller scale Albert Schweitzer, in that he ran his hospital in what modern hygiene would call an untidy, messy way, believing that the very simple people of the area would be less scared if it did not look too antiseptic. His memory of frequent arguments with British authority in the past enhanced his genuine delight that we should have wanted to come, tempered only occasionally by a slight suspicion that there might even now be a catch in it somewhere. We were glad to have made friends in this way.

The monsoon period of 1956 brought two sensational events, one local and the other world-wide. It had been known for some time that Chinese forces were in occupation of a remote spot in the Wa States in the north-east of Burma. The Government were understandably anxious not to create alarm and despondency by revealing this publicly. But finally U Law Yone, the very independent-minded editor of the English language newspaper, *Nation*, decided he could bear it no longer and came out with the story. At once there was great alarm. Had the Chinese, who were suspected of continuous quiet infiltration, suddenly started an invasion of Burma? It emerged gradually that either the Chinese had made a mistake or that, more likely, this was a Chinese way, repeated later in India on a large scale, of drawing attention to a difference of opinion about the real line of an undemarcated frontier. The dispute over this and a more important area further north continued for some years and was finally settled by General Ne Win.

The second event was the Egyptian seizure of the Suez Canal. I listened that evening to all the radio news and comment that

I could pick up. There was an insipid comment from the BBC and a more robust one from Australia which got the main point – that you cannot conduct international relations as the Egyptians had done and expect peace to survive. The Burmese Foreign Office, under James Barrington, a highly intelligent Anglo-Burmese, as Permanent Secretary, had grasped this point immediately. I did my best to play on it. In my last interview with Barrington before my transfer home he told me that there was much sympathy with our case, but that it did not help us to bristle so much politically or to rattle so many sabres militarily. I of course reported this helpful non-aligned comment.

In the middle of these events I was instructed, for reasons which will appear later, to return to London. I decided that, after nearly three years in Burma, I ought to do what was, in Burma, something exceptional, to make a formal farewell public speech, and this was arranged with the active Rangoon Rotary Club.

Although the speech was carefully worded, it was very frank and the implications were clearly critical. After paying tribute to the warmth of Burmese-British personal relationships, I expressed strongly the hope that, as nearly all Burmese foreign exchange earnings were in sterling, exporters from sterling sources should in future be given a better chance of competing in the Burmese market. I also urged that the treatment of much needed foreign investment should be such as would attract that investment, and that fair and efficient treatment should be accorded by the Burmese authorities to those from abroad who were resident in Burma because of such investment. 'I do beg you,' I finished, 'not to make it too difficult for your friends to help you.'

The speech was remarkably well received in the local press. On re-reading it now, I am tempted to say with Dean Swift, 'What a genius I had when I wrote that. . . .' I doubt if I have done anything quite like it again – and that is a tribute to our staff in Rangoon and to Burma itself.

And what, in terms of concrete results, had we achieved? In measurable terms not as much as I had hoped. We had lost a military mission and the conditions of our trade had deteriorated.

Hopes of a different British presence in terms of investment and aid had been limited by the limitations of British economic resources and by Burma's decision to leave the Commonwealth. But against the tide of events the British political position and relationship had remained good: we had, I think, made the Embassy both a business-like and a hospitable concern, both of us and our staff concentrating a great deal on the exercise in local personal relationships which, as between free countries, is the stuff of diplomacy. I hope my successors found it a useful legacy. For us it has meant many abiding friendships.

When I revisited Burma in 1959, the ruling party had split and power had passed to General Ne Win. The General formed what might be called a technocratic government, efficient, authoritarian and not unimpressive. There was an atmosphere of shirt-sleeve activity and purpose; one only asked oneself whether the arrangement was really temporary or would tend to become permanent.

Ne Win produced a most surprising and creditable answer. In April 1960 he handed the government back to U Nu. It was democracy's last chance for some time to come. But, sadly, it was not taken. Instead of reading accurately the lessons of what had happened and pursuing a stabilizing policy, U Nu set about fulfilling his conscientious dream of making Buddhism the state religion of the country. This effort, superfluous in a country in which Buddhism was the official religion in all but name, caused much disturbance and uncertainty.

When Pat and I visited Rangoon in January 1962, the British Chargé d'Affaires, Dick Slater,[3] and his wife gave a party in their garden. It was a great gathering of our many friends from politics, the civil service, the business community, the diplomatic corps and the navy and air force. Only the army were absent. Nobody had accepted or refused. The military had just faded into darkness, and the telephone was not answered. It was no surprise that two months later there should have been a second Ne Win coup.

This time there was no efficiently technocratic government.

[3] Richard Slater was Ambassador to Cuba, 1966–70, and High Commissioner in Uganda, 1970–72.

Ne Win, having failed to secure useful political backing from the U Kyaw Nyein–U Ba Swe group, had allied himself with the left-wing dogmatists. U Nu, U Kyaw Nyein, U Ba Swe and U Raschid were all detained for the next six years. So was Chief Justice Myint Thein, later allowed the most limited access to his distinguished, dying wife. A medical institute run by a gentle and respected Indian physician, Dr Suvi, was taken over one night and its director bundled into the next aeroplane for India. Foreign business was proceeded against with a blunt weapon. Life was made impossible for Gordon Luce and his wife and they had to leave the country: to make Burma uninhabitable for two such wise, patient people required real genius. The economy ran rapidly downhill and in a short time Burma, the country which stood above all things for self-sufficiency in rice, was suffering from a rice shortage.

From all this performance one must in fairness exempt external policy. Ne Win's policy was one of keeping Burma's head down. This was entirely right. When non-alignment went anti-West, Burma swayed with the wind; when it edged back again, Burma did the same. For this reason there was no national political quarrel with Burma from any quarter. The Burmese performed their once a century act of retiring into their shells and viewing the rest of the world with some disdain. But the effect on individual Burmese was deplorable. Burmese are delightfully direct and unaffectedly cheerful people. Under this regime, they became dull and rather priggish, totally contrary to the national character. They looked round to see whether the Chairman was going to hear about them in a Big Brother manner and they prudently took no risks. Yet Burma with its gentle climate, its supply of natural products and its freedom from over-population survives these things and indeed accepts them for a time as an alternative to the democracy which might have become too difficult to manage.

All this has been something of a sadness for Burmese and for lovers of Burma. However, there has been one way in which we have sought to pay our debt of affection to that country. Our home in London has always been and I have no doubt always

The author with U Nu, then Prime Minister of Burma, 1954

The author of the article at a recent Buddhist Annual meeting, Penang, 1941

will be a home for Aung San's family. It remains our hope that his daughter Suu Kyi, who was married from our house, and his son Aung San U, both exceptional young people, will in their time be able to do some service to their country whose government in this time has done so little for them.

H

London

1956-1960

In the summer of 1956 Pat flew home to cope with the transfer of the boys from preparatory to public school. As the monsoon pursued its course in Burma, half a day wet and half a day dry, it seemed that we should complete three years there and expect to be moved in the New Year of 1957. But early in August 1956 a telegram came in with the ominous prefix 'Decipher yourself.'

I began to decipher. 'The Secretary of State is proposing a reorganization in the office. . . .' So it was to be a transfer home.

Since 1953, when Roger Makins who had specialized in economics work left his Deputy Under-Secretaryship in the Foreign Office to become Ambassador in the United States, the top economic work had been carried by an Assistant Under-Secretary, that is, one rank below. It had been very competently done, but Whitehall, like an armed service or a Communist government, is a hierarchical place and, however good your Assistant Under-Secretary, the fact that he is an Assistant (the Number Three level) suggests that your department attach that much less weight to that particular branch of policy. Therefore, in the Whitehall subconscious, the Foreign Office had demoted economics.

It had become very clear by 1956, however, that economic developments in Europe would mean a notable increase in economic diplomatic work, and Mr Selwyn Lloyd now proposed to create a full-time economic Deputy Under-Secretary. That was the post I was offered. I was asked whether I could move out of Burma and be ready to start at the Foreign Office in six weeks. Pat came back for the farewells; we paid a brief visit to Bangkok, flew home, found for our immediate needs a bed-sitter in Bina Gardens and I started work on 15 October.

What, I have often been asked, was the Foreign Office doing with an economic department? Wasn't finance the business of the Treasury and commerce that of the Board of Trade? The concise answer is that the mathematics of international trade and finance do not necessarily correspond to political and diplomatic realities. The duty of the external policy department is to watch over and participate in policy formation and execution. This is not just a matter of advising on tactics, though this is in itself very important. It is a matter of understanding the real issues and constantly warning, guiding and hinting with knowledge and tact, and if necessary insisting that a divergence between economic and political interest be referred to the Cabinet. As I have explained in a previous chapter, this requires no merely dilettante knowledge of what is under discussion and a deeper knowledge takes time to acquire.

A classic case of where an economic case went politically wrong was the famous Treasury note to the United States Government in 1932, in which it was explained in elegant and pellucid prose that it would really be much better for the United States if Britain and others did not pay their 1914–18 war debts. The logic and self-interest of this document were so overwhelming that it created explosions of fury in the United States, which reached right into the early period of the Second World War. Whether a strong Foreign Office economic operation could have affected this presentation can never be known, but it would have been its job to try.

Suez

Before I became immersed in economic matters, I found myself involved in one of the great crises of our time. It was clear from the moment I started work in October 1956 that there was something very odd and very wrong with the atmosphere in the offices and corridors. People sensed that big events were impending. They did not know that; they only knew that, to a degree unprecedented since Munich, they were not being consulted or even allowed to know.

Then an odd thing happened to me. Less than a week after

I had started Pat Dean[1] came into my office and said that there was an inter-departmental body called the Middle East (Oil) Committee which had been dealing with oil mainly from the point of view of defence in which field he was the Deputy Under-Secretary. It had now been decided that the oil question was preponderantly economic, and, as I had arrived as the new Deputy Under-Secretary (Economic), it was proposed that I should take over the chairmanship. This was in fact a piece of administrative readjustment, but against the background I have described it seemed peculiar.

On Sunday evening, 28 October, a fortnight after I had joined the office, we were dining with colleagues when news came over the radio that Israel had invaded Egyptian territory. On Monday morning my Treasury opposite number rang up and said politely, 'You seem to be arranging a war. As we shall have to pay for it, could we know what it is all about?' I disclaimed responsibility for the war, but agreed that the request was reasonable. It was arranged that Pat Dean and I should call at the Treasury on the Tuesday morning. Sir John Maud, Permanent Under-Secretary for Fuel and Power, would also be there.

By that time Dean had been briefed about the statement which the Prime Minister, Sir Anthony Eden, was to make in the House of Commons that afternoon. There was to be an ultimatum to both sides, but there was also to be bombing of Arab airfields. I said that if one single Arab were killed in this first bombing, there would be hell to pay. But it was difficult to know how to react except by agreeing to meet again as soon as something definite was known. We went away a little stunned to think over the possible consequences.

So we were involved, side by side with the French, in an equivocal side-by-sideness with the Israelis. During the Second World War, I had developed the practice of having wherever practicable a radio on my desk to give me the news at all critical

[1] Sir Patrick Dean, lawyer, Deputy Under-Secretary (Defence), Foreign Office, 1956–60, U.K. Representative at the UN, 1960–64, Ambassador in Washington, 1964–69.

moments. When I came in on the Wednesday morning, 31 October, I found that the radio I had ordered had been delivered overnight. I tuned in to the first news broadcast and heard that British bombers had been in action over Egypt. During the war one had listened times without number to such announcements; one had breathed hard and hoped hard for both success and survival. Now, somewhat to my dismay, I could only hope that nobody would be killed on either side.

Then began the dreadful wait for the expeditionary force to plough its way over six days from Malta while the controversy raged at home. I had decided right away that this was all a terrible mistake in decision and execution, and wondered what one could do. A few people in the Office had at once spoken of resignation. Retired members of the service invited to support the Government line on the BBC were reluctant to do so. Information officers abroad received no guidance at all, since the Office had none to give and nothing beyond the Prime Minister's statements was coming from the politicians. Resourceful people like my old firm in the United States invented explanations of their own.

In this atmosphere of initial perplexity turning into despondency and resentment, I consulted various of my colleagues about what one could do. Apart from the rights and wrongs of the situation, the action we were taking seemed so utterly out of the character of post-war, United Nations Britain and of the Prime Minister himself. It has been suggested that at this point I 'led a revolt' in the Foreign Office. I did something perhaps a little less spectacular than this, but I had indeed arrived at a point when, despite all my ignorance of the subject, I could not do nothing. On the Friday I wrote, after several attempts, a confidential note to the Permanent Under-Secretary, Sir Ivone Kirkpatrick. It said that in economic work I had exceptional opportunities of talking and listening to people in the Office at all levels. I thought it important for those in authority to realize that the overwhelming majority of people in the Office felt that our action had been a bad mistake. I agreed with this myself, and wanted to express urgently the hope that we could work ourselves out of our present position through the life-line now extended by Mr Lester Pearson on behalf of the Government of Canada.

It may seem odd in this age that I did not march in somewhere and bang on someone's desk, or that no one sent for me to ask me to explain myself. My way of expressing my view owed something to my total newness back in the Office after seven years' absence and in a new job and to my inexpertise on Middle Eastern affairs. But it also reflected the feeling of those days. Not only in the Foreign Office but elsewhere in Westminster, many people seemed to be skirting round the issues and not committing themselves on a situation in which they knew so little and felt that it was only too easy to hurt others or get hurt themselves.

I was alone in London the week-end following my note. I walked for miles along the Embankment and up from Chelsea to Campden Hill, trying to think the problem through. I listened with the greatest concentration to the Prime Minister on the television that Saturday night and to Mr Hugh Gaitskell, the leader of the opposition, on the Sunday night. I hoped that, if the Government had been wrong, Mr Gaitskell might give the right answer. Sadly I realized that party politics were not quite capable of this. As I observed at the time to a friend on a newspaper which had taken the opposition view, 'If only you had said that the arbitrary seizure of other people's canals lowered the standard of international behaviour but . . ., I would have been with you all the way. But you didn't, and the opposition didn't.' So there was nowhere to go.

I do not know what precisely happened to my note. But it led, or helped to lead, to an urgent top-level official meeting on the Monday morning at which Kirkpatrick did his best to answer questions to which there was no answer. For instance, if we and the French occupied the Canal and marched on Cairo, and Nasser escaped to a neighbouring Arab country, what was supposed to happen then? Suffice it to say that, after a fortnight of drama, with a military half-victory in our hands, but with almost universal hostility in the United Nations and with financial pressures and pressures on our oil supplies mounting rapidly, we did indeed avail ourselves of the Canadian life-line.

Throughout this crisis my reactions had been largely instinctive – 'gut-feeling' as we have come to call it. But there were two good reasons, one constitutional and the other international, why I as an official felt as I did. Under our constitutional arrangements, officials give advice and Ministers, whether individually or as a Cabinet or Cabinet committee, take decisions. If they take decisions without first taking advice, they may decide things of great importance without knowing the full background of detail, of opportunity and danger. There is no other source from which they can expect to find such advice presented in an orderly, convenient, comprehensive, and, as far as possible, unbiased form. That is what professional advisers are for, and one only puts in the qualification 'as far as possible' because the giving of professional advice is a human and not a mechanical activity. Ministers of course have no obligation whatever to follow the advice given by officials: they may well have sounder instincts on individual problems, and it will be for them to judge the politically possible. But the obligations on them to be aware of the background as presented by their professional advisers, though not a formal one, is a practical one of vital importance. They disregard it at the nation's peril.

When one presents the subject in this way, the parallel between Suez and Munich becomes dreadfully clear. Just as Mr Chamberlain did not choose to have full advice from the Foreign Office in 1938, so did Sir Anthony Eden tragically avoid it in 1956. In general Conservatives tend to be less touchy about advice than their opponents, and it is sadly ironical that on the occasion of our two foreign policy disasters in my time, it was the Conservatives who did not so much reject advice as decline to hear it.

The lesson was not wholly learned even then. Some years later I had a fierce argument with a friendly Minister when the Government had breezily decided to give an increased bacon quota to a Commonwealth country without remembering to find out (through a half-minute telephone call) that the gesture would mean taking away that amount from someone else and that this would have a serious economic effect on a highly sensitive foreign country.

My diplomatic objection to Suez derived directly from experience. I did not agree with those who argued that the right thing would have been to go in with parachutes and clear the whole thing up in a few days. This could have led to limited short-term success, but it would have solved nothing. By our part in promoting and drafting the United Nations Charter, we had pledged ourselves to promote a more adult method of conducting international relations. The method had suffered some failures and would still be struggling for years to come for more general acceptance – many governments, notably the Soviet Government, have over recent years acted as though these intentions had never existed. But for Britain to go back on so genuine an intention and to adopt, for however righteous a reason, the old forms of the use of force, seemed to me to be a fundamental and tragic denial of those things for which in the past the Prime Minister among others had fought so hard.

It is not true to say, as some liberals too highly charged with emotion said at the time, that this performance marked the end of our ability to act effectively in the Middle East. This was disproved by the skilful little operation in 1961 in which, side by side with some highly embarrassed Arabs, we helped to defend the independence of Kuwait against an Iraqi threat. What it did mean was that with a divided public opinion (to my mind the vital influence) in the Suez crisis, and a thinly lined exchequer, we could not, even in alliance with the French, take on a hostile world. It also meant that, in the longer run, the process started by Mr Dulles in mishandling the Aswan Dam case and driving Arab States into Communist arms was bound to be confirmed and accelerated to the detriment of the Western position. This might have happened for other reasons; but it was sad to have given it avoidable assistance.

After the cease-fire, there remained two loose ends, one personal and one political. The personal one which hung over many of us was whether to go on if the Government did not change its outlook on what had happened. One very wise man said to me, 'Regard this as the Great Aberration.' Provisionally I did, and the agony was resolved by the resignation on 9 January 1957 of the Prime Minister on genuine grounds of ill health. One of the happier things about our national political life is that, looking back on Anthony Eden's career as a whole, the country, including many of those most virulent about Suez, has thrown a veil of forgiveness over this episode. Lord Avon has rightly become a respected *éminence* and has not forfeited the gratitude which the country owes him for so many years of effort to achieve a better world.

The other loose end was the huge one, 'What ought our policy now to be?' I had never served in the Middle East and, except for a week-end in Khartoum, had never visited it. But the accident of having taken charge of the Middle East (Oil) Committee led straight to basic policy. In the vacuum of secrecy no official policy committee existed, and the so-called Oil Committee was the best suited of any existing body for picking up the pieces. Perhaps a chairman with a general knowledge of international affairs rather than specialized knowledge of a bitterly-divided area was a suitable umpire. At any rate, after a series of intensive high-level meetings, Sam Falle[2] of the Foreign Office and I sat down in the bow window of the Gore-Booth bed-sitter to work out a total policy. I cannot speak too highly of Sam's contribution. A good Arabic scholar with an intuitive sense of the meaning of new movements in the Arab world and with a capacity for indignation carefully disciplined by official responsibilities, he provided just that local bone and sinew that the enterprise needed.

Between us, we compiled a paper covering the whole spectrum of the Arab-Israel world and it provided a most comprehensive working basis for a policy for the immediate future within our means, military and financial. As events displaced the then Iraqi and Syrian regimes and slowed down economic progress in these countries, the ideas which might have held good at the end of 1956 became rapidly less valid. In any case, what had happened had left too many scars for any succeeding government to adopt

[2] Sir Samuel Falle was Ambassador to Kuwait, 1969–70, and before that Head of the UN Department of the Foreign Office, 1963–67. Since 1970 he has been High Commissioner in Singapore.

a paper bound to contain criticism. But at least the essay was commended by the committee and proved a help to all those engaged in the work of repair.

At this point I was able to bow out of an involvement in Middle Eastern affairs which could have become an embarrassment for expert and inexpert alike. The Middle East (Oil) Committee became a Committee under Treasury chairmanship for watching over our oil supplies generally, and Middle Eastern affairs as such passed back into well-practised hands.

I assumed full-time charge of the three economic departments, Economic Relations, European Recovery and General Department, with a watching brief of a general kind over our relations with the United States. In the period autumn 1956 to summer 1960 there were two external economic themes which persisted throughout, the national balance of payments and the future economic relationship between Britain and Europe. Suez gave us a balance of payments shock. But some brilliant financial diplomacy in Washington by Lord Harcourt[3] restored confidence, and from then on, while preoccupation never ceased, there was no total crisis.

The worry which weighed on many people most days, and on one department under my supervision all day every day, was the relationship with the European Six, first within the framework of the OEEC and then more broadly. Since the collapse of the European Defence Community in late 1954 under French opposition, the relationship had been thought of almost entirely in the economic context, though within the wider political framework of NATO – political justification for Britain joining the Community came at a later date. Developments were tortuous and sometimes tense, and they had momentous repercussions on the future.

---

[3] Lord Harcourt, chairman of Morgan Crenfell, also of several insurance concerns, was a member of the Radcliffe Committee, 1957–59, and of the Plowden Committee, 1962–64. He was UK executive director of the International Bank and of the International Monetary Fund, 1954–57.

Negotiations with Germany

But my first task during my high-level apprenticeship was a bilateral negotiation. The Foreign Office had been seeking quietly and persistently to get our relations with post-war Germany on to a more sensible basis avoiding either gush or rancour. The two Governments had set up, at the official level, an Anglo-German Economic Committee of which I now became the British Chairman. Meeting alternately in Britain and Federal Germany the Committee dealt mostly in general, confidential discussion, but a new negotiation was coming up about 'support costs' – the amount which Germany would pay towards the expenses of British forces in Federal German territory, and this was entrusted to our Committee.

The period was, one might say, late transitional, between original automatic payments by the German losers of the Second World War and agreement between equals. The British argued that the stationing of British troops in Germany imposed a special burden on the British balance of payments, which the Germans should meet at least in part. The Germans replied that the British troops in Germany were there at least in part for the defence of Britain.

My German opposite number was Dr A. H. van Scherpenberg ('Scherpie'), a blonde, stocky, red-faced diplomat, who looked, as his name implied, more Dutch than German. He was immensely industrious and able, though he took on so much that he was exactly twenty minutes late (known by the Germans as 'one Scherp') for every appointment. But he was friendly to Britain, where he had served, and anxious for agreement.

When the negotiations started I said that, while we really needed £67 million to cover costs, we had tried our best to bring this down and would settle for £60 million. Van Scherpenberg replied that, having looked for every conceivable source of money, given German requirements generally, they could not possibly manage more than £42·5 million.

At this point, of course, one does not bow stiffly and give up. You turn the bilateral negotiation into a multi-dimensional one, in which you and your opposite number start to negotiate with your own respective sides. After a little over a week, I had obtained some discretion and Scherpie got to the point of asking, without commitment, whether we would be 'interested' in £50 million. I replied substantially, 'Yes, interested.' By this time Scherpie and I knew, independently, that, if there was to be agreement at all, we would come out at something like £50 million plus a couple of small bonuses to us to make up for our greater concession in terms of figures. For a moment the whole thing looked like being over in a week. Not at all. The German side appeared to go completely to sleep, while we had detailed work to do including hours which I spent late at night with an Embassy typewriter dissuading our side from telling me that I was to carry out my instructions and not bother them with bonuses under a different heading. The Germans were in fact squaring their Finance Ministry and ensuring that the French and Americans would not ask on behalf of their troops sums which would upset any pledge to us.

Suddenly, after three weeks, things moved again, though a not very felicitous message from the British to the German Government caused a setback. Then we had what we christened an '*Entklammerungssitzung*' (bracket deletion session) in respect of both sides' reservation until only one pair was left, concerning a date for a particular payment. Scherpie passed me a note: 'I can't suggest May 15th, but I might get it accepted if you propose it.' After a few minutes on some formal points, I said that, at the peril of my reputation, I would be prepared to suggest May 15th. The German delegation rose like partridges from the stubble, were absent for twenty minutes (one Scherp), and, after suitable expressions of apprehension by Scherpie, accepted the date and it was all over.

I have only sketched fragmentarily the complications of six weeks of negotiation. In a detailed negotiation between two governments amenable to parliamentary and public opinion, you cannot rush things, however real the goodwill. Nor is there the slightest use in trying to judge progress by day to day expressions on the faces of people leaving meetings. Negotiation is a mixture of perceptiveness and grind, and in this I was totally grateful to the admirable team from the British Embassy, Bonn, and Government departments at home who prevented me from going wrong.

Strategic Controls

Much of 1957 was devoted to going over and over the difficult question of policy towards Europe, to which we shall return. But one major item of policy surfaced and came rapidly to a head in 1958. Late in 1957, the French raised in general terms the difficult question of the control of strategic exports to Communist-controlled Eastern Europe. These controls flowed naturally from the situation in the late forties when the Soviet Communist advance overwhelmed Hungary and Czechoslovakia, and it was difficult to see how far this advance was likely to go. There was no question of exporting actual arms and ammunition to Eastern Europe. But there was also strong demand by the Americans and in Western Europe for control over items which, while not being classifiable as arms or ammunition, contributed materially if indirectly to Soviet armed strength. The somewhat eccentric gift by Sir Stafford Cripps in 1946 of two Rolls-Royce Nene engines to the Soviet Government was seen as something which should not be repeated.

Accordingly the main NATO powers, including the United States, Britain, France and allied-controlled Germany, set up outside NATO a committee for controlling strategic exports to Eastern Europe. This Committee worked out in 1950 a list of such goods which was revised in 1954.

In the mid-1950s military and scientific development passed through many changes. The Soviet Union exploded its first hydrogen bomb in 1953 and achieved a world 'first' in the launching of the Sputnik in 1957. These achievements made a number of the previous restrictions look absurd. Moreover, the development of defence technology and theory had led at that time from concentration on massive conventional war to a doctrine of smaller conventional forces, less massive equipment and a great reliance on a nuclear response.

On the political side the death of Stalin in 1953 had removed the extreme feelings of tension which had prevailed since 1945. Thereafter, and particularly during the brief Malenkov interlude in 1953–54, it seemed right to think in terms of a more relaxed relationship, subject always to vigilance about the future development of Soviet doctrine and policy.

By the end of 1957 it was accepted that the 1954 strategic control rules would have to be revised. Following on the French initiative, the British Government undertook a more precise one in January 1958. I was personally involved as chairman of the Inter-departmental Committee on Strategic Controls. In this committee views naturally differed. The Board of Trade were properly anxious to promote exports and therefore to liberate as many items as possible. The services' concern was precisely the opposite, the maintenance of security. The Foreign Office was somewhere in between, concerned like the Board of Trade to increase exports, at any rate if people would pay for them, but also mindful of security and of the importance of carrying the Americans with the rest of us. This was not going to be easy, since a Republican administration, with Mr Dulles as Secretary of State, was likely to be extremely cautious about concessions to Eastern Europe.

Under my general responsibility for relations with the United States, I visited Washington in February 1958 and took the opportunity to raise the matter with Mr Douglas Dillon, at that time Under-Secretary of State. I said that opinion in Europe was getting impatient and that there was danger that, unless the Co-ordinating Committee would adapt itself to new ideas, individual countries might start making their own unwritten rules which would lead to an unfortunate breakdown of the system.

It was in due course agreed that the Co-ordinating Committee (COCOM) should attempt a revision of its lists. New criteria for definition were drawn up and between March and June the Committee went completely through the lists. At the end of this study there were still sixty-eight disagreed items. There was also a disagreement of substance. There had been three categories of control, namely embargo, quantitative restriction and a 'watchlist'. The British wanted to abolish everything except a short, clear embargo list. The Americans felt this to be dangerous and argued strongly for the retention of the watch-list for the purpose of observing developments in respect of the items on it.

To try to improve on the sixty-eight disagreed items and reconcile the policy differences, it was decided to hold a two-day high-level meeting of COCOM in Paris on 18–19 July 1958. The sessions, presided over with efficiency, patience and humour by Olivier Wormser of the French Ministry of Foreign Affairs, were like a stock exchange or auction in reverse. A disagreed item would be presented and the heads of the delegations had to decide quickly whether they could made a concession – the Americans whether they could release something or the British and Europeans whether they would continue controls on something which they would prefer to release – given the balance of concessions already made or likely to be made.

I had two great advantages, reasonably flexible instructions and a superb 'second row'. This consisted of Philip Homan of the Board of Trade and Bill Cranston of the Foreign Office. Both knew every item by heart and shared a combined sense of responsibility and desire to get on. The Americans had done some remarkable homework, and at the end of two breathless days the sixty-eight disagreed items had been reduced to three. Since the Americans had done the Europeans proud by their flexibility, the British conceded the merits and principles of a watch-list. A number of minor items and side-issues were handed back to the permanent representative who cleared them all by the end of July.

This had been an almost miraculously successful occasion, and it is worth pausing a moment to consider the reason why.

When the sittings began, it was on a basis of general identity of aim, namely, a reasonable form and degree of control, with a sufficient difference between the parties to warrant a high-level conference. Those who conferred knew their subject thoroughly, or had advisers who did. (It may seem curious, but these conditions are not always fulfilled.) There was excellent chairmanship. There was flexibility of procedure, with time being allowed for talks outside the conference itself and mobility in the conference room. But above all things, the conference took place at the right time, when both the Americans and the Europeans were simultaneously prepared not to be too dogmatic and to take advantage of this dispositon.

These are the crucial ingredients of successful conferring. The Foreign Offices of the world are apt to bore the peoples of the world by calling for 'suitable timing' and 'careful preparation' for international conferences. They are right. A shock conference can occasionally work. Sometimes international meetings take place at fixed times like the NATO Ministerial meetings in June and December or the convergence of Foreign Ministers at the time of the United Nations General Assembly; one can only hope and pray each year that this imposed timing will not be too awkward or embarrassing. But if, in a conference called for a particular purpose, you can get the various planets I have mentioned to converge, you may achieve your miracle. And despite all I have said, a slight element of the truly miraculous will outlive this earthbound analysis.

Aviation, Aid, and Other Business

One subject of great difficulty and sometimes disagreeableness was that of international civil aviation. Before my arrival the so-called General Department which dealt with international functional matters such as aviation, telecommunications and shipping had been absorbed into the Economic Relations Department. My first effort was to de-absorb them without delay. The motivations and *modalités* (as the French untranslatably call them) of these subjects are quite different from those of straight economic policy: if a department which was likely to be too large anyway took charge of both, the General Department items, however important, tended to be the Cinderella of the operation.

Re-engagement in the civil aviation field was naturally exciting, coming as it did at a time when after too much time spent over testing, Britain was trying to retrieve the Comet disaster and to develop the Britannia. But for the politically-minded official international civil aviation negotiation had its emphatically disagreeable side.

Its hard-headedness and hard-heartedness seemed total. This was an area, one was told, in which one could not afford to oblige political friends or disoblige the not so friendly. It was pointed out with ruthless logic by the airlines, supported by the Ministry of Civil Aviation, that the only way to secure much-needed commercial rights (the right to pick up and set down passengers) was to use to the full such bargaining power as we had. This consisted in control of landing rights in Britain and the British dependent territories which were then still very extensive. Our need for facilities and the financial danger of over-supply of services were, it was argued, so great that we simply could not waste any of our bargaining power in what appeared to the experts to be political charity. In our balance of payments situation there was no contesting this argument which was used equally toughly by our competitors. The best we could do was to press the marginal case and try to ensure that hard technical and financial argument did not, at least in manner, break political eggs.

Supervision of this specialist subject involved me in frequent contact with the BOAC and BEA of the time. The contact with the former was extraordinary. The Chairman of BOAC was Mr Gerald d'Erlanger and the Deputy Chairman Sir George Cribbett, a veteran of the Chicago Conference. Personal relations were always most amiable, but the Corporation was going through a period which in some ways recalled acutely the Chicago Civil Aviation Conference of 1944. As chief negotiator for BOAC, George Cribbett was inclined to disappear into bouts of total secretiveness followed by sudden requests for diplomatic support in situations which might have been avoided or at least foreseen if he had consulted us sooner.

The relationship with BEA was exactly the opposite. They always knew exactly what they wanted and were prepared to tell us. The late Lord Douglas of Kirtleside sometimes conveyed these wishes to the Office in terms of rudeness to the point of insult. I enjoyed this enormously. One knew exactly where one was and why; one could answer back in kind and if, exceptionally, there was any uncertainty one could always ring up Mr Anthony Milward and get a direct and coherent answer.

Another activity of promise and further interest was Overseas Aid. The great preponderance went to the Commonwealth and was not within the Foreign Office's competence, though there were important items under such heads as the Economic Co-operation Programme of the Central Treaty Organization,* which concerned us. Sir Paul Sinker, Director-General of the British Council, said that he would like to talk over something which, between us, we seemed to be mismanaging. There were cases in which confusion was caused to the authorities in developing countries by the British Embassy or High Commission and the British Council both offering the same technical assistance to the same organization, or the same scholarship to the same individual. So we set about forming a machine for conciliation. We were eventually authorized to form a committee under my chairmanship provided that it was firmly understood not to be a committee. This invention illustrates in one act the sensitiveness, rigidities and flexibilities of Whitehall. Suffice it to say that my non-committee eventually became the Department of Technical Co-operation under Mr Robert Carr, which later was transformed into the Overseas Development Ministry.

The formation of a committee could not, of course, settle policy with ease and despatch. The Colombo Plan in Asia and CENTO co-operation in the northern tier of the Middle East had settled into well-defined, if in the latter case modest, routines. The desirability of doing something similar in Africa was emerging. But Whitehall departmental interests and Ministerial responsibilities in Africa were sharply divided. The Commonwealth Relations Office was interested in South Africa (which did not leave the Commonwealth until 1961), Southern Rhodesia and Ghana; the Foreign Office in Ethiopia, Liberia and the dependent territories of Continental European powers; while the Colonial Office were having a difficult time in large areas of East Africa and elsewhere. My own view was that, despite these

* CTO: Originally the US, Turkey, UK, Iran, Pakistan, Iraq. Iraq withdrew after the coup d'état of 1958.

difficulties, we should boldly go for a Colombo Plan for Africa. But both fear and finance were too strong and I eventually undertook to be quiet, even in confidential discussion, if the opposition were also silent. A junior Minister broke silence and so, quite vainly, did I.

It was just at this time that my favourite prophet, Edmund Hall-Patch, emerged from Africa after a tour as Chairman of the Standard Bank of South Africa. 'My dear,' he said, 'I have channels that other people don't. These people' (with a magnificent sweep of arm over Whitehall) 'have no idea what's coming to them. And it's coming very, very soon.' Such was my private and confidential draught ushering in the wind of change.

Routine punctuated by crisis is not the whole of life, even official life. In 1950 my parents had bought at Hook Norton near Banbury a house consisting of two cottages placed L-shaped in an acre of garden. The children spent holidays there when we were in America and Burma. Later, as we worked in London, it became a week-end breath of fresh air and the scene of one family Christmas after another. From there we organized ourselves in 1958 for the first great camping tour. David, Christopher and Celia had seen America and Asia; it was time to be introduced to Europe in the only way we could afford and we set off with two borrowed igloo tents to learn camping the hard way. We took in the Brussels Expo, Luxembourg, the Lorelei Rock, an ice-cream in Switzerland, the Roman theatre at Orange (but was it built by *real* Romans?) and that most vivid of moments when the three young capered on the third tier of the Pont du Gard Roman aqueduct in the usual high wind while the parents gritted their teeth and gazed determinedly in the other direction.

There were sadnesses too, the death of my father at the end of 1958 and the sudden collapse of my brother's health in early 1959 before a cancer which could not be halted. There came in the end the regretful abandonment of Hook Norton. Had it been a little more of a dream house or a little nearer London, we might have hung on. But in 1960 we were off again abroad and my mother could not be left to live there alone. So we bade it good-bye at Easter 1960. We have passed by periodically and looked over the gate gratefully since.

Visit to Japan

Two senior civil servants briefly halted in conversation on the Horse Guards Parade constitute a quorum. Under this heading Sir Edgar Cohen, Deputy Under-Secretary of the Board of Trade, and I halted for a few important minutes in the summer of 1959 by the First World War Guards Memorial. A British General Election was coming up; so was a conference in Tokyo of the General Agreement of Trade and Tariffs. I mentioned to Edgar that Ministers might not wish to be in Japan on Election Day. In that case, I said, I would be glad to stand in and make the formal speech and the informal contacts which are the normal functions of the President of the Board of Trade at GATT conferences. I added that I was personally interested since Pat's mother was still living in Yokohama.

The personal interest turned out to be irrelevant, as Mrs Ellerton visited us instead. But the President of the Board of Trade agreed with my diagnosis and kindly asked me to go.

I travelled via Rangoon and Manila and in Tokyo I duly made the formal speech, and then went with some other delegates on a tour of Nagoya, Kyoto and Osaka. On my return to Tokyo I attended a lunch in Vere Redman's house to meet a group of British business people interested in exports to Japan. They were deeply pessimistic, saying that the personal approach to Japanese business through the giving of *geisha* parties had gone far beyond the budget of any small or middle-sized firm. Consequently there was really very little business to be done. I asked rather despairingly whether one could not give the right Japanese the right cup of coffee at the right place at the right time. A man looking at that time rather *outré* in a coloured shirt and a notable beard said that you could and he did. But, he said, there was little interest from industry at home.

On return I wrote a rather fierce memorandum. I pointed out that except for the sale of an atomic power plant, British high-level commercial effort in Japan was practically non-existent. We were doing a mere three per cent of Japan's external trade. It was not easy to get in, but the Americans (with natural advantages), Germans, Swiss, Swedes and Austrians had found it worth while. Why not the British? The post-war hangover had gone on too long. The Japanese Prime Minister, Mr Kishi, and the Foreign Minister, Mr Fujiyama, had visited Britain. And Mr Ushiba, the very able economic specialist in the Japanese Foreign Office, had urged upon me the early conclusion of a commercial treaty, over which both sides had hesitated for so long.

I recommended a high-level political visit to Japan, the early conclusion of a commercial treaty even if that meant giving up some reservations about cheap Japanese products, particularly textiles, a new industrial and commercial attitude towards exports to Japan and much greater hospitality towards Japanese visiting London. Subsequent events were remarkable. In 1961, Sir Norman Kipping, for so many years the dedicated Director-General of the (then) Federation of British Industries, paid a first visit to Japan. In 1962 a Commercial Treaty was concluded. Between 1957 and 1970 internal trade increased five and a half times. An Anglo-Japanese Committee was set up in 1963, in the framework of which the Foreign Ministers of the two countries seek to meet each other yearly in Britain and Japan alternately. Members of the Royal Family have visited Japan and re-established an historic relationship between what are now two constitutional monarchies and in 1971 the Emperor of Japan visited Britain.

Of course all this did not result from one visit or one memorandum. A necessary historical process was at work. But I happened to go to Japan at a moment when this process could be given a push. And despite all the horrors of the Siam Railway I still wonder a little at the post-war unforgivingness of the British as a whole.

Europe
At the time I returned to the Office in 1956 the question of Britain's future economic relationship with Western Europe already had a considerable history. By 1948–49 the feeling had

been present in Paris that Benelux (the Belgium, Netherlands, Luxembourg Union) might develop into a wider union. In 1950 came the launching of the Schumann Plan and the idea of a European Iron and Steel Community. The mechanics of the launching had not been happily handled and Mr Bevin had been upset by them. Moreover, if you want to interest the British in a package, you cannot do so by telling them that, if they will take your absolute principles on trust, you will then find out that the package will be to your advantage. This was so much so that even French writers have suggested that some at least of the promoters of the Plan may have wished to scare off the British for fear of the latter's predictable hedging and delaying tactics in subsequent discussion. The upshot was that when the time came to decide whether or not to join the Iron and Steel Community, the chance was let slip, less through malignity than through a kind of weary and sceptical indifference.

In the early fifties, the idea of a united Europe continued on the march. Britain in the person of Mr Eden played a notably constructive part when the idea of a European Defence Community was blocked on French opposition. But the next real test came in 1955, when the future Six, having started on economics in place of defence, clearly were making purposeful progress towards an institutional breakthrough. At this period, British officials were participating in consultations with their European colleagues.

The Six set September 1955 for a Ministerial discussion of the next, crucial step. The British Government were invited to send a Minister to be present. A Minister was not available and the offer was made to send a senior official. The Six replied that they were not interested in anyone not of Ministerial level.

I have always regarded this episode as something of an emotional turning point. It does not reflect great credit on either side. At a moment of this importance a Minister (not necessarily a senior one) should have been made available. The refusal by the Six of an official equally looked unnecessarily discourteous. If there had been a reciprocal will, there could have been a mutual way.

There was now no stopping the development of the Community. The Brussels discussion went ahead and the great moment came on 3 June 1955 at Messina, when agreement was reached on the many points which became the Treaty of Rome. An Italian colleague, not necessarily a romantic, has told me that, as they stood on the terrace overlooking the straits, they wondered at, without quite comprehending, the dynamic which had led them to an unprecedented and almost unbelievable result.

The British were not entirely convinced even now that the road from Messina would lead to Rome. But it was necessary to consider whether, assuming Britain could not join a Community, there should none the less be some response to what the Six were doing. If nothing was done Britain and other European countries would wake up one day wholly unorganized for confrontation with an embryo customs union from which they would have been excluded. Moreover, the main upholder of European economic unity, the OEEC, would be badly damaged if six of its members created a barrier between them and the remaining ten.

By the time I took up my post, the British Government had chosen as its response a plan for a European Industrial Free Trade Area. For the understanding of subsequent events it is necessary to be a little technical about this. The idea of a Free Trade Area was that manufactured goods would circulate with nil tariffs within the whole OEEC area, and thus between the six and the remainder. The United Kingdom would thus be taking the risk of opening its market freely to manufactured goods from German, French and other European industries. But this was a limited concession because arrangements within the Commonwealth could expose European goods coming to Britain to a kind of competition which British goods entering the Common Market would not suffer. The objection was also raised that goods coming into Europe from outside would come in to the free trade area country with the lowest external tariff and then be forwarded to any other destination within the free trade area without paying the difference. This objection consumed a great deal of time, though wartime experience had shown that mechanisms could be created to cope with it.

Agriculture was omitted from the British plan and the omission was buttressed by strong arguments of Commonwealth and domestic interest. Yet if the proposed Free Trade Area were to exclude free (i.e. tariff free) circulation of agricultural goods, the vitally important if markedly less efficient agricultural economies of France and, even more, Germany would derive no benefit from the plan, and Italian fruit and vegetables would also fail to profit. Thus the doctrine on which the Free Trade Area proposals were based had from the start some anti-incentives for members of the future community.

The period 1956–60 divided itself neatly into two. The first lasted from the launching in 1956 to the breakdown in December 1958 of the Free Trade Area proposal. The second lasted from the launching in early 1959 of the proposal for the European Free Trade Association (EFTA) of seven non-members of the Six to the effort thereafter to get back on to some reasonably friendly basis with the Six after the estrangement of the mid-fifties.

When I found myself confronted by European questions, I badly needed education in the change of economic circumstances in Europe since 1949, when I had last been familiar with the details, and this high-level apprenticeship took longer than was ideal. It is a distinction between political and economic work that a trained diplomatic observer can usually absorb the essentials of quite a detailed political argument in a very short time; the faculties required are quick comprehension and sound judgement. In economic work, there are no short cuts. If mathematical and statistical material is involved, there are no paragraphs which can be skipped without the thread of argument being lost.

The department was well-informed and competent. But, with hindsight, I feel that neither we nor our posts in Europe had quite caught the wind of change that was blowing through the Community countries at that time. What should have been clear was that, whereas up to to, say, 1955, it had been assumed that a radical economic reorganization of Western Europe would not be possible without the participation of Britain, the only major OEEC country not overwhelmed by defeat or occupation, the Messina meeting had changed all that. Certainly there would be a wish to go ahead with rather than against Britain if possible. But from the moment of the signature in 1957 of the Treaty of Rome, the preservation and development of that Treaty would have at least for a time a total priority in the external economic policy of the signatories.

After a series of talks in the first half of 1957 with individual countries of the Six, it became clear that, if the Free Trade Area proposals were to have a chance, we should have to add to our normal inter-departmental machine a proper negotiating set-up, something which would have been known later as a task force. Accordingly in August 1957 a special section was set up in Gwydyr House in Whitehall under Mr Reginald Maudling as Paymaster-General supported by John Coulson[4] and a small but expert staff. Some progress was made. But the Six, primarily concerned with building up their own institutions and settling their own practices and procedures, greeted the prospect of a new negotiation with at best *ennui* and at the worst suspicion.

In the first months of 1958, political crisis deepened in France and there was a desire on the British part, perhaps more laudable than wise, to relax the pressure while things sorted themselves out. But there seemed to be informal agreement in May 1958, at the time of the de Gaulle take-over, that during the summer the Six would do some real homework in order to be ready for the opening of detailed sessions in the autumn. A note received from the French Government in the summer was very negative in tone, but was not regarded as invalidating the agreed procedure.

When the autumn came, it was found that the Six had done little or no collective homework after all, and the situation was rapidly approaching a showdown. Four days of meetings were arranged to take place in Paris on Thursday and Friday, 17 and 18 November, and the subsequent Tuesday and Wednesday. As the main negotiations were in the hands of Mr Maudling's group,

[4] Sir John Coulson, Secretary-General of EFTA in 1965–72, was Ambassador to Sweden, 1960–63, Deputy Under-Secretary of State at the Foreign Office, 1963–65, when he was also Chief of Administration of the Diplomatic Service.

it was not necessary for the Foreign Office as such to take a principal role in the Paris meetings. But Denis Wright,[5] the Assistant Under-Secretary, and I went alternatively to important meetings as political advisers. Denis was designated for these particular sessions.

On November 18, before returning to London for the weekend, Mr Maudling gave a lunchtime talk in Paris to the Anglo-American Press Association in which he expressed cautious hopes of progress. Simultaneously the French Minister of Information, M. Jacques Soustelle, was saying in a somewhat offhand manner at a press conference that of course there was no prospect whatever of the Free Trade Area proposals being agreed. The effect on the British was one of total consternation. The matter of the statement was bad enough; the offhand manner, before we had realized that we were in a period of elaborate discourtesy, made the mood far worse.

When the delegation returned to London the same evening, I was in the country, visiting my father who was very ill. It was in fact the last time I saw him before he died. Denis rang me up and said that, after prolonged thought, the delegation had arrived at the conclusion that they simply could not return to Paris for the remaining scheduled meetings. I remember feeling one of those bumps at the pit of my stomach. I wondered whether this was really right, and whether we should not have gone back and blandly sat waiting for apologies and explanations. Later I met European colleagues who wished that we had done this. But it is worth remembering that, while this might have gained a debating point, the result would not have been different.

What was arranged was that the Ministers of all the OEEC countries would meet in Paris on 5 December to review the situation. The meeting which would be held in private would last for one whole day but not more. The Chairman would be Mr Derek Heathcote-Amory, the Chancellor of the Exchequer, and the chief British spokesman, Sir David Eccles, President of

[5] Sir Denis Wright was Ambassador to Ethiopia, 1959–62, and to Iran, 1963–71.

the Board of Trade. The French would be represented by their Foreign Minister, M. Couve de Murville, the Germans by Dr Erhard, then Minister of Economics. The meeting had to be decisive for the future direction of policy.

This turned out to be unquestionably the worst conference I have ever attended. The meeting started with the presentation by M. Couve de Murville of a resolution recommending the closest relations between the European Community and the Free Trade Area. This was one of those too clever pieces of diplomacy which irritated everybody, including the remainder of the Six. The proposal assumed with a blandness of wording that the question we had come to discuss, whether the Community would take part in the proposed Free Trade Area, had already been decided in the negative. The British delegation, who had prepared themselves for various eventualities but not this one, could not, in the time, give any decisively constructive turn to the debate, and frank speaking by Sir David Eccles only caused M. Couve de Murville to say he would not negotiate under threats and to walk out of the meeting.

The embarrassed Five tried to rescue the situation by working out and introducing an amended resolution on behalf of the Six. This would not have satisfied the Free Trade Area proponents, but would at least have taken the sting out of the Couve de Murville draft and might in other circumstances have led to progress. But tempers were by now thoroughly roused. No rapprochement seemed possible in the plenary session, and limited talks of great length in which the Germans and Americans took part failed to bring relief. I did my best to see whether any middle-of-the-roaders on either side, like the Italians or the Danes, could do anything to help. But the Italians were at the time very close to the French and unable to move and in any case time was too short. At the resumed plenary, recrimination broke out again, and eventually the chairman, at my suggestion, made an appeal for a dignified and conciliatory conclusion. As the delegates parted, some of them were hardly saying good night to each other.

Why was this gathering such a shambles? First it had to take place at a particularly unfavourable moment, preceding developments having left the Governments with no freedom of manoeuvre. There had been much study of the subject but no possibility of agreeing on how to handle the meeting so that proceedings began with a shot-gun draft resolution. The parties were not converging unless by converging was meant a collision course.

Such a background was bad enough. But even this kind of situation can be cushioned if the physical conditions are right. But they were not. An absolute *sine qua non* of such a conference, particularly a high-level one, is freedom of movement by the second and third rows. (NATO understands this very well and provides for it.) Many a dangerous development can be forestalled by the little note or verbal message from A to B, saying anything from 'Our delegation is stuck; can you help?' to 'How about a cup of coffee?' But the Conference Hall of the Château de la Muette, hitherto so satisfactory, simply could not cope with the inundation of top brass with expert retinues, so that any attempt to move around was totally frustrated and rear rank conciliation practically out of the question. Some of the delegations, including our own, were a bit overwhelmed by their own size, and the long waits endured by normally over-busy people increased the already massive irritation.

Even so, there is still one other possible healer – time. But governments had grown impatient and had given themselves the inside of a day. This was hopelessly short, and after the first few minutes the conference hardly had a chance. Perhaps, given our later knowledge of the methods and convictions of General de Gaulle, one must conclude that it never had a chance anyway. But its inbuilt defects themselves assured failure, and one could only sympathize with the Secretary-General, M. René Sergent, whose patient efforts at conciliation had ended so badly.

So the Free Trade Area initiative broke down with a crash and in some bitterness not so much between individuals or even between governments in their bilateral relations as between the Six as an institution and those outside who felt that the Free Trade Area initiative, however misconceived, had been rejected without explanation or even courtesy. This feeling of bitterness pervaded the atmosphere for the next year or more.

After Christmas 1958, it became urgently necessary to consider in Whitehall what, if anything, should be done next. On the bilateral front there were trade negotiations to be picked up, notably the renewal of our agreement with France. On the multilateral side, we were faced with the immediate question of whether we should leave things as they were, or look for means to foster or even institutionalize co-operation among the proponents of the European Free Trade Area, who had shown a striking unity in the final Paris debate.

I led the British delegation in talks in the Quai d'Orsay in which the French team was led by Olivier Wormser. This was a straight haggle between the two countries about quotas of goods which were sensitive in terms, mainly, of mutual competition. Each side wanted to export more automobiles to the other; we wanted the French to take more whisky, and they in turn wanted us to take more wine, flowers and fruit.

Again I had excellent support, notably from the remarkable Miss Moira Dennehy from the Board of Trade. Through a perpetual cloud of cigarette smoke Miss Dennehy spotted anomalies in French customs arrangements which the French negotiators had not perceived themselves. In the middle of the negotiations, a characteristic minor tragedy occurred when the British Government, no doubt forgetting about its negotiating team in Paris, increased overnight the duty on cut flowers. Next morning one of our French colleagues came in complaining with sonorous justice, '*Hélas, mes pauvres anémones!*' But agreement was in the mutual interest and we reached it.

At the end Hugh Ellis-Rees, our resident Ambassador to the OEEC, and I had a quiet brood with Wormser in his office overlooking the Seine. There was no mutual reproach but we reflected over whether there was any European substitute for what had failed. We tried out, as many did before and after, the concept of a preferential tariff area for Europe which would leave the Six with their Customs Union and their unified tariff and put the rest of us in a favourable tariff position. But this fell down, as always, on the objections that the GATT rules, while permitting out-and-out customs unions of Free Trade Areas, forbade the creation of new preferential systems. We looked rather glumly through the bare trees to the Elysée Palace, the official Residence of the French President. 'It will all depend on what comes from over there,' said Wormser.

On the multilateral front the question which posed itself to the British Government was whether the countries which would have been ready to join in a Free Trade Area with the Community would be prepared to join, for instance, in a Free Trade Area with each other. And if they were willing, would the enterprise be worth while?

This was the theme of a top level official meeting held under the chairmanship of Roger Makins. The question contained an important emotional element. If we felt that we should go ahead, were we merely wanting to hit back at the Six for the sake of hitting back? One by one round the table we found ourselves unanimously in favour of recommending to Ministers that we should explore this idea of a European free trade grouping of such members of the OEEC other than the Six who wished to join. Taking this view I myself was influenced in part by indications that there were similar feelings in Stockholm. One of the great virtues of the OEEC had been the bringing back of the Swedes with their competence, expertise and high quality industry into Europe. After the departure in 1953 of Dag Hammerskjöld to New York to be Secretary-General of the United Nations, the Swedes had tended to fade away again into an Arctic twilight. A Free Trade initiative with their active participation should reverse this tendency. There was also for us and for some others the harder-boiled national consideration that, if there were no organization of the non-community members of the OEEC, individual members might well disappear, economically and commercially, into an area from which Britain would be excluded.

The project realized itself with astonishing speed. Under the leadership of Hubert de Besch of Sweden and John Coulson, negotiations proceeded through the spring and in June 1959 a project was submitted to the Ministers of seven countries. A draft Convention was initialled in November. It is pleasant to record that when, in 1965, Frank Figgures[6] of the Treasury, the first Secretary-General, had done five years of distinguished service, there was a unanimous demand for John Coulson to succeed him.

This remarkable performance was only clouded in two ways. For reasons which I have never quite fathomed, the press took against the EFTA idea. No doubt it was a lesser substitute for the frustrated European Industrial Free Trade Area and no substitute at all for an enlarged European Community. No doubt it lacked the balance of larger proposals and left Britain despite its foreign exchange crisis an excessive preponderance in an unbalanced group. But in fact the EFTA initiative was positive and by no means unimaginative; it was also personally and politically heart-warming, and led to a great expansion of trade between the members.

The other point, unsatisfactory to us, which the formation of EFTA again brought out was the curious insensitivity of the American Administration to the problem which these European developments presented to us. It was entirely acceptable that the Americans should put their full weight of policy and senti-ment behind the European Community. To them this meant revived economies, political strength and the realization of an ideal. The possibility that a united Europe behind a common external tariff might present balance of payments problems to the United States still seemed distant enough not to weigh in the balance against all-out support.

Against this clear and immediate background, the complexities of the British situation and the hesitancies of British policy stimulated neither comprehension nor sympathy. The Community was a right thing, and the British should see this and use their political ingenuity and diplomatic skill to find a way in somehow.

[6] Sir Frank Figgures, Director of Trade and Finance, OEEC, 1948–51; Secretary-General to EFTA, 1960–65; Second Permanent Secretary to the Treasury, 1965–68; Director-General, NEDC, 1971–73, and Chairman of the Pay Board, 1973.

The Commonwealth, a baffling concept in American eyes, seemed an unreal distraction from the obvious course. To the British, however, with most of Africa not yet independent, the dilemma was real and obvious.

The European Industrial Free Trade Area was not the only casualty of December 1958. So long as the sixteen members of the OEEC maintained an individual equality in the organization, so long could it transact business without hesitation or inhibition. The moment that six members, including two of the most important, began to feel an obligation to speak with one voice and to adopt policies aggressively different from what the rest could accept, hesitation and inhibition began to appear. The 'Europeans' and the French Gaullists for their different reasons were not particularly sorry. To the Europeans a sixteen-member organization of countries with many differing political and economic objectives was either a brake on progress towards true unity or a respectable waste of time. To the Gaullists a small organization, which, as they assumed, France could dominate, was preferable to a large one in which the British could be expected to thwart at least some essentially French purposes. Gradually from 1956, and much more rapidly after the collapse of the Free Trade Area enterprise, the OEEC began to lose its significance.

This politico-economic development was reinforced by other economic trends. Apart from the distribution of American aid, much of the life-blood of the early OEEC had flowed from the work of technical committees, charged with promoting the production and fair distribution of goods and services scarce in the initial post-war period but now in abundant supply. The conclusion from this could have been that the organization should be brought to an end. But this would have meant cold-blooded destruction of an expert and experienced body, and Governments preferred to think in terms of transformation. So on 21 December 1959, the heads of government of the United States, Britain, France and the Federal Republic of Germany issued a declaration to the effect that a new organization should be set up which would have the United States and Canada as full members and should among other things further the development of the less developed countries. A meeting of Ministers of thirteen OEEC countries followed this by agreeing on a Resolution to set up a 'group of four persons' acting in their independent capacities to draw up plans, including, if they thought it appropriate, a draft international instrument for consideration by governments. The next day, 14 January 1960, a meeting of twenty ministers of member-countries of the OEEC and countries associated with it and a representative of the European Economic Commission approved the resolution. On 28 January the four persons held their first meeting and on 7 April they presented their report, including a draft convention. Even in complicated economic matters, governments can sometimes move quite fast.

It was agreed that the group should consist of members from the United States, Britain and France and one of the smaller countries. For the latter, the Greeks were very quick off the mark and put forward a first-class name in Professor Xenophon Zelotas, Governor of the Bank of Greece. The Americans appointed Mr W. Randolph Burgess, US Ambassador to NATO, the French M. Bernard Clappier, at that time Under-Secretary in the Ministry of Commerce. On the British side, the failure of the Free Trade Area enterprise and the success of the EFTA negotiations had somewhat diminished the working pace in the Foreign Office, and I was invited by the Government to represent the United Kingdom. Inevitably, amid loud disclaimers, we became 'Four Wise Men', a description without either scriptural warrant or, we felt, current validity. But at least it was a very congenial foursome.

I lived in Paris for about six weeks from February to April 1960, in a small apartment in the Avenue Kléber, owned by relatives of the late Chaliapin. We heard evidence from all OEEC countries, from a number of international economic organizations and, unofficially, from a few distinguished individuals like M. Paul-Henri Spaak. It soon became apparent that the emphasis of the future work of any organization would have to be on economics and, in the widest sense, finance. The Italians,

I

with Southern Italy no doubt in mind, laid special stress on development, and once they had suggested inclusion of the word 'development' in the title, there was, despite the suspicions of the British Treasury, no alternative to putting it in.

In the writing of our report Mr Zelotas took over the financial chapter, I dealt with history and miscellaneous items. Mr Burgess, an admirably patient chairman, performed the particular service of persuading his government that an organization working by unanimity could afford to retain the OEEC power of decision. We felt it important, also, to leave the door open for commerce, since finance and development could not be discussed without it. But there were known to be French suspicions on this front, and the drafting of a chapter was entrusted to the quietly ingenious Bernard Clappier. After a time he came back with the shortest introductory speech on record: 'Please don't alter a word if you can help it.' We didn't.

When we reported after just over two months we commended to member governments a complete new look for OEEC, and appended a new draft convention. A convention based closely on our draft was signed on 14 December.

One can never foresee accurately the result of an enterprise of this kind. We (or those of us who pressed for it) may have been over-optimistic in hoping that a specifically trade function could be retained by OECD; nor have the powers of decision transmitted from the old organization to the new proved as important as seemed possible. But on the finance and development side we had foreseen correctly. Despite the European origin of the new body, the title which imposed itself upon us, Organization for Economic Co-operation and Development, did not contain the word 'European'. We had felt that a future organization would have to be more than a purely European agency with North American associates. It would have to include machinery for organized co-operation with other main manufacturers and aid-donors in the mixed economy, non-Communist world, such as Japan. We were also right in expecting continuous importance to attach to economic reviews. These have maintained a high standard and have incidentally been revealing about the

British economy, not always to the comfort of British Governments. Any fear that such activity would obstruct or duplicate the work of the existing, world-wide organizations such as the International Bank and Fund has proved groundless. The tenth anniversary was celebrated in December 1970 in an atmosphere of confidence and with a formal declaration looking forward particularly to a wider scope for development co-operation in the 1970s.

In the spring of 1960 there was a growing feeling in Whitehall that the time had come to take some conscious step towards changing the sultry atmosphere hanging over relations between the Six and the Seven. But since the Six had much to work out among themselves, we felt that, if there were any more to be made, it would have to be by us. In any case, it was desirable to show that EFTA was not a small-scale hostile reprisal to a major imaginative enterprise, especially as the Stockholm Convention pointed towards a wider European Community in the future.

It was exciting to be working on this problem in one mind with that great public servant Sir Frank Lee, now Secretary of the Treasury, who in big questions always found it natural to think above and beyond departmental interests. Out of this process came accord between ministers and officials that, before the summer Parliamentary recess, a major speech should be made in the House of Commons, bringing the public position of the British Government up to date.

It fell to Mr Selwyn Lloyd to make the speech, his last speech as Foreign Secretary, on 25 July. It was one of considerable length and complexity. He began by recognizing the need for political and economic unity in Europe, spoke warmly of the Community and, on Britain's position, said, '. . . if Britain were to be regarded as outside Europe, we could not fulfil our complete role in the world. Nor do I believe that Europe would be complete without us.' He listed the main British reservations vis-à-vis the Community – the Commonwealth connection and the free entry of Commonwealth goods, the difference between British and Community agricultural policy, difficulties about commercial

policy and about international institutions, but presented these
not as insolubles but as difficult problems. The Six, Mr Lloyd
recognized, were 'not at present prepared to discuss long-term
solutions'. At the same time, quoting a resolution in the Committee for the United States of Europe that Britain and other
countries should become members of the community, he said,
'I think it would help if we could be given some indication of the
attitude of the Six towards the special problems I have mentioned.'
Altogether the speech showed a new mood and a new approach
even if many of the positions taken up were positions from which
there would later have to be retreat.

The effect of this speech was to give the incoming team at
the Foreign Office, Lord Home and Mr Edward Heath, some
freedom of manoeuvre. The Government could, over the next
year, choose whether to stand pat on previous policies or to
change ground, up to and including an attempt to join the Community. In terms of our politico-economic relations with Europe,
it was at least a constructive end to what, despite some successes,
had been a disappointing period.

Thus my service in the Office from 1956 to 1960 ended with a
feeling of some accomplishment over Europe after all. The
question remains, could we have done better over Europe?
With hindsight, of course we could. We could have understood
quicker and reacted earlier. In that event the tone of relations
with the European Community by 1960 might have been more
cordial but I doubt whether events themselves would have
been greatly different. The inertias in the early and mid-fifties
were to my mind too great for us to have got in on the European
ground floor. There was an immense load of them – reaction
to the unhappy presentation of the Schumann Plan, the indifference
of the British iron and steel industry to the European Iron and
Steel Community, a certain insensitivity to the momentum of
the European idea, the existence of large dependent areas of the
Commonwealth in Africa, South-East Asia and the Caribbean,
the claims of efficient domestic and Old Commonwealth agriculture, and the attraction of the Commonwealth idea whether as
a source of imports and a market for exports, or as a political and

cultural ideal to the exclusion of others.* All those things continued to converge on public and political opinion and to convince
it that to add to other national problems a plunge into a European
Community would be visionary and irresponsible.

But, as we have seen, 1960 pointed the way to a new stage
of the journey. It was only to be a stage, since it ended with an
ironic echo of a phrase made famous by another French general,
'*Ils ne passeront pas.*'

* I do not include our relationship with the United States. This relationship
would remain special anyway. But whatever course we took, our influence
with the United States would decline. If we remained separate from Europe
our voice would carry that much less weight. If we joined the Community,
we would be speaking as one among many.

India

1960-1965

In July 1959, the Permanent Under-Secretary, Sir Frederick Hoyer-Millar, sent for me and said, 'About your future – would you like to be the official candidate for appointment as High Commissioner in India?' Malcolm MacDonald's appointment was coming to an end in the autumn of 1960. There was likely to be a General Election in the autumn of 1959, and it was not possible to say whether a newly elected Government would want a political or a civil service High Commissioner in Delhi. Meantime it was necessary to propose an official candidate. The Commonwealth Service had no one of comparable Asian experience available, and Derick had been asked to sound me.

I said I felt this was a great and surprising compliment which I would of course gladly accept.

In September I was told that the Government had accepted me as the official nominee. In October the Conservatives were returned to power again, and in November when in Tokyo for the GATT Conference I received a telegram saying that I should regard myself as designated for the post. This was immensely exciting. But it introduced a period of some strain. When a new appointment is made, it is a good principle to keep it confidential as long as possible, simply because the moment the appointment is announced, the existing holder however eminent or popular becomes the 'retiring' Ambassador or High Commissioner, and people locally begin to say, 'Oh, we thought you'd gone.' So, since Malcolm MacDonald would not be leaving India until October 1960, Pat and I would have to sit on our secret some nine months.

This had one very sad result. We were looking forward more

than anything to having long talks with Lord and Lady Mount-batten about India but had conscientiously 'stayed away' until my appointment could be announced. Then, with a sickening suddenness, we read in the newspaper of 20 February 1960, that Lady Mountbatten had suddenly died on a tour of South-East Asia. Her overtaxed strength had finally given way and a great link with India had gone.

We sat on our secret until one May morning in 1960 when Harry Hodson, then editor of the *Sunday Times*, rang up Pat and began, 'As you are going to India . . .' Pat rang me up in surprise and alarm. But everyone agreed that there was nothing to be done or said; to 'refuse to confirm or deny' means these days to confirm. At least Harry had not acquired the information through us. So the Government of India were hurriedly informed (the formal process of seeking agreement was not insisted on in the Commonwealth family) and on May 17 the announcement was made.

We wanted to make, before publication, a private announce-ment to our family. Santha Rama Rao's theatre version of E. M. Forster's *Passage to India* was running in London and we took David, Christopher and Celia to see it. On returning home we told an astonished family why we had chosen this play.

Premature announcement had one advantage. Prime Minister Jawaharlal Nehru was coming to London in June and any anxiety lest meeting him should lead to premature publicity was now removed. His sister, Mrs Vijayalakshmi ('Nan') Pandit, was Indian High Commissioner in London, and through her we had a pleasant family introduction to the great man. On a hot summer afternoon he was sitting in a cool dark corner of the small recep-tion room of the Indian High Commission residence. His greeting was, 'So you are to be our guests?' It was a kindly welcome and Panditji* later told Mountbatten that he would keep Pat and my-self 'under friendly scrutiny', appreciating, I think, that events had

---

* The suffix 'ji' (pronounced 'jee') is a neat Indian method of expressing respect. Lal Bahadur Shastri became in due course 'Shastriji' and so on; 'Pan-ditji' was better than 'Nehruji' since 'Pandit' also indicates respect. The process of earning the suffix is entirely informal.

put us into a political dimension in which we had not worked before. In 1961 events placed something of a strain on the 'friendliness', but I do not think we ever quite forfeited it.

Mr Nehru talked about agriculture. It was an odd conversation to look back on later, for while Nehru had a great feeling of affection for the people of the vast Indian countryside, the nuts and bolts of agriculture seemed to have for him much less appeal than the romance of dams, hydro-electric power and new, large scale factories. Agriculture was something his ministers had to take over, and it was only after his death that the green revolution followed.

Despite the year's warning, it had been very very difficult to rehearse even privately for India. Economic work had been extremely concentrated, and even after Mr Lloyd's speech of 25 July, there had been much tidying up to do. I managed to re-read Kipling's *Kim*, still much the best pocket magnifying glass through which to look at North India, and I had, like all my generation, lived very consciously with all the phases of the Indian independence struggle. But there was so much to learn and I could have done with much more time to study.

After a short family holiday in Devon and the usual briefings, including a profitable day with Malcolm MacDonald, we set off by air for Gibraltar to catch the P&O liner *Arcadia*. It was so full that we had only been able to get very moderate accommodation.

From Bombay onward leisurely progress ceased. We were rushed in the early morning from ship to airport, arrived in Delhi in mid-morning; and directly after lunch I was presiding over a meeting in the High Commission to discuss with Buckingham Palace officials the final arrangements for the visit by the Queen in two months' time.

The pace continued. We arrived on a Thursday. On the Sunday Mr Nehru was officially opening the public sector Heavy Electricals plant near Bhopal, being built with British Government aid and technical help from Associated Electrical Industries. He had invited us to attend. The Indians, like the Burmese, made arrangements for me to present credentials at once. The short carriage drive, the inspection of the guard in the courtyard and the courtesies in the *Rashtrapati Bhavan* (President's House) recalled much of the best standards of the British tradition. We can be proud of these legacies without being nostalgic; Indians can also be proud of having accepted them and made them their own.

The pace continued as I paid calls on the Prime Minister, who was his own Foreign Minister, and on top officials of the Ministry. We then braced ourselves to an early morning flight to Bhopal in, we were told, the Prime Minister's special Ilyushin. Somebody tactful on the Indian side evidently intervened; we took off in the Prime Minister's special Viscount, and I travelled with Mr Nehru in his cabin. When we landed a tiny little man in a Gandhi cap came to greet us. It was the Minister of Commerce, Lal Bahadur Shastri.

We were taken to a large amphitheatre, containing some twenty-five thousand people. Mr Shastri opened the proceedings in Hindi and I was asked to say a few words. I spoke, in English, for literally three minutes, starting by saying I had never addressed more than six hundred people before. This to my surprise got a laugh; I had not thought there would be so many who understood. Then the Prime Minister spoke in Hindi, making generous allusion to AEI's help and going on to talk about economic development. We toured the great plant, still in very embryo stage, and had a lunch at which Mr Nehru told us the story of Arjun* and advised us not to get the 'pan' habit (chewing a green leaf in which are wrapped spices including betel which made the mouth temporarily bright red). He added: 'You must come to my Sunday School later.' So at sunset we sat in the front of an immense audience which poured quietly in from the country round about. He talked to them in the gloaming as intimately as you can talk to so many people at once. He was obviously improvising, and tantalizingly so, since I could not then – and

---

* The battlefield dialogue in poetic form between the warrior Arjun and the Lord Krishna constitutes the Bhagavad Gita (Song of the Lord) a basic text of Hindu philosophy. It covers human motivation in its many aspects and more particularly the conflict of pacifism and the obligation in certain circumstances to fight.

never did – find anyone who could give me a simultaneous
translation. (Later I learned enough Hindi to follow his theme
if not his text.) We flew, tired and virtuous, back to Delhi. As
we left, Shastri said to me in his thin attractive voice, 'Excuse me,
please do not misunderstand me, you did not speak like an
official but like a politician.' It was a heart-warming compliment
and a happy start to the 'friendly scrutiny'.

If later events, procedures and atmospheres are to be understood
we must now stand still and look around. A British High Commissioner had to make up his mind about the effect and influence
of the British past. And it was necessary to achieve some comprehension of the personalities and influences in the Indian present.

In forming any view about India it is important to remember
that from 1192 AD, when Prince Prithviraj was defeated and
killed in battle outside Delhi by the advancing Muslims, until
1947 there had never been a Hindu-controlled India. Some
rulers, notably the rulers of Jaipur and Jodhpur in the north and
others in the extreme south, had managed even at the height of
the Moghul Empire to secure non-interference. But the sub-
continent was in essence Muslim controlled and Moghul power
only began to be seriously threatened after the death in 1707
of the Emperor Aurangzib.

It so happened that this weakening of central power in India
coincided with a period of great economic expansion in Europe,
where Britain and France had emerged as the main rivals, and it is
by no means absurd to see the subsequent British Empire in
India as one of the great climaxes in the Anglo-French struggle
projected overseas.

As Moghul authority receded, defending itself with more
skill than resources, the continent suffered constant depredation
and lawlessness, and it was not until General Lake captured
Delhi in 1801 that decisive British authority over India began.
The next period was one of relative content, known as the 'English
peace'. The canals and highways of the Moguls were reopened, the
Grand Trunk Road reconstituted and the beginnings of just
administration and English-style education were laid. British
colonels in remoter outposts administered justice, hunted tigers

and studied, drew and painted the landscape, the animals, the flowers and the birds.

The mid-Victorians were in more of a hurry. India must be made strong externally against the growing menace of expanding Russia and more efficient internally against corruption and mismanagement. It was a forward policy supported by a military establishment which had lost nothing in bravery but a great deal in understanding, so the old forces of religious and national tradition swelled in protest and in 1857 the Mutiny exploded.

The Mutiny was indeed a mutiny and not a conscious and forward-looking national uprising. It was conservative in ideology and it was fortunate for India that the British were victorious. But, equally, the Mutiny was not devoid of national origins, and the British never quite recovered from it. More conciliatory policies followed, of which the founding by Allan Octavian Hume in 1885 of the Indian National Congress was a logical and humane offshoot. Little could it be realized at the time that something had been born which would become stronger than the post-Mutiny British themselves.

In this period also was born that strange phenomenon of British society in the non-white countries of the Empire, the social segregation of the races. It is a phenomenon which increasingly hurt the people of the country and which becomes, as the years go by, increasingly difficult for later generations to understand. In 1869 the Suez Canal was opened. From then on the journey from Britain to India was a safe one lasting three weeks instead of a dangerous one of three months, and it became much easier to establish British family life in India. It was not perhaps surprising that in a country of such a different climate, language, religion and way of life British civilian and military wives should have gravitated into a self-sufficient society. Yet it was a great failure of effort and foresight, a failure which Latin colonizers have not committed, a failure not just by wives but, with honourable exceptions, by at least two generations of Britons of both sexes. Their successors have had a hard time picking up the pieces.

We need not relive here the 1920s and '30s. We can say that

with their conflicts and friendships, their chivalries and their
stupidities, these years were peculiarly Indian-British phenomena
into which the outside world did not intrude. On the one hand a
Viceroy, on being told he could not bring an Indian friend to an
exclusive British Club in Bombay, founded a club of his own,
the Willingdon Club, which outlives its exclusive rival; and when
Mahatma Gandhi was ill British authority agreed tacitly to look
the other way while sundry friends 'wanted' by authority
visited him in his confinement. On the other side, one sultry day
in Amritsar in 1919, after some peculiarly nasty riots accompanied
by deaths, destruction and rape, the British Commander, General
Dyer, surrounded a crowd in Jillianwallahbagh, a large enclosed
space with only a few very narrow exits. Believing he was saving
the Punjab from chaos, he gave his troops the order to fire
on a crowd, including women and children, that could not
escape. He did not change history but he won waverers to the
nationalist cause and became a symbol for the more bitter elements
of the struggle.

In the end, after the British had rightly held on for the duration of the war, Mr. Attlee took the great decision that we must
go and that, under the management of Lord Mountbatten, we
should go with the utmost speed. Friendly Indians have said we
went too fast. The thought is kindly, but, in my view, mistaken.
The decision once made, the right course was to go without delay.
And if the end was accompanied by tragedy which Gandhi
diminished but nobody could prevent, at least there was no
tragedy between India and Britain, and the new era began with
fair prospects of good relations.

This, with such brevity as almost to constitute a parody, is the
background against which a British High Commissioner worked.
A fierce left-wing professor once greeted me at one of our own
parties with the comment, 'You poor man, with the weight of
the Empire on your shoulders.' I could reply crisply, without
too much stretching of conscience, 'Yes, it is an advantage.'

In 1960 and for the next three and a half years India continued
to reflect to an astonishing degree one man, Pandit Jawarharlal
Nehru, its first Prime Minister. Astonishing because to an extent

for which they are not always given credit, the Indians maintained fully democratic institutions. Yet within this framework, one man stood alone. And as the plane bringing the British party in 1964 to attend his funeral circled Delhi airport, I remember reflecting that, for me as for countless others, not only the state of India but the detail of India reflected or somehow expressed this one man.

When I subsequently wrote some reflections on Nehru, I described him as 'infinitely the most distinguished man in India'. This was the one way in which I could arrive at the essence. For Nehru was, by mathematical reckoning, a highly fallible mortal. He was neither an orderly administrator nor a particularly effective orator. He had some odd and not always very helpful friendships and sometimes tended to avoid problems, internal or external, with a laugh or a turn in another direction. He could be, at his worst, superficial, peevish and occasionally unworthy. And yet he inspired the most remarkable devotion, and the gap when he left was felt continuously and intimately all over his country and beyond. Why?

First, his appearance. Nobody ever suggested that he looked 'like' anyone else. The fine straight nose, the curling lower lip expressive of anything from gaiety to petulance were both unique. The effect was always enhanced by an elegance of appearance which, for all its simplicity, was carefully managed; there was always the small rosebud in the buttonhole of the *achkan*. A Gandhi cap added an air of jauntiness which took twenty years off his appearance.

And then he embodied a tremendous past. He was the quiet reserved boy at Harrow, son of a rich and fashionable Allahabad family. By lonely thought and conviction he had arrived at the desperate conclusion that he must dedicate his life and, what is often forgotten, his immense capacity for work, to the cause of the independence of his country. In this sacrifice, in which after much agony, his family joined him, he passed eleven whole years in prison. During those years he was able to think out what he had done and why. I shall never forget the impression made on me by his early books. This was no Oxford Union orator, but someone who had tried to think out the great problems of his country with passion and had ended with little real malice. Perhaps in later years there was a kind of self-indulgence, leading to occasional lapses of good temper and good taste. There were certainly self-deceptions and evasions of unwelcome reality. But, more important than all these, there was always a rapport with the people as a whole and the weaknesses could be forgiven as part of a life of such magnitude and devotion.

In the conduct of external politics, Nehru as Prime Minister must be given the great credit of bringing into operation the concept of a Republic within the Commonwealth which saved the Commonwealth from disruption. (There were those in India who welcomed the idea as a method of keeping Britain separated from the United States, but I am sure there was a positive side to Nehru's concept.) He was also the author of the doctrine of non-alignment, a much better and more flexible philosophy than neutrality, since it enabled an adherent to approximate to one side in the ideological struggle on one point and the other on another, according to the merits of the case. Unhappily, largely because of the views and behaviour of some of India's associates in the non-aligned group, the concept lost some of its credibility. Nehru's own professions seemed to give the East the benefit of a doubt not accorded to the West. Whatever he may have said privately to the Russians, and he was reported to have been bolder than others, it was dispiriting to run into extenuations of the Soviet renewal of nuclear testing in the atmosphere and the construction of the Berlin wall which would not have been allowed to the rest of us. This was not non-alignment but a double standard.

Writers of political autobiography describe Nehru as one of their most difficult 'opposite numbers'. He could be a man of moods to a degree that made business difficult. He did not shirk seeing people if they had a claim on him, but he was quite capable of being there in the flesh – and saying nothing at all. As time went on I used to warn people, particularly those like British business leaders, with whom Nehru had little in common, that if they asked for an interview they must realize they were running the risk of this silent treatment. On other occasions he could be relaxed, humorous and understanding.

There was constant speculation about what would happen when his increasingly lone figure left the scene and the Congress Party came to its inevitable division.

The British High Commissioner in Delhi lives in just the right place. When independence came, the British could have had any building they liked as a High Commissioner's residence, including a selection of Maharajahs' palaces. Wisely Mountbatten and the first High Commissioner, Terence Shone, chose 2 King George's Avenue, an Indian Civil Service bungalow previously inhabited by the head of the Department of Education, Health and Lands. The residence lies three minutes by car from the Secretariat and seven minutes in the other direction from the office compound. There was a plan to give up the residence and transfer the High Commissioner to the compound, a project ferociously resisted by several High Commissioners including myself. I dislike diplomacy-by-compound which tends to isolate diplomats from the local every day world. And the residence, modernized by successive High Commissioners, notably Malcolm MacDonald and ourselves, is an ideal mixture of informal 'lived-inness' and official convenience and dignity.

And there is the garden, more like a miniature park. (We held two miniature cricket matches in it.) Malcolm MacDonald has written the last word on the innumerable birds. We cherished a family of mongoose, but we concentrated on flowers. With the help of the Horticultural Institute we created several rose beds including a display of McGready's Sunset outside the terrace where we often had our meals.

If I go on somewhat about houses and gardens, it is because in our diplomacy, especially as you grow senior, your house and garden are a place for both family life and official business. Even in days where traditional ways of life are questioned, the British concept of home is admired and enjoyed by others, and I would not wish to see the day in which British entertaining had all to take place in public places. In any case, diplomacy is a partnership business and if a husband and wife have any sensitivity at all, the quality of the place where they live can contribute immensely to contentment, concentration and efficiency.

In Delhi an establishment like ours needed something of a private army to keep things in order. Since India is a country where for many years to come people will outnumber jobs, I feel no compunction about this whatever. Our domestic team needed plenty of organizing and we had much help over this. There is only space to mention Pat's Australian cousin Beth Corry. She came for a few weeks and stayed for four years. She was totally serene, industrious, unselfish and humorous. She addressed everybody in the restryned Stryne they use at Adelaide (it was always a 'gaaden paaty'), and everybody always knew what she wanted and did it. Sometimes one gets a better break than one deserves and there is no way to thank Beth adequately.

The Queen's Visit

The Queen and Prince Philip arrived in India on 21 January 1961. The initial moments were nervous as I sought to present to Prince Philip diplomatic colleagues whom I could not possibly identify for certain after two months. I saw nearer and nearer as we approached an enormous man whom I had never seen before. Fortunately he said in a loud voice 'Mongolia'. We had no relations with Mongolia at the time, but you cannot let a small thing like that stand in the way of saluting the Queen.

The arrangements for this tour had been made with immense thoroughness and good sense on both sides. Mistakes of organization during the visits of Messrs Bulganin and Kruschev and of President Eisenhower had been studied and remedied, and the tour of three weeks was remarkable for the absence of comic stories beginning 'Do you remember when . . .?' A great deal of the credit for this goes to Raschid Ali Baig, Chief of Protocol, on whom fell the day to day responsibility for the whole programme. Enormous and enthusiastic crowds in Delhi, Calcutta, Madras, Bangalore and Bombay were efficiently marshalled and controlled, programmes were adhered to punctually and sensible provision had been made for periods of rest. The Queen and

Prince Philip saw ancient and modern India alike. The Taj Mahal, Sarnath (the place where Buddha first preached), and the burning ghats of Benares represented the older India. The British-built steel plant at Durgarpur and the Indian Atomic Energy research establishment at Trombay near Bombay showed something of the new.

Moreover Governments and people had taken a sober and balanced view of the meaning of the visit. It did not mean a recapture of Imperial grandeur or an Imperial relationship. It meant that the Rani had come back to greet and be greeted by the people of India. As the Queen said herself in her address to anything up to a million people in the Ramlila Ground in Delhi, 'This visit sets the seal on the new relationship between Britain and India.'

Apprenticeship

Meantime I had started the normal apprenticeship of learning how things worked. One item which had worried me was that much of what was said and done in India seemed to be greeted in Britain with disappointment. It seemed to me that this might derive from regarding India as a member of the Commonwealth family that had gone somehow wrong. I felt that for purposes of both operation and morale, it would be much better to look at the situation the other way round; we should regard India as a foreign country in which for a number of reasons we had some advantages. With this approach, the disappointments seemed less, and the benefits more real and heartening.

I also found that we needed considerably to alter our methods of work. My predecesor had a unique genius for Asia and somehow carried the whole continent in his head. I told my staff that they must regard me as a bureaucrat who needed constant advice, positive and negative, or I should make a mess of it. I also made it clear that if I personally could not attend something to which I was invited, somebody else probably could. On the other hand things were not to be arranged to 'spare' the High Commissioner; a kindly thought, but demands must be judged on their diplomatic merits.

In dealing with the Indian Government, one started with the fact of Mr Nehru being his own Foreign Minister. It was an advantage to have a certain right of access to the head of government. But it also meant that one was concerned to spare him secondary matters which might otherwise have been taken up with a separate Foreign Minister. I mentioned my self-restraint once to Mr Nehru: 'I've noticed it,' he replied.

There was a junior Minister in the Ministry of External Affairs, Mrs Lashimi Menon, who became a great friend. She was probably too forthright in the expression of personal views to be a good party politician, but she was a strong 'liberal' anti-imperialist and one respected her frankness. But business was in the main conducted with 'the Secretaries'. These were R. K. Behru, the Secretary-General, M. J. Desai, the Foreign Secretary and Y. D. Gandevia. All were top ranking civil servants.

There was a diplomatic corps of some sixty missions. In Delhi where the wide streets eased traffic problems, it was not an intolerable chore to call and return calls in accordance with diplomatic custom. It is a good custom. It is better to know your colleagues rather than spend your time wondering who they are. As for the return call, it is often *le deuxième pas qui coute*. In any case in these years the Delhi diplomatic corps contained an exceptional number of interesting and original people like the liberal and sensitive German Ambassador G. F. Duckwitz, later State Secretary in the German Foreign Office. The most remarkable sequence consisted of three American Ambassadors. First there was Ellsworth Bunker, a sugar magnate turned professional diplomat, indeed one of the few diplomats of whom I have never heard criticism. A wise, humorous and almost saintly man, he lost his delightful wife, Harriet, soon after leaving Delhi. In our time he manifested further wisdom by marrying his talented counsellor, Carol Laise, by then appointed Ambassador to Nepal. Meantime Ellsworth himself served with his proverbial distinction for one supremely testing year after another as Ambassador in Vietnam. His successor in Delhi was Professor J. K. Galbraith. I had to run all the time to keep up intellectually and physically with all the six foot eight and a half inches of Galbraith;

but I had two good cards, professional knowledge and an ability to be greatly impressed without necessarily agreeing. From my point of view the two years were most enjoyable and very fruitful because, according to the evidence of his staff, Galbraith, perhaps because of his Canadian background, did not fall into the error committed by some American liberals of feeling it reprehensible to be seen with the British in a country the latter had once ruled. So, particularly during the Chinese invasion, the co-operation between the American Embassy and our own was constant and intimate, with effects among other things very helpful to India.

Galbraith was followed by Chester Bowles who had been American Ambassador in Delhi from 1952–53, an old friend of India with a mind as wide-ranging as Galbraith's was incisive. If American policy towards India did not in later years give total satisfaction, it was not the fault of the efforts of this trio. Indeed Galbraith's efforts to persuade the United States to build the fourth public sector steel works in India were absolutely right, and the failure of Congress to approve was a sadly symbolic moment in the Indian relationship with the West.

The Congo

1961 turned out to be a year of political flurries. Two of the more important were Britain's first effort to join the European Community and the proposed legislation to restrict Commonwealth immigration. On the first, Mr Peter Thorneycroft visited Delhi and was able to assuage a good many Indian anxieties. It became clear that temperate zone agricultural exports would be affected and not tropical products. Later, some quiet economic diplomacy produced an abolition of the much resented 18 per cent excise duties in Europe on tea. But Indians rightly remained concerned about the fate of future industrial exports to Britain.

On immigration there was at the official level a great deal of righteous indignation over the British decision to limit the inflow from the Commonwealth. This overlooked the essence of the problem for Britain. British Governments had striven to maintain a freedom of immigration for Commonwealth citizens which no other Commonwealth country had attempted. Sooner or later this would have, however regrettably, to cease, if there were not to be a severe social explosion in Britain. The argument with India never reached crisis proportions because Mr Nehru took the broad line that he did not see why an Indian Government should busy itself with aiding the flight of Indians from India. The problem also had its lighter moments as when an enterprising gentleman lifted several hundred freely available application forms for entry to Britain and was found selling them in Jullundur for a rupee apiece.

But one political question suddenly ran Indo-British relations into great difficulty and indeed to near disaster. This was the Congo. There the Belgians, after forseeing independence in some years' time, all at once proclaimed it for 30 June 1960. The mineral-rich province of Katanga seceded from the new Republic, a bloody civil war ensued and Belgian interests behind the Katanga mine operations were blamed for this by the Nationalist Congo Government. Both because of local personalities and of our intimate relations with Belgium, Britain's role in the Congo aroused deep suspicions in the minds of Indians. As I entered Mr Nehru's office on 4 November 1960 for my first official talk he was, no doubt advisedly, fumbling among sheets and sheets of teletype. 'Look,' he said indignantly, 'Belgians, Belgians everywhere. Nothing but Belgians.' Against a background of knowledge not fully up to date I did my best, and then did better at subsequent interviews, to argue that Belgian industrialists and business people had a right, almost an obligation, to be there contributing their wealth and skill to the Congo's development. International opinion appeared fairly well satisfied that armed and mercenary Belgians had left. However, he could not be expected to be much reassured by this.

The fighting continued, especially in Katanga province, and in February 1961 the Indians decided to respond to a United Nations request under a Security Council Resolution for an Indian contingent to join the UN peacekeeping force. This was a courageous step. There was considerable doubt whether the decision, despite Nehru's sponsorship, would go well with an Indian public opinion still conscious of the Gandhian doctrine of non-violence; and the Russians, having attempted a clumsy and unsuccessful intervention in the Congo 'revolution', were not at all keen that anyone else, including the United Nations, should intervene. Moreover the financial implications were not at all clear. None the less the Government, with Krishna Menon as Defence Minister, went ahead.

British hesitations about UN involvement in hostilities in Katanga province were interpreted by much Indian opinion as letting down the United Nations, covertly assisting unregenerate Belgians, or failing to support the Indian contingent. There were confused stories about alleged British reluctance to allow passage across Northern Rhodesia (Zambia) of Ethiopian aircraft on their way to help the United Nations forces.

During the hot and damp weather in July and August, the High Commission sustained one serious and one tragic loss. First, my Deputy, Morrice James, was transferred to be High Commissioner in Pakistan. It was a natural promotion, particularly as Morrice had done invaluable work in Karachi during the Suez episode. But his experienced advice in Delhi was going to be sadly missed. The Counsellor and Political Adviser, Martin Anderson, became my chief adviser on matters political. He was a serious, kindly, infinitely hard-working man with a sense of humour turned on unexpectedly just as you were beginning to forget he had one. In August he drove up rather tired to the hill resort of Kasauli and was expected back next evening. As I was awaiting three guests for dinner, the telephone rang; someone had seen Martin's car wrecked against a tree by the side of the road. Two hours later our fears were confirmed. Martin had clearly been killed instantly.

So I suddenly found myself very short of political advice. At that point the Congo rushed back into the news. The mood between India and Britain had deteriorated again. Some fighting had broken out in Katanga between United Nations (including Indian) forces and elements understood to be mercenaries. Commenting on the fighting, a BBC report had contained the expression, 'brutality of Indian troops.' Indian sensitivities had also been aroused by reproaches levelled against India at a non-aligned Conference in Belgrade that they were soft on 'colonialism'.

On 17 September Mr Nehru held a formal press conference. He dealt with various matters, but the leading and most quoted part was devoted to an explanation of events in the Congo. He spoke about 'foreign mercenaries' who escaped removal by UN forces and 'to some extent with the permission of the United Nations . . . took refuge in various consulates, notably the Belgian Consulate.' Then came the following passage, copied from the verbatim text:

'It is apparent that some of these people, the foreign officials, organized resistance to the United Nations. Firing started, in this whole affair, from the Belgian consulate building where those foreign mercenaries were taking refuge. Obviously I cannot go into details, but the main or the surprising thing is that the United Nations is being criticized and condemned by some countries, notably, the United Kingdom and, of course, Sir Roy Welensky of Rhodesia for the action it took. It simply means that the United Nations is a good body when it supports the policies of a country; it is a bad body when it does things off its own bat! That shows how even last year, the whole weight of some of the great powers was cast on the side of the separatist, obstructive elements in the Congo, and the elements like Mr Tshombe who is accused of one of the most brutal murders in history, that of Lumumba; they are the heroes of some of the great powers. I think the whole thing is perfectly amazing and scandalous in the extreme.'

These words, mentioning only Britain in addition to Belgium and coming with all the constitutional and personal authority of the Prime Minister, could only be constructed as a sign that Indian public opinion ought to express condemnation of British conduct.

Much worse was to follow. On Monday 18 September, I was summoned, on Mr Nehru's instructions, by Gundevia. He said at once 'I am instructed to have a quarrel with you.' He then rehearsed the various items with which we were charged – obstruction of the United Nations, sympathy with 'mercenaries' and delay over permission for the Ethiopian aircraft to overfly Rhodesia. I immediately replied to Gundevia that I was glad to have this opportunity of a quarrel with him. His Prime Minister, without the courtesy of a warning from one Commonwealth Government to another, had launched a formal attack on my Government at a public press conference. There was quite enough in that to quarrel about. We wrangled away on the basis of our respective information and points of view and were still doing so when the dreadful news came in of the death of the United Nations Secretary-General Dag Hammarskjöld in an air crash at Ndola in Northern Rhodesia. That a connection would surely generate itself in India between Nehru's press conference and the Ndola tragedy was obvious to us both. We could only part on a note of acute apprehension.

Next morning all our fears were realized. The *Indian Express*, not normally hysterically anti-British, said 'Never, even during Suez, have Britain's hands been so bloodstained as they are now.' The Indian language papers followed suit. Our very well-informed and perceptive Press Officer, Ben (Dunelm) Brown, simply said, 'The Press is terrible,' and asked whether I felt I could give a press conference. I asked how much time we had in hand if we were to make the national press effectively the next morning. The reply was 'About ten minutes.'

There was no question of consulting London. A press conference meant repudiating the Prime Minister of India in India before an audience, mainly Indian, of whom many, if not ill-disposed, would be at least sceptical. On the other hand in terms of Indian public opinion, things were about as bad as they could be, and if nobody said anything, there would be lasting damage to relations. And we had one advantage. Thanks to the Foreign and Commonwealth Relations Offices at home and especially to our very efficient Ambassador in the Congo, Derek Riches, we were now very well informed and up to date. I would certainly know more about the latest events in the Congo than anyone else present. So I decided to go ahead.

On entering the hall in the High Commission, I invited the assembly to stand for a minute in memory of Dag Hammarskjöld, both as Secretary-General and as a close personal friend of mine (there was no false sentiment about this). I then gave a full statement of British Government policy in the Congo. I recounted the British pledge to work for the unity of the country within the existing boundaries and with Katanga contributing its resources to a united Congo. We had certainly had our anxieties about the use of force in Katanga. So had Mr Hammarskjöld, and that was why the Secretary-General and a British Minister, Lord Lansdowne, were both in the Congo. The decision to go to Ndola to meet Mr Tshombe was Mr Hammarskjöld's own. I confirmed that permission had been given to the Ethiopian aircraft to fly to the Congo and that we objected to 'pirate' aircraft flying round Katanga. It was a long session and there was much more besides. Only the last question was off-side: 'Was I criticizing remarks by Mr Nehru?' 'It is not for me,' I replied, 'to criticize remarks by Mr Nehru.'

We then went home to await results. They were extraordinary. They were also immensely creditable to the Press Trust of India and the individual correspondents and newspapers. The Indian press carried what I had said at length and in detail with good understanding and objective headlines. The heat came off almost instantaneously. The Secretary of State for Commonwealth Relations, Duncan Sandys, sent a heart-warming telegram. Within a week, an understandable interval, the Indian Ministry of External Affairs dissociated itself from any suggestion that Britain had had anything to do with the death of Mr Hammarskjöld. When I next saw Mr Nehru, he was splendidly bland. Of course he had had 'no intention of attacking the United Kingdom'.

So while one cannot in one press conference 'restore' a position which has changed, we in Delhi could allow ourselves a quiet smile over a comment sent to one British newspaper, that: 'the current of anti-British feeling is running in this capital too strongly by now to be reversed by [Sir Paul's] remarks.' If you have never seen a current change, well, I have. And I do not care to think what might have happened to our relations if no one had done anything about it.

Life in India was never uniform. We were bound to come back again to colonies and former colonies, but it was not only on the political front that we were embattled. In the same late summer of 1961 we fought the weather as well. There was sudden and overwhelming flooding. 2 King George's Avenue is at a flood confluence point where the water comes down from the President's House and decides what to do next. I looked out of the window one morning to see a boat gliding by. The water had come within an inch of the top of the steps leading into our house. All the carpets had been taken up and the water had meantime found its way round the verandah and was spilling into the staff quarters. I sloshed around in shorts and gym shoes trying to help. There was not much to be done then, but we improved the drainage and defences later.

In the compound the devastation was more technological. For aesthetic purposes the electricity generators had been sunk below the ground level. But no one had thought out the weather probabilities and the flood water had sailed in, fusing the electricity and ruining machines. So we sweated away without air-conditioning or fans or even punkah-wallahs for several weeks. And we built a few water-thresholds, asking permission later.

In the middle of it all, I had an invitation which I found most moving. A Feroze Gandhi Annual Memorial Lecture had been instituted in honour of Mrs Indira Gandhi's late husband. Shri H. C. Heda, a Congress MP, invited me on behalf of the organizers to give the first lecture. It had to be on a political subject as Mr Gandhi had been a politician *par excellence*. I expressed surprised pleasure, but added that the only political subject I could lecture on would be the relationship between politicians and civil servants. This was accepted. The meeting was presided over gently and judiciously by Lal Bahadur Shastri, Mrs Gandhi was present and the answering voice to my talk was that of Dr V. K. V. R. Rao, a born controversialist later to be Minister of Education. The talk owed most of itself to a combination of personal experiences and Herbert Morrison's excellent book,[1]

[1] Herbert Morrison, *Government and Parliament – a Survey from Inside, 1954.*

and was very kindly received, but what I really learned from the experience was that the word 'official' in India still reflected in some degree the period when officials had put present Ministers in prison. This meant an emotional approach to officialdom very different from ours.

But we were soon back in the wars. In the autumn, an unofficial conference was held in Delhi about the Portuguese colonies. Mr and Mrs R. K. Nehru invited us to meet some of those attending. I talked with Dr Kenneth Kaunda who was in a mood of self-pity and gloom. He said everything was going wrong in Northern Rhodesia and he would not reach independence without trouble. I told him with risky confidence that he was wrong and did not seem to know his British. Mercifully I was right.

But the Conference had more purpose than chat. As at Belgrade a few months earlier, pressure was put on India to do something to prove its true anti-colonial status. There was, it was pointed out, something to be done. The British and the French had had the sense to hand over power in India; the Portuguese maintained the pretence that Goa, in Western India, was part of metropolitan Portugal. Why should not India move in and take over?

There was clearly some hesitation about this. But by the end of November rumours began to circulate that something was in the wind. Immediately on return from a business visit to Calcutta, I went and saw R. K. Nehru and said I did not like the atmosphere at all. Were the Indians really going to take matters into their own hands and use force in an international dispute? Naturally the reply was indefinite.

I received an overnight telegram from London approving my having taken this line in advance of instructions, and instructing me to make the expression of our concern official. I went to see M. J. Desai, who denounced the Portugese for shooting at Indian ships; I counter-reproached him for not in that case asking Portugal's NATO allies to help relieve the situation. The subsequent week I saw Prime Minister Nehru himself and remonstrated; he banged the table and I suddenly remembered Mrs Gandhi once saying to me in jest, 'When my father bangs the table, don't believe a word he says.'

Events were developing fast. Troops continued to move. The Brazilian Ambassador made an ineffectual gesture of mediation. Vice-President Radhakrishnan tugged me by the sleeve at an MCC Test match in Delhi and said 'Can't you do something about this nonsense?' The American Ambassador, Kenneth Galbraith, floated a last minute idea for pressure on Portugal. The editor of the ruthlessly left magazine *Blitz* said to me, 'I have told Krishna Menon that if there is no attack on Goa by this weekend there will be trouble for him.' India was in the grip of forces beyond the reach of diplomatic action.

On the morning of December 18th, we heard that Indian troops had marched into Goa against little or no resistance. One of those hopeless telegrams came telling me to tell the Indians they ought not to have done it. Going on record can be right, but we had done this in essence already and this expostulation was futile. However, it was not a case for quasi-heroic questioning of orders, so I asked to see Nehru thinking he would refuse. To my astonishment he agreed to see me at noon. Both of us knew what the other would say and that we had nothing to add to what we had already said. The talk petered out and we ended by discussing the beauty of the Montezuma rose he had brought back from the Rose show we had attended the day before.

Behind all this there was genuine tragedy. Nehru was totally caught between two ideals, the ideal of good world behaviour and the ideal of liberating colonial peoples. One flatly contradicted the other. I have no doubt whatever that the agony of his choice hurt him very much in a way that he would naturally never admit, and I contend to this day that while he showed much resilience in the two years that were to come, he was never quite the same again.

Trade, Finance and Aid

Amid all this political excitement there was perpetual and complicated commercial, industrial and financial business to be done. There was a British investment in India of a value variously estimated but well over £300 million. The trade between Britain and India in 1960 amounted to £301·4 million.

There was also a very considerable aid programme of which far the biggest contribution went to the Durgapur Steel Works.

Our objectives were clear. In trade we were anxious to keep up the mutual flow as high as possible, subject to the vexed question of limiting cheap textile imports from Hong Kong, India and Pakistan. Industrially we were concerned to protect as far as possible the British investment as it expressed itself in industry and commerce. There was increasing emphasis on investment in production and manufacture. The age of making and remitting profits purely on export and import trade was clearly coming to a close. Financially, India carried on with extraordinary endurance at the bottom of an empty barrel. If therefore trade was to be kept going, the level of imports from Britain would be greatly dependent on the wise use of credits by Indians and British alike.

In doing our best for British interests, we did not lose sight of the interests of India and the developing world as a whole. In 1960, much economic opinion still held hopefully to the take-off theory. The idea was that once a basis for the production of power and steel had been laid under the first three Five Year Plans, the Indian economy had the capacity and skill to expand rapidly, if not into self-sufficiency, at least into something comparable with a Western industrial economy. In income per head, India is a very poor country (say, $110 a year in 1970) but it is not altogether poor in resources such as iron ore, limestone, coal, foodstuffs and, of course, human capacity. But the take-off theory underestimated the adverse influences – the difficulty of generating capital, the scarcity of skilled (as opposed to untrained and unskilled) management and labour, and the difficulty of producing in India, in addition to traditional exports like tea and jute (the world demand for which was inelastic), enough industrial goods saleable outside in conditions of market competition. Finally there was the overwhelming rise in population. The foundations of steel and hydro-electric power production on a large scale laid by Mr Nehru's government and the Indian planners have proved to be good ones. But far more was needed than could be foreseen or afforded or, indeed, achieved in so short a time.

To deal with these problems we had a sizeable Trade Commission headed by a senior Trade Commissioner, Harold Bailey, a member of the Board of Trade serving on secondment. As Harold was also a member of my staff, the organization in Delhi was coherent and operated well. The financial side was looked after by a seconded Treasury adviser. In the other main cities, our organization was unsatisfactory. No doubt through laudable mutual deference, the Commonwealth Relations Office and the Board of Trade had agreed that the Deputy High Commissioner and the Trade Commissioner should be of equal status. This meant that if they were agreeable people, they were tempted to defer to each other while the business flowed by; if one of them wasn't, far too much time could be spent on protocol and suspicion. The Plowden Report of 1962 brought this impasse to an end; meantime we did our best.

For anyone used to export drive activities in, say, the United States or Federal Germany, commercial diplomatic work in India was something of a nightmare. The only way to help exports was to see that licences for particular imports of raw materials, spare parts, etc, were not reduced from year to year and to watch for opportunites where India simply had to buy something so that British industry got a chance and a fair deal. What could not be attempted was an export drive which would simply increase India's expenditure in sterling or lead to pointless switching from one British export to another. It was also necessary from time to time to help firms to arrange remittances to Britain both of fair share of profits after Indian taxation and also of the earnings of expatriate employees who needed the money at home for education, holidays and the like. Given the balance of payments situation, the Indian record on remittances was good. It was recognized by British firms (some quicker than others) that Indianization of senior staff must be accelerated, and the Indian Government accepted that, if British capital was invested in India, there was a case for the presence of some expatriates with responsibilty for its use. The situation for expatriates only became really difficult after the Indian devaluation of 1967, which could not carry with it an automatic rise in rupee salaries.

The problem of supplies and machinery was very difficult. Barter with Eastern Europe had already assumed large proportions and it was usually possible to get some kind of Eastern European machine to do a particular job. But despite the quality of some machinery from the Communist countries, particularly Czechoslovakia, many firms, not only British, were often desperate for machinery from the West.

This was where aid and credit came in. Either means could be used to produce new resources. The biggest single effort by Britain in this field was the £90 million Durgarpur steel works, a project constantly demanding the High Commission's attention at all levels. In the British time, Indian steel production had been only 900,000 long tons (1947); this output was wholly inadequate for a large country in search of take-off. Accordingly in the 1950s, the Indians invited the main steel producing countries to build large modern steel works for them in the public sector. First the Russians, then the British and Germans accepted. A British steel works construction expert who visited all three when they had gone into production said to me, 'Durgarpur (British), probably the most modern plant in the world: Rourkela (German), also a very fine plant indeed: Bhilai (Russian), ugly, much too large and dangerous for the workers – but produces a hell of a lot of steel.'

Durgarpur's problems involved both management and labour. The plant had been built by a British consortium. The general manager of the construction was Douglas Bell, a tough Scots getter-doner. Once he had finished and the plant was handed over to the Indians, the latter felt bound to appoint an Indian general manager. Partly for political reasons they chose a retired Indian civil servant from Bengal. The Russians, faced with the same problem, had quietly kept control of Bhilai. The British, much more vulnerable to criticism, kept experts at Durgarpur but had to be very careful not to interfere in control. This was particularly important in Bengal where labour could become very difficult. In the end, however, production was so unsatisfactory that Hindustan Steel decided, the Indian Government concurring, that the only thing to do was to invite Douglas Bell, as having constructed the plant, to come back and run it. He was still in India, tired and ill. He and his wife came to stay and I urged him to try. With great public spirit he consented. At the cost of bearing a bit severely on the machines, he did a brilliant job of raising output to where it ought to be.

Then began stage 3, further labour trouble from the Communist section of the labour force, who objected to the new emphasis on efficiency. The High Commission were once more involved in quietly successful negotiations with the able and agreeable Minister, Dr Sanjiva Reddy, and through the unpopular but still effective Calcutta 'boss', Atulhya Ghosh.

This story shows the degree to which British officials had to become involved in a public sector industry in the interest not simply of the reputation of British construction but also of India itself. And it always had to be done with the goodwill of those in India who were responsible. It was a business involving much patience, but gratifying when it worked.

Another industrial development was very important in quality if small in volume. Norman Kipping, the untiring Director of the Federation of British Industries, arrived in India with an idea that part of British aid might be tied to the purchase of spare parts and small components by British-owned or British-Indian partnership industries. Many businesses, in difficulties about import licences for these crucial items, were threatened with closing down. There was some official questioning on our side but I was strongly for this ingenious plan. The Indians accepted it, and it operated well and most usefully under the name, needless to say, of 'Kipling loans'.

On our tours there were numerous visits to factories – there were so many with a British interest that I visited very few others. The best were exceedingly good, like Ashok-Leyland in Madras for instance, and some of the pharmaceutical factories like Glaxo in Bombay. Others showed badly the effect of lack of new capital, a lack due partly to growing discouragement in Britain, for balance of payments reasons, of the export of capital, and partly

because of growing official disincentives in India to the development of wealth. In general the Indian Finance Ministry did its
best, under the remarkable official leadership of L. K. Jha, to
make intelligent taxation exceptions in favour of industrial
expansion. But the general tone, for political and ideological
reasons, was the other way; it reached an absurd moment when
an application by the Tata firm for a licence to produce a million
more tons of steel a year financed by the firm itself was turned
down. The story was that the firm was too large already; the
ideologues had not learned or chosen to learn that in these days
a firm cannot be too large if you have control over your country;
the lessons of Iran in 1951 had not been accepted.

None the less, the position was never as bad inside India as it
seemed from without. There was striking economic and industrial
progress and, in many places, a real partnership between British
and Indian effort. This continued to the end of my time, when one
of my last acts was to brief a powerful British delegation to an
International Chamber of Commerce meeting, led by Sir Duncan
Oppenheim. A British High Commission or Embassy does not
sell goods. But, as has since become much better understood,
there is a long way between offering a desirable product at a
good price to a developing country in financial difficulties and
finally effecting delivery. A good official representation can
sometimes do a lot to help along that way.

Aircraft

There was one form of export which concerned both trade and
defence and which brought about a complicated series of successes
and failures – aircraft. In some cases our efforts involved us heavily
with high politics and personalities.

The most successful storm followed by calm concerned the
Avro 748, a quick take-off turbo-jet, highly practical as either
a big official or small passenger plane, particularly in mountainous
country. Under the direction of Krishna Menon as Minister of
Defence, this plane was being built under licence at Kanpur
(Cawnpore), and Krishna Menon invited me to visit the plant
with him. He was constantly blaming production delays on

Avro's. The latter went through an awkward time in which there were three small fires at their factory in Britain. Krishna Menon did not hesitate to say with his best sarcasm, 'When Sir Roy Dobson does not wish to send me something, he burns down his factory.'

The moment we arrived at Kanpur, the factory director, a retired Indian Air Vice-Marshal, launched at me a tirade of abuse of Avro's and of Britain generally. (He apologized afterwards, saying you always had to talk like that in the presence of the Minister.) I answered back, if less violently, reserving, as it turned out, my stronger language until after I had seen the factory. When I had been round, and talked with both Indian engineers and a patient team of British technicians, I told Krishna Menon that building aircraft was not like putting together bits of Meccano; you needed these days a proper factory layout and production plan, and he would never produce aircraft satisfactorily the way he was going.

You could talk like that to Krishna Menon. The argument went on, including dinner for three which I gave somewhat later for Menon and Sir Roy Dobson. Krishna Menon dashed from a party at which he wore Indian dress to put on a dinner jacket. I fear I was underdressed. The guests got on rather well. Later, after Krishna Menon had disappeared from office, the factory was improved and aircraft were produced which gave immediate satisfaction.

Disappointments had their lessons. The Indians began during my time to think of replacements for their ageing Viscounts. The resident representatives of BAC and Hawker-Siddeley and travelling sales managers did their best, but I felt that our case was not getting near the top. So I called on the then Minister of Aviation. I had plenty of sales talk but suffered from the disadvantage imposed on all of us at that time that, after taking up the BAC 111 (which seemed the 'readiest'), I had to say that we also had a splendid aircraft called the Trident. The idea was that the British Government must not favour one British enterprise against another. This practice left many customers in the developing world confused by the absence of one officially sponsored

K

'British' offer. In this case the Indians deferred a decision
and in the interim bought second-hand Caravelles.

But the aircraft question which got us all into high politics was
the provision for the Indian Air Force of an up-to-date fighter to
succeed the splendidly successful Hunter. (It would have been a
wonderful thing for the balance of payments if we could have
reconstituted the Hunter assembly line in about 1960.) The options
open to the Indians were the French Mirage, the British Lightning,
the Indians' own HF 24 with a developed (British) Bristol engine
and the Russian MiG. The Americans could offer nothing on the
sort of terms which might have interested the Indians; they were
also much involved with the Pakistanis. The Mirage would have
been in many ways ideal and there were those in the Indian Air
Force who would have opted strongly for it; but there was not
much encouragement from the French. The Lightning was
generally felt by developing countries to be too complex and too
expensive and a single seater was wanted. So, to a degree which was
not apparent at the time, the field was narrowed to the Indian plane
with a British engine and the Russian MiG, both to be manufactured
in India.

In May 1962 there was suddenly a story in the press that India
was going to opt for the MiG. I knew then and it subsequently
became more generally known that, while Britain claimed no
right to dictate to India what aircraft the Indian Air Force should
make or buy, there was a clear understanding between Lord
Mountbatten and Mr Nehru that the Indian Government would
consult the British Government before any decision was taken.
Accordingly I went round at once to Krishna Menon and asked
what was going on.

He was not displeased at being asked, and confirmed the
story generally. He was very angry about the leakage. He added
various technical explanations. As Mr Nehru's undertaking
was a very delicate personal matter, I did not want to rush into
discussing it with Menon. Meantime the latter went ahead with
his plan. It was a period when he enjoyed an almost uncanny
ascendency over the Lok Sabha (Indian House of Commons).
His rather frightening personality, his incessant activity and his

nearness to the Prime Minister (including a house just outside the gate) seemed to make him impregnable. When he put the MiG proposition to the House, all sorts of people would have liked to ask questions. But somehow nobody dared. The Air Force as such could of course say nothing.

I began to think that we were going to say and do nothing ourselves. Home leave was due at the end of June, and we intended to take the new route across the Soviet Union, visiting Moscow and Leningrad on the way. The Soviet Ambassador, Mr I. A. Benediktov, and his wife came to lunch with members of his staff. We had a hilarious time, and, as his first name was Ivan, we christened the Russian doll he had brought for Joanna 'Natasha Ivanovna'.

Then came one of those set exchanges of telegrams. Set inward telegram (basically): 'The Secretary of State feels it is time he revisited India. He does not wish the High Commissioner to change any plans.' Set reply: 'I am grateful for the Secretary of State's consideration, but I think it would be misunderstood if the moment he arrived the High Commissioner left on leave.'

Mr Sandys arrived and said he would be taking up the MiG question with Nehru. As it was a delicate one, he would wish to do this alone. I agreed. Generally it is a bad principle for a visiting minister to leave the resident representative out of a high-level talk. This is because the omission of the Ambassador or High Commissioner suggests, however unintentionally, that there are things which the resident representative is not allowed to know. This suspicion permanently damages his utility. But, particularly in the Commonwealth where there are special personal relationships between ministers, there are justifiable exceptions.

Mr Sandys had a long and painful interview with Mr Nehru who admitted that he had 'forgotten'. It was the only way out but it was sad, and it was clear where the fault lay.

Many felt that, with the cold behaviour of the Russians to the Indians at the time of the Chinese invasion, the project might fall through. But I myself always felt that the Russians, having seen their opportunity, would come back to it, and that the Indians would feel far too committed to go back to their own project. This is indeed what happened.

It had been a grey, damp June, and with this physical and political atmosphere I was not sorry to be on leave.

We betook ourselves again to the igloo tents. Christopher was doing voluntary work in North-Western Greece on a housing project for refugees from Albania, initiated by the United Nations Association. With this as our objective we visited on the way south Pavia, Milan, Florence, Siena and then Rome. Then on via Naples and Pompeii to camp at Sorrento. We followed round the wonderful coast road through Positano and Amalfi and across the Mezzogiorno via Metaponto to Brindisi, then by ferry across to Igoumenitza. (I swear I heard someone in a lower deck call in a foreign voice 'Zere is a lady in my cabin. Vere is ze berth controller?' Had he heard the joke before or wasn't he a foreigner at all?)

We slept in the open on Christopher's location. Then with him we 'did' Greece from Missolonghi to Mycenae and from Athens and Sunium to Olympia. There were of course bathes and rests, but sight-seeing among the young was beginning to wilt as we went back up the pre-autostrada east coast of Italy. Ravenna and Venice were none the less irresistible. It was all a dream for the adults, and an appetizing cocktail for the young.

Chinese Invasion

However, we had left a worry behind us in India. For some time there had been more concern than usual about Chinese activities near the border. Despite warnings dating from the mid-fifties Mr Nehru had hoped beyond reasonable hope to maintain or recapture with the Chinese Communist Government something of the cordial relationship which had been established after independence with the Nationalist Government of Chiang Kai-Shek. There was in fact no prospect of this. The Chinese had been methodically seeking to settle any frontier problems with neighbours such as Burma and Nepal. Opposite India, however, they were expanding their strategic communications westward, partly through territory claimed by India. There were considerable areas of undemarcated frontier and there was patrol activity on both sides. Krishna Menon was in a mood of some exaltation about the ability of Indian patrols to take on Chinese opposition on the same scale.

During the summer, harassment had continued, and in September General Kaul, the Chief of Staff of the army, had been sent to take command in Assam. Many questioned this appointment since General Kaul, though a very pleasant and civilized man, was lacking in the tough combat experience that might be needed. But there was no immediate expectation of anything more serious.

We returned to India on 9 October and our first engagement was at Simla on the thirteenth. The Dalai Lama was to visit and bless several Tibetan children exiled from their homeland and being cared for by the (British) Save the Children Fund in Simla. The 'reunion' in Simla was a touching scene. All children are attractive; Tibetan children proudly displaying new garments best described as bright-coloured woollen dressing-gowns, were wholly entrancing. And an extra poignancy was added to the occasion next day. The lesson in the Anglican Church was read by Lady Alexandra Metcalfe, Vice-Chairman of the Save the Children Fund, whose father, Lord Curzon, had worshipped there as Viceroy.

As we were thus peacefully engaged, the situation not so many miles away in Asian terms had changed suddenly and completely. The Chinese had decided that they had had enough of playing toy soldiers on the frontier. As soon as we had returned to Delhi, M. J. Desai was ready with a relief map showing what he understood to have happened. At the Thagla Ridge in the North East Frontier Area the Chinese, he said, had suddenly scrapped the unwritten rules by which grazing on the frontier was controlled and had moved forward. It was not clear what they wanted or how far they would attempt to go. Nor, from what was said, did the Indians appear at this stage to want more than sympathy. The mood was one of defiance, 'kick the rascals out.' But of the truths of relative strengths and real intentions little seemed to be known.

We did our best to report fully. When we had done this, I retired to have a think and came to the conclusion that if things became serious, the attitude of Pakistan would be crucial. There would be a chance to re-establish a degree of unity in the sub-continent, but equally there would be a temptation to the Pakistanis to work for a short-term discomfiture of India regardless of longer-term considerations. It seemed to me that the British Government could play some part in averting a divisive and short-sighted choice. And I telegraphed drawing attention to this.

It is important to try to feel the edgy atmosphere of that moment. Our recent relations with the Indians had not been notably happy. The Pakistanis remained members of CENTO, and therefore allies, though it was becoming steadily more apparent that they regarded the alliance principally as offering some support in their rivalry with India. There was a tendency in Britain to sympathize with Pakistan which had, in the eyes of British public opinion, a somewhat better case over Kashmir than had India, while the latter had tended to be non-aligned eastward and to lecture westward. Any approach made to Pakistan was therefore bound to be cautious.

For some days we all lived in something of a twilight. The Indians were understandably taking the line that they could manage. If they had rushed immediately into pleas for help this would have meant that Krishna Menon's stewardship and General Kaul's generalship were in question from the start.

I was therefore at first chary about recommending any pre-cipitate word or action out of London. But during the week it began to become obvious that the Indians could not hold on to the Thagla Ridge and that worse was to come. The way became rapidly open first for encouragement and then for military aid. I delivered a message of support and encourage-ment from Mr Macmillan. Over the next week-end, as the situa-tion deteriorated, the whole 'team' in London worked as people had done in the war to get the first consignment of Western aid to India. Krishna Menon, however, begged me not to make publicity out of our effort. This was manifestly a tiresome and obstructive request. But he was still Defence Minister and spoke, whether truly or not, in the name of the Prime Minister, and I felt bound (to the displeasure of our compatriots in India) to comply.

As soon as it became clear that aid was welcome we set about organizing it. This was immensely difficult. The Indians had little systematic knowledge of what they had and what they needed – except that they needed the earth. There was also to my mind a great danger that the Americans, the Australians, Canadians and ourselves, all of whom offered help, might start competing with each other instead of with the Chinese. In one of our talks, which were then taking place daily, I suggested to Galbraith that we should set up an informal joint body to see that this did not happen. His reply was characteristic. 'Paul, you must be a genius; I was going to suggest it myself.'

Meantime there was a great demand for clothes and other aid for the *Jawans* (soldiers) and Pat set up at 2 King George's Avenue through the Delhi Commonwealth Women's Association one of those working parties which were so memorable in many Embassies in the Second World War. Indian ladies poured in to sew, knit and pack, and great enthusiasm remained as long as the hostilities lasted.

It was now becoming wholly obvious that the Krishna Menon régime in the Defence Ministry had failed to provide the means to resist invasion. There had been brilliant ideas, but many of them were unsustained, and the prosaic items from small arms and ammunition to clothes for altitude campaigning had been disastrously neglected. Criticism of Krishna Menon rose rapidly in volume. Mr Nehru appeared unwilling to respond, the situation in the Congress Party grew tense, and one Congress Member of Parliament was reported in the press as saying angrily to the Prime Minister, 'If you will not let Menon go, you will have to go yourself.' This was perhaps the nearest Pandit Nehru ever came to disaster during his seventeen years of Premiership. There was no doubt that Menon was a special friend of the Prime Minister but there was no rescuing him now. After a short relegation to be Minister in charge of Defence Production he was finally out. A new team took over with Y. B. Chavan from

Bombay as Minister of Defence and General J. N. (Muchu) Chaudhuri as Commander-in-Chief: this was a really strong combination of the two most capable people available.

Hostilities continued to take an obscure course. The Chinese offered a cease-fire and a talk between Nehru and Chou En-Lai and then a twenty-mile withdrawal by both sides. But the Indians were now aroused in a manner normal to people who had not been expecting this kind of behaviour and were still confident.

Returning from engagements in Ahmedabad and Bombay on Sunday 18 November, we heard the worst. At Chusul airfield in Ladakh, the operations were being well conducted and the Indians were holding on. (It was possible also that the Chinese had only a limited diversionary objective on that front.) At Walong in the far north-east, too, the troops had done well. But they had finally been overwhelmed and were in retreat. On the Sela Pass in the North-East Frontier Area, there had been total disaster. The Chinese had outflanked the Indian positions over high, snow-covered ground, and there was nothing, as far as could be ascertained, between them and the military and economic centre of Tezpur on the Brahmaputra River.

All the aid we could bring could do little about this. The question was 'what the Chinese would do next'. On this my mentor throughout was the Canadian High Commissioner, Chester Ronning. Mrs Ronning once said to me 'My first language was Norwegian, unlike my husband's which was Chinese.' Ronning had grown up in missionary surroundings in China and had an extraordinary feel for Chinese psychology. He maintained throughout that the Chinese had in mind a precisely defined limited operation and that when they had carried it out, they would turn round and go away. So we waited in growing apprehension to see whether they would be true to form or whether the plains of Assam would be too great a temptation for the Chinese Commander.

On 22 November I was suddenly able to congratulate Ronning, for the Chinese had done exactly what he said. His reaction was 'My goodness, I nearly lost my nerve.'

Apart from obtaining information, channelling aid and helping to sustain morale, British representation in India had had another difficult duty, the safety of British subjects. A great many of them were concentrated in Assam either in tea gardens or in the Burmah Oil Company oilfield and refinery. An evacuation is almost impossible to get right. If you are too quick and eager and nothing happens, your community will ask you why you panicked. If you are too slow, why did you dither and allow Messrs X, Y and Z to be overrun by the invaders? Nearly all the work on this had to be undertaken by Eric Norris, the Deputy High Commissioner in Calcutta. Eric got rapidly round the state of Assam, summed up the situation accurately, got splendid help from the hard-pressed Indian Air Force, and we ended up right almost to a man. It was a truly remarkable effort.

Of course, when I went to make my annual speech to the British community in Calcutta a few weeks later, there were known to be a few grievances. I started, in an excited atmosphere, on a long explanatory speech and then remembered in the middle that I had left out the most important point. 'Apart from anything else,' I said, off the cuff, 'if you have been upset and displaced please remember this is not the fault of the British Government, the British High Commission, the Indian Government or the Indian forces; keep on reminding yourselves that this is the fault of the Chinese.' This kind of elementary truth gets forgotten by people in distress. I did not hear any further complaint.

There has been much debate, political and academic, on the background of this invasion. In it much criticism has been levelled at the Indians. Their attitude, it is said, was first complacent and then rash, their boundary case was unproven and their military performance disappointing. There is something in all these criticisms. What is too often forgotten is that they were the victims of a piece of organized forcible aggression deep into their territory. Even if the Chinese had a case and did go home, there were casualties and damage and there had been a serious breach of international law and custom. If there is anything for which the civilized world ought to stand, it is for the rendering obsolete of this kind of international behaviour. It shocked me very much when a British theatrical company came from

Pakistan to Delhi having been so brainwashed in Pakistan as to object at first to allowing a contribution from the takings to go to the Indian Red Cross. This basic issue has too often been forgotten in the detailed discussion of claims and counter-claims and needs to be firmly restated.

As for Chinese objectives one can only repeat what came to be the local interpretation. Indian economic progress had been outstripping Chinese. The Chinese for their part had been mending their frontier fences with their neighbours, but had seen that, whereas some might be willing to compromise, the Indians would not. Therefore the Indians must be taught a short sharp limited lesson about who was the leading Asian power. Perhaps the Chinese also thought that there would be a much more complete Indian collapse, social as well as military. When this did not happen and Indian unity was aroused instead, the Chinese with long lines of communication and still limited resources prudently turned back.

Meantime life for us had become much easier. For example we had had difficulties with India over Nepal, the recruiting ground for Gurkhas who had to cross Indian territory to reach their British destinations. Illegal and destructive inroads from Bihar into the *terai* (lower country) of Nepal constantly troubled the situation, and there seemed to be no stopping them. I was now asked from London for advice on whether we could raise the subject again with the Indian Government. I raised it without further ado with Mr Nehru, who was very helpful. He said that the Indian Government had gone after the border problem energetically, and there should be no more trouble. He was as good as his word.

But the biggest dividend, if temporary, showed itself on 22 November. As a result of the war news and of desperate appeals from India for help, the Secretary of State had decided to come to India personally and had arranged with the United States Government that their Number One elder statesman, Mr Averell Harriman, should come too. Mr Sandys had been unwell and would be coming on 24 November; meantime the Chief of the General Staff, Field-Marshal Sir Richard Hull, and Mr John

Tilney, MP, Parliamentary Secretary in the Commonwealth Office, would be arriving that very day. The scene at the airport was one of immense, crowded enthusiasm. It seemed utterly appropriate that in India's hour of need the Commonwealth, and particularly Britain, should be there. As we talked about it at lunch, we had no illusions about how long such a mood between two nations can last. But at least Pat and I could say from our experience, 'How wonderful it is for Britain to be really popular, even if it may only be for a brief moment.'

Kashmir

Mr Sandys lost no time in making it clear that one of his chief objects in coming to India was to see whether in the existing fluid situation, some real step could be taken towards solving the Kashmir problem. This problem injected continuous poison into the Indo-Pakistan relationship. It was already easy to foresee that a generous arms aid programme for India would arouse suspicion among Pakistanis that, if the Chinese did not return, the arms could be turned in their direction.

The problem was one of immense complexity and only the barest bones of it can be given here. In the 1830s and '40s Kashmir, despite its Muslim population, was part of the empire of Ranjit Singh, the famous Sikh leader. After his death, his empire dissolved in bloodthirsty feuds. The British intervened, separated Kashmir from what was to develop very successfully as the Punjab, and installed Ghulab Singh, the Hindu ruler of a hill-state, as ruler. Muslim Kashmir having been ruled by a Sikh prince, the substitution of a Hindu ruler raised no serious problems at that time.

When a hundred years later independence came to India and Pakistan, the princely rulers, who had a direct relationship with the British Crown, were invited to opt for India or Pakistan. The then Maharajah of Kashmir simply failed to decide, and the status of Kashmir after Independence Day was uncertain. The question why he failed has never been clearly answered. The most reasonable conclusion is that he may have hoped to preserve an independence from both countries to the political and economic advantage of Kashmir. The result, however, was that Pakistani tribesmen, with the unquestionable connivance of the Pakistan Government, advanced on the capital, Srinagar. There was a panic appeal by the Maharajah to Delhi for help. The reply, quite correctly, was that if Indian help was wanted, the Maharajah must accede to India. He did, and Indian troops arrived in the nick of time to hold Srinagar airport against the invaders.

From this has risen a dispute not yet settled. Technically India is in the right as the Maharajah finally acceded, even if in circumstances which should have been avoided. On the other hand, India expressed to the United Nations a willingness to hold a plebiscite to confirm this result and then rejected all suggestions on how to hold it. The Indian Government has held in detention Kashmiris who wished to advocate a plebiscite. A cease-fire line watched by UN observers ran through the beautiful Kashmir Valley, leaving most of it in Indian hands; each country consolidated its hold on the parts effectively occupied by it and there the situation remained.

The Pakistanis felt strongly about Kashmir because of its Muslim population and the assumed preference of its people. In any case, they could argue, access was easier from Rawalpindi *via* Murree than direct from the Indian plain. The Indians, apart from their legal position of strength, could argue that at least Ladakh was not Muslim and that, as the only way there led through the Kashmir Valley, India needed control. Also, with time, the doctrine grew stronger and stronger that the presence in India of a Muslim state was vital to proving beyond all doubt that India was indeed a secular country and not theocratic or exclusively Hindu.

The perpetuation of the Indo-Pakistan feud was bad enough for the sub-continent. Worse than that it hamstrung the foreign policy of India and deprived it of an effectiveness in world affairs which might otherwise have been exercised to the general advantage. Because the population of Kashmir is overwhelmingly Muslim, the opinion of the Muslim world on this dispute is bound to incline towards Muslim Pakistan. In order to counter this, India had to do two things. The first was to find a strong ally in debate. The Russians decided to be sponsors of India to a degree to which the Americans, though allies of Pakistan, did not become patrons of Pakistan in this context. Secondly, Kashmir being Muslim, the Indians had to lean over backwards not to upset in any way the feelings of the Muslim countries from North Africa to Indonesia. Thus the freedom of India to help the world as an impartial umpire in various difficult situations, a role which otherwise Nehru would have welcomed, was ruled out. An impartial Indian voice in the Middle East, for instance, could have been most telling.

This was the daunting controversy into which Messrs Sandys and Harriman plunged in a continent where compromise is not second nature. However, in the atmosphere prevailing immediately after the Chinese invasion, both India and Pakistan showed a readiness to talk, and there was no immediate resentment in India at the idea. But there were two immediate difficulties, one of which nearly wrecked the talks before they began. First, what should they be called? This may seem trivial, but it ran straight into one of the main psychological issues. In Pakistan it was widely held that, if Kashmir could be settled (no doubt with considerable concessions to Pakistan), there would be nothing else for the two countries to quarrel about. Indians were disposed to argue that, on the contrary, if Kashmir were settled, the Pakistanis would find something else to quarrel about. Therefore they would have liked the talks to have been given a general title like 'Matters of mutual interest,' while the Pakistanis would have preferred 'Talks about Kashmir.'

The bigger problem was whether talks could be launched in such a way as not to create an atmosphere prejudicial to their success.

Mr Sandys, having signed on 27 November an arms aid agreement with the Indian Government, went off to Rawalpindi with Mr Harriman to discuss with the Pakistan Government the text of an announcement of talks between the two countries.

On Thursday the twenty-ninth, a statement was made that the two countries: '. . . have agreed that a renewed effort should be made to resolve the outstanding differences between their two countries on Kashmir and other related matters so as to enable India and Pakistan to live side by side in peace and friendship.'

This looked very satisfactory, and 'Kashmir and other related matters' was an ingenious compromise wording, so I went off at 6.00 next morning to fulfil engagements in Calcutta. Half way through the day I heard that all hell had broken loose. Nehru, strongly pressed in Parliament about the formula, was driven into saying: 'Anything that involved an upset of the present arrangements would be very harmful to the people of Kashmir as well as to the future relations of India and Pakistan. I explained to them our basic principles and how it was not possible for us to bypass or ignore them.'

This provoked at once a storm of resentment and suspicion in Pakistan. For air transport reasons, I was literally in baulk in Calcutta; there was no way to get back to Delhi in time to help. However, Mr Sandys, who had not left the sub-continent, turned his plane round at Karachi and came back to Delhi to try to mend the situation. He and the Deputy High Commissioner, Ronald Belcher, worked all night with M. J. Desai and in the early morning a formula for a statement was produced for the approval of a none too pleased Mr Nehru. It read: '. . . there has never been any question of pre-conditions or of any restrictions on the scope of the talks which the two Governments are initiating or on the consideration of any solution which either Government might wish to propose.' The statement was approved and reached Rawalpindi in time to prevent disaster in the Pakistan Assembly. Mr Sandys' rescue effort had been heroic, but inevitably it left scars.

The way was now open for discussion and an Indian team led by Swaran Singh arrived at Karachi on 26 December. The Pakistanis meantime were known to have been in touch with the Chinese. On the day of Swaran Singh's arrival, the Pakistan Government announced that they had reached agreement with the Chinese on a border settlement. On any reckoning, this was an intolerable discourtesy. But it was worse than that. A border agreement included agreement on the frontier of Pakistan-held Kashmir. But India claimed the whole of Kashmir, so that in Indian terms, if the Pakistanis had given anything away, they had given away Indian territory.

I had occasion some years later to ask Mr Zufilkar Ali Bhutto, at that time Foreign Minister of Pakistan, why the Pakistanis had done this. He replied, 'Because we knew they [the Indians] were not coming in good faith.' 'Why, then, did you ask them to come at all?' There was no answer to this question. And of course there is no answer.

However, Swaran Singh with exemplary patience stayed on and the series of talks began. Views were wide apart and the Americans and we could not push the negotiators as our status was that of friends in need rather than participants or possessors of any authority. American thinking developed eventually in the direction of seeking to persuade India to give up a little more of the Vale than had previously been thought possible. I did not myself feel that this would lead to an answer. Morrice James and I visited each other at intervals to make sure we did not get into a mutual row. We did some planning on what we would do if we had to produce a proposal for a solution. (I must make it clear that we never did.) It became obvious to us that there was no possible division of the Vale because (a) the Pakistanis would not be satisfied if they had no say in Srinagar and (b) the Indians must have authority in Srinagar as commanding their only land route to Ladakh. If those two premises were accepted, the only hope was some kind of mixed regime for the Vale, either under or without United Nations auspices. In the uncompromising climate, this could not be said to be a very promising idea either, though as the talks neared deadlock, I did suggest to Mr Nehru that it might be the only way out.

At the fourth meeting in Calcutta we got nearer to cases. Bhutto presented to Galbraith and myself a preposterous proposal leaving precisely two districts in the whole area to India. We both called it nonsense. He than challenged us to produce a better. Galbraith at once said that that was not the idea. Indeed it was not; an Anglo-American plan, on the legitimate assumption that it would have satisfied neither country, would have been an object of execration in both.

I felt after Calcutta that we might have got somewhere, since there could be discerned on both sides an unwilling, even unconscious, acceptance that Pakistan was in any case going to keep Azad Kashmir and Baltistan (the west and the north of Kashmir) and India Ladakh and Jammu (east and south). This left the most difficult item, the Vale, undecided but it channelled the argument into one manageable item. What I had underrated was the degree to which the steam had gone out of the negotiations. The Pakistanis had signed their border agreement with China. The Indians had suddenly discovered what a recognition of substantial Pakistan interest in the Vale might mean and did not like it at all.

So this set of talks came to nothing. There was one more effort. Thinking switched to the possibility of mediation, and Mountbatten used all his powers of persuasion to secure Nehru's agreement to the idea, and there seemed a chance of progress. Further efforts were made in an extraordinary week in Delhi in May 1963 when Lord Mountbatten, Mr Sandys, Mr Dean Rusk, Secretary of State of the United States, and Lord Selkirk, British Commissioner General in South East Asia, were all in Delhi together. But the mediation idea also faded when the Pakistanis demanded impossible conditions.

There was, in that Delhi week, one moment of Anglo-American drama. We had sorted out with Mr Rusk a method of handling the next stage which did not involve further action in Delhi, but overnight Mr Sandys thought up a new formula for mediation which he wished to try on Mr Nehru before leaving. I was apprehensive because Mr Rusk had left and could not be consulted on the change of plan; however, we had a quietly constructive meeting with the Prime Minister after which Mr Sandys asked me to do a telegram to Karachi. In his book Galbraith[2] has graphically described the scene when he came over to protest. His description of his own dramatic performance in

[2] J. K. Galbraith, *Ambassador's Journal*, Hamish Hamilton, 1970, p. 570.

inveighing against these proceedings first with me and then with Mr Sandys is accurate enough. But it omits to mention that I had been instructed by Mr Sandys to consult the American Embassy before further diplomatic action was taken, which meant that, if Galbraith were to object, Mr Sandys would not carry the matter further. I arranged the second of two meetings in a smaller room where the stage was less suited to histrionics and this crisis was averted. Ken Galbraith afterwards wrote me a kindly and generous note praising the poise of the British High Commissioner.

I have one further personal memory of that week, the departure of Lord Mountbatten. As Mountbatten boarded the plane, the only two people on the apron were Mr Nehru and myself. As the aircraft took off, I turned and looked at Panditji in profile. He looked suddenly terribly lonely.

1963–1964

There is a legend that the ground gained at the time of the Chinese border conflict for Indo-British relations and by the West generally in Indian eyes was dissipated by the effort to bring about a Kashmir settlement. Naturally the immense good will created by military aid could not be maintained at its initial strength. It is also true that there were elements in India who sought to exploit the difficulties of the Pakistan relationship expressed in the Kashmir negotiations to turn opinion against the West. But in practical terms, events in 1963–64 did not develop to destroy what had been gained.

There was in the first months of 1963 a steady consolidation of the work of military aid. The British team under the leadership of Major-General Peter Glover, settled down to expert co-operation with their colleagues from the United States, Canada and Australia. Relations with the Indian Defence Ministry were much less complicated and temperamental under the new Minister, Y. B. Chavan; and relations with the Indian Chiefs, General Chaudhuri, Admiral Soman and Air Vice-Marshal Arjan Singh, were close and harmonious. Joint air defence exercises were held in the course of the year. Lengthy and by no

means simple negotiations resulted in a plan for the development
of the Mazagon dock in Bombay for the production of Leander
frigates under licence for the Indian Navy. All of us had to pay
constant attention to our assurances to Pakistan that this build-up
was not intended against anything but a possible renewal of
Chinese aggression, a basis understood and accepted by the
Indians.

The Kashmir issue, being unsolved, was far from dead. But its
survival did not prevent the continuance of the better relationship
which military aid had brought about.

There has also been a tendency to suggest that efforts were
made to force India into SEATO or into some other Western
combination. This again is a distortion of the nature and direction
of the many general discussions of the future security of India.
The invasion had brought about a sudden understanding in
India of the strategic vulnerability of the country in the face of
air attack from the north. The Indians began to cast about for new
forms of self-defence. Was there any way of assuring such defence
by air warning systems, a stronger Indian fighter force and some
kind of international guarantee? Discussions of this kind continued
over the next two or three years but without concrete result. The
Americans and the British were hesitant about extending commitments any further, and there were also hesitations on the
Indian side about any proposal which would compromise the non-
alignment policy.

In the time of lessened tension which followed the Chinese
invasion there were two matters which kept a number of us busy
in Delhi. One was the Indian Institute of Technology. There
were four such institutes in India with external sponsorship,
the American in Kanpur, the German in Madras, the Russian in
Bombay and our own at Haus Khas, just outside New Delhi. The
moving spirit in establishing the British sponsored institute
in the Delhi area was Professor M. S. Thacker, a remarkable man
who seemed to give India a 'first' in inventing a man who could
be in two places at one time. The Indian Government provided
the land and buildings, British industry the machines and the
British Government some ten professors. There were at intervals

difficulties between scientific inspiration and Indian administration but the institute grew steadily in size and performance.

Another was the British School in Delhi. Indian and British educational objectives and methods were naturally diverging. For lack of a local school aiming at British examinations, people who could not afford or did not want a boarding school education for their children began to decline appointment to Delhi. The feeling came to a head among families with education problems that we ought if we could to organize a local British school. We started organizing it in March 1963 and by July we had a school of sixty-seven pupils from sixteen nations in temporary accommodation, permanent premises being almost unobtainable. But one day the Indian Minister of Works, Shri Mirchand Khanna, sent for me and offered us an ideal piece of land not far from the High Commission offices. The Government, he explained, were making this offer because, while we naturally taught the British syllabus, we catered for all nationalities and races without discrimination. I was almost too surprised to say 'thank you'. When Pat and I revisited the School in 1970, it had a building and over 230 children aged between five and sixteen from thirty-six countries.

Travel and Visitors
One of the principal activities of a High Commissioner is, of course, travel. During our tour of over four years we managed to see something of every corner of India except for one area in central India which we would have visited had we stayed for a month longer. In past ages travel in India used to be immensely full of circumstance and not a little romantic. Even when the railway age succeeded horses and elephants, the romance remained.

Now an air service takes you from Delhi for anything up to a thousand miles. A car ride takes you to your immediate destination, anything from eight to two hundred miles. Then comes a whole series of visits to people, factories, dams, tea gardens, universities, British Council operations (an outstanding performance in India), hospitals, temples, Governors, Chief Ministers and more and more ordinary people. Pat and I always did these journeys together if it could possibly be managed. This, apart from being infinitely more enjoyable than going alone, was immensely important professionally. India is rightly proud of the activity of women in its public life, and Pat often had valuable programmes separate from mine.

Some of these visits were regular, such as the December visit to Calcutta for the meetings of the Associated Chambers of Commerce and the United Kingdom Citizens Association, and similar dates in Bombay and the annual get-together of the United Planters' Association of South India (UPASI) at Coonoor in the Nilgiri Hills. On all journeys there were speeches, short and long, press conferences, heavily scented garlands of marigolds and frangipani and photographs galore.

The one impossibility was a casual visit to an Indian village. A manifestly official European, here today and gone tomorrow, was something extraordinary even in the 1960s. When he arrived, however informally, everybody stopped 'doing' and stood and stared. Of course one learned about the village, but it had ceased to be itself.

There were a few general rules. One was not to embark on a curry without being sure that your glass of water was by your side; the curry might be infinitely hotter than your hosts admitted. A taste (which I fortunately had) for very sweet and not necessarily very hot coffee was invaluable. And a general capacity for endurance enjoyment and appreciation is the basis of making these purposeful wanderings the pleasure we always found them.

Vivid moments remain in mind like one on the speakers' platform at Annamalai University in Madras State (Tamil Nadj). As we waited amid what seemed to me to be the deafening chatter of 3,000 students for the moment to begin, the Vice-Chancellor, Sir C. P. Ramasvany Aiyar, bellowed into my ear, 'This silence is most remarkable.' He then went very serious and added, 'In a year, a third of these young people will be without jobs.'

In 1964, Gundevia suddenly rang up and asked me whether I still wanted to go to Nagaland. I had applied some considerable time before, but there was a chronically tense situation between the Nagas hostile to the Indian connection and those who accepted it and had the support of the Indian civil and military authority. This had made visiting unsafe. I think an exception may have been made for me as the British had a tradition of friendship with the Nagas, and a visit of this kind might be hoped to do marginal good. I accepted at once.

We drove up under military escort from Dimapur in the plains to Kohima where the Japanese advance to India was finally stemmed. The famous tennis court battlefield is preserved in concrete and, just below, the inscription stands:

> ... for our tomorrow
> They gave their today.

We were welcomed by a hall full of Nagas friendly to the Indians who received us with the wobbling contralto hum which is the national greeting. We discussed endlessly with the Governor, Vishnu Sahay, the intractable problem of reconciliation. It was clear to everyone, including the 'friendly' Naga Government, that whatever the prospects, the two sides would have to talk.

The tour brought to us on several occasions in Delhi a visitor who was always announced as 'Excellency, there is a man in the garden who does not give his name.' I began to know that it would always be the Rev. Michael Scott. Living among the 'hostiles,' he taxed his physique to the utmost in efforts for peace. But I did have to suggest to him that, if he were to make a contribution to reconciliation, he would have to discipline in public his devotion to the people among whom he lived.

Delhi is on Routes UK 1, US 1, UN 1 and many other main highways of the world. With a foresight which other nations including Britain might have practised, the Indian Government had built a fine conference centre, the *Vigyan Bhavan*, beside the broad avenue leading from the Secretariat to the India Gate. So Delhi lay on a general Conference Route 1 as well. Thus we never lacked guests, old, young, important, exciting, eccentric, normal, invited or totally unexpected.

Perhaps the finest hand of top honours which fate dealt to us was the combination of Sir Saville Garner, head of the Commonwealth Office, Sir Percival Griffiths, Professor Sir Isaiah Berlin and Lady Berlin and the Archbishop of Canterbury and Mrs Ramsey. I have a recollection that we were all exceedingly brilliant though I cannot remember a word anyone said. The Archbishop's visit, for the meeting of the World Council of Churches, ended, in our absence on tour, in splendid climax. He invited thirty Eastern Orthodox priests to a party. Ninety came. Dr. Ramsey was equal to the occasion but the Comptroller got accidentally locked into the wine-cellar.

For Sir Percival Griffiths our house became an Indian home from home. This remarkable man had volunteered in British days to succeed no less than three British officials who had been assassinated by Bengali terrorists in Midnapore. He had survived to became a British member of the pre-independence legislature and since independence had been the dyamic elder statesman of British commerce and industry in India. It was good to feel that he could relax completely with us.

Sir Malcolm Sargent came as conductor of the visiting London Philharmonic Orchestra, who under his baton played the Indian National Anthem in a way that spellbound the audience. Sir Malcolm as a guest was every bit as intense as Sir Malcolm on the podium. Everything was done with emphasis, so much so that when he opted to rest in the garden, so the legend went, the birds considerately suspended their rehearsal. I warned him that the price he would have to pay for our hospitality was Joanna (aged seven) practising the piano from 8.00 to 8.30 each morning. He was as kind as could be and later sent Joanna a series of records of Gilbert and Sullivan, as conducted by himself with that passionate vitality which brought back life into music which had become somehow too solemn. He added a standing invitation to rehearsals of the proms. He became very much part of our lives when we returned home in 1965 and I listened on the radio in real agony to his last poignant appearance at the Albert Hall. His 'style,' the seriousness of his musicianship and his kindness and encouragement to Joanna showed amply how he had been able to do so much for music, and particularly for music for the young, throughout his life.

I must also recall a frequent distinguished guest. Duncan Sandys, my Secretary of State. Mr Sandys is a controversial character and would hate to be anything else. His methods of work were, as he knew, exhausting for others if not for himself. But he was a delightful guest, taking a warm interest in the words and deeds of the younger members of the family. And it was a special bonus when his French wife, Marie-Claire, came too. Occasionally a slight but delicious French accent could be heard round the house, explaining, 'I was only looking for my husband.'

The Passing of Jawaharlal Nehru

As 1963 moved on the pace of political life both in India and between Britain and India seemed temporarily to slacken. Mr Nehru was finally showing signs of old age though he went on working as hard as ever, until he collapsed at the end of a Congress conference at Bhubaneshwar in Orissa. There were troubled questionings about the Congress Party's future and the lack of new blood. Then, for us, Kashmir raised its ugly head again when the matter came once more before the United Nations Security Council.

Pat Dean, our representative in New York, sent me an outline of his intended speech which seemed eminently sensible. In its final version it came out more formally and the Indian delegation took against it. The Press Trust of India sent a highly prejudiced account to the Indian Press. The Indian special delegate, Mr M. C. Chagla, withdrew his acceptance of an invitation to a reception by the British delegation. (A militant Hinduism in the shape of the Jan Sangh party was growing in India and no doubt an Indian Muslim in this position, confronted by Muslim Pakistan, had to show himself more Hindu than the Hindus or lose part of popular confidence.)

There was an immediate press uproar in India. Very fortunately I had an appointment with Lal Bahadur Shastri, then Home Minister, and again our communications proved excellent. A quarter of an hour before I was due to see him I was handed a copy as clean as it could be made of Pat Dean's speech. I gave it to Shastri. With that extraordinary fairness which characterized all that he said and did, he said slowly, 'You cannot expect me to agree with everything you said, but I understand why you said it.'

The episode ruffled the atmosphere but not more. A multi-party delegation from the Lok Sabha (Indian House of Commons) came to see me in protest. The argument boiled down into a fascinating discussion of why, given that Lord Mountbatten, a close relation of the Queen, had become the first Governor-General, Britain was not more pro-Indian. I tried to explain that, when Lord Mountbatten took this office after independence he, so to speak, became an Indian and could not therefore occupy in Britain the position of political authority which they imagined. There were tough words and no ill-feeling.

Even then Kashmir would not lie down. Mr Nehru decided to release Sheikh Abdullah, the Muslim political leader in Kashmir who had started as pro-Indian but had subsequently advocated the plebiscite and had been kept thenceforth in detention. There was hopeful talk of a move towards reconciliation between the Sheikh and the Prime Minister. But progress was slow and when the Sheikh on a tour abroad entered into some talk with a Chinese representative, any hope of progress understandably collapsed.

We were due for home leave in March. Shortly before leaving, Pat and I called on Mr Nehru to say *au revoir*. He was sitting quietly in a comfortable garden chair under a sun umbrella on the terrace of the official residence. He was relaxed but very quiet. When he was like this, it was usually the family things which interested him, whether his family or ours. But this time he did not react at all. We seemed to be just going through the motions.

So I changed the mood. I mentioned that everybody in Britain was looking forward to seeing him in London at the forthcoming Commonwealth Prime Ministers' Meeting. He came to the surface like a man who has come out of a dive. 'Oh yes,' he said, 'I am looking forward so much to going to London again.' A conventional remark in most contexts. But not in this one.

As we left, I thought of the beautifully descriptive passage where Galsworthy describes the tranquil passing away of Old Jolyon. The character was not quite appropriate, but the scene was. It was the last time we saw Panditji alive. Two months later he was quite suddenly struck down and on 27 May he died, still in harness. I have a feeling that for him dying in harness was a happy and even a peaceful departure.

Leave was at first a rest, then a sudden flight back to India for Nehru's funeral. At Delhi there fell on the Cabinet Secretary, Sir Burke Trend, and myself the unforgettable duty of being driven in slow procession from the Prime Minister's Residence to the funeral *ghat*, a normal twenty minute drive which took us two hours and three-quarters. Hundreds of people insisted on shaking hands through the car window. Everybody guessed who we were. 'It is Chester Bowles.' 'No, it is Lord Mountbatten.' There was sadness, of course, but I carried away the feeling that in that crowd the main sensation was one of gratitude that so many people had come from so far to pay Panditji a last tribute.

Just as we were preparing to fly back, there was a flurry in the aircraft which was hurriedly stopped. Someone had spotted an Indian official car arriving. It was Lal Bahadur Shastri coming to thank our party, Sir Alec Douglas-Home, George Brown and Lord Mountbatten, for having come.

Shastri and Retrospect

So it was back to leave and an eventful family summer. We gave on David and Christopher's joint twenty-first birthday, with Celia (eighteen) as co-guest-of-honour, one of those parties to which parents nerve themselves once in a lifetime. David in the meantime had got a good degree in history, married Jilli Valpy with whom he and Richard Bullock had driven to Delhi the year before, and got into the diplomatic service. So 1964 was an *annus mirabilis* for him.

When I returned to post-Nehru India, there had already been some excitements. Shastriji had plunged into the overwhelming task of being the first Prime Minister of India after Nehru by impossibly overstraining his energies and suffering a heart attack. The difficulty of succeeding Nehru remained, and Shastriji seemed disinclined, partly through a natural diffidence, to force himself or his ideas on his colleagues or the country. But his government was a good one by and large, and the country and the world waited to see what would come of it.

One of his earlier duties was to attend a non-aligned conference in Cairo. This was probably the least non-aligned of all non-aligned meetings. Shastri did his best in an opening speech to be non-aligned, but the tide was overwhelming and on the return of the Indian delegation one newspaper had the headline 'non-alignment anti-West'. An official of the Ministry of External Affairs complained to me that the 'Cubans had been an awful nuisance' – and then the idea of Dr Castro's Cuba being non-aligned caught his sense of humour and he burst into delighted laughter.

Lal Bahadur Shastri was very keen to visit London, and arrangements were made for the beginning of December. The media and public threw off their accustomed indifference and showed a real interest in the successor to Nehru. There was broad discussion on many things including the future defence of India and on the remaining questions of dependent territories in the Commonwealth. Mr Shastri was interested in what Britain could do to help over the first and uncompromising in his pressure for independence of even very small communities on the second. When he left, I asked him the banal question whether he had enjoyed himself. He replied in his charmingly direct way, 'It was very nice but there are too many televisions.'

I went back to India convinced that there would soon be changes in our lives, and just after Christmas came a letter saying that I was to be the next Permanent Under-Secretary at the Foreign Office. I prepared mentally for the difficult period in which no one knows but yourself that you are going. But on the evening of 3 January 1965 came a frantic telegram saying that the appointment of John Freeman as my successor had leaked (it was a great period for leakage), and that my appointment as Permanent Under-Secretary was being announced at once. Would I please tell the Indian Government before tomorrow morning?

I managed to locate Gundevia at a party so my duty was done. The news was in the next morning's press. Tuesday was the morning for my weekly meeting with all the senior staff. When I came in they all stood up and applauded. This was one of those moments so spontaneous that one finds oneself bereft of anything clever, elegant or statesmanlike to say. I could only mumble the one thing which I most sincerely meant; that this appointment was a great tribute to the consistently fine work done by the High Commission over the last four eventful years and that I wanted to thank all present for their part in it.

The accent in London was on speed of movement. So having dashed off a letter of welcome to John Freeman, I did a quick calculation. January was already totally booked, February could be divided into one week in London, one week flying round India to say a few good-byes and a fortnight to organize ourselves out of Delhi. Departure date would therefore be 1 March. The chief sufferer would be David Scott, the new Deputy High Commissioner, who was due to arrive at the end of January and would get a few introductions from me but no guidance or proper attention at all.

Before departure there were two memorable events, one symbolic of the moment, the other pointing ominously to the future. The first was the death of Sir Winston Churchill. I learned it on the afternoon of a Sunday on which we had arranged for a dinner in honour of Sir James Cassels, the new British Chief of the General Staff. The ranking guest was to be General Muchu Chaudhuri, the Indian Commander-in-Chief. I gave myself a few minutes thought. The orthodox thing would have been to cancel. I rang up the General and asked him if he would agree that instead of cancellation we should have the dinner as a seriously commemorative occasion. I would invite him to say a few words to which I would respond. I realized, I added, that Sir Winston might not always have been India's favourite British statesman, and would entirely understand if he preferred cancellation. The General said that he would be delighted to do as I proposed. The evening was interesting and dignified.

A memorial service was arranged in Delhi Cathedral. I put the same point to Mr Shastri, adding that, if he would wish to attend, I was sure the Cathedral authorities would be glad to arrange a time to accommodate him. Mr Shastri accepted, saying that Friday, the day of the Service in London, was a busy cabinet day in Delhi, but that he would adjourn the cabinet for the time of the service. As for the service itself I insisted on an American share. Members of the American Embassy joined with our mission in ushering and I also arranged inclusion of the Battle Hymn of the Republic. Mr Shastri and eight of his colleagues attended. It was a gracious and understanding act, immensely appreciated by the British and Commonwealth communities.

The other event concerned, once again, Indo-Pakistan relations. In the autumn of 1964, the Indian Parliament had approved an amendment of the Constitution which made Kashmir an integral part of India. Since this put one more obstacle in the way of an agreed settlement, it was a little surprising that Shastri should have agreed – no doubt it was a subject on which he was not disposed to contest the views of his colleagues. Meantime signs of tension were beginning to appear in another quarter, the Ran of Kutch. In this remote corner of north-western India, there was doubt about the exact frontier and there were signs that force might be used. General Chaudhuri came over for a quiet talk and told me that we should take this danger very seriously. According to Indian information Pakistan's preparations were on a scale which could hardly be exclusively defensive. We ought to know that help might be needed to prevent armed conflict. Of course I reported this. The excellent policy and diplomatic job done by the Commonwealth Relations Office and the British High Commissioners in the two countries came after my time. General Chaudhuri's warning had been very valuable.

The last two weeks were spent inevitably in eating and (soft) drinking ourselves out of Delhi. Special and appetizing South Indian breakfasts with *idlis* (a tasty but by no means light South Indian pancake) were a fattening start for the day. There were parties of every kind, including one given by our Indian staff at the High Commission where I made my second only speech in Hindi. Our host at the diplomatic farewell was the Soviet

Ambassador Mr Benediktov, who had become doyen of the diplomatic corps. We learned that he intended to invite the representative of the East Germans to the party. The same channel carried back a message that in that embarrassing case the guest of honour might necessarily fail to appear. In the end the East German representative, whom we could identify, did not appear, but Mr Benediktov 'happened to have an East German friend there as a house guest'. So we both won, and Mr Benediktov was generous in his hospitality to us personally and to the High Commission staff.

My last interview was with Lal Bahadur Shastri. He was running behind schedule, crowded with engagements. But he was as always serene and kindly. I said that in this last interview before leaving India, I would like to speak to him as Paul Gore-Booth and not as British High Commissioner. I said I had been round India and found that, despite riots and protests against this or that, his name carried great respect and affection. People did however ask why Shastriji did not intervene a little sooner and use his prestige more strongly to quiet things down. He replied, as near as I can recall it, 'I am glad you spoke to me like that. I must tell you something. It is our, the Congress's, fault. We encouraged our people to behave like this against the British. Now we must pay the price.'

That is why, without any criticism of his successor, I am sure that India, Britain and the world could have well done with a little more time with Lal Bahadur Shastri. In 1970 'Rajaji' (C. J. Rajagopalachari, the Congress politician who became the first Indian Governor-General) said to me, 'Nehru was the man we had to have: but to my mind Shastri was in some ways the better man.' Like most things said by Rajaji, this has an uncommon if provocative shrewdness.

A year later Shastriji did pay a special price – the price of Kashmir. His efforts at the Tashkent negotiations cost him his life, another victim of that nagging deadlock. When his affairs were settled after his death, it was found that he had no earthly possessions at all.

On Sunday 28 February, we paid a quiet, private visit to

Rajghat, the memorial to Mahatma Gandhi. At 8.00 pm that evening David Scott and I folded up my valedictory despatch. At 8.00 am on 1 March Pat and I set out for our last official journey to the airport. A considerable crowd had gathered there. At the last minute there was a rustle. Mrs Indira Gandhi had arrived. This was a final very generous gesture, and we were both very silent as the plane drew away from our home of the past four years.

It always seems possible to prove logically and statistically that India is on the point of collapse. This is a very dangerous thing to do. It is dangerous because for an identifiable five thousand years people have contrived to exist in this sub-continent of extremes of nature and vicissitudes of all kinds and to have become and remained strongly and recognizably Indian. Others may despair about Indian poverty, but there is a feeling of civilization about the poorest person in India. Arguments and crowds sometimes get out of hand, and there are those who descend below civilization like the Naxalites of West Bengal. But, as anyone who has lived in India knows, there is something about Indian tradition, character and method that keeps things in motion when in theory they ought to stop.

I am often told that this realism is heartless. How can you bear to live among the poverty, the hunger and the homelessness of so many? A sense of history does not fill an empty stomach. The answer is that it is no good going to India if it is too much for you. As an official you must do what you can within the framework of national policy and your ability to influence it. As a private citizen, you can help great causes; or you can give 'a cup of cold water in Christ's name,' or in any other name, to an individual or community, knowing that, if enough people, undaunted by the magnitude of the problem, do the same, there really will be a difference.

As I left India, there seemed to be three great dangers; economic collapse, divisive tendencies and a further deterioration in relations with Pakistan. Economic difficulties related particularly to the balance of payments and did indeed force a devaluation two years later. It may be that the economic problem has transferred itself to the danger that prevailing doctrine may further retard and inhibit the creation of wealth. India with its population problem cannot afford this.

Divisive tendencies were strong in 1965. There was a danger that in future non-Congress State Ministries might reject reasonable control by the Central Government and a longer-run fear that linguistic division might prove too strong for political unity. Subsequent political events have drastically reduced any early danger of states getting out of central control.

Linguistic disunity on the other hand became an issue when Nehru was still alive. There was the possibility of a collapse of English as the only country-wide language, before an indigenous language was ready to take its place. Nehru saw this danger and ingeniously anticipated it by turning English, due to be demoted from official status in 1965, to the status of 'associated official language'. This gave official sanction to the prolongation of the unifying mission of English similar to that of Latin in the European Middle Ages. Hindi had now time to assert itself as the universal language and to come to terms with the use in state universities of regional vernaculars.

Apprehensions about the Indo-Pakistan relationship were, sadly, only too justified. In the summer of 1965, something like 1947 repeated itself and Pakistan irregulars sought to seize an opportunity for a coup in Kashmir. But the Chinese had done the Indians a good turn in 1962, and the new command structure and personalities caused the Indians to surprise themselves and some of their less knowledgeable friends by their performance in repelling the attack.

As for relations with Britain and the West, there was at the time I left a slight drift westward. This caused the Russians to remonstrate with the Indians in a manner to which, I would hope, a British Government would have given a dusty retort. On one occasion when Mrs Gandhi was Minister of Information, I told her that many people including myself found it a bit hard to take that on All-India Radio every country was open to criticism except the Soviet Union. I was rather glad when my comment was leaked (not by the British High Commission) since many

Indians felt that way and thought the practice damaging to Indian self-respect. India had every right to a friendly relationship with the Soviet Union: as R. K. Nehru once imaginatively remarked to me, Central Asia ought to be a highway and not a barrier. Moreover, from 1965 onward defence aid to India from Britain and the United States became hesitant and it was legitimate for Indians to take the view that, if they were to have a clash with Pakistan, scruples about intervention in an intra-Commonwealth quarrel could inhibit British defence aid for reasons which would in no way obstruct Russian aid, particularly given Pakistan's rapprochement with China.

All the same, those who care for the success of the Indian experiment will watch anxiously lest India, having obtained independence from the leading imperial power of yesterday, should lose some of that independence to the leading imperial power of today. And it would be a pity if the non-alignment of yesterday should lead through forces either within or outside the control of India to an involvement in the power struggles of the Communist heartland tomorrow.

British relations with India were relaxed as we left, and despite British hesitations about defence aid, they remained so for some months. My view was that if this continued, we could influence Indian policy and thinking a little but not much. We did until the war with Pakistan in 1965. Then according to Mr Harold Wilson, 'C. R. O. officials briefed me on the situation and in-veigled me into issuing, on September 6, a statement – justified as they said by cast-iron evidence – condemning India for an act of aggression.'[3] Mr Wilson adds that he was wrong. It may well have been that some of the advice was faulty. But to put the blame for the subsequent damage to relations with India, which lasted for years rather than months, on officials is neither appropriate nor convincing. The statement involved two decisions which were wholly political – a decision to intervene in the argument at all and a decision to take sides in an intra- Commonwealth dispute. And at least on Mr Wilson's showing, the state-

[3] Harold Wilson, *The Labour Government 1964-70*. Weidenfeld/Joseph 1971, pp. 133-4.

The author with Mr Aneurin Bevan, Rangoon, 1955

H.M. The Queen's visit to India, 1961

The author with Mr Nehru and Vice-President Radhakrishnan, watching a Test Match in 196

ment could have waited until the return of the Commonwealth Secretary the very next morning.

After their slow recovery, Indo-British relations by 1973 were
reasonably relaxed again, though during the time both trade
and standing were damaged. None the less, there is a permanency
to the Indian-British relationship, not a love-hate relationship but,
rather, a genuine affection blown about with periodic gusts of
exasperation. This is not an unhealthy relationship and does not
affect the great talent for personal affection in which India is
so rich.

At the farewell dinner which the Foreign Minister, Sardar
Swaran Singh, gave for us, I said I wanted to emphasize one
particular virtue of diplomatic life in Delhi, the unfailing accessibility of people whom one needed to see. In some countries
which pride themselves on being civilized feigned absence or
sickness is used as a political or diplomatic tactic. I had always
regarded this as sophisticated boorishness and not even as an
advantageous device. The Indian practice, I said, was courteous,
genuinely civilized and deeply appreciated, and I wanted to
take the opportunity to express my thanks both professionally
and personally for it.

Indians and British will not always agree. But the British do
still and will continue to be a little proud that they handed over
the brightest jewel in the imperial crown to the rightful owners
before they had to. For this they are not so foolish as to ask for
thanks. But they like to be assured that the owners are getting
on all right and not losing their independence or their democracy
in the process.

L

London

1965-1969

On Becoming Permanent Under-Secretary

The process of becoming Permanent Under-Secretary is an inscrutable one. There is even now a predictability about becoming a hereditary monarch or peer, but the only predictable thing about the turn of the year 1964–65 was that Harold Caccia was due to retire at sixty and that a successor would have to be found.

There were other relevant factors. Lord Harlech was coming away from Washington. It was known that a Labour Government would be likely to appoint someone with political background to represent Britain at the United Nations. What this meant was that the Government, principally the Foreign Secretary and the Prime Minister, would have to make some decisions.

It is arguable that there ought not to be even this amount of predictability about change, and that in these days sixty ought not to be the retiring age. The answer, which I believe to be presently acceptable, is that in a diplomatic service if you do not retire people at sixty you cannot give the fifties sufficient authority or the forties sufficient responsibility to make them feel the career worth while.

I had paid my respects to the then opposition leadership in the summer of 1964 and had, at Mr Wilson's suggestion, a long talk with Mr Patrick Gordon-Walker, the Foreign Secretary designate, When I came to London with Mr Shastri in December 1964, I called on Mr Gordon-Walker in the Foreign Secretary's room at the Foreign Office. We sat in front of a roaring fire and discussed the practicability of regional policies, the Secretary of State being interested both in Europe and in Asia, particularly South-East Asia. Not a word was said about future appointments.

When the appointment was announced, Mr Gordon-Walker wrote me a kindly letter. But his political ill-luck persisted, and there was something a little poignant about never serving someone who must have had much to do with my appointment and had the right to expect that we should be working together for several years.

So, two days before my visit home on 31 January 1965, I had mentally to change gear to meet Mr Michael Stewart. I renewed acquaintance after a gap of thirty-five years. After we had talked a little about his new position, he asked me for my comments on other Secretaries of State. I started with the great Lord Salisbury and came down to the present day. I got about a 95 per cent mark but stupidly left out the wrong one, Arthur Henderson. This was because in the few papers I had seen of that period, anything anyone else said seemed to be trumped by a minute from Ramsay MacDonald. But I did underline the immense admiration of all my generation in the service for Ernest Bevin.

I started work in the Office on 10 May. I chose this date for an historical reason. I had started my acquaintance with Germany when relations were tolerable. I had seen them propelled by a madman to unimaginable depths, stay there and then very gradually convalesce. Now that the Queen was finally visiting the Federal Republic, I wanted to be in office when reconciliation was ceremoniously confirmed. That visit ended with the slow progress of a lit-up *Britannia* down the Elbe as the vast crowd on the banks sang that haunting folk-song

> '*Muss i denn, muss i denn*
> *Von dem Staedli hinaus . . .*'

Having consciously but by no means uncritically worked for reconciliation, I found this a very emotional moment. Professor Münch would have felt the same way.

The routine had already begun. At 10.30 am on 10 May I was again sitting at the head of a table and the back of a desk wondering how I had got there. I had not been given to much thinking on the lines of 'what would I do if . . .' because, given the various posts to which I could have been sent, this would have been a waste of intellectual energy. In any case I felt that before I judged I had better know, and before I knew I should need a little time.

On Being Permanent Under-Secretary

The Permanent Under-Secretary of any department of Government is the senior official or civil servant in that department. The word 'permanent' is accurate in the sense that, if there is a change of government or of Secretary of State, you do not have to move out or even go through a formal process of resignation and reappointment. A Permanent Under-Secretary could have an objection of conscience to a new Government, but the necessities of British external policy largely impose themselves on succeeding governments, and officials normally carry on without difficulties of conscience. As for the rest of the meaning of the word 'permanent', the one thing that is certain when one begins is that on a particular date, unless there are very exceptional circumstances, your permanence will cease. Perhaps the continental 'Secretary-General' is less misleading.

What governed the whole of my life in this final period was the circumstance that, apart from the Secretary of State, the PUS was the only person in the Office whose obligation it was to have some knowledge of everything. In 1965 'everything' meant foreign countries and international organizations. A similar obligation in Commonwealth affairs rested on the Permanent Under-Secretary of the Commonwealth Relations Office, Sir Saville Garner, who had the further responsibility of being head of the Diplomatic service, unified in January 1965 under the recommendation of the Plowden Report. It might have been thought that this combination would have created an impossible relationship between the two Permanent Under-Secretaries, much of whose work was bound to overlap. Fortunately such a relationship depends in the main on personal attitudes; I had already been working with and for Joe Garner in India, and in seven years together over the wire to and from India or down the

passage in London we never had any trouble. Since the amalgamation of the two offices in 1968, the Permanent Under-
Secretary of the Foreign and Commonwealth Office has the
same obligation over the entire area.

Of course, internal communication in the Foreign Office
and its successor, the Foreign and Commonwealth Office, being
exceedingly good, a number of people, both Ministers and officials,
have an excellent general knowledge of events and policy. But
whereas, generally speaking, this overall knowledge is a matter
of choice, with the PUS it is obligatory. If there is any sign of
policy or action becoming discoordinated, it is the PUS's responsibility to see that this is put right at once. This cannot be done
by rule of thumb. It presupposes an organized individual ability
to distinguish what is going right from what needs encouragement or correction. It also means readiness to initiate and, very
important indeed, to be sympathetic to the spirit of initiative.

Several things follow. First there are the personal points.
One must have a capacity to read quickly and listen intelligently,
and an ability to judge the right moment to intervene – in other
words a sense of priority. On this point I had been deeply impressed by what Winston Churchill wrote about the North
African land battles of 1941–42. He criticized General Auchinleck,
possibly unfairly, on the ground that he was too diffident about
personally intervening when things might be going wrong. But
the contrary proposition has almost equal virtue. When at the
time of the Foreign Office/Commonwealth Office merger we
sought outside advice, an old and vastly wise friend looked me in
the eye and said 'How do you ensure that you, as Permanent
Under-Secretary, have the control that you should have over
policy and action?' Before answering I took much longer to think
than usual. Eventually I replied, 'Largely by silence.' What
I meant was that, if you have a high-class, experienced and loyal
team – loyal that is to the Secretary of State, the government and
the country – then your estimate of character and capability and
of current information will tell you how things are going. It will
advise you how far you can trust each of your departments and
senior colleagues to do the right thing in the right way without

being fussed from above. Equally you acquire a sense of what is ill-directed or a waste of time. Of course one is not always right; an early telephone call can usually put that straight. But there is so much going through the Office day by day that an attempt personally to 'control' everything would constipate policy and its execution and kill off the Permanent Under-Secretary.

You also need above all a private secretary who has the same instinct, and the courage and judgement to decide on his own what to let you in for and what to keep off your desk, and when to tell you, in a way that you will accept, if you seem in danger of going wrong. I must pay my whole-hearted tribute to the three private secretaries I had in my time, Nicholas Gordon-Lennox, Patrick Wright and Richard Baker. In their different ways they all without exception used their experience, good sense and good temper to such effect that I don't think I ever had cause to say 'Why didn't I see this?' or 'Why did you let me do that?'

Part of the discipline involves the PUS in refraining from having favourite subjects. Of course one country or one subject may interest him as a person more than another and he is likely to be better at one subject than another. But one of his principal functions is to keep a balance all round, and too great a specialization could undermine his ability to do so. The necessary overall knowledge and the function of preserving that balance and consistency of policy meant that, although I was the senior official, I could not be the permanent leading expert on the detail of any particular question, geographical or functional. What I could do was to ensure that particular interests did not disturb the general direction of policy. This function assumes particular importance when it becomes necessary to weigh, say, the claims of European policy against involvement in the Middle East or, once in the Middle East, to measure the conflicting claims of the Arabs and the Israelis.

Against this background I felt I should involve myself personally in critical points of major crises such as the de Gaulle attack on NATO, the Kosygin visit and its Vietnam repercussions, and the six-day Middle East war. I also made a practice of attending certain important international occasions such as the meetings of the United Nations Assembly in each September-October and the Ministerial meetings of NATO in December which were also a kind of *Club des Sécrétaires-Généraux*. These short but important visits kept alive both personal contacts and a feel for atmosphere which in turn made advice more sound.

All this may sound a little grandiose and it is well to remember that Permanent Under-Secretaries are by no means exempt from the rule that governments are ineluctably compelled for Parliamentary, press or personal reasons to spend a lot of time on things which in proportion to the cosmos in general are very trivial.

Such is the doctrinal description of running an organization at the official level in a way adapted to the temperament and capacity of a particular individual. It is not necessarily *the* way, though it does contain a percentage of inevitables. As I prepared to return to London, I was conscious of one lack in Foreign Office organization which I had felt in my previous period in London. There was a remarkable cross-fertilization of ideas and information through the circulation of documents, and there were plenty of meetings between the Ministers and officials concerned to discuss particular policies and actions. But precisely because people were well-informed and knew what they were doing, there seemed to be no regular machinery by which you could be a bit officious and question what other people were doing in their own fields. You could not easily ring up someone in cold blood and say, 'You seem to be making a hash of disarmament,' if you happened to be specializing in East Africa. Yet a little mutual abrasion between generalists and specialists and between specialists themselves would, it seemed to me, be a good thing.

The needed machinery came into being suddenly and by historical accident. When the Labour Government took office in October 1964, the Foreign Secretary, Mr Gordon-Walker, was largely absent seeking election to Parliament. There could thus be no firm top-level Ministerial direction of day to day foreign policy. So Harold Caccia set up a short daily morning meeting of senior officials. I urged him to keep it going even when the emergency was over. It was exactly what I wanted as a permanent institution.

Thenceforth the Under-Secretaries met every morning for never more than half an hour under the chairmanship of the Permanent Under-Secretary, with the head of News Department (ie the Press Officer) and the Secretary of State's Private Secretary. Decisions, even under already agreed policies, would not normally be taken, pending advice from expert departments. But the meeting developed arguments and attitudes and pointed the way in which the day's business should be organized for decisions, where needed, by the Secretary of State or other Ministers. The plain man could get his word in, and no one could get too many words in. The meeting was also an invaluable launching pad for bright new ideas which could be rapidly tried out and, if considered promising, be remitted to the Planners. Thus a small and not very original administrative reform grew into a new and more efficient way of handling day to day business.

With these various aids to knowledge and efficiency, it might be thought that the Permanent Under-Secretary with a reasonable capacity for delegation could have a well organized and not too exacting life. On this I at once consulted all my surviving predecessors. All agreed that, if you were to be reasonably thorough and properly accessible (a point to which I attached the greatest importance), you would have to make up time outside rather lengthy office hours. William Strang, my senior and remarkably youthful predecessor, said he used to work a good deal in bed; Ivone Kirkpatrick used, I knew, to get up frighteningly early. Derick Hoyer-Millar worked immensely fast, but had even so to make up time at the expense of official receptions and during the weekend. When in a BOAC aircraft over the Arabian desert in 1966, I was confronted with a questionnaire unexpectedly inquiring 'How many hours do you work a week?' Counting the business meals, formal and informal, the red boxes taken home and the solid backlog papers done during the week-end, I conscientiously wrote 'eighty hours'. The sharp end of this calculation was that five nights a week there was an hour and a half's work to be done between 11.30 pm and 8.00 am. I started by doing it at night; my physique took charge at half time and indicated a strong preference for 6.30 to 8.00 am.

All this exercise of management and direction is subject to one overriding qualification. Speaking of the PUS, Mr Michael Stewart used the term 'my senior adviser'. Like anybody else in any Government office, the PUS is the servant, however senior, of the elected representatives of the people. This is not because the politicians are necessarily wiser or better informed. Often they are not, though as an admirer of the political virtues I dislike the one-time fashion among civil servants of decrying politicians. The reason is that the country is dedicated to a system of democracy by choice of the people, and not to one of appointed meritocracy. It is unwise ever to forget this.

Entirely consistently with this I came to the job with one very strong conviction, a conviction which I know to be strong throughout the diplomatic service. I am passionately convinced that the Permanent Under-Secretary, like all his colleagues, is a counsellor and not a courtier. It is his duty, as it is that of the whole Office, to give honest, intelligent and fearless advice. It is not a diplomatic officer's duty to find out what a Minister 'might like' and then devise means of gratifying him or her. This in turn does not mean an insensitive disregard of the Minister's known views and of political possibility; but it does mean a willingness to try your arm and say your piece, more particularly if it represents the general view of the Office as a whole, even if the advice is unwelcome. Once policy has been debated and determined, then comes the time to organize the best way of carrying it out and justifying it.

This was perhaps the strongest conscious view of my new function that I brought to the Office. It did not present notable difficulties since the policy issues throughout the period did not, with a few exceptions, involve the Office in conflict with its own Secretaries of State. The difficulties were much more between members of the Government themselves. And when domestic and international objectives conflict, officials can only go so far. The real battle takes place in Cabinet.

General Themes, 1965–1969

There were in this period, as in my previous time in London, two or three themes which accompanied policy-making throughout. The main one was, as ever, finance. Our economy was far too vulnerable to short-term pressures on the balance of payments for a steady external policy to be planned and adhered to. A month's bad trade figures, or a disparity in interest rates leading to a sudden inflow of 'hot' money and an inevitable and inconvenient outflow later, could upset the best laid calculations. This was never really overcome until the last year of Mr Roy Jenkins' stewardship as Chancellor of the Exchequer. Meantime it led towards a financial-defence-foreign policy operation of great complexity with moments of great bitterness which endured until 1968. This was the policy of keeping national defence expenditure within a sum of £2,000 million at 1965 prices.

I shall come back to the events of 1967–68. But it may suffice to say here, as a general thread of the argument, that the national defence budget at the beginning of the period involved an annual payment across the exchanges of some £500 million. Given that very strong trade competitors, notably Federal Germany and Japan, had no such burden, this represented a direct and indirect handicap to our efforts to promote growth on a basis of balance of payments equilibrium and a reasonable rate of social progress. Of course such a burden can be borne by a medium-sized country if the people are in a mood to sustain it or are not consulted about it. But while there were bitter differences of view on what ought to be done, Parliament and people in Britain were decreasingly inclined to maintain, either on their own or as members of alliance, overseas commitments which seemed of diminishing appropriateness to the post-Imperial period. In any case a Labour Government would not have pressed them to do so.

Thus there began in 1965 a series of Defence Reviews which must have greatly depressed the armed services, for whom one had much sympathy. For the Foreign Office, as for the Commonwealth Relations Office, the main interest was to seek to avoid cuts which involved an ill-timed repudiation of political commitments. Thus to seek to withdraw from a defence commitment to Kuwait in 1965 would have been extremely bad foreign policy; by 1968 it could be quietly and smoothly negotiated at the diplomatic level in the light of intervening developments in the Arab world.

Another permanent ghost at the feast was Rhodesia. When I left India, I was clear in my mind that there were only two serious outstanding further problems of withdrawal, Aden and Rhodesia, and I thought they were both insoluble. In a sense we 'solved' Aden and my fifty per cent error was a compliment to British flexibility. Rhodesia was not primarily a Foreign Office problem; it was dealt with initially and largely at a high political level, though the Foreign Office became more and more involved as we chased smuggling vessels and their ownerships from the high seas to Panama via the US to Greece, tried to discover whether the South African Government, as a member of the United Nations, would help at all and, increasingly, advised on likely developments in the United Nations itself.

The earlier proceedings on this matter do not make very happy remembering or reading. One of the great difficulties was the idea prevalent in the summer of 1965 that, if the British Government were too obviously working on what would happen should Mr Ian Smith unilaterally declare independence, this might incite him to do so. This doctrine tended to be quoted when we in the Foreign Office worried about inadequate information and we had to suspend worrying. But he declared it anyway, and the necessary information was not there.

It became clear all too soon that Rhodesia would survive the first impact. The only effective preventive would have been force, and the military and political objections to this would have been immense. Hence we could only do our best to impede the Rhodesian economy and try to see whether the process would bring about a settlement consistent with the original Five or subsequent Six Principles. To the irritation of the South Africans we sent a couple of people up to the Beit Bridge between South Africa and Rhodesia to see what sort of a channel that would be if South Africa did not play; one's private deductions could not be very cheerful. At the United Nations in October 1965, the atmosphere was suspicious. Britain appeared to be claiming that the matter was a domestic one (which legally it is) and yet doing nothing effective about it. Mr Stewart had a very difficult time with the heads of African delegations. Perhaps fortunately we could not foresee that the question would still be with us five years later; such foresight was hardly possible in 1965. Indeed at one juncture, the period of the *Tiger* talks with Mr Smith in December 1966, it would have been within an ace of being wrong.

On such matters there was in May 1965 preoccupation rather than crisis, so that I had the advantage of not plunging straight into crisis before getting the feel of the Office. Much of the external scene was business as before. There were routine meetings of SEATO and CENTO. A Commonwealth Prime Ministers' meeting was taking place in June. In Borneo the confrontation between Dr Soekarno's Indonesia and Malaysia, involving the maintenance of some 50,000 British troops in Malaysia, continued expensively and apparently interminably. In the Middle East things were 'normal,' no war and no love. Our relations with the Soviet Union were also normal: fundamental disagreement on political outlook but no serious irritants in the day to day bilateral relationship.

With the Johnson Administration in the United States our relations were good. Mr Wilson and Mr Gordon-Walker had visited Washington soon after the 1964 elections in both countries and Pat Dean, the new Ambassador there, developed a very valuable relationship with an administration which, as time went on, became an increasingly strange being. In London, the Amercans had a superb Ambassador in David Bruce. He and Ellsworth Bunker have been two of the outstanding diplomats of our time.

On a few fronts there was movement. In Europe, while there was no particular movement in NATO – only growing signs of an unco-operative mood on the part of the French – there was a revival of interest in our economic relations with the Continent. There was something of a conscience in Whitehall about the sudden imposition in November 1964, for balance of payments reasons, of a surcharge on imports from EFTA, a measure conveniently forgotten when President Nixon did something similar in 1971. This all led to an effort, strongly advocated by the Prime Minister, to see whether there was any way in which there could be constructive corporate contact between EFTA and the European Communities. From my past experience I had little faith in this; events had shown that the corporate approach could really only lead to frustration or to talk of a European preferential area in breach of the General Agreement on Trade and Tariffs. On this occasion too the absence of results supported the view of those who held with increasing emphasis that the one item worth discussing was whether a new approach to the European Communities aiming at British membership could be attempted and, if so, how and when.

There was also movement on the disarmament front. The situation inherited by the government had not been an easy one. There had been efforts in the NATO framework to establish a Mixed European Force as a means of integrating Germany into the Western nuclear effort without allowing any German finger on the trigger. Russian concentration was almost wholly on debarring Germany from any connection with nuclear effort, and on the acceptance of what was then called a non-dissemination treaty, precluding the spread of nuclear weapons. The two objectives, a mixed force and a non-dissemination treaty, need not have been incompatible, but the difficulties of integration within NATO proved so great that the argument never took place.

To cope with disarmament the government, amid some derision from the opposition, appointed Lord Chalfont a Minister of State in the Foreign Office in charge of disarmament, and equipped him with an expert team. Progress was necessarily slow; the future historian will find himself unable to endure the tedium of reading the minutes of Geneva meetings. But out of this work, with the persistent efforts of Lord Chalfont and Mr Fred Mulley and their official teams at home and in Geneva, there came a non-proliferation treaty, signed on 1 July 1968, a treaty on the use of nuclear weapons in outer space and a first step towards

a treaty prohibiting the use of chemical weapons in warfare.

The one problem which tended to be permanently both acute
and chronic was, of course, Vietnam. As with some of the really
obstinate conflicts in the world, it is almost impossible to say
where this one exactly 'began'. One could go right back to the
original French colonization of Indo-China, or to the French
defeat at Dien Bien Phu in 1954 or to the United States reservation
at the 1954 Geneva Conference about the unification of Vietnam
or to the decision in 1959 by the North Vietnamese to make good
by force their claim to unification of the country which they had
failed to achieve by negotiation, or to the American feeling of
obligation to help the South Vietnamese to resist. In theory the
Americans could have withdrawn from that obligation at any
time; in practice, once they had given a pledge of support to Ngo
Dinh Diem when he assumed the government in 1954 with the
consent of the Emperor Bao Dai, it was always painfully difficult
to find a way out and equally difficult, in dealing with people
as sharp-witted and complicated as the Vietnamese, to insist too
bluntly on the rapid creation of a state capable of defending itself
without outside military assistance. Certainly Ho Chi-Minh, as
leader of the resistance against the Japanese and the French, had
some claim to control a united Vietnam; balancing this claim were
the claims of sympathy in the United States and elsewhere for
the 900,000 Vietnamese who had fled from the North in preference
to submission to Communist rule. In these conditions the Americans sought for five years to assuage their national conscience by
sustaining South Vietnam with an ever-increasingly large flow of
advisers, estimated in early 1965 to have reached 20,000 strong.

With the British management of the victory over the Communist rebellion in Malaysia in mind, I once asked a distinguished
British officer whether a similar operation was in his judgement
practicable in Vietnam. Would it be possible to seal off South
Vietnam at a particular parallel and render the country south of
that parallel safe. His reply was, prophetically, 'You could not
do it without the power to give orders' (which we had been able
to do in pre-independence Malaysia, and the Americans could not

do in Vietnam). He also emphasized that, whereas the British only had to defend the Kra Isthmus, twenty to thirty miles across, against infiltration by land, South Vietnam is a crescent-shaped country with a long, exposed land frontier.

Early in 1965, the presence of even 20,000 American advisers became clearly insufficient to hold the position against the skill and determination of the Vietcong within and the North Vietnamese infiltrators from without. The situation drastically changed when, in February 1965, the Americans took the decision to bomb North Vietnam, and I remember my immediate fear that the Americans might have greatly over-estimated the military effect of bombing. In any case why on earth start bombing when the Soviet Prime Minister, Mr Kosygin, was actually in North Vietnam? If the idea was to show that effective protection from air attack could not be provided by the Russians, that could be shown any day. On the other hand, a bombing in Mr Kosygin's presence ensured that the Soviet Union would have to do its best for the North Vietnamese in the way of missile defence if aircraft could not be made available. Unhappily the explanation appears to have been all too simple; a failure, through a structural weakness in the United States Government, to co-ordinate political and military thinking and action.

By May 1965 the Americans had about 40,000 combat troops in South Vietnam. At the same time President Johnson in a speech at Baltimore on 7 April had offered to open peace talks and to provide a billion dollar development loan for South-East Asia. In May the Americans executed a bombing pause, too short a one to give the North Vietnamese a chance to respond. But the difficulty was, and remained so for the next five years, that in this war there was no drawn battle. Either Hanoi agreed to a cease-fire leading to an abandonment of its objective in using force; or the Americans would have to go home, leaving South Vietnam too weak to defend itself.

The policy of Mr Wilson's Government, maintained with considerable political courage throughout these years, was not to condemn the Americans, but to respect the good faith of their effort and try when possible to act in the cause of peace. At the same time the British Government made it clear that there were limits beyond which US military action would compel British 'disassociation'.

One of the great problems for the Government in forming a Vietnam policy was the nature of the opposition. One evening I sat at dinner next to an attractive and well-known actress. 'What right,' she said with total indignation, 'have the Americans to be in Vietnam?' 'You do know,' I replied, 'that they were invited?' Abrupt change of subject. The opposition consisted of people who sincerely felt the North Vietnamese were the true nationalists, people who felt that a possibly unjust peace was better than arbitrament by war, especially after the public had seen enough of this war in the back parlour, people who preferred probable Communist oppression to a regime which they believed to be inefficient and corrupt, people who saw something of killing from the American/South Vietnamese side and did not realise, or care to realise, the hideous and methodical murders of civilians and their families carried out by the Vietcong and North Vietnamese and not available to the television cameras, and people who simply wished the Communists well and the Americans ill. The United States Government machine did not help by their inarticulateness. They had a respectable case but one rarely heard it and people whose emotions are stirred and whose reason is baffled are suckers for the most articulate voice. The media, including the American media, were of little help to the Americans. Those interested at the time will remember a documentary advertised by the BBC which turned out to be a virulent anti-American film produced in Canada, and the very limited coverage given to a highly distinguished Independent Television interview with the Secretary of State, Dean Rusk.

Since the Americans had shown themselves disposed to negotiate, Mr Wilson secured agreement at the Commonwealth Prime Ministers' meeting in June for a Commonwealth Peace Mission which never proceeded. Hanoi had gone hard. Mr Wilson then sent Mr Harold Davies, Labour MP for Leek, on a special mission to Hanoi. One could but advise, with all the respect due to Mr Harold Davies' personal qualities and knowledge of the area, that his mission also could only be a failure. There seemed at the moment nothing that we could do.

Mr Stewart tried very hard on his visit to Moscow in the following December to get some kind of response from the Russians in the way of help in shortening the conflict. But the Soviet attitude at that time was of total refusal to be involved. And there, essentially, the matter remained for the British Government until the Kosygin visit to London a year and a half later.

United Nations and Moscow

Meanwhile it was time to consider what should be said in the United Nations Assembly. It was the first appearance by a Labour Foreign Secretary for fifteen years and Mr Stewart was anxious that his Assembly speech should have specifically United Nations content. A careful reading of the Charter discloses a weakness in the chapter entitled 'Pacific Settlement of International Disputes' (Chapter VI, Articles xxxii–xxxviii). The chapter enumerates various forms of solution and says that the Security Council 'may investigate any dispute or any situation which might lead to international friction . . .' It also establishes the rights of members to bring such disputes or situations to the attention of the Security Council. But there is little more by way of guidance either in the Charter or in subsequent documents on what should or could actually be done, and the United Nations has suffered from this weakness. Accordingly the British delegation submitted a resolution calling for examination of this question and Mr Stewart spoke to it.

The debate when it came was unsatisfactory. A combination of Dr Nkrumah's Ghana and the Communist countries was responsible for the idea not being pursued. The East Africans were not sympathetic since, in the suspicious atmosphere at that time, they saw a connection between the proposal and the British unwillingness to use force against the Smith régime in Rhodesia. The idea has been kept alive, but this and subsequent debates showed how far ahead British thinking is on this point than more or less anybody else's. The Soviet Government has remained strongly opposed to our proposal.

The speaker in the Assembly immediately after the Foreign Secretary was the representative of the United Arab Republic. The UAR had 50,000 troops in the Yemen at the time, and the delegate spoke with bitter scorn of the stationing of troops in other peoples' countries. 'It would be fun to be able to make a speech like that,' observed Mr Stewart. But no one intervened to say so; interpolation is not *de rigueur* in the General Debate.

In December I accompanied the Foreign Secretary on his first visit to Moscow. I had made one visit on an Air India flight in 1963 in which I stayed with Humphrey Trevelyan and did some sightseeing. I find Moscow much the most evocative of the old imperial cities. This is partly because of the way the three European monarchies departed from history. The Hohenzollerns with Kaiser Wilhelm II at their head marched, even goose-stepped, out of history; the Hapsburgs, with the almost endless reign of Kaiser Franz Josef II, fossilized out. The last Romanovs, with their autocracy and their poignant family tragedy, went out with a rattle of bullets and a sigh. This sigh still echoes in the older houses and beneath the golden domes of the churches which survive.

By contrast this second visit was up to date, comprising a series of meetings with the Soviet Prime Minister, Mr A. N. Kosygin, exchanges formal and informal on a whole series of subjects, the signature of a consular convention and a press conference. Mr Kosygin has a sombre look. But sometimes, right at the end of an earnest discourse, a quick, attractive smile flits across that grave face. He is also most extraordinarily well-informed, and seemed to carry in his head facts and answers about anything. Since Mr Stewart has the same kind of *gravitas*, there was a very satisfactory personal rapport.

A helpful presence was that of Mr V. V. Kuznetzov, a Deputy Minister in the Soviet Foreign Office. His pleasant personality and diplomatic skill aided in turning tough arguments into smoother passages. The discussions did not reveal anything greatly new, the Russians taking their then orthodox anti-German line on Europe and declining to express interest or suggest activity in Vietnam. But the press conference at the end was extraordinary. Mr Stewart, without endorsing the American position, suggested that there might be a side to the case other than that of Hanoi. No doubt the Soviet journalists as professionals had some inkling that this might be so, but many of them had never heard it expressed with such authority, and this gave the conference an atmosphere like the first night of a new thriller. I thought it would never stop. But the Soviet reader did not benefit much.

At the end of the visit Mr Stewart arranged for a visit to the Soviet Union by Mr Wilson early the next year.

Altogether it had been for me an enjoyable and profitable experience. Apart from meetings with the Russians, it was also most useful as a look at Moscow as a post under my official responsibility. It can be hard enough to understand the shades of meaning in messages from posts you know well; when you have little or no knowledge of a post or the atmosphere of work in it, your judgement can easily go astray.

One wishes indeed that people generally could be reminded more frequently what it is like to serve at a post like Moscow. Of course you have the attraction of being in a city where history is being made. But you are also living in the capital city of a régime obsessed with espionage and 'bugging', and you lead your life on the basis that if you have something really confidential to say, you do not say it but write it down on a piece of paper and pass it to the person in the next armchair for perusal and immediate destruction. This is not science fiction nor political preconception. It is just a way of life, and you get used to its rhythm. But it is hardly the natural way to live.

De Gaulle and NATO

As Mr Stewart was indisposed, I reported to the NATO Ministerial Council in the same month as the visit to Moscow. I found in Paris a strong feeling that in the New Year President de Gaulle might well take some action which could weaken NATO. At a press conference on 9 September, the President had spoken to the effect that by 1969 at the latest, the Alliance must 'end

the subordination . . . described as integration'. The French
Ambassador had said to me, 'You think there should be more
integration; we think there should be less.' The Ministerial
meeting meantime had proceeded further in the integration
direction by setting up machinery for extended consultation on
nuclear matters.

The blow fell on 21 February 1966 when, again using the press
conference technique, President de Gaulle announced that:
'While not going back on the Atlantic Alliance, France will . . .
continue to modify the arrangements that exist, in so far as these
arrangements concern her.' In effect, France would withdraw
from all integrated activities. In later announcements the General
made it explicit that French forces would be withdrawn from
all integrated commands, and requested the withdrawal by April
1967 of NATO military headquarters and installations from
French soil. France would still be part of the alliance but no longer
part of the organization.

Theoretically it would have been possible to carry on in this
way. And NATO did indeed receive one of those 'you can stay
here if you like' invitations for the political as opposed to military
headquarters of the Alliance to remain in the specially constructed
premises in Paris. But in practice the French decision, besides
seriously weakening military security, could, through its obviously
political motivation, have dangerously weakened the political
cohesion of the members, and do so before any form of balanced
reduction of forces had been agreed with Eastern Europe. It
had to be reckoned that some members of NATO might,
without necessarily following France's example at once, diminish
their support. This might be followed by a chain reaction
between military withdrawal and political disunity. Moreover
de Gaulle had acted at a moment when two loyal NATO
members, Belgium and Italy, had no government with a popular
mandate and Britain was about to enter a general election.
Unless therefore positive diplomatic action were taken there was
a real danger that NATO might begin to melt away.

The first thing was for NATO to give itself a post-crisis
guideline. The best demonstration of holding fast would be a

declaration by the NATO Council minus France that the fourteen other members would continue to operate under the 1949 Treaty.

In such a crisis the first reaction is apt to be cautious to the point of flabbiness. Then, if the crisis is to be overcome, the international organization involved needs leadership, both from its principal officer and from at least one leading member Government. On the official side there was nothing to worry about. The Italian Secretary-General, Signor Manlio Brosio, has been one of the outstanding international officials of these times. In NATO, unlike most organizations, the Secretary-General presides over Council meetings. The post therefore needs very special qualities of fairness, understanding and calm. Signor Brosio had these attributes in exceptional measure and quality. Moreover, although his English and his French were both manifestly Italian, he could turn either on at a moment's notice and both were entirely sufficient for his and the organization's purposes.

On the Governmental side the position might well be difficult. Of the major powers, France was out. The United States could no longer step in and organize a European and Canadian team, and in any case this would have meant a direct retort to President de Gaulle's anti-American gesture and there was a general desire not to make things worse. A German lead would not be accepted and the Italians had not the military or political strength to undertake it. If NATO was to survive, a rapid and determined initiative would be needed from Britain.

The Minister of State, Mr George Thomson, promptly visited capitals of NATO countries. In Paris, our permanent representative on the NATO Council, Sir Evelyn Shuckburgh, an immensely experienced and energetic colleague, undertook the main day to day negotiations. But in a situation which combined such urgency and complexity it is wise to use all your resources. The Foreign Office was always good at instructing British Embassies abroad, but we sometimes tended to forget that our best friends, and the people who understand the British position best, ought to be found among the Ambassadors and High Commissioners accredited to London. Appointment to London is much sought after, and the quality of heads of missions is generally very high. So we urgently invoked their help too. There is risk in carrying on the same talks at both ends of lines which can very easily get crossed. But this was an occasion for taking risks.

For more than three weeks we wrestled, argued, drafted and re-drafted. Finally on 18 March the declaration was made. It read:

> The North Atlantic Treaty and the Organisation established under it are both alike essential to the security of our countries.

> The Atlantic Alliance has ensured its efficacy as an instrument of defence and deterrence by the maintenance in peacetime of an integrated and inter-dependent military organisation, in which, as in no previous alliance in history, the efforts and resources of each are combined for the common security of all. We are convinced that this organisation is essential and will continue. No system of bilateral arrangements can be a substitute.

> The North Atlantic Treaty and the Organisation are not merely instruments of the common defence. They meet a common political need and reflect the readiness and determination of the member countries of the North Atlantic Community to consult and act together wherever possible in the safeguard of their freedom and security and in the furtherance of international peace, progress and prosperity.

Once the declaration had been made, the other problems, though delicate, could be decided in a less tense atmosphere. The Ministerial meeting of the NATO Council in June confirmed what had been done so far and an elaborate technique was set up for having meetings of the fifteen including France, and others of fourteen without France where France would have been welcome but preferred not to attend. Eventually in December 1966 it was decided to accept a cordial invitation from the Belgians and build a new headquarters in Brussels, where NATO was given a warm welcome and its presence enhanced the city's growing claim to be a genuine European capital.

Would a NATO collapse have mattered? This is a fair question, and there are uncertainties about NATO, ranging from the willingness or otherwise of European member countries to pull their financial weight to doubts about the credentials of the Greek Government. For all this there remains a post-1945 Western European and Atlantic concept of life and government in progressive evolution which still needs protection from pressure and subversion. So long as this remains so, we cannot afford to be without a NATO.

In 1966 there was a further reason for preserving the integrated organization. It was still important for Germany as a friend and ally to be seen to be subordinated to the mutual disciplines of alliance. A rather dislikeable colleague from a hard-line East European country once made to me, without provocation, a searing attack on the Germans. I thanked him for his rousing pro-NATO speech and did not wait for his answer.

So, as I write, NATO persists. One cannot expect France to walk back into it – this is the vice of the gesture the General made. But at least in a period of national retreat, quietly vigorous British diplomacy contributed vitally to maintaining international security.

Far East and SEATO

In June 1966 I presided in Hong Kong over a Conference of British Heads of Missions in the Far East, with Lord Walston as Minister in attendance. It came up with the general and sensible consensus that South-East Asia could only solve its problems by the right form of regional organization, notably the development of ASEAN (Association of South-East Asian Nations). The Association had the advantage of being politically cautious rather than doctrinally non-aligned and could thus cut across alliance or non-alliance boundaries.

From Hong Kong I flew to Australia where I took a week off, visiting Sydney, Melbourne and Adelaide where I stayed with Beth Corry and had the pleasure of meeting masses of Pat's relatives. I joined with zest the cliché group which says, 'If I were thirty-five years younger, I would seriously think of settling in Australia.' There seemed to be room, enthusiasm and masses to do if you were prepared to work hard and keep your Pommie complaints to yourself.

In Canberra we found concern about the implications of British defence cuts. Mr Stewart did his best with a speech in which he pledged publicly that if ever Australia were in serious trouble, Britain would come to her support. But the upshot was not wholly satisfactory. The British were seeking some kind of assurance that, if we were compelled for one reason or another to retreat from Singapore, the Australians would give us military. naval and air facilities. The Australians for their part were being cagey about facilities in order that we should not contemplate leaving Singapore.

But in a way the most interesting part of the trip was a night stop at Jakarta. We very nearly missed it altogether because there were no night landing facilities at Jakarta; we just got to the point of no return in time. These few minutes gave us a fascinating evening with Mr Adam Malik, the Foreign Minister of post-Soekarno Indonesia.

It will be recalled that the putsch of September 1965 which would, with Dr Soekarno's consent, have put the Communists in power, had failed owing largely to the failure to assassinate all the generals. A moderate régime under General Soeharto had taken over and had conducted its relations with Dr Soekarno extremely carefully in order not to provoke reaction. Indeed the situation was still so touchy that General Soeharto had sent a message to the effect that, since this was the first high-level British visit since Soekarno had failed, he would prefer the talks to be between Foreign Ministers and not to involve himself. But over and after dinner Mr Malik made it clear that the new Indonesia would wish to let confrontation with Malaysia and therefore Britain die out, normalize relations with Britain and other Western countries, and rejoin the United Nations international organizations which Dr Soekarno's Government had left.

Tensions of July 1966

We returned to a month (July) which at the time I called 'lurid'. The country was only just beginning to recover from a very expensive and disrupting seamen's strike. The foreign affairs atmosphere had been agitated by an extension of American bombing in Vietnam and Mr Wilson's dissociation of the British Government from bombing targets 'touching on the populated areas of Hanoi and Haiphong' which to some went too far and to others not far enough. Then the balance of payments figures announced on 4 July were bad. There was heavy short selling of sterling. Nervousness was increased by a briefing apparently given by someone from M. Pompidou's delegation during his visit on 6 and 7 July, suggesting that in the French Prime Minister's opinion devaluation of sterling might be unavoidable.

The pressure on sterling continued. The Government, acutely divided within itself on whether the countervailing policy should be restraint or, as Mr George Brown preferred, devaluation, worked in a state of great tension, producing among other things a sudden demand for cuts in overseas expenditure of 'at least £100 millions'. In the middle of it all, Mr Wilson was confronted with the dilemma of keeping or breaking an engagement with the Soviet Government in Moscow; he could hardly break it, but the visit looked a little irrelevant. In the end the 20 July restraint measures restored the situation, but the episode had been a great strain on the Government and its servants and on public opinion.

Such situations involve particular difficulties for the conduct of foreign policy, and there is no agent so efficient for the destruction of the external operating capital of a country like Britain as a sudden requirement on overseas services to save a particular percentage of expenditure. This process costs more than it saves in the immediate future (because of compensation for breaches of contract, premature dismissals, etc) and may in the end prove misdirected or unnecessary. Yet in conditions like those of July 1966, no Foreign Secretary could just say 'no'.

Mr George Brown Arrives

The July crisis swept by, as such crises will, and when Parliament had risen, Pat and I drove off with Joanna and camping gear to a very fine camping site overlooking the Dordogne, recommended by Morrice and Elizabeth James. We visited ruins of castles where in the fourteenth century the English forces under the Black Prince and their French adversaries glowered at each other behind impregnable walls. We then went south to look at Carcassonne and on to the crowded Mediterranean seaboard where we finally found room at a camp with the splendid name of *Camping Mer et Soleil*.

After spending a delectable morning, totally incommunicado, on a restful beach, I thought I ought to re-establish contact with the outer world. I rang up the Dordogne camp. Several agitated voices seemed to come on the line: '*Ah, Monsieur, il s'agit de quelque chose d'une* extrême *urgence . . . on vous prie de téléphoner instamment à l'ambassade de Grande Bretagne à Paris.*' Consternation. 'Yes, there was a matter of extreme urgency. No there was no international crisis.' So I was on the next train to Paris in a couple of hours.

By breakfast time in Paris the answer was public. George Brown was to become Foreign Secretary, Michael Stewart moving to the Department of Economic Affairs. On the rest of my journey home I thought and wondered. On my two sudden sad flights to India to the funeral ceremonies of Pandit Nehru and Lal Bahadur Shastri I had had long talks with George Brown. He had expounded his ideas for a Department of Economic Affairs separate from the Treasury. It sounded comparable to the highly successful German Economics Ministry under Professor Erhard, except that the German Ministry was predominantly laissez-faire in outlook while Mr Brown's ideas naturally concentrated on planning and on growth adapted to social objectives. I found his ideas most exciting. I had always felt that the Treasury as a whole had an undeserved reputation for short-sighted meanness which came through public confusion between its policy work on the one hand and the budgetary and establishment work on the other. Given the apparent success of the German experiment there might be advantage in creating a department concentrating on the broader aspects of economic policy and released from the psychological bondage of the annual budget.

Mr Brown has recounted how and why in his view the experiment failed. But from the point of view of one outside the DEA it was not yet clear that it had failed. So I looked forward to Mr Brown's dynamic originality and to the effectiveness, on behalf of foreign policy, of his standing in the Government and the Labour Party. There were indeed stories about his temperament and, immediately more worrying, about a reputation he had acquired for hostile comment on the Foreign Office in Whitehall meetings. But these were not necessarily abnormal challenges, and the Office prepared itself to welcome its new master warmly.

We started off in a rousing manner with a meeting at which Mr Brown and his ministerial team met the Under-Secretaries, specialist advisers and heads of departments, perhaps a hundred people. He made it emphatically clear that 'foreign policy will be run from this building'. He called for the maximum free discussion between ministers and officials on all matters and said that he proposed to follow up energetically items of foreign policy with which he was not yet familiar. He added that he also proposed to introduce a form of submission of documents which would replace the traditional argument followed by conclusion: documents in future would state the problem, advance as briefly as possible the department's recommendation and only then present the argument and background at greater length.

I replied for the Office, warmly welcoming Mr Brown personally and saying that everybody would be greatly heartened by his assurance that the Foreign Office under his leadership would effectively control foreign policy. I also personally welcomed Mr Brown's preference (which had also been Mr Bevin's) in the arrangement of submissions.

There was then, as Mr Brown has described, a rapid series of meetings over the week-end, including a private discussion between Mr Brown and myself. It was at once apparent that on a wide range of policy subjects there was little or no difference of view between officials and the new Secretary of State. In particular there was a close identity of view about the promotion of European unity, in so far as this could be done, within the framework of a wider Atlantic alliance. (Mr Brown has said himself that he thought the Office were making relations with President de Gaulle more difficult than they need be; we shall see the progress of this idea later.) We were also in accord with Mr Brown's perspective on world policy and his view that Britain should pursue an individual role suitable to the country's capabilities and resources.

Coming from his previous work, the new Secretary of State was particularly keen on planning. We had an instrument ready in a small but strong planning section under the leadership of John Thompson. The story of the section had been one of much trial and a good deal of error. In its earliest stage from 1949 it became too much of a residual department for work not naturally falling in the competence of others. A revived planning section in the fifties had so much to do in the field of NATO planning that the rest of the world went without. Papers 'in depth' on non-NATO matters depended on the excellent work of the Research Department which, however, looked factually and analytically backwards rather than purposefully forwards. Planning work also suffered from planning papers being submitted to detailed scrutiny by senior people who had not the time to supervise them properly.

In the sixties we at last got it right. The Planning Department dealt with the whole world of foreign policy and the Planning Committee, of which I was chairman, commented only on ideas and left the commas to others.

There are severe limits to planning possibilities in an external department. When you are planning governmentally for your own people, things are difficult enough. When you are 'planning' for a world of over one hundred nations over most of whom you have little influence, your powers of foresight are very limited. None the less, if you set your mind away from but not out of touch with day to day work, you can foresee what may happen and what, if it did happen, would be beneficial or damaging to national interests and world peace. So when in 1968 the Fulton Committee very properly recommended that Government departments should have planning sections, it filled us with helpful virtue to be able to say that we had been trying it out for nineteen years already.

Thus we seemed all set for a vigorous and positive pursuit of policy within the framework of national capability. In some respects this was indeed achieved. But there was a difficulty of atmosphere which I shall refer to later but which must be touched on here, since otherwise the picture of work over the next year and a half would be distorted.

From the first there was a feeling of strain, apparent from the autobiographies of both Mr Wilson and Mr Brown, between No. 10 Downing Street and the Foreign Office. This relationship is rarely an easy one.

Foreign Affairs are the responsibility of the Foreign Secretary, and when the Foreign Secretary is a powerful character and a skilful operator, the Prime Minister may advisedly leave him alone. The classic case of this is Attlee and Bevin, which is not to suggest that Attlee was not master of his own Cabinet. The opposite situation prevails when the Prime Minister is an outstanding authority on world affairs, having perhaps been Foreign Secretary himself; then Foreign Affairs may be extensively waged from No. 10. The pattern of Palmerston and Russell in some ways repeated itself in that of Eden and Selwyn Lloyd. But if the relationship is less definite there can be great difficulty. While the Prime Minister's 'primacy' is not constitutionally that of the President of the United States, it is real. He is clearly bound to intervene in various contexts such as difficulty in the cabinet, or direct dealings with the head of a foreign government. In the case of Mr Wilson and Mr Brown, the background was one of a strong shared loyalty to the Labour Party beneath which there survived feelings aroused by a fierce contest for the leadership which Mr Brown had lost. Loyalty to the party tempered any outward exhibition of the strain, but within government it was real and perceptible. And it needed and, I think, received constant and mutually understanding attention from the five people principally

concerned, the two principal Private Secretaries at the Foreign
Office, Murray Maclehose and his successor Donald Maitland, the
Secretary at No. 10 responsible for liaison within the Foreign
Office, in this case Michael Palliser, the Cabinet Secretary, Sir
Burke Trend, and myself. Perhaps the job of the man at No.10
is the most difficult. He has two loyalties; he is the servant of the
Prime Minister but he is bound to keep closely acquainted with
and reflect the thinking of the Foreign Office at all levels on
the international situation. Palliser managed both with great
skill.

Europe and Anglo-French Relations

Mr Brown's immediate interest was to get moving in the matter
of relations with the European Communities. One of his first
initiatives, on which I accompanied him, was a visit to Mr Michael
Stewart in the Department of Economic Affairs to make sure that
the two departments continued to see eye to eye on this. The
histories of the two departments were a bit different. In the DEA,
under the leadership of Mr Brown and his Permanent Under-
Secretary, Sir Eric Roll, the external thinking had been strongly
European. In the Foreign Office ideas developed the other way
round. Sir Con O'Neill had come in 1965 from his post as
Ambassador to the European Communities to be Deputy Under-
Secretary of State in charge of Economic Affairs (the position
I had held from 1956-60). The attempt in 1965 to bring
European countries together through a new corporate relationship between EEC and EFTA had had no useful sequel. It was
becoming clear that nothing short of a new attempt at membership of the EEC by Britain and others could break down the
developing economic and political wall between Europe and
ourselves.

It was not, however, to be assumed that Foreign Office Ministers
would instantly agree with this diagnosis and 1965 and the first
half of 1966 saw much time devoted to discussion and analysis
of possible policies. By the time the change of Foreign Secretaries
took place, there was agreement in the Foreign Office at all levels
that a new approach ought to be attempted. By wholly different

processes, the DEA and the Foreign Office had arrived at an identical view.

The consequences were remarkable. A great deal of preparatory work had been done in Whitehall and it was soon possible to have papers ready for presentation to the Cabinet. On 22 October 1966 Mr Wilson put forward to his Cabinet colleagues the idea that he and Mr Brown should at the end of the year make a tour of the capitals of the Six to see whether there would be sufficient receptivity to a British initiative to make a formal application for entry worth while. Mr Wilson announced the plan in the House of Commons on 10 November and the visits were duly made between January and March 1967. The Cabinet discussed the results of the visits at the end of April and on 10 May, after a three-day discussion in the House of Commons, the House voted, with a tremendous majority of 488 to 62, to present an application. Mr Brown has recounted the stratagem he employed at a Ministerial Western Union meeting to ensure that the application was formally presented in a way that could not run into procedural objections.

Consideration of the British application by the Six did not proceed very fast. Procedural difficulties presented themselves, and on 28 November General de Gaulle ceased to be enigmatic and pronounced a total veto. The question which poses itself was whether this veto was inevitable and could have been anticipated and whether, given its possibility, the British Government and Parliament were right to have taken the risk of presenting the application without assuring themselves of France's benevolence.

The answers to this query are very complex. On his visit to London in the summer of 1966, M. Pompidou, while being wholly non-committal, had given the impression of welcoming the apparent movement of British thinking in the direction of an application. From then on the French attitude continued unclear. General de Gaulle was consistently non-committal during the Wilson-Brown visit to Paris in January 1967. By the time the application was presented, it could be said that the French Government had thought aloud in the British presence in terms of doubt and even criticism, but had never said that the answer would be 'no'.

This was not very promising but there were grounds at least for hope. There was, at the beginning of 1967, a perceptible stir in France in favour of British entry. Five members of the Six were known to be in favour. It must have seemed to many in France that in the circumstances a solitary veto was a course to be avoided if possible. Perhaps matters could be strung out procedurally and the British would tire of the effort. Or perhaps others of the five would develop doubts and decide that the Community should develop further before considering new applications. Time might avert the necessity of a veto. In the end it did not.

On the British side the timing practically decided itself. Membership of the Community seemed the only direction in which to go. With the impulsion of this view and the dynamic leadership of George Brown which, as it were, swept up the Prime Minister in its wake, British opinion began to move rapidly towards favouring the idea. Mr Brown did some superb advocacy. On one occasion he invited me to attend his presentation to the TUC International Affairs Committee. It was model pleading among friends and his audience were wholly convinced. Once a tide like this starts you can no longer modulate it to suit diplomatic timing. The whole Government apparatus moves into the rhythm – even that part of it which is opposed to what you are doing. So the application was made, and this turned out to have one great advantage. The Government rightly decided to leave the rejected application on the table. It was ready waiting when the General had gone and the time came round to try again.

The failure of the 1967 attempt to join the European Community raises the whole question of the British relationship with General de Gaulle. The stature of the General, physical, intellectual and historic, was such that his personality dominated the French and, to a great extent, the European scene. This tended to produce in those with whom he dealt the feeling, 'If only I am allowed to deal with this man, I can fix it.' Thus it was that the General's

The author visiting an aircraft factory at Kanpur with Krishna Menon in 1961

The author and his wife and family, New Delhi, 1960.

personality, combined with his personal (as opposed to political) courtesy, convinced many people that, if only the General could be approached in the right way, our troubles with France would be over. It became a kind of legend that de Gaulle presented a great chance for Anglo-French relations to which the only obstacle was the pig-headedness of the British Foreign Office.

People with this outlook did not have the advantage of the advice once given to me by a loyally Gaullist French colleague. 'Let me describe to you,' he said, 'an interview with de Gaulle. You go in and, with perfect courtesy, the General explains his point of view. You then explain your point of view. The General, having listened with perfect courtesy, presents his point of view again, and the interview is over.'

And in this case points of view differed widely. Britain stood for the strengthening of NATO; the General sought to weaken it. We stood for the strengthening of the United Nations; the General refused to contribute to the expense of that most positive activity, peace-keeping, and abetted Soviet moves to transfer important decisions outside the United Nations. We wished to join the European Community as an equal partner; the General wished to prevent it. Where British interests in the Middle East or in Nigeria were under political pressure, the General's habit was not to help, sympathize or even discuss; it was to infiltrate into the situation and seek to substitute French influence for British.

This almost endless catalogue had an emotional and historical background, dating back possibly to Joan of Arc and certainly to the eighteenth and nineteenth centuries, when larger French ambitions were frustrated by the inconvenient British who were then gallantly prepared to forget what the French found only too easy to remember. The list traversed the wartime relationship of American incomprehension, and what de Gaulle held to be British obstruction not to mention British support for the independence of Syria and Lebanon. (It neglected, of course, Eden's efforts to reserve a proper seat for France at the post-war Great Power Table.) More lately the General, as the acknowledged

M

saviour of France, foresaw for his country perhaps a greater role than, in the changed world, it could hope to play.

Against this background there was only one possible policy, insurance. It would have been emotional lunacy to write off the Entente Cordiale because of irritation with the latter-day policies of a difficult great man. As I told a group of French correspondents who visited me in my room, we were meeting in the room where Nicolson had worked for Grey and where Vansittart had prophetically discerned the evil prospects of Nazism and cherished the friendship with France. The right policy to my mind was to find things in which French and British worked closely together in a way which would outlast the anti-Anglo-Saxon attitudes of the French President. One obvious item was the Concorde project. For this reason, I personally and the Foreign Office departmentally, consistently supported its continuance when it was under threat. There were other projects too which met varying fates and one of the main anxieties concerned the effect on future relations with France of our wholesale withdrawal in 1968 from European space projects.

This point of view involved outstaying de Gaulle. It meant holding on to our intention to join the Common Market by invitation of the Six. There were of course possible compromises and, in the context of General de Gaulle's Presidency, it would have been possible to do a deal with him for a kind of special British relationship with France, in a tacit if not explicit anti-American basis, by which we would have enjoyed a special association with the Common Market through a special association with France. This was tempting to many, but seemed to me doctrinally undesirable as a basis for European unity, nor did it accord with a certain moral obligation towards those members of the European Community who had maintained a consistent support for British membership.

All this, if we may escape from the time schedule for a moment, is relevant to the famous 'Soames incident' of February 1969, of which Mr Soames was the victim rather than the agent. When Mr Soames's entirely welcome appointment was made, all the official advice was that there would be a waiting period during which he would be building up a position in France but that not much could be done on the European front.

Before the famous lunch took place I had retired and so do not know the details. It was natural that Mr Soames should seek occasion for an intimate talk with the General. But any such conversation was bound to be, in the European context, immensely sensitive. It was bound to deal, or appear to deal, with the British application, still on the table, for admission to the European Communities. The five members other than France, including our best friends and supporters, the Dutch, would be nervously concerned about what was going on, and their concern would be increased by the periodic outbursts of Tory Gaullism which, for all they knew, might have affected Mr Soames.

The matter was therefore not one of convenience or inconvenience or of Mr Wilson's immediate problem on his simultaneous visit to Bonn. It was a matter of good faith with the Five that they should know what was being said. Naturally the French official reaction to our telling the Five was strong, since our action closed the way again to any advance other than in the direction of the stated British objective, admission by unanimous invitation. If these things are looked at not as an instant problem susceptible to snap judgement, but in the longer perspective, who can say that the result was fatal?

The truth was that we had to outlast the General without losing our links with France. By this criterion we did not do badly. The time to work on a link is not always today. Sometimes you may have to wait while people write solemn treatises explaining that you are doing nothing because you do not know what to do. The policy might have failed. But it did not. Within a month the General had gone.

Vietnam and Kosygin

In earlier reference to the Vietnam story we have seen that from the spring of 1965 the United States was thinking and speaking in terms of a peaceful solution of the conflict. But suggestions such as a development loan to the area were from the Communist point of view irrelevancies if not intrusions, and the climate was in no way favourable to negotiations. Apart from anything else both sides were clearly confident that they could win.

In the autumn of 1967, however, the Americans were in better directed search of something which could be negotiable in terms of North Vietnamese psychology and the real military situation. The prevalent idea was that, if the United States could contrive to make two concessions against one by the North Vietnamese, this could lead towards a cease-fire and negotiation. The idea assumed concrete form in what became known as the 'Phase A – Phase B' programme. Phase A would be a published American cessation of bombing; Phase B would be an assurance of a cessation of North Vietnamese infiltration into the South in exchange for an American de-escalation of reinforcement for their forces in Vietnam. This approach seemed to hold some prospects of progress.

The story of the end of 1966 and the beginning of 1967 is one of how this plan, largely through administrative muddles, ran into the sand. The principal events from the British point of view were a visit by the Foreign Secretary, Mr Brown, to Moscow in November 1966, and the visit to London of the Soviet Prime Minister, Mr A. N. Kosygin, and his delegation from 6 February to 13 February 1967. Detailed accounts of these matters are given by Mr Harold Wilson[1] and by Mr Chester L. Cooper[2] and a shorter one by Mr George Brown.[3] These men were directly involved. It says something for the complexity of the story that there are curious variations in these accounts. For instance, Mr Brown has Mr Gromyko present; Mr Wilson and Mr Cooper, correctly, do not. Both Mr Wilson and Mr Cooper appear to underestimate the strength of the Soviet delegation. True, it contained a good deal of secondary façade, but Mr Kosygin's chief advisers were Mr Soldatov, a Vice-Minister in the Soviet Foreign Office with strong party connections, and Mr

[1] Harold Wilson, *The Labour Government, 1964–70*, Weidenfeld/Joseph 1971, p.345.
[2] Chester L. Cooper, *The Lost Crusade*, MacGibbon & Kee, 1970, p.342.
[3] Lord George-Brown, *In My Way*, Gollancz 1971, p.143.

Falin, a very bright, up and coming official who later became Ambassador in Bonn.

The detailed accounts already published exempt me from attempting yet another, though I shall have some judgements to make on their conclusions. I was myself present at the formal meetings though not at private meetings confined to Ministers. This did not, however, prevent me from knowing what was going on.

When Mr Brown went to Moscow in November 1966, he was provided with a detailed explanation of the 'Phase A – Phase B' proposal. He tried this out on Mr Kosygin and Mr Gromyko and found them unimpressed. This has been attributed by both Mr Brown and Mr Wilson to the fact that similar ideas would by then have been coming to Moscow through the channel of the Polish Ambassador in Saigon, Mr Lewandowski, who had been attempting to act as an intermediary on the spot. It was clumsy diplomacy by the Americans not to tell the British Government that they were using a parallel track in a different way, and I am also not convinced that the Americans were wise in the choice of the Polish channel. But I do not agree that this destroyed the usefulness of Mr Brown's intervention. On the contrary, as Mr Cooper has pointed out, Communist governments constantly employ the identical approach from different sides (the proceedings of disarmament conferences are full of it). Simultaneous advocacy by British and Polish intermediaries would have enhanced, not weakened, credibility. There was no point in the British claiming to be 'mediators' as though they had invented or had some special copyright in the American plan.

None the less this lack of information ruffled the mood which preceded what was going to prove a tense occasion anyway. It was tense because there is a special tension attaching to major contacts between Britain and the Soviet Union, for reasons which I shall describe in a later section on diplomacy and ideology. There was, of course, general tension over Vietnam. There was also tension, perceptible to the Russians, between the Prime Minister and the Foreign Secretary. In these situations it is not always easy to help.

There were two aspects of the visit which are worth a mention before we consider Vietnam. First, Mr Kosygin made in his famous Guildhall speech, attacks on two of Britain's allies, the United States and Federal Germany. Quite apart from any question of sentiment, it is one of the few remaining courtesies in international affairs that a foreign guest, when allowed the courtesy of a formal public speech, should not abuse it by attacking the friends of the host country. And it does not enhance the self-respect or the respect abroad of the host Government if it fails, as happened in this case, to put in a public word for its friends in reply.

Secondly there was useful work with the Soviet delegation on lesser mattters, notably the highly practical offer by Mr Callaghan, recorded by Mr Wilson, for the settlement of the First World War debts. Many months of negotiation were still required, but it was a constructive step. One evening we held a several-ring diplomatic circus in my office at which a number of secondary matters were usefully discussed with Mr Soldatov and his official colleagues.

The top-level meetings plunged immediately on Mr Kosygin's arrival, on Monday 6 February, into discussion of Vietnam. The Russians at once referred to an interview given to Wilfrid Burchett by the North Vietnamese Foreign Minister, Nguyen Duy Trinh, in which the latter said that 'only after the unconditional cessation of US bombing and all other acts of war could there be talks'. (Mr Wilson describes Mr Burchett as 'an Australian journalist'; Mr Cooper, more accurately, adds 'communist'; this is important, since Communist governments exploit independent journalists as mouthpieces, but with someone who is an admitted communist they tend to be more careful about the authenticity of what they say.)

The interest shown by the Soviet Prime Minister in the Vietman question and Foreign Minister Trinh's statement caused the British Government rightly to think that there had been two significant moves which might be exploited in the direction of peace – a positive statement by the North Vietnamese (though consisting of an unsaleable offer made in a negative tone) and the willingness of the Soviet Government to advance from its position of total detachment. The question was whether this limited advance could be extended.

Mr Brown thought he detected in the Soviet attitude a possibility of reconvening the Geneva Conference of which Britain and the Soviet Union were co-chairmen. Britain had always been willing to do this; the Soviet attitude had been wholly negative. Mr Wilson throughout the first three and a half days bent his energies to the search for some variation on the 'Phase A – Phase B' approach which might have some attraction for the Russians and, through them, for the North Vietnamese. (Mr Kosygin gave it to be understood that the Russians were in close touch with Hanoi.) It could not, of course, be assumed that the Russians would move beyond the Burchett interview, but it was worth trying. It was also urgent, because the truce agreed on for the traditional *Tet* (New Year) holiday in Vietnam would start on Wednesday 8 February, and finish on Sunday afternoon, 12 February. There seemed just a chance of moving the whole matter forward. Mr Wilson and Mr Brown had also the advantage of the continued presence in London of Mr Cooper through whom any proposal could be checked immediately with Washington.

It was on this basis that discussions proceeded on 7, 8 and 9 February. By the evening of the ninth (Thursday) Mr Wilson was able to present to an interested Mr Kosygin a text which corresponded with the 'Phase A—Phase B' plan, a text accepted by Mr Cooper as consistent with United States Government policy and telegraphed back by him 'for information'. It seemed that the ball was now satisfactorily with the Russians who, it was assumed, would see what they could do.

Later on the same evening, Mr Kosygin and party were due to go on the night train to Scotland. At about 10.00 pm there was a telephonic warning from Washington that an important message was on its way. When it arrived in Downing Street, it was an utterly bewildering shock. Phase A and Phase B had been stood on their heads; the cessation of bombing and the abstention from augmentation of American forces would only take place *after* the North Vietnamese had given assurance that they had actually stopped infiltration.

By the time the new version had been typed out, Mr Kosygin was on the way to the station. Downing Street was faced with a genuine split-second dilemma; should the new version be sent with top urgency to the station to catch Mr Kosygin, or was there any alternative course? If it were sent, any prospect of successful negotiation was pretty certainly dead. If it was not sent, Mr Kosygin would be going off to Scotland under a serious mis-apprehension and a misleading text might have already gone to Moscow. Mr Wilson accordingly decided that Mr Kosygin must have the new text, and his private secretary got it to him just in time.

Mr Brown is very critical of this decision, which was taken without his being consulted. With the gift of hindsight, I can see quite clearly what the action should have been. A message should have been sent to Mr Kosygin to say that we had received a worrying message from Washington which we were checking with the Americans; meantime the Soviet Government might wish to suspend any current discussion and action. I was at home and was not consulted either. I am not going to claim that I would in fact have got the answer right had my telephone rung; at the end of a hard tiring week, one is as certain of giving right advice as a footballer in the ninetieth minute of a cup-tie taking a penalty with the score at 0 – 0.

Mr Brown is, in my judgement, technically right. But I think the error was not simply technical. I have alluded to strains within the British team at the top level. When such strains exist, there is almost certain sooner or later to be an error of top level decision and this was it.

The rest of the story can be told quickly. The next morning, after consultations with the Prime Minister, I held a meeting in my office at which the American Ambassador, Mr Bruce, and Mr Cooper discussed the situation with Mr Brown's private secretary, Murray Maclehose, the Foreign Office Vietnam expert, Donald Murray and myself in order that we might all be clear what the situation really was. We also had the task of urging on the Americans that the truce be prolonged until Mr Kosygin left London. This was not difficult to urge; with bombing of North Vietnam having begun when Mr Kosygin was in Hanoi, it would have been tragic farce if it had restarted now with Mr Kosygin in London discussing Vietnam with us.

We had further discussions at Chequers on Mr Kosygin's return from Scotland and a revised formulation was finally presented to him at Claridges Hotel in the early hours of Monday 13 February, the truce having been prolonged by a few hours. But, of course, it was not possible to get back to the formula which had interested the Soviet Prime Minister on 8 February.

At 12.00 noon, British time, on that same Monday Mr Kosygin took off for Moscow. There was only one more thing to do. I was determined that no chance whatever should be taken of any further mistake. There might be the slightest glimmer of hope out of Moscow before the bombing restarted on Monday evening, and there must be no possibility whatever that Mr Brown or his department had missed it. So I arranged a minute to minute schedule, rang the Soviet Ambassador twice and kept the connections going throughout. But Moscow had gone dead. At 5.40 pm bombing was resumed.

From this severely compressed account, we must ask ourselves several questions. Was Mr Kosygin really interested in the 'Phase A – Phase B' formula? Why was there the astonishing reversal of form in Washington which left the British negotiators with their credibility gone? And was what Mr Cooper calls the 'Tragedy of Errors' really a lost chance of peace in Vietnam?

If the traditions of Russian history remain unchanged, we shall probably never know what Mr Kosygin or Moscow thought. So speculation is permissible. I am much inclined to believe that Mr Kosygin, thinking in Soviet terms, saw some hope in the formula which could be read as meaning that the Americans would take two overt steps (cessation of bombing and abstention from reinforcement), while the North Vietnamese would only take one step which would not have to be announced publicly (cessation of infiltration). This equation might have some appeal in Hanoi. When the matter came to President Johnson's personal

M*

attention, it could well have struck him that a bargain as un-balanced as this, against the background of frighteningly large North Vietnamese troop movements during the truce, would be politically intolerable, and that his position could become indefensible unless at least infiltration actually stopped before bombing ceased. Mr Wilson's judgement is 'the hawks had won.' One could, however, equally say 'the North Vietnamese troop movements had shot down the doves'. Not even the Pentagon papers throw any light on this point. Either way, it was a sad thing that at this crucial moment the American governmental machine at the top level had failed to operate coherently.

Had a great chance for peace been lost? Probably not, because some of the detailed snags in 'Phase A – Phase B' would have emerged and held negotiations up for months; the later Paris talks are evidence for this. But it was a great let-down when a hopeful situation was destroyed by bungling and the hope banished that the encounter could at least have registered infinitesimal progress.

The Middle East

I have mentioned that when I came to the Office in 1965 the situation in the Middle East was 'normal' – no war, no love. Our own relations with the area varied from country to country. If, on the whole, our relationships with monarchies and sheikh-doms were better than that with more radical Arab régimes (I avoid purposely the word 'progressive'), this was from no theore-tical preference for feudalism. Political relationships contain an element of reciprocity. If a particular country has a certain regard for your interests and a certain capacity to discuss mutual problems with flexibility and without dogma or rabble-rousing, this naturally has some effect on your own attitude.

As between the Arabs and Israel, British policy could only be one of balance. The state of Israel had been born in 1948 amid a mixture of compassion for the Jewish race, combined with admiration for its great qualities, and disapproval of the methods used by Zionist organizations to bring the new state into exis-tence. For the Arabs there was the survival of an old affinity between the desert-dwellers and English 'wanderers'. As time went on, the Arab world developed a great economic importance to Britain as the source of over 70 per cent* of British oil supplies.

The most important and most difficult relationship for Britain in the Arab world was that with Egypt. This was partly because Egypt was much the most articulate of the Arab countries, whether from the wide-spread voice of Cairo radio or the views of the many school teachers from Egypt working in schools and universities throughout the Arab world. Since 1956 our relationships with the UAR had been extremely difficult. This was not because of any personal pique in our diplomacy. It was because from 1956 onwards Egyptian policy was to disrupt any influence or standing Britain might have in the Arab world, and to espouse and advocate an extreme form of doctrinal anti-colonialism which in the name of non-alignment harassed us in our dependent territories: needless to say there was no simultaneous criticism of the unwelcome hegemony of the Soviet Union over Eastern Europe.

Egyptian philosophy in 1965 was enunciated with great eloquence at a luncheon for four given by the able and agreeable Egyptian Ambassador, Hafiz Ismail, to Mr Michael Stewart and myself. The 'spokesman' was Mohammed Heikal, the famous editor of *Al Ahram* and at that time very much the voice of President Nasser. Mr Heikal spoke in apocalyptic mood. The people of Britain and Egypt were great people. They had a profound respect for each other. They were worthy antagonists. But destiny had decreed that antagonists was what they would be. We might deplore our destiny and seek to mitigate it but nothing could change it.

We naturally disputed this. But the point to remember is that, when the mouthpiece of the highly able Head of State and Government in an important country pronounces in this manner, you may discount some of the eloquence but you cannot simply pretend you have not heard. Nor could you pretend, if you lived in the area, that you had not heard Cairo radio.

---

* 71.4% in 1971.

None the less it was important to try to maintain the best possible relations in the circumstances. On the personal level the attempt was by no means disagreeable, since Egyptians are extremely agreeable people. Accordingly, when on the Rhodesian question the UAR Government in 1965 broke off diplomatic relations, a position of frustrating paradox was reached in which, contrary to the mutual interest, there was no official communication between us and the leading state in the Arab world.

Meantime there were occasional ominous portents. In November 1966 there was a raid by Egyptian MiG aircraft over the Negev area of Southern Israel. One awaited a word of criticism by the Secretary-General of the United Nations who was not wholly reticent in such comment. None came. In the same month the Israelis undertook a punitive attack against Jordan. Even granted the unsettled state of the Jordan-Israel frontier, this seemed an extraordinary act since, if there were ever to be peace on the frontiers of Israel, the Jordanians were the most likely people to promote it.

On 16 May 1967, at about 6.00 in the morning, my bedside telephone rang. The Resident Clerk at the Foreign Office said that President Nasser had ordered the United Nations Expeditionary Force to leave the Egyptian frontier with Israel. This force had been guarding the land frontier for ten and a half years and the post of Sharm-el-Sheikh which commands access by sea to the Southern Israeli port of Eilat. The Israelis had not helped their case by refusing to allow the UNEF to operate on their side of the frontier. None the less this was a brusque order by President Nasser to the United Nations to get out.

It is still not wholly clear why President Nasser took this action at this time. It is known that the Syrians either feared or thought they feared (a slight but important difference) a punitive Israeli attack similar to that on Jordan. It is also clear that the move initially must have had Soviet connivance, though it is not clear (and may never be) whether this connivance was active or grudging. But it was immediately apparent that the situation was a grave one.

After an early talk with the Foreign Secretary I went on to what was perhaps the most depressed session of the morning meeting that I can remember. The Israelis had clearly been 'framed'. Unless the Secretary-General of the United Nations intervened at once, Israel would at one diplomatic stroke be deprived of such protection as the UNEF could give. Israeli shipping was already barred from the Suez Canal; the fortification by the Egyptians with the Russians' aid of Sharm-el-Sheikh would further impede access by sea to Israel. The action had provoked a sudden crisis, not just a normal flurry, and if the United Nations did not act, the Israelis would have to submit or act forcibly themselves.

To the great disappointment of those who could read the inwardness of this situation, the Secretary-General, U Thant, without consulting the Security Council declared the UNEF non-operational preparatory to withdrawal. Since this decision was strongly questioned in many countries, the United Nations Secretariat took the unusual step of circulating a document explaining its legal necessity.

Mr Brown's view is that 'all this is legalistically true, but wise men faced with big events whose consequences are immeasurable, shouldn't in my view act as though they were working in a solicitor's office conveyancing property.' The word 'legalistically' is, of course, prejudicial; a General Assembly Resolution is an Assembly Resolution and though not mandatory, not to be lightly brushed aside by the Secretary-General. The 'conveyancing' parallel is unfair; apart from the legal position, U Thant had become identified with the so-called non-aligned thesis and was therefore not disposed to tackle President Nasser head on. In any case, a Buddhist background predisposes the individual temperament to meet the dilemmas of crisis with resignation or, at the most, conciliation, rather than drastic initiative. But for all this I believe, as I believed at the time, that Mr Brown is right in substance. There was only one way to head off this crisis. That was for the Secretary-General to send to Cairo a message saying 'Hold everything: am already en route to see you.' This would have put at risk the dignity of the Secretary-General and the authority of the United Nations. But this authority had already been brushed aside and the Secretary-General must on occasion take the ensuing responsibility on himself. I am sure that this is what Dag Hammarskjöld would have done.

It would have been hypocritical to press the Israelis to react with resignation. The question was whether anything could be done to reassure them until some stability could be restored. We took the obvious line with Arab ambassadors; one of them quoted me back later, 'Yes, you warned us that if we put on the pressure too hard, the Israelis would have no alternative but to fight.'

One idea tried out was whether, through a limited naval movement, freedom of access to Eilat could be maintained. Britain could, no doubt, raise the men, but we had few ships and no money. The vulnerability of ships passing Sharm-el-Sheikh was obvious, and there was a disposition internationally to thank us for a good idea and invite us to go ahead and carry it out. In the end, ideas of naval intervention were swallowed up in wider conflict.

On the morning of Monday 5 June there was a repeat of the telephone routine. A message said that in response to spottings on radar the Israelis were in action against UAR forces. Again I went to the Office as soon as I could and found Mr Brown and Denis Allen discussing the situation. We all felt like the captain of the ship in the middle of a typhoon, storm raging around and a curious calm at the centre where the captain could do nothing but wait and hope he was facing in the right direction.

There was very soon something to do with great urgency. Owing, I think, to a state of near panic, the Jordanians picked up on their radar something which they identified as American and British aircraft flying acrosss Israel to attack them. The story was manifestly wildly false, but against the background of 1956 it was also immensely dangerous. It would be believed very easily in all Arab countries and would be immediately used by ill-disposed people as a windfall for all anti-British and anti-Western propaganda. The only course was to respond at once, not as part of the general information effort but as a special task force operation. The operation was brilliantly successful. The story became rapidly known as the Big Lie and very soon was discredited world-wide except in Arab bazaars and in places where you believe what you are told to believe.

Meantime the Israelis bombed and swept all before them. Against Syria they secured the strategic Golan Heights whence it had been all too easy to shell the plain of Galilee, against Jordan, the rest of Jerusalem and the West Bank area, and against the UAR the whole of Sinai up to the Suez Canal which was not, however, crossed. It was total victory, and among those free to think for themselves and with no special interest to defend, it was an immensely popular one. The question was how would the interested parties use or misuse it.

First into large scale diplomatic action came the Soviet Government. They had, as was later learned, expressed concern to the UAR Government about the development of events. As a compensation they put forward in the United Nations General Assembly a completely pro-Arab motion requiring that the Assembly: (1) Vigorously condemn Israel's aggressive activities and continued occupation of part of the territory of the UAR, Syria and Jordan and (2) demand that Israel should 'immediately and unconditionally' withdraw its troops behind the armistice lines. At the time the significance of this move was almost wholly missed. It meant that the Soviet Union had attached itself so explicitly to one side in the contest that it had no role for some time to come in the restoration of peace.

The stock reply was, 'Oh well, the Americans are equally committed to the preservation of the Israelis.' This is a line for the gullible. All members of the United Nations are committed to the protection of the independence of other members. With its large Jewish community, the United States would certainly be active in upholding this principle on behalf of Israel. But the Americans have interests and friendships in the Arab world too. Thus, while the United States would inevitably gravitate into being the chief protector of Israel, the immediate, real effect of the Russian action was to make the Soviet Union completely partisan with an interest in making the Americans appear equally partisan.

It was important that the Soviet motion should be defeated. Admittedly it would not, if carried, have had a stronger force than recommendation. But that recommendation would have had some weight as a United Nations pronouncement and would, in effect, have ruled out the United Nations in Israeli eyes, and those of others, as a suitable agent for conciliation or mediation.

So I accompanied Mr Brown to New York in June for the Special Assembly meeting and we worked as one does, night and day, together with Lord Caradon and his resident British delegation, in favour of a more moderate motion. This was successful and a way was at least left open for progress under UN auspices, if and when progress became possible.

These events at New York in the summer left the position about machinery for future peace open. The Israelis said that they would negotiate with anybody. The Arab attitude was that they would not negotiate with anybody before total Israeli withdrawal. Both positions were entirely understandable but they left no way open for any approach towards a peaceful settlement and no great disposition among the parties to seek one acceptable to both sides.

Since the United Nations had thus remained an appropriate intermediary, the question was how, in these unpromising conditions, to get it moving. The Russians and Americans were ruled out as initiators; the French were also ruled out, because General de Gaulle had switched the spontaneously pro-Israel sympathies prevailing in Governmental circles in Paris into a pro-Arab policy. The British were no longer decisively powerful in the Middle East, although we were still physically in Aden and the Gulf. But for reasons of mixed sentiment and interest we happened, alone of the permanent members of the Security Council, to be exactly in the middle of the argument. The alternatives were, therefore, that a resolution should be worked out and presented by a small power with assured support, or that if larger power support were considered more authoritative, we might undertake this ourselves. In September, Lord Caradon and his colleagues saw the first signs of possible acceptability of a British initiative if this were launched at the right time.

A Security Council Resolution on a difficult subject requiring negotiation and compromise is not something placed on the table, debated freely and quickly, and voted on according to conscience. Confidential discussion is essential. But, more than this, under Chapter VII of the Charter a Security Council Resolution can be binding on the members of the United Nations. Therefore, before a draft resolution could usefully be placed on the table, there had to be days or even weeks of urgent but quiet negotiation involving constant communication between delegations in New York and home governments.

As soon as signs began to appear that a British initiative might achieve a result, our own machine was completely geared to bringing this about. It was an exciting experience watching the pieces gradually coming together. Although the Americans were not acceptable as sponsors, the text had to be acceptable to them. It had of course to be acceptable to the contending parties. The third world with whom Lord Caradon and his deputy, Sir Leslie Glass, had especially good relations regarded the effort with relief. The question was whether a formula could be found which the Soviet Government could also accept. So it is not surprising that it should have taken two months to arrive at a formulation with a good chance of acceptance. The Soviet Government, no doubt largely because it was represented in these discussions by Mr Kuznetzov, agreed to do so. When success was achieved on 22 November, we sent a really whoopee telegram to the delegation.

Mr Brown, to whose dynamic persistence in this initiative all honour is due, has explained the advantage of the final text. It established the principle of withdrawal of Israeli forces without explicitly requiring them to restore every inch of the former frontier. It terminated all states of belligerency and guaranteed territorial inviolability to all states in the area, and therefore, if made effective, could banish the spectre for the Israelis of perpetual warfare. It requested the Secretary-General of the United Nations to send a special representative to the Middle East to: 'establish and maintain contacts with the States concerned in order to promote agreement and assist efforts to achieve a peaceful and accepted settlement in accordance with the provisions and principles in this resolution.'

U Thant appointed Dr Gunnar Jarring of Sweden who had had similar experience in Kashmir, as special representative and a certain guarded hopefulness became for once permissible. Another positive step was the re-establishment of diplomatic relations between Britain and the United Arab Republic, resulting in two excellent appointments, those of Sir Harold Beeley to Cairo and Ahmad Hassan El Feki as Egyptian Ambassador to London.

El Feki had been my UAR colleague in Delhi. He was an incredibly hard worker and a terrifying chain smoker (his wife said, 'I can do nothing about either'). He had manifestly come to London to make up Egypt's lost ground and we had some excellent discussions. I told him that, if we were to make progress, it would not be enough for the UAR representative in the United Nations to make speeches: there would have to be a document signed by the UAR Government – the exact kind could be worked out in the United Nations. He agreed.

In the Office we also did some homework in depth by appointing another task force, this time under Sir Richard Beaumont, our former Ambassador in Baghdad, to work out, in the way Morrice James and I had sought to do about Kashmir, a possible settlement of the dispute, not for use internationally but as a guide to our own thinking. An obvious comment is, 'Why not launch it?' The answer to this is not just that an adverse reaction to an initiative might hurt the national ego. It is that if a good plan is launched by the wrong people at the wrong time it not only discredits the launcher but it also discredits the plan. If we were the right people to launch Resolution No. 242, we were not the right people to launch at this moment a project for final settlement.

Given these favourable developments at the end of 1967, why, four years later, were we so little further ahead? There is the sheer obstinacy of the problem itself. It contains two famous blind spots. The Arabs find it impossible to imagine their way into the Jewish soul in which the history of Jerusalem, of Zion, of Canaan is the whole history and faith of a race – a race always courageous and talented, sometimes misguided and insensitive, constantly persecuted and exiled and always infinitely pertinacious. For their part the Jews, or at any rate the Zionist Jews, claiming their fundamental right to a small piece of land, cannot conceive that the people whom they have evicted from that land survive with an inextinguishable hatred against the evictors. Until both sides make first the mental and then the political adjustment, progress will be slow and not real.

But for some time after their military triumph the Israelis had it in their power to be magnanimous. After such an emphatic victory, and on the assumption that no Arab state would sign a document on which there was also an Israeli signature, the objective could have been to secure a formal unilateral declaration, signed by the Arab states, covering non-belligerency, and unmolested passage through the Suez Canal and to and from the Gulf of Aqaba. In return for this and for some marginal territorial concessions, the Israelis could have offered early military withdrawal. But the Israelis developed a preoccupation with the means rather than the end. They insisted that there must be direct negotiations between Israel and this or that Arab country. This, they kept on saying, was on the point of happening; we must be patient. But it never did. In this argument, from which we could not dislodge them, the Israelis frittered away their chance of a settlement and far too much of the sympathy they had enjoyed in June 1967. Dr Jarring did his best, but time slipped past. Egypt lost President Nasser, whose flair could eventually have helped, and various American initiatives petered out – five years after the June war there was still no sign of peace.

President Nasser is a figure who will bear much study in the future Mr Brown says that British foreign policy 'underrated' him. I do not think that after 1956 the British underrated his ability. It may be that they underrated his flexibility. Given the course of non-alignment and given what was said and done by Cairo over many years, it was natural to suppose that President Nasser would continue indefinitely to work against the British interest. It was tempting also to think of him in company with Nkrumah and Soekarno whose vanity and egoism eventually brought about their downfall. But in fact when Britain was in trouble in Aden, Nasser found himself in trouble in the Yemen; suddenly London and Cairo became colleagues in adversity and a degree of dialogue, fortified by the personal contact brought about by Mr Brown, developed usefully. It was only sad that, having conspired and fought his way out of the arms of one imperialism, he and his country should in the end have found themselves in the arms of another.

Honours and Awards

The useful phrase, 'other related matters', borrowed from the Kashmir argument, is a reminder that being Permanent Under-Secretary is not only a matter of high politics, economics and diplomacy. I once asked my uncle Alwyn Scholfield what he did all day as University Librarian. He replied, 'I sit at my desk and am interrupted.' So it is that the determination of policy, its expression and execution are interrupted by a stream of episodes which are not in the main line of policy but which can, if not properly handled, damage morale and even policy itself. Work in this category can be positive. But a lot of diplomacy is such that, while action neglected can lead to trouble, action taken merely leaves things no worse than they were before.

One matter which was time-consuming and not a little distressing was the argument about honours and awards. Everyone who looks twice a year at the two full newspaper pages of names of people receiving anything from the highest award to the most modest medal asks himself whether the system is not a little out of hand. Yet anyone who looks around among his friends or down the columns of a telephone book does not find himself overwhelmed by the company of people with letters after their names. There are world-wide variations in attitude about these matters. Some feel that there should be no honours at all. Others, including developing countries like India and Burma or a Communist country like the Soviet Union, take the view that at least some recognition of services to the country is appropriately and inexpensively conferred in this way.

In a written answer in the House of Commons on 21 July 1967, the Prime Minister referred to criticism that the proportion of honours going to the Home Civil Service, the Diplomatic Service and the Defence Services was higher than that which normally goes to those in other walks of life. There would therefore be further reductions over and above those in the previous ten years in the honours accorded to the Home Civil Service, and corresponding reductions would be made over a period in awards to the Defence Services and the Diplomatic Service. The effect he explained, would be to halve the number of knighthoods over the period and materially to reduce awards in the Order of the British Empire.

The effect on the Home Civil Service was the greatest. This was because with the growing complexity of government and the greater responsibilities thereby falling on civil servants, the size of the civil service was bound to grow. Thus the proportion of civil servants receiving awards and particularly higher awards would diminish. Such a change needed to be handled with sensitivity and understanding.

The media slapped themselves on the back and said how much better it was that footballers and pop-singers should get awards rather than 'dull civil servants'. No civil servant or diplomat is in the least jealous of pop-singers and footballers receiving honours; they join the applause, especially when Britain wins the world football cup. But the essential point is that people who are publicly successful get rewards in terms of fame and finance. The civil servant is condemned to 'dullness' not because he or she is in fact duller than anyone else, but because as part of the compact with government under our constitutional system he is anonymous. The compensation to him for refraining from public utterance and renouncing exceptional financial reward is partly an assured career and partly an award which may not have material value but at least says, 'Well done, good and faithful servant.' Neither the Government nor the media saw fit to remind the public of this.

I had no personal interest in this matter since by the time it arose I had for all practical purposes passed the post. But I argued hard and explicitly on behalf of my diplomatic colleagues because becoming a 'Sir' is one of the tools of the trade, and on behalf of my home service colleagues because people who by previous standards would have earned distinction were going to be denied it.

These matters are not perhaps greatly important on the day of judgement if there is one. But in the atmosphere of 'anti-Civil Service' which heralded and followed the publication of the Fulton Report, owing as it did something to the psychology of 'the jealous society,' I thought myself bound to make my feelings known. I hope the system will continue to be applied with flexibility (otherwise Buggins rides again) and with the generosity which should inform relationships between government, its servants and the public.

Spies and Security

Another immensely preoccupying subject was that of security, espionage and treason. In a world of nation states divided by strongly held ideological views these problems are bound to exist, especially when one side in the argument is strongly addicted to espionage as a method of securing information. Communist authority remains in some degree wedded to the psychology of conspiracy, and as the revelations of 1971 about the strength of Soviet espionage in Britain showed, there is evidently plenty of information to be acquired in Britain to make its acquisition by secret means appear desirable. The agents and double agents of Tudor times reproduce themselves in the Philbys and Vassalls of today.

In the immediate post-war years the depth and persistence of Soviet penetration were not at first realized, and personnel structures and policies were in no way geared to the security needs of the time. Hence the failure by the Foreign Office to guess the significance of the physical and mental breakdown of Donald Maclean in Cairo in the late forties. In this particular case it was not easy to be right. In the period 1942–45 I often worked closely with Maclean in Washington and thought I knew him well. He was a tall, quiet, attractive man with an apparently tranquil, settled family life and a professional ability that was quite outstanding. When hard pressed you could leave it with perfect confidence to Donald.

I saw him once after 1946 when I called on him in 1950 as head of the American Department of the Foreign Office. I was appalled at the aspect of *dégringolade* (falling to pieces) which he presented. But I still had no suspicion that, as I now believe, he had contracted an obligation to Communist masters which had remained dormant during the war and was now in the last stages of repayment. It was not just a lack of perception on my part. The mood of the times was such that official and public opinion were simply not prepared to accept as true what the dramatic events of the early fifties would reveal: the security betrayals of Fuchs, the flight of Maclean and of the useless Burgess, the prosecution of Alger Hiss in America, and the activities of later and lesser disloyalists in Britain all showed the depth and magnitude of the problem.

In my years at the Foreign Office we had a sudden and most intense outburst of public intelligence fever round the most remarkable spy of all H. A. R. Philby (unlike most people I never had the privilege of calling him 'Kim'). After the Maclean and Burgess case, the Foreign Office never again put its trust in Philby. But nothing could be proved and a Parliamentary question in 1955 caused his name to be publicly cleared. He was given a relatively minor post in the Middle East from which he duly defected. His name hit the public in 1967 when an immense series of articles appeared in the *Sunday Times* about him, with ancillary television and other publicity.

The content of the articles does not matter. They were based on an attempt, following fashionable doctrine, to prove that the success of Philby had been due to the prevalence of an old-boy network in the wartime intelligence service. The thesis was blown out of the water in short order by Professor Hugh Trevor-Roper. In a brilliantly incisive article in *Encounter* Trevor-Roper wrote from inside knowledge, not attempting to prove that the intelligence service was perfect, which it was not, but showing that the particular accusation was wholly ill-founded. It seemed to me a pity that the *Sunday Times* by its failure to publish Professor

Trevor-Roper's article missed a wonderful opportunity of making journalistic history. It did, however, publish an editorial disclaiming any intention of benefiting the Russians by its disclosures.

All this speaks for itself as a peculiar agony for the diplomatic service and the security authorities while the uproar lasted. The only thing you can do is a lot of very delicate, detailed work (one slip can wreck it) to make as sure as you can that there is nothing currently wrong and then ride the trouble out. But riding trouble out is not just sitting still, and careful research in conditions of public tension is no rest-cure. In the end, like other onslaughts, this one did not prove of indefinite duration. Morale was maintained and Mr H. A. R. Philby emerged as a remarkable and ingenious, if hardly admirable, character.

Finance and Defence
Our ability to help much further in the Middle East was sadly limited by further financial trouble. In October 1967 it became clear that devaluation was this time unavoidable. All one could do was to urge at a meeting with Ministers that we should aim at devaluation with a difference, not just more of the same. The machinery for passing advance confidential information to Commonwealth and other Governments worked with its normal fluency, and devaluation was announced on 18 November.

There was then something of a policy pause. Mr Callaghan resigned as Chancellor and Mr Roy Jenkins replaced him. Complaints began to arise that nothing was being done to exploit the devaluation through either a renewed export drive or an import saving review. Then suddenly the economic situation exploded in a most unwelcome impact of domestic politics and economics on the conduct of external affairs.

With preparations for the 1968 Budget in hand, the Government were about to find themselves once again in great trouble over restraints on domestic public expenditure. There was much pent-up demand, particularly on a Labour Government, for new expenditures on social services which had had repeatedly to be cancelled or put off. The leadership concluded that the price of preventing domestic expenditure from rising above its existing level was insistence on an actual lowering of expenditure overseas. Expressed abstractly, the proposition sounds logical and acceptable. But in fact, as Mr Wilson has explained, it deeply divided the Government. Mr Wilson rightly says that, in defending himself against further or accelerated cuts in defence, the Secretary of State for Defence, Mr Denis Healey, could 'call on Foreign and Commonwealth Office support'. Since the whole period was tense and disagreeable to a degree, it may help to explain why.

The Defence White Paper issued in February 1967 had announced that 'by the mid-seventies, British forces would have left South-East Asia.' During the year this withdrawal had begun to be accepted by our Commonwealth friends in the area as inevitable. They had, however, been given reassurances about the immediate future which would afford time for discussion and readjustment. In the Middle East also reassurances had been given that no immediate withdrawal was intended. Suddenly these reassurances were all reversed.

The 1968 White Paper would announce withdrawal from South-East Asia not by the mid-seventies but by the end of 1971. There would also be withdrawal from the Gulf not just in principle but by the end of 1971. True the 1968 White Paper spoke of 'consultations' with the Governments concerned in both areas. But these 'consultations' were the kind which the Commonwealth most dislikes, advance confidential information of what the British Government intends to do anyway.

One must not over-argue the case. The economic saving of withdrawal from the Gulf was in fact unimportant – some £12 million a year. But in the Office there had been some anxiety about an indefinite prolongation in the Gulf of a 'special position' which might involve us in internal struggles in the Arab world. In South-East Asia, too, there was no doubt that sooner or later the big establishment at Singapore would have to be run down; an arrangement for alternative facilities in Australia was an obvious objective. What assured opposition by the Foreign and Commonwealth Offices was the disastrous effect of these proceedings on our relations with friendly countries.

In relation to the Americans the move was particularly dis-comfiting. It came at a time of no progress towards peace in Vietnam. Further trouble was to be expected and it came with the *Tet* offensive by the Vietcong and North Vietnamese in the same month as the issue of the White Paper. I joined Mr Brown in Washington where we had a gloomy interview with the United States Secretary of State, Mr Dean Rusk. He was as always quiet and patient. But he did go so far as to say that, although he was not a man of strong language, he must not be taken to lack strong feelings. The British Government had one piece of luck; the F 111 aircraft turned out a failure and we made a real saving by cancelling the contract for it. But altogether the episode was a grim one. It was grimmer in the context of coincid-ing with the beginnings of a significant Russian naval expansion and of the realizaton that some of the strongest supporters at home of our withdrawals in the East were equally going to oppose any compensating commitment to Europe.

Again one must not over-argue. Savings on balance of payments ensued. But a credibility gap had been created which was not easily or quickly closed. The external departments could only work for the modest little paragraph at the end of this recital of withdrawals: 'We shall, however, retain a general capacity based on Europe, including the United Kingdom, which can be deployed overseas as, in our judgement, circumstances demand, and can support United Nations operations as necessary.' It was a reassuring card of re-entry.

Latin America

Ever since I can remember, the Foreign Office has fought a lone battle, supported by a few enterprising friends like Sir George Bolton, the then Chairman of the Bank of London and South America, to maintain a national interest in Latin America. To the Treasury that continent remained an unpromising place from which it was impossible to collect debts; to the Board of Trade for many years it was a market that was hardly worth while compared with most others. Neither point of view was un-reasonable. Only Japanese, Germans and, sometimes, Americans seemed to take an interest and make money there. The British share of trade was, in 1967, a miserable 5 per cent of Latin American imports: against our imports of £288 million we only exported £149 million. There were a few shining exceptions like some aircraft sales in Chile and Central America, but the general performance was mostly unimpressive.

Latin America is a continent where the memory of British aid to the liberation of many republics from Spain and Portugal is such that it might have happened yesterday instead of a hundred and fifty years ago. Consequently modern disinterest on the part of Britain leads to sadness among our many friends in that continent and can cause fragile morale in British Missions. On the other hand, a little attention brings big dividends. I arranged, therefore, with Mr Brown that Pat and I should spend a month there, the whole of March 1968, visiting, as it turned out, ten countries.

In such a programme there could be no question of precise negotiation. But I could at least make contact with presidents and governments, show that we had not forgotten the continent, help the various Embassies with a first-hand understanding of developments at home, and listen to their problems of policy and housekeeping. Pat could very usefully talk with wives both personally and in the name of the very active Diplomatic Service Wives Association. In advance I brushed up with Señor Honor, the head of the Spanish section of the Foreign Office Language School, the Spanish I had learned in internment in Japan. We composed an invaluable document christened '*el discurso general*' which would have been intolerable as a speech but contained a most useful series of paragraphs from which an introduction to a speech could be devised.

In Brazil we spent much time with my opposite number, Dr Sergio Correo da Costa, who almost immediately after became Ambassador in London. There were no touchy problems, but there were tiresome matters of housekeeping in the new capital of Brasilia. This immensely ambitious project had paused slightly in its spectacular advance; but as one Brazilian remarked, 'It will succeed and we shall work much harder in that climate than we do in Rio.'

In Argentina we arrived at a tense moment, two days after Britain had removed the embargo placed for health reasons on the import of Argentina's main meat export, beef, but retained that on the much smaller item, lamb. The British understandably regarded this as a generous gesture; the Argentines simply took it as a supreme insult to Argentine lamb. Such are the problems of politico-economic diplomacy.

My opposite number, Dr Mazzinghi, the Ambassador, Sir Michael Creswell, and I discussed trade, a successful arbitration recently carried out by the British on the land frontier between Argentina and Chile, the difficult problem of a further arbitration in respect of the Beagle Channel in the south and the obstinate deadlock over the Falkland Islands (Malvinas) where British sovereignty upheld against an Argentine claim led to total cutting of communication between the islands and the nearby mainland. We then paused. Was there anything further to discuss? Well, maybe . . . indeed yes, there was a small current difficulty. Thus we finally entered discreetly and, in the end deeply, into the acute current discontents, making a little progress over the hump and paving the way for the immediately forthcoming visit of the Minister of State for Agriculture. Even in an age of international rudeness, there are still right and wrong ways of getting at the really sensitive core of a problem. At last we adjourned and the Argentines served lamb for lunch.

Christian Democrat Chile was awaiting with friendly and relaxed anticipation the visit of the Queen. There was a possible atomic order round the corner (ultimately achieved). The British Council's Institute buzzed with the coming and going of innumerable students of the English language and British institutions and literature, and we had a delightful evening *folklorica* as guests of the Foreign Minister and his wife.

So it went on. I had insisted on going to little-visited Bolivia (airport of La Paz: 13,000 feet, and in the Embassy residence a cylinder by the bedside in case one ran out of oxygen in the night). I called on that impressive ruler, General Barrientos, who governed with a sternness softened by knowledge of local dialects; his death in an air crash cannot have helped his country.

There were more discussions in Peru, on the point of a military-revolutionary development arising from frightening differences between rich and poor and from national bankruptcy caused by the uncontrollable expenditure on President Belaunde's development schemes. A Hovercraft had come sensationally up the Amazon and Britain was on the map.

We went to steadier Colombia and sensationally developing Venezuela, where a small plane threaded its way through sky-scrapers to land in the middle of the city. Then after a night in Panama we had a gathering of British Ambassadors to Central American countries in San Salvador. Finally came a visit to Mexico. I looked out of the aircraft window and saw a triangle in a hazy sky. In a piping voice the stewardess announced 'It is Popocatepetl.' It was a great moment I had been waiting for since childhood.

In a long talk with the Mexican Foreign Minister, Señor Antonio Carillo Flores, I raised that least welcome of subjects, Gibraltar. Right round the continent I had reproached various Governments for betraying their historical tradition by voting for the absurd United Nations Resolution recommending the transfer of Gibraltar to Spain, whatever the known wishes of the Gibraltarians. All of them had taken the implied line that they wished the question would go away. They knew what I meant but, political liberation from Spain having been accomplished, '*Hispanidad*' (Spanish-speaking solidarity) took over; and one could not go against it whatever one's ex-colonial conscience might say. Mexico alone had abstained. Yes, said the Minister, they had had a hard debate in the Mexican Foreign Office, but self-determination had held out as a principle against '*Hispanidad*,' and much to the displeasure of the Spaniards, Mexico had not voted for them.

I could wish that there were space to write more of that continent with its great natural beauties, it immense and un-forgettable variety in unity, its spectacular riches and ominous poverty, and of the efficient hospitality of Government after Government and Embassy after Embassy. It must all be taken for granted. Except that wonderful afternoon by Lake Titicaca in Bolivia when there was low, brown cloud over the landscape as, with our hosts, the Ambassador and Mrs Ronald Bailey, we sat in an estate car, munched cold chicken and shivered. Suddenly, the cloud began to move away, a curtain literally rose from the landscape, revealing mile after mile of the splendid Andes contour, bathed in sunshine.

Mr Brown Resigns

As we were sitting in La Paz, oxygen cylinders at our elbows, a telegram came in from Denis Allen, saying that there were persistent rumours of a change of Foreign Secretary; unlike previous ones, these looked serious. I could not help reflecting that, if I had been at home, I should very likely have found myself seeking to restrain Mr Brown from a course which could only end his political career. But in La Paz I was exempt by distance from this responsibility and could only listen. Next day came the news of Mr Brown's resignation and Mr Stewart's return to the Foreign Office.

As there was at the time also one of the recurring gold crises, I naturally sent a telegram saying that, if the Secretary of State wished, I would come home at once, and I made provisional arrangements to do so. The reply I had been hoping for came back: carry on with the tour. If anyone else had been appointed, I should have had to return; since Mr Stewart and I knew each other well, there was no such immediate necessity.

We returned via Washington. The atmosphere in a city where we had so enjoyed ourselves for seven years was ominous and depressing. Shopping which had been a pleasure had become a penance, a search for what was not there among people who did not care. Small wonder; the fearsome Washington riots of May 1968 were only a month away. I wrote back to Denis Allen saying that to a degree we might find it hard to imagine in London, the United States was in serious trouble with itself.

Indeed it was in those months that the supreme irony of Vietnam was playing itself out. The Americans had continued through 1967 their search for negotiation. Meantime American military strength in Vietnam remained around half a million men and the North Vietnamese continued their build-up both in their own territory and in the demilitarized zone (this had ceased to be thought odd). This build-up expressed itself finally in the great offensive which burst out in the *Tet* festival, a period traditionally associated with truce (a circumstance also not thought strange). The offensive rocked American and South Vietnamese defences up and down the country; casualties were estimated at 6,000 US and South Vietnamese soldiers dead.

When it was over the offensive was seen to be a tremendous military failure. The North Vietnamese had put the most immense effort into it. With its repulse they ceased for the ensuing period to menace the security of the South. But the offensive had done its political work. While consciousness of the extent of the North Vietnamese defeat slowly grew, American political morale finally cracked. In April President Johnson declared his intention not to run for a second term as President. By the time the Presidental election came round in autumn 1968, Presidential candidates could only promise early evacuation and hope that somehow this could be accomplished without dishonour. I had in Washington another testy dinner conversation. A liberal Congressman informed me that all the Americans had to do was to install a coalition government in Saigon and clear out. I replied waspishly that this was indeed what they might have to do and they would not like what they saw when they looked behind them. I don't think he liked me.

Sherlock Holmes

The immediate crisis to which I returned in April was neither the change of Secretary of State, nor the international monetary strains, nor Czechoslovakia's Bohemian spring. It was entirely personal. For reasons for the disclosure of which, to use Dr Watson's phrase, 'the world is not yet prepared', I had become President of the Sherlock Holmes Society of London. This august and scholarly body had long planned a quiet week's holiday in Switzerland with an occasion or two in period costume. On our return from Latin America, I found that the excursion had become a matter of world interest. 'Anyone who has not been buried alive in a coffin for thirty days knows that the Sherlock Holmes Society is leaving for Switzerland at the beginning of May.'

It had been tacitly understood that the President of the Society should where necessary impersonate the Great Detective. It was now clear that this would mean a repeat single combat with Professor Moriarty on the narrow path overlooking the splendid Reichenbach Falls, in the full glare of international television. The question posed itself, 'Could the functioning Permanent Under-Secretary of State for Foreign Affairs and Head of the Diplomatic Service undertake this hazardous assignment?' I decided that, by virtue of his other office, he had to. But it would be wise, I thought, for him not to be away more than the minimum forty-eight hours needed for this crucial encounter.

I submitted a minute to Mr Michael Stewart assuring him that in my absence, Mr Mycroft Holmes would take charge of the Office. I waited with some trepidation for Mr Stewart's reply. It was splendid. It said: 'All right. But don't return in two years' time via Tibet.' Mr Stewart knew his Sherlockian business. But I must say that when we paraded at London Airport, in front of buzzing and clicking cameras, Mr Holmes in deer-stalker and Inverness cape and Miss Irene Adler (Patricia Gore-Booth) in 1890s costume with a hat burgeoning with feathers, I experienced as never before the sensation of 'in for a penny, in for a pound.'

The triumphant progress of the Society through Switzerland, the delighted friendliness of the Swiss, the six encounters with Professor Moriarty (only room for two television cameras at a time) and the bestowal of the freedom of Meiringen on Mr Holmes must be described at another time. After I returned the house was knee-deep in press-cuttings. We had precisely two expressions of criticism, one from the extreme right and the other from the extreme left. The Government and the Diplomatic Service survived, and the matter passed gaily into television and diplomatic history.

Bohemian Spring

The gay interlude had come just at the right time. The rest

of 1968 and the one month of 1969 left to me were to be full of events. They included the whole gamut of subjects political, economic and administrative, and there was to be everything from accomplishment to tragedy. The tragedy was already visible on the horizon.

In February the hated Novotny régime in Czechoslovakia had been overthrown and a new spirit was stirring in the country. Something was happening for which many thinking people had hoped for years, an attempt to run a Communist society on a basis of human, personal freedom. Since the Czechoslovaks had an inter-war tradition of successful democracy, the movement, under the leadership rather than control of Alexander Dubcek, grew like wildfire. Something new in European history began. It was exciting and happy, but it had its dangers and fear was felt in the Office and elsewhere that this new movement by its very momentum might overrun its capacity to survive. Would the Russians allow it to live?

By the end of July, when Parliament adjourned and Pat and I left London for a few weeks' rest, the question was still un-answered. There were troop movements by the Warsaw Pact powers and threatening sounds and gestures from Moscow. Since the answer was still not clear, some contingency planning was necessary.

There was no great difficulty about our attitude if current developments continued; we would be sympathetic to the Czechoslovak popular movement without doing or saying things which would unnecessarily provoke the Russians against the Czechs or ourselves.

There were differences of view about the likelihood of a tragic ending to the Bohemian spring. There were some who held that the decision would be based on defence considerations, the question whether the Warsaw Pact defence system could tolerate a Yugoslavia in Czechoslovakia. I myself felt that the decision would be based on the much wider ideological considerations with which I deal later. At any rate, if the worst were to happen to the Czechoslovaks, we must be ready with a policy and a reaction.

N

In terms of travel time Czechoslovakia in 1968 was far nearer than Mr Neville Chamberlain's remote and little-known country of 1938. But two things had drastically changed. The Soviet-controlled régime imposed on Czechoslovakia in 1948 had kept the non-Communist world at a political distance. Moreover the balance of power in Europe was totally different. In 1938 it was conceivable that Britain could threaten and indeed carry out armed intervention to help Czechoslovakia. In 1968, the power of the Soviet Union and the existence of the nuclear deterrent made it impossible to think in these terms, even if there had been a disposition among the Western countries to intervene. And the tragedy of the 1956 Hungarian revolution had taught the free world not to offer false expectations.

The only possible policy therefore would be to bring to bear any pressure that could be brought by world public opinion. Soviet intervention therefore should not be regarded as a little local European trouble, but as a matter of world importance necessitating United Nations attention.

Alternative policies having been prepared, Pat and I went for our much needed rest to a quiet valley in north-eastern Italy. From there we watched the brilliant Italian television coverage of the tragedy, as Russian tanks rolled over Czechoslovak liberty and the people watched and prayed silently in Wenceslas Square. Our preparations for recourse to the United Nations had been adequate, and there was no need for me to come officiously back for their execution.

In the United Nations there was a censure of the Soviet action which was nearly unanimous. One exception was India. A good friend from the Indian diplomatic service called on me soon after and complained that if we had been ready to 'deplore' instead of 'condemn,' India could have gone along. For once, for all my efforts at comprehension, I was cross with my Indian friends. I said that we both condemned and that the only difference between us was that we had had the guts to say so.

Merger
As we were sitting in March in remote La Paz listening to radio

reports of the resignation of Mr George Brown, we also heard, with considerable surprise, the last sentence of the Downing Street statement: 'The Prime Minister proposes to bring about the amalgamation of the Foreign Office and the Commonwealth Office into a single Office. He has asked Mr Stewart to supervise this and to be responsible for the new Office. During this period Mr Thomson will continue in Cabinet as Secretary of State for Commonwealth Affairs.'

The announcement of the amalgamation was a complete surprise. The subject had been discussed in the report of Lord Plowden's Committee, published in February 1964. That Committee had felt that while such an amalgamation 'should be the ultimate aim . . . to take such a step now would be interpreted as a loss of interest in the Commonwealth partnership.' But the Plowden Committee did recommend, as an 'urgently needed reform,' the creation of a unified Diplomatic Service instead of the existing separate Foreign and Commonwealth Services. This unified service came into being in January 1965.

Things could not stop there. From 1965 to 1968, not only was the new, unified service getting used to itself; the two departments were at the same time organizing ways in which there could be joint management and procedures, so that members of the new, unified service should not remain subjected to differing routines and disciplines. Contentious matters, such as widely differing filing systems, a more intimate and sensitive feature of most people's daily lives than the making of high policy, needed resolving and claimed much patience. But the logic of these developments was obvious. Most official thinking had put this merger some four of five years ahead; I thought of it as coming sooner than that, but no one had predicted 1968.

I felt at once that this was a good decision and an exciting and highly welcome challenge. For me personally it set a target date. With Joe Garner's retirement on 1 March, I had become Head of the Diplomatic Service, and my retirement date (sixtieth birthday) was 3 February 1969. It seemed to me that we could amalgamate quicker than that if we organized the process right, and that this was what the Government would wish. The one awkwardness was that Morrice James, having become Permanent Under-Secretary for Commonwealth Affairs on 1 March, had his department abolished a fortnight later. Ability is not normally recompensed in this way.

On the steps toward the merger, my immediate thought was that everyone in both offices must be consciously involved. We had an excellent administration of the unified service under the ideal leadership of Sir Colin Crowe. But this basic change could not just be 'left to the administration'. Everybody's life and work were involved. Accordingly I set up a committee of three, consisting of Colin Crowe, Dennis Greenhill, my successor-designate, representing the Foreign Office and Jack Johnston representing the Commonwealth Office, to meet daily at the start to direct the operation and to report at least weekly and more if necessary to Morrice James and myself. At the other end, everybody was to be asked for ideas so that no one should feel left out of the process or estopped from making suggestions.

I was also extremely keen to have outside wisdom brought to bear on our affairs. I would like to have revived in 1968 the proposal that Messrs McKinsey or the equivalent should examine our administrative structure. But there was now no time for this. Instead, I organized something which had never happened before, two 'working dinners' in my office. These consisted of equal numbers of Foreign and Commonwealth Office officials and people from outside who had had top responsibilities in both government and business or had expert knowledge of government administration applied to external affairs. The former included personalities like Lord Aldington who had been Minister of State at the Board of Trade and was chairman of a bank; Lord Franks who had been head of a government department, an Ambassador, chairman of a bank and head of an Oxford College; and Sir Leslie Rowan, former First Secretary at the Treasury and subsequently chairman of Vickers. The second category contained senior people from industry and communications, and academics such as Dr A. F. Wheare, head of the London Graduate School of Business; Professor Bernard Crick of Sheffield University; and Mr Donald Watt, lecturer at the London School of

Economics. We circulated in advance a paper summarizing our problems. On both occasions we had fascinating and most profitable discussions on Government organization.

What transpired most vividly was that the complexity of Government is such that it is theoretically remarkable that anything happens at all. Assuming that, say, a bank has staff (including numerous branches) and a Board of Directors under a strong chairman, the pyramid of command is logical, coherent and intelligible. In a Government department such as our own, the process of an important and difficult decision is remarkable. It may originate at the top or the bottom; it passes through a hierarchy or a sort of sub-cabinet or both, and is approved explicitly or tacitly by the chairman (the Permanent Under-Secretary). It then goes to a second level, the second sub-cabinet being the departmental ministers or such as are interested, with the Secretary of State as chairman. Thence it goes on to the real cabinet whose chairman is the Prime Minister. Even the cabinet does not necessarily have the final word, since Parliament can, and occasionally does, insist on a final word of its own. Thus modern government simply cannot afford sloppiness of structure or efficiency. It follows also that presentation has to be thorough, accurate and clear, since the more important the decision, the more likely it is that decision-making will be influenced by people powerful in their own right who do not know the subject until it is presented to them for decision.

This analysis led to agreement that one of the most crucial problems is the efficient relationship between what are known in management as 'line' departments (geographical or functional) and 'staff' departments responsible for the personnel and facilities to enable the line departments to function properly. This is elementary in theory, but it was not so easy in practice when the main staff department was in one building, and most of the line and special advisory departments were in sixteen others.

Apart from this distinguished external advice, we had numerous working parties of our own. A particularly valuable study was done by Sir Thomas Bromley, an Ambassador *en disponibilité*, who went through the entire accommodation and did what no

N*

one had ever done before – tried to group departments and their servicing units (registries) into blocks to replace the haphazard arrangements brought about by years of improvization and false economy. The main building does not allow a contemporary standard of efficiency but the improvement was remarkable.

There were awkward personnel problems too. The Commonwealth Service, before amalgamation, had been a small one, and posts had been expanding as new territories became independent and new High Commissions were required. This meant rapid promotions. The Foreign Service was much larger and there was no proportionate increase in the number of independent non-Commonwealth countries. Accordingly Commonwealth Office personnel felt that in the amalgamation of the services followed by the merger, their promotion had slowed down unfairly. Foreign Office personnel, for their part, felt that Commonwealth colleagues had come into the combined list at too high a level. One could only point out firmly that the two complaints cancelled each other out; however unjustly this might have worked out for a particular individual, the collective rough justice was undeniable.

By midsummer, Morrice James and I reported to our Secretaries of State that the new firm could open for business on 1 October. This turned into a splendid piece of one-up-manship. An urgent request came down from highest political authority: would we please slow down a bit as the date suggested would coincide with the Party Conference. We consented to 16–17 October.

On 16 October we held a meeting which included ministers, senior officials and, at my insistence, representatives of all branches of our activities including cipherers, telephonists and doorkeepers (my office called it 'your Tolstoy party'). There were speeches by Mr Michael Stewart and Mr George Thompson on the themes of true merger and, in particular, of the Commonwealth idea and ideal not being swamped in the wider organization (Mr Stewart made a particular point later of seeing all Commonwealth High Commissioners individually to convey this assurance to them). I made a speech of compliments and thanks to the two Secretaries of State, emphasizing in particular Mr Stewart's clear-headedness and calm and Mr Thompson's exceptional instinct for the conduct of international affairs. I added, as reported correctly in a gossip column, that the whole thing was obviously a racket by the Order of St Michael and St George, the order particularly associated with diplomacy.

At midnight a small gathering collected in my room; Morrice James, Pat, Nicholas Barrington from the Secretary of State's private office, Richard Baker and myself. As Big Ben struck midnight, we drank a series of toasts: the Queen and the Commonwealth Office proposed by me, the Foreign Office proposed by Morrice and the Foreign and Commonwealth Office proposed by me. No doubt the announcement in Parliament that day had been the official beginning of the new order. But our little ceremony was the Service's farewell to the past and greeting to the future.

The Duncan Committee

The merger was not the only major administrative operation of 1968. In the somewhat panicky atmosphere of early 1968 it was natural that the demand should be revived in the Government for economy in the handling of our overseas representation. My professional reaction was that we had been spending the last three years methodically working through the reforms proposed by the Plowden Committee and that it would be pleasant if we could be allowed to get on with a little uninterrupted diplomacy. However, I had to agree that this further review was unavoidable. A tough negotiation followed in resistance to terms of reference which would have meant, like the trial in *Alice in Wonderland*, 'Sentence first, verdict afterwards.' The result was a compromise in which the sharp-end sentence said that the Committee was to: 'bear in mind, in the light of the current need for the strictest economy, the importance of obtaining the maximum value for all British Government expenditure and the consequent desirability of providing British overseas representation at lesser cost.' One does not need to be a professional logician to see that the word 'consequent' is in fact inconsequent. But this did not matter since the phrasing left the committee a very free hand.

The choice of the members of the committee was most important. A great deal of current opinion about representation abroad was highly subjective, and it would have been quite possible to find ourselves confronted with people holding totally preconceived ideas. Whatever may have been later criticisms, the service and the country were fortunate in the choice of Sir Val Duncan, Sir Frank Roberts and Andrew Shonfield. Sir Val was the Chairman of a very successful international company, Rio Tinto Zinc, Andrew Shonfield had strong economic and journalistic background for a study of the Service and Sir Frank Roberts had just concluded a highly varied career with an outstandingly successful five years as Ambassador in Bonn.

The news commentary on the appointment of the Committee was pretty bizarre, but characteristic of the time. One gentleman informed us that 'until the very eve of last year's (1967) Middle East War, the guidance from the Foreign Office was that the situation did not look very dangerous.' The narrative has shown that our feelings were precisely the opposite. On the other hand some good points were made, notably the question whether our political reporting, enormously diminished since 1939, might not still be excessive.

I gave evidence in early September, concentrating on the importance of permanent presence as opposed to spasmodic visits if diplomacy is to be effective. We were able to bring the Committee up to date about the immense concentration on commercial work since the mid-fifties; it was of interest to find that in administrative jobs abroad the number of officials engaged in commercial work (392) was greater than those (379) on the wide-ranging classification 'political work'. The variety of our secondment and training programmes was striking; it included secondments to such industries as Leylands, ICT (the predecessors of International Computers Ltd) and English Electric, with more under negotiation. 50 per cent of the junior administrative officers were going through a Treasury economics course (not enough; but the limitation was not of our choosing). Nine hundred people were doing language training, over half through the Foreign Office Language School and Laboratory, started in 1965. It was an impressive showing.

The report came out in July 1969 and therefore is not part of this narrative. It provoked some shocked reactions. The passages on the shape and purpose of the Service were somewhat over-stated and the distinction made between what the Committee called 'areas of concentration' of our diplomatic effort and the rest of the world was too stark. The chapters on commercial work tended to give too much the impression that nothing had been done hitherto. But I have always assumed that these comments were underlined for the purpose of making important points in a way which would catch the deaf ear and the blind eye. There were some admirable 'nuts and bolts' recommendations, parti-cularly about handling property overseas and about more travel and less correspondence. There were weaknesses too, notably on information work which the Committee did not seem to under-stand. But to people in the Service who have grumbled, I always quote Chapter 2, paragraph 5. I quote it here: 'We have been impressed by the quality of the Diplomatic Service and by its team spirit. It is highly regarded in other countries. Successive mergers though desirable in themselves, have perhaps sometimes made it harder to maintain the high standards which the Service demands of itself. But by and large we have found it well adapted to its present tasks and with the capacity to adapt itself to new roles and new requirements.' Nobody in such circumstances could expect a better verdict than this. When it was pronounced, public nonsense about the Service dramatically ceased.

Nigeria
Thus my service was drawing to an end amid a multiplicity of administrative activities. But political problems did not just sign off.

Overshadowing everything was Nigeria. The civil war had broken out in July 1967. But the impact on British opinion grew steadily with its progress. This was due partly to the disagreeable necessity of providing arms to one side in a civil war in a Com-monwealth country, but even more to the astonishing public relations campaign carried out by and on behalf of Colonel Ojukwu's régime in the former Eastern Region (Biafra), consisting since May 1967 of the East-Central State, Rivers State and the South-Eastern State. I need not describe this campaign, as this has been done most vividly by Mr Wilson. But the stream of propaganda, with accusations of wholesale starvation and atrocities amounting to genocide, the evidence of which was later shown to be most inadequate, induced what I can only call a hypnotic state in much of public and intellectual opinion and large sections of the media of information. I received on behalf of Mr Stewart a delegation of intelligent, humane and distinguished people who came to plead the Biafran cause. What disturbed me immensely was their quiet-voiced extremism. No virtues were allowed to the Federals, no vices to the Biafrans. This just could not be right. Apart from any absolute judgements, the great majority of the Organization of African Unity, in opting for the unity of Nigeria, could not be acting out of sheer perversity. I knew from my public relations experience that a public relations success by one side implies a failure by the other. The apparent inertia of the Federal forces for long periods, added to the inarticulateness of the Federal Government, sometimes made it very difficult to keep steady.

The sane arguments for remaining loyal to the Federal side were overwhelming. The Federal Government was the heir to the British Government. Fragmentation in Nigeria was going to give rein to infectious fragmentation all over Africa. Failure to help Nigeria with any arms would not have meant useful pressure for peace but immediate replacement of British by Soviet arms, an irrevocable political price for achieving nothing. Besides, it was not discreditable for a country like Britain which lives by industry and trade to have in mind its own interests, an investment of £200 million in Nigeria. Nor was it foolish to bet that the Federals were going to win since eventually they did. (But, contrary to frequent allegation, I never heard anyone in the Foreign and Commonwealth Office us the cruel phrase 'quick kill'.)

So through all the dark days of demonstration and brainwashing, we stuck to our advice and Mr Stewart stuck to his view. But what perhaps does not fully come through even in Mr Wilson's account is the feeling of demoralization which the campaign sought to induce. On occasions it was very nearly successful, as at a moment in December 1968, when a combined attack on the Government over Nigeria and over possible concessions to Argentina in the Falkland Islands brought Mr Michael Stewart back from India before the end of his programme. Not until well over a year later did the end come in Nigeria, the human agony having been prolonged by the help cynically provided to Ojukwu by the French under the orders of President de Gaulle. Suddenly, in January 1970, it was over, just as another political onslaught on the steadiness of the British Government was being prepared. No one could have been more relieved than my former colleagues, unless it was the people of Nigeria themselves. A slow kill had been even more cruel than a quick one.

Commonwealth Conference, 1969
Before I retired there was one more major political event. A meeting of Commonwealth Heads of Government was due to open in London on 7 January 1969. There were vivid unhappy memories of the 1966 meeting, nearly wrecked by ill-temper over Rhodesia. While there was a desire to avoid a repetition, there were also muttered fears that, whatever anyone might desire, this might indeed happen. If it did, Commonwealth Heads of Government might never meet again.

Since this was to be the first major operation by the newly merged Foreign and Commonwealth Office and Morrice James had left to be British High Commissioner in India, I decided to assume personal responsibility for the official level preparations. I took charge of the briefing, admirably assisted by the newly-formed Commonwealth Co-ordination Department, arranging to delegate all the rest of my work so far as it might interfere with daily and nightly attendance at Commonwealth meetings.

The crucial moment was at the very beginning. Mr Wilson's comment is: 'In the advance discussions there was complete agreement on the agenda.' Indeed so – in the end. But it is of some interest to recall how that agreement came about. For if it had not, the conference would have been very different indeed. According to the custom of such meetings, the top officials meet on the eve of the opening session to check arrangements and procedures and agree the agenda. On this occasion the draft, presented by the Commonwealth Secretariat, began with a general discussion on the world situation and followed with Rhodesia. We had had some inkling, through our channels, that an East African representative would move that Rhodesia should be taken first. The motive was understood, but the change might alter very much for the worse the whole mood of the conference. I went to the meeting prepared for this. Sure enough, the Zambian representative moved for change. He spoke with moderation and was promptly and dutifully supported by the other East Africans.

There was a pause. The Chairman, Mr Arnold Smith, Secretary-General of the Commonwealth Secretariat, then asked, quite properly, whether it was the wish of the meeting that this change be made. Silence. Rhodesia was a sore subject and no one wished to challenge the East Africans in any way on the issue if it could be avoided. I then asked to speak. I said that we much respected the deep feelings held on this subject in East Africa and we appreciated the measured terms in which the amendment had been moved. None the less, since the meeting was a meeting of Commonwealth leaders from all parts of the world, it seemed more appropriate that a discussion of world affairs should come first. On the other hand, since Mr Wilson wanted to controvert silly stories in the press that he was seeking to avoid discussion of Rhodesia, it was important that this item should come second. There was a short supporting intervention from Canada. Another silence followed. Then came a most welcome comment from Ghana that this seemed reasonable and we were home.

Mr Wilson handled the ensuing meetings with skill and aplomb. He comments that 'the communiqué went through more quietly and speedily than in any previous conference I attended.' There is a background to this too. The communiqué was of enormous length (seventy-five paragraphs) and evening after evening till late into the night Jim Bottomley and I sat there guarding or amending paragraph after paragraph. Most of the time, I took the word and Jim advised me; when it was Rhodesia, Jim, who knew almost as much about Rhodesia as Mr Ian Smith, took over and I advised him. We had difficulties with India over phrases about disarmament, about which I had a pleasantly tough negotiation with the very able Shri P. N. Haksar, Mrs Gandhi's private secretary. We had difficulties with Pakistan about almost everything. But we showed up our work in unanimous good order.

The Commonwealth communiqué is always dull reading. But it is much more important than is ever recognized, for it represents a consensus among some thirty countries of different areas and races and interests. And if confidence is observed as it was in 1969, the communiqué is unique of its kind since it comes out not from public display of convenient and popular attitudes, but from sober private discussion. And as one attended that particular series of discussions, it impressed me strongly to hear twenty-three Heads of Commonwealth Governments speaking and even more to observe twenty-two of them listening. There will always be danger that this world-wide, inter-racial high level *causerie* may one day break down. If it does, then the world will be deprived of a certain political enrichment and, in my view, Heads of Commonwealth governments should be very wary of disparaging it.

Curtain

So we were at 15 January and it only remained to wind up the show, visit colleagues in Whitehall and departments in the Office to say good-bye. The day before I left I met a group of press people for a discussion. It was not a very lively occasion – I think I was by then too tired to spark. But for one moment the meeting woke up when a correspondent suddenly said, 'Are you telling us that the Foreign Office is always right?'

Happily I was not too tired to give what I think to have been the right answer: 'No human institution is always right. But never forget that, in the two great crises of my time, Munich and Suez, when, by later universal consent the judgement of a

British Government was grievously wrong, the sense of the Foreign Office was right.'

So we had come to the end. After all the drama we finished, like *Der Rosenkavalier*, on a small but happy note. Someone came in and reminded me that I had always been fussy about getting the cluttered Foreign Office corridors cleared; the Ministry of Works, he said, now begged to report that they had just taken away 'thirty-nine lorry loads of junk'. Pat, Richard Baker and I took a brief, relaxed supper together. At 11.50 p.m. I left my desk to say good-bye where I had begun, in the cipher room. Then at 11.59 I stepped for the last time as of right into a Foreign Office car and, as we drove out into Downing Street, Big Ben struck midnight.

Perspective

In this narrative I have retraced, albeit sketchily, the early years and professional life of one British diplomat. From the story there will, I hope, have emerged some impressions of the processes and challenges of mid-twentieth century diplomacy. On that basis it would be possible to call it a day, but this would mean leaving out some of the things which still need to be said if there is to be a well-rounded answer to the question: 'What did it all feel like and what did it all mean?' Such an answer includes the nature of diplomats and what is required of them, what they are like and what they are not like, and what are the pressures on them, professional and external, ranging from family problems to the world ideological conflict.

One day in Delhi I had a visit from an International Bank team touring South Asia. I thanked them for giving us some time to talk with them, to which the leader replied, 'Oh no, we always go to the American Embassy for a thorough economic analysis and the British High Commission for a sound political judgement.' This compliment implied a sense of proportion and perspective in the British Mission. An instinct of this kind underlies the constantly recurring phrase in diplomatic reporting, 'as seen from here,' meaning that the sender may be satisfied, preoccupied or alarmed but realizes that the recipients, while respecting his views and feelings, have to take account of the same situation as seen from elsewhere. Proportion and perspective have to be the constant allies of day to day diplomacy and hence the daily battle between detail and the wider view, or rather the battle to fit the detail into the proper place in the bigger context.

A total comprehension of thirty-five years of world history is probably beyond the human understanding. But at least the writer of this narrative has an obligation to present something of the accompanying perspective – as seen from here.

Diplomacy and Diplomats

'These, then, are the qualities of my ideal diplomatist. Truth, accuracy, calm, patience, good temper, modesty, loyalty. They are also the qualities of an ideal diplomacy.

"But," the reader may object, "you have forgotten intelligence, knowledge, discernment, prudence, hospitality, charm, industry, courage and even tact." I have not forgotten them. I have taken them for granted.' *Harold Nicolson.*[1]

'A diplomat is a man who always thinks twice before saying nothing.' *Dr Herman van Roijen.*[2]

It would be wonderful, if a little overpowering, if all British diplomats could tick off Harold Nicolson's list and show up a 100 per cent result to some heavenly High Commission. Of course none of us can do that or anything near it. But if one looks at the list with cold sobriety, it is astonishing how often diplomats have to apply a great many of these qualities if they are to make any sense either to their government or to themselves. I shall not seek to prove it. But Harold Nicolson's reminder contains so much that is true of what the profession demands, that it can stand as a Platonic 'ideal of a diplomat' or a Kantian '*Diplomat an sich*' (diplomat as such).

I will, however, try to bring out some of the capacities and qualities which a diplomat uses specifically today and also explain some of the difficulties he encounters in reaching and sustaining the ideal. I would not claim that the modern diplomat sets a defined ideal before him. British people are not like this. Diplomacy is a job. None the less the job, if it works out right, can in a curious way create the ideal as you go, particularly if you have the perception and the humility to profit from observing the merits and weaknesses of others.

Some capacities are special features of modern diplomacy and it must therefore be underlined that they are additions to and not substitutes for basic virtues such as reading fast and

[1] Harold Nicolson, *Diplomacy*, p. 126.
[2] Dr Herman van Roijen, Netherlands Ambassador in London, 1964–70.

writing and dictating clearly. Modern custom necessitates the former but does not necessarily encourage the latter.

At home, diplomats, like home civil servants, are often called 'faceless'. In fact, like both home civil servants and public faces, they differ from each other immensely as individuals. They are felt to be faceless at home because, if they say anything publicly at all, they say it very very carefully, since under our constitutional system public saying is done by politicians. Even the most cautious and deferential public statement of Government policy by a civil servant can lead to trouble. Hence the aptness of Dr van Roijen's remark.

However, in these days the diplomat abroad in a country where there is freedom of speech, and even where it is partially restricted, will need among other things to show his or her personality and character by being publicly articulate. Above all things, he or she will need to be wholly adaptable. Diplomats must be able with equal spontaneity and calm to walk backwards out of the presence of the Emperor of Japan, to sit on the floor of an Indian village school and talk with a saint or make a speech at the drop of a hat at an occasion on which the chief speaker, the Megalopolitan Ambassador, has somehow failed to turn up. I have done them all. They must be able to contrive anything, bear anything, eat or drink anything and appear to like it, and to be surprised by nothing. And all this must be done without loss of sensitivity or courage.

Adaptability needs to be collective as well as individual, and the demands on the collective adaptability of a diplomatic mission can be heavy and sudden. A declaration of war, an internment and an evacuation show some of the qualities needed. In recent years have been added, lamentably, the burning down of Embassy residences and offices, often with the collusion of the local government authorities, and the kidnapping and even assassination of personnel. As in the theatre, the show must go on as best it can, and so it does. By contrast with these afflictions, minor adaptations can be interesting and even gay. In Delhi our main reception room became a periodic rehearsal room for the revived New Delhi Symphony Orchestra, and when the MCC visited India we set diplomatic protocol aside and invited to a reception only people who regardless of rank could step up to a lonely stranger and talk cricket.

When I say that a diplomat must be able to contrive anything I do not mean anything underhand. Embassies have latterly taken on a greatly enlarged task, the good or indifferent performance of which directly affects the value of the post and the reputation of the Service. Because of fast air travel, the number of visitors to countries abroad goes on increasing. Most of them are self-supporting professionally as well as financially. But some have or develop a legitimate claim on the help of diplomatic or consular expertise. Therefore a good Mission will, as far as local conditions allow, know how to contact practically anybody.

Of course, in a large country a small Embassy cannot know everybody. Its principal customer is the Ministry of External Affairs and its principal material the political, economic and commercial situation. But it may be called upon at the shortest notice to serve and help any visitor – a Cabinet Minister, industrialist or trade unionist, a delegation of doctors or a chess champion or a footballer in distress. You do not need to know the visitors' opposite numbers personally, though it helps if you do. But you do need to know how and where to find them (the Ministry cannot always be relied upon to know) and, if necessary, to enlist sympathy or help.

In a paragraph in his article in the *Sunday Times* of 7 April 1968, unfortunately not reproduced in his book, Lord George-Brown wrote: 'My very first impression of the Foreign Office and my very last was one of its quite extraordinary professionalism.' The comment is highly perceptive. Diplomatic professionalism is not always understood because it is a professionalism involving capacity and experience differing from recognizable and describable attainments such as engineering or finance. Sir Val Duncan's Committee rightly described diplomats as 'professional generalists'. The profession, however much it may formalize itself in terms of documents or etiquette, is essentially one of human communication between people who talk different

languages and have different thought-patterns and temperaments, not to mention histories and geographies. It has to include multilateral as well as bilateral communication; this has
meant, since 1945, an instinct for Conference Diplomacy. This
combination of instinct and experience must include a sense of
priority and cost-effectiveness, and readiness to subordinate
routine to the historic or the unique.

Some aspects of diplomatic professionalism abroad is being
on duty for twenty-four hours a day, seven days a week. A
diplomat is not at his desk or telephone all that time. But there
is no time during the seven days when the post is off duty and no
time when a diplomat and his wife in their contact with others
revert to being private citizens. There is therefore no exemption
from attending receptions celebrating the national day of one
country after another. Absence is noted and presence appreciated by the hosts; absence of mind is no excuse for absence of body.

I do not want to fall into the fallacy of appearing to suggest
that, because there are certain standards, all diplomats are good
diplomats. This cannot be so in any profession. In diplomacy
some people start with a rush and then somehow, whether
through illness or through over-rapid development of talent,
slow up or cease to develop. Some may be unlucky and have a
series of unrewarding assignments and become disillusioned.
Others may just scrape into the service, lie fallow for a time and
then show true quality in a crisis, after which they never look
back. Needless to say, all the qualities and capacities enumerated
apply to women diplomats exactly as they do to men. A woman
officer adds a dimension to a Mission's knowledge and 'feel'. I
have owed a great deal to Dame Barbara Salt who but for a
calamitous illness would have been our first woman ambassador,
and to Elizabeth Barraclough, Information Officer in Burma,
who rejoined us in Delhi at my request.

An immense amount depends on wives. I want to pay them an
unreserved tribute. Diplomacy is a partnership game *par excellence*.
A good pair is worth considerably more than two good individuals, and of the pair the wife has just as arduous a job as the
husband, with rather less of the excitement in not knowing all

that goes on marked 'confidential'. The partnership role of wives will continue, but there may be changes in how it is practised. Many will be trained to this or that profession, which they may be able to pursue in the country to which they are sent, or they may not. In one country I know of, a doctor tried for two years to find how to spend a few voluntary hours each week in an over-crowded, under-staffed hospital, and never succeeded; on the other hand a physiotherapist wife was called in urgently to unstiffen a distinguished visitor's neck and was promptly success-ful. No doubt there will be in the future diplomatic husbands to whom the same compliments will apply.

Anything may push you on; anything may throw you out of your stride. And somehow the Personnel Section have to keep track of what is happening. On this I am bound to say that diplomats, good or indifferent, are remarkably sound and objective judges of each other. Moreover, I doubt whether there is any profession in which there is less atmosphere of gunning for each other or working to get the other man's job than British diplo-macy.

The weaknesses which can develop are unexpected ones. I myself think that the main affliction which a diplomat can deve-lop is the loss of ability to listen. If you serve in a series of posts which though interesting are not of great daily interest in Britain (and the British, despite their imperial past, can be astonishingly insular), you have to become an actor without an audience. It is then very tempting consciously or subconsciously to create an audience that is not there, and the habit can grow even in diplomatic company. If you stop listening, you stop learning, and self-importance takes the place of authority. The alternative is not a leaden silence. One can only say 'watch it'.

An occupational weakness, not so visible from outside, is the failure to develop an ability to delegate – an insistence throughout life that because one can do things better one must do them all. In diplomacy this can easily grow, because advances in promotion do not necessarily mean advances in range of com-mand. You do not rise from company to battalion commander all that often; indeed a post to which you are sent on promotion may be less large and less central than the department you have left.

Failure to delegate is in any case an affliction of the body bureaucratic. The Foreign Office has a good tradition but sometimes it slips. The day after the 1968 merger, therefore, I issued to the new department a circular on this subject which, I am happy to say, has become Civil Service department doctrine. I will only quote a very small extract, referring particularly to junior officers:

'. . . the rule is: if you can rightly decide, do so. There are some snags about this (a) you may be wrong; and (b) your judgement may be right but someone above may feel he should have been consulted. The answer to (a) is that we are all wrong sometimes, but there is no need to make a habit of it. As for (b) I can only ask those whose first impulse is to say "I should have been consulted" to think again and encourage venturesomeness rather than timidity.'

Having talked about reality, I must reluctantly take a little time off to talk about images, the late sixties having been a great period for image-worship. The basic stereotype of a senior official of the Foreign Office, seemingly beloved of cartoonists, is a gentleman of eighty, preferably wearing striped trousers and a buttonhole. He has to look like this because otherwise you cannot use the word 'mandarin'. In the Cliché Secretariat, which has taken over some of the duties of Dickens's Circumlocution Office, the use of the word is compulsory.

I have searched many years for a mandarin – in fact I was tempted to call this book, 'In Search of a Mandarin'. I found two in the 1930s, but later research has been less fruitful. More seriously, the misconception arises from a traditional view of a small Foreign Office of spacious days with the occasional giant personality, like Sir Eyre Crowe, as the official head. Now senior people, who have in any case to retire at sixty, are part of the general high speed scramble conducted at the non-mandarin pace imposed by events.

It is also important to remember that the Foreign Office is in the Aesop's Fable sense less of an oak than a willow. It has its convictions but, like any other department, it needs and wants ministerial leadership. This is neither total wisdom nor a corporate spirit of 'passed to you please'. It is practical wisdom, because everyone knows that, however right you may think you are, you need a senior minister with political qualities if the department's views are to prevail in Cabinet. If he does not agree with those views, it is your duty at home or abroad to argue, and his (or hers) to decide.

It follows also from the willow simile that officials do not go around being 'shocked'. I like to think that, if a Secretary of State decided one summer that all meetings with him should be held on the lawn outside the Foreign Office building, the reaction would not be 'shock' so much as a minute saying 'Does the Secretary of State wish us to indent for a centrally heated marquee for winter use?' Innovation is usually taken in its stride these days. So is the swing of the pendulum method as one Secretary of State's way of doing things differs from another's.

Another misconception is a by-product of the generally excellent ITV film made by Associated Rediffusion in 1967 under the leadership of Clive Irving. The team were welcome and admirable guests, astonished and delighted that they could talk to anybody and take pictures practically anywhere. People responded spontaneously, and Mr George Brown loyally refused to be inveigled into saying that there was anything peculiarly troublesome about being in charge of the Foreign Office. The team were appalled, and rightly, by the 'magnificent slum' as they called it in which we worked. But they fell a little into the trap of supposing that if you work in palatial Victorian surroundings, you cannot help acquiring a palatial Victorian outlook which you apply to policy. Exactly the reverse is true. Policy execution for today and planning for tomorrow is a conscious, continuing battle against an office environment handsomely designed for the purposes and methods of the day before yesterday.

There is also the class image, beloved of professional class-warriors and productive of proper anxiety among those who seek genuine equality of opportunity. I am sure there has to be a university degree standard for admission; second-class honours is the right minimum level since coherent thinking and use of language is basic to the trade. Before Labour came into power in 1964, we had started visits from the Office to try to interest universities other than Oxford and Cambridge in diplomacy as a career, but without great effect. Mr Stewart insisted that we step up the campaign and he also gave a working dinner for redbrick Vice-Chancellors. Their general theme was that what we had to offer was fine; we had simply to persuade possible candidates from redbrick that diplomacy is a human world, relevant and accessible to them.

One day a Labour Minister asked me if colleagues from non-privileged backgrounds were in fact getting any responsible jobs at all. I said I didn't like classifying people in this way; I was interested not in who they were but what they were. The demand was persisted in and I produced a list of four names on condition that it be immediately destroyed. The Minister was handsomely grateful and impressed.

Good diplomats spring from all sources and prejudice must remain abolished and not simply be transferred.

More reluctantly still, I must take up one or two points in Lord George-Brown's book, *In My Way*. This is not from any desire to revive ageing argument. It is because when a former Foreign Secretary commits himself to print on the team who served him, his comments must be considered authoritative unless someone with knowledge comments further on them. There are a few items on which I cannot avoid doing this.

In his book Lord George-Brown complains, as all modern Foreign Secretaries understandably complain, that: 'A Foreign Secretary's day is incredibly full.' He describes the many activities and goes on: 'As Deputy Leader of the Party I was of course also very involved in Party work both in Parliament and outside it . . . and so by evening I had already worked a very full day.' He continues: 'But round about 6.00 pm the bowler-hatted chaps would start wending their way home or to their clubs, depositing as they went the papers, the minutes, the telegrams which they thought I should deal with that night.'[3] Then, suddenly, by a magic stroke of the pen we are transported out of reality into the World of Wooster, on our way to the Drones Club. Forty years ago this would have been good clean fun with the chaps. But the modern permissive society has its solemnities and some of Lord George-Brown's many readers will take his word-pictures exactly as they are written. So they deserve a short but solemn commentary – in my way.

If a statesman who is an active deputy leader of the government political party feels he can also take on the work and responsibilities of the Foreign Secretaryship, he must expect that the price of this temporary power and privilege will be 'doing the files' by night; there are some which simply have to be done if the Foreign Secretary is to keep up to date. It really is not worthy in this context to take a side-swipe at the less important people who would no doubt quite like to have seen the Secretary of State all day and have instead to leave papers for him to study later.

The picture is also distorted in detail. Many officials in these days cannot afford clubs. I myself was a member of a club for thirty-five years and cannot recollect ever seeing the inside of it 'around 6.00'. Hardly anybody wears a bowler hat these days (I last wore mine in 1936) and civil servants don't 'wend'. Many of them catch post-commuter trains to suburbs of London well away from the Office since they cannot afford to live near the centre. A proportion carry home with them brief-cases containing non-confidential material to read at home, having been too busy with confidential material all day.

I may appear to be heavy and humourless in my comments. But recalling once again the prevalence of image-worship à la mode, I have felt bound in all loyalty to put the picture straight.

I must also comment on Lord George-Brown's account of personnel policy and management. First I would say that, subject to a qualification that I make later, Lord George-Brown was extremely perceptive about people. He made a number of

[3] Lord George-Brown, *In My Way*, Gollancz 1971, p. 163.

excellent decisions on appointments which he describes. Some were his own; more were what might be called 'consensus decisions' in that they came up through the appointments machinery and his and our views coincided.

The machinery itself is serious and thorough. At the top level a meeting of some twelve Under-Secretaries is held at regular intervals with the senior administration officials and the Secretary of State's private secretary present. A plan of suggested forthcoming moves and promotions is circulated in advance by the administration. In the late 1950's the custom arose of inviting ministers to be present if they wished; this was later formalized so that two Ministers of State came reguarly, one specializing on Commonwealth and the other on Foreign Affairs. A board of this size is needed in order to be sure that there is sufficient personal knowledge of diplomatic officers and their wives stationed all round the world. The ministers, apart from contributing their own ideas from acquaintance in London or visits abroad, could satisfy themselves that there was no injustice within the service. The recommendations of this board were all submitted to the Secretary of State who, in cases of outstanding importance, consulted the Prime Minister. There are five similar committees going down the seniority ladder except that Ministers only attend the senior one. This arrangement provoked the following comment in the House of Commons in November 1968 from Mr Edward Heath, who takes a strong personal interest in personnel and management matters: 'The system of promotion by the joint meetings of the Under-Secretaries, with the Permanent Under-Secretary in the Chair and Ministers present is, I believe, in many ways the most effective and for members of the service the most satisfactory system of promotion which exists in Whitehall.'

Lord George-Brown gives the impression that, when he arrived at the Office, everything was in a muddle which he proceeded to tidy up. Actually, when I came to London in February 1965 to discuss the hand-over with my predecessor, Harold Caccia, and the then Chief Clerk, Sir John Coulson, they were able to brief me not only on the appointments already approved by Mr

o

Gordon-Walker and Mr Stewart, but also the current thinking in the administration about the next one hundred or so people on the list in preparation for the time when proposals would be presented to the appropriate board. Punch-cards and computers have made this process a little less laborious, but a very personal watch has to be kept over mechanical results.

Of course the board and the ministers are not always right. Someone who is very good in country A turns out, inscrutably, to be much less good in country B. More frequently, a sudden severe illness, a new international job or the birth of a new country occurs, and overnight you have two round holes for which the administration can offer you at once three high-quality square pegs. The man who would have been perfect has just gone elsewhere (where he is also perfect). So not every posting can be ideal all the time. But ever since, under Derick Hoyer-Millar, I had first to do with appointments, I have been most impressed with the care and integrity with which the process is conducted.

As to the individual people mentioned by Lord George-Brown, obviously I do not want to go over past cases. I join with him now as I did then in great satisfaction that Denis Greenhill was designated as my successor. But I must remark that, if the case of Sir Con O'Neill only cost the Foreign Secretary an amiable glass of sherry, this is a great tribute to Sir Con's diplomatic tact, and an unconscious underestimate of the agonies of those immediately and not quite so immediately concerned.

My last comment is on structure. I agreed strongly with Lord George-Brown that the Foreign Office needed an expert economic adviser over and above the operational economic departments. Both he and I tried hard and failed to get one; we were competing with the inflated demand for economists in the earlier period of Labour Government, and no one was forthcoming. Later the problem was neatly solved by the Commonwealth Office contributing to the merged department an expert economic section under David Holland.

But I am doubtful about an array of home-based experts in the Foreign and Commonwealth Office, with little or no experience of service abroad, advising the department and the Secretary of State expertly on the business of other goverment departments. Ideally we could have more than we do. For instance, I started negotiations for a scientific adviser. But the scale on which British Government operates with the consent of Parliament would not allow any great extension of this, and experience in the United States suggests that there is a danger of multiple abrasions if there are too many checks and balances.

This is not a matter of 'breaking tradition'. One does this all the time. In 1967, because we did not think that export promotion was going ambitiously enough, we set up with the concurrence of the Board of Trade an Export Promotion Department, thereby breaking the traditions of both departments.

But I think that in Lord George-Brown's critique, a deeper psychological point is involved. There is a sentence in *In My Way* which I have found particularly thought-provoking. Speaking about getting the right people into the right jobs, Lord George-Brown says: 'Like everybody running a business, you tend to be pretty sure of the views of the men you have met and liked; rather doubtful about the men you have met and not liked; and very uncertain about the views of the men you have never met at all.'[4]

I see the point, and it may be valid particularly in politics. But it is not a principle I would apply myself. I always start a new job with the assumption that, if someone whom I don't particularly like is in a position of responsibility, there must be some reason why he got there, and the dislike may arise from some failure of judgement on my part as much as from some deficiency on his. Sorting things out on this basis may take longer, but I do not see how, in taking over a going concern, you can do anything else without unnecessary risk to justice or morale. The weaknesses will show up all right if the organization as a whole is any good.

This is not an 'old boy' attitude, but human commonsense. If things have to be done differently and people won't do them differently then you have your crisis and something has to give. But I do not, as if in some official Cold Comfort Farm, start by

[4] Lord George-Brown, *In My Way*, Gollancz, 1971, p.129.

suspecting the presence of 'something nasty in the wood-shed'.

Lord George-Brown read the Duncan Report and felt disappointed to find in it no 'genuine reform' of the Foreign Office. I wonder whether this is not a will o' the wisp. The truth is now that the Office goes on, in this rapidly moving age, 'reforming' itself all the time within the cramping limits of the 'magnificent slum'. I hope this spirit continues – the new arrangement wrung out of the Treasury about property abroad after so many years is a good example. But it is probably true that nothing ever reforms itself quite fast enough purely from within. The members of the service itself, individually and through their Association, and those genuinely interested outside, will have to keep the pressure going, knowing that there will never in the nature of things be a final answer.

Diplomacy and Ideology

One reason why the British people have found it difficult to measure what is going on around them is their dislike of thinking in ideological terms. It is odd that the British, with all their inventiveness and their facility for launching religious movements, should be this way. In British history the substitute for ideology has perhaps been the instinct to identify the next group in the queue for the removal of grievances, from the Barons in the Great Charter down to everybody left out in the social reforms of the twentieth century. This instinct is to be found even in religious controversy. By contrast, perhaps the only genuinely ideological interlude in the modern sense of the word was the short eleven-year Cromwellian 'reign'. Therefore if your real desire is to see a Communist Britain, it is no good saying 'I am a Communist. The more fruitful approach is, 'I am not a Communist but . . .' The failure to recognise that other people do think ideologically, not just in terms of philosophy but also in terms of method, can lead to frightening errors of judgement and policy. Anyone who has suffered from well-meant advice that a well-fed ideologue is less dangerous than a thin one knows that such advice is based on little knowledge of what happens in ideological societies. And the doctrine that national or economic interest is always stronger than ideology is likewise fallacious.

We need not spend long over Fascism and Nazism since both of them, in terms of Mussolini's Italy and Hitler's Germany, are still dead. But it is important to recall them for a general understanding of the twentieth century. Mussolini's Fascism was to a remarkable degree lacking in doctrine. The main doctrine was: '*Mussolini ha sempre ragione*' (Mussolini is always right). One searched in vain in Italian bookshops for anything comparable to *Mein Kamf* or *Das Kapital*. Indeed Mussolini has been quoted as saying, 'Fascism is a desire for action, and is action, it is not a party. For we do not believe in dogmatic programmes.' None the less, Fascism was a real thing and a dislikeable one. More importantly, once Nazism had started on its internationally aggressive way, Fascism had no alternative but to follow. It was the non-recognition of this, not only by Chamberlain but even by the infinitely more perceptive Vansittart, that caused hope to linger far too long of inducing Mussolini to stay out of major war.

On Nazism I was, like most of my countrymen, at first wrong. Feeling, like many, that the Germans had a case against parts of the Versailles Treaty, I had ploughed through *Mein Kampf* in 1939 and could not believe that anyone who came to political power could possibly go on like that. Perhaps in that day and age we did not take what passionate people wrote seriously or literally enough: nowadays we may be in danger of the opposite mistake. In any case *Mein Kampf* to some extent defeated itself by its incomprehensibility. But it did not take long, especially if you went to Germany, to see emerging something intensely evil in both doctrine and action. Even in 1938, however, the British public would not believe it. In this sense Neville Chamberlain, virtues and weaknesses, represented the British public. Failure to heed the right professional advice (unhappily the wrong professional advice was coming from Berlin) and the belief, not confined to Chamberlain, that personal contact could cure the disease, both contributed to the briefly popular débâcle of Munich. The basic mistake by those who misread the portents was the refusal to think in terms of the other man's ideology.

In the end the British public came to know all about Nazism and dedicated themselves to its destruction. It collapsed in 1945. Thereafter, unlike Mussolini's Fascism, it had a kind of ghastly half-life. This came partly from the lasting horror of what had been done and, worse still, done in cold blood, partly from the necessity for the German people, so many of whom had looked the other way, to learn what had really happened, and partly from the properly tenacious memories of the Jewish people. There were other less admirable reasons: a tendency by British people and communications media in less good times to reassure themselves with past heroics, and the assiduous repolishing of such memories by those minded to deflect criticism from the doctrines and actions of communist totalitarianism.

Communism

Manifestly the most important ideology of the time, and the one which persists, is communism. Beginning with the profound social analysis of Karl Marx, it established itself through a Russian conspirator of genius, Lenin, as the government philosophy and method of a great country. There followed the régime of the man whom Edward Crankshaw has described as a 'tyrant of genius,' Stalin, whose successors have alternatively demoted and rehabilitated him to the present day.

In analysing the nature of twentieth-century communism, it is wise to think back to what actually happened in 1917. The Russian Revolution took place in March of that year when, under military defeat, social unrest and administrative collapse, the autocracy abdicated. For the next seven months, the people of Russia enjoyed the only time of freedom in their history. Meantime the Germans accomplished that most brilliant short-term piece of political warfare, the transit journey of the communist conspirators from Switzerland through Germany to Russia via Sweden and Finland. And in October 1917, as people went to meetings and attended committees in Petrograd and Moscow, the communists took over. An election was held in February 1918 for a constituent assembly to draw up a new constitution. The assembly turned out to have a non-communist majority; this inconvenient nonsense was suppressed by force and never allowed to recur.

It is now necessary to consider why, despite this violent beginning and subsequent uglinesses, there was at the time and still persists a sympathy with the communist Soviet Union. I believe myself that the best explanation lies in the simple proposition that the events of 1917-18 represent to many a major triumph of 'us' over 'them' – 'us' being interpreted as those who are, or feel themselves to be, the oppressed elements of society. In Russia a group claiming to represent the majority had got rid of a corrupt and inefficient minority government. Their method of establishing supreme power within the revolution might seem crude and disfiguring; the hope would persist that authority might become more civilized as the revolution moved from self-defence to development.

This hope held on through the ghastly purges of the 1930s and created the illusion that the Soviet Union, in 1938, might be the ally which would keep faith with not only ourselves but with Poland and Rumania too. Ideologically this was not possible. On this point there could in the end be an approximation of view between Chamberlain and professional students of foreign affairs to whom, after all the stream of denunciations of Nazism from Moscow, the Molotov-Ribbentrop pact of August 1939 was shocking but predictable perfidy. The immediately subsequent contribution of the Soviet Union was to invade Poland, annex the Baltic States and attack Finland.

When Hitler kicked Stalin into the war on the allied side (and this is not too strong an expression), the Churchill Government in Britain acted entirely rightly in effacing the past and wholeheartedly welcoming the new ally. There then began a period in which, under necessary wartime censorship, the British Government, armed services commands and the Diplomatic Service had one view of the Soviet Union as an ally and the public another. To the public, the Russians were simply our massively intrepid if suspicious allies – very true as far as it went. But Government knew about the Katyn massacre. They knew all about the ghastly affair in 1944 when the Russians advanced to Warsaw, encouraged the Polish Resistance to revolt openly and then stood idly by while the Poles were massacred by the Nazis. This was cold-blooded doctrinal and class war at the expense of a gallant ally which had suffered so much already.

The post-war period would thus begin with the Government conscious and the public ignorant of things that had happened. And when for a short time the United States Government appeared to acquiesce in this ignorance, the situation nearly caused Mr Bevin to go out of office and tell the unbelieving world.

It was right not to precipitate the issue. But the Western hope of a German people, with lessons of Nazism so starkly before it, invited freely to elect a government of its choice faded into the imposition and maintenance by force of a communist régime in Soviet controlled Eastern Germany. Some thinking people then began to foresee the hard foreign policy and diplomatic road ahead. We would be confronted with a powerful government dedicated to the simultaneous pursuit of an expansionist national policy and the spread of Marxist-Leninist ideas and methods (both of equal importance), the whole being run by an interlock-ing directorate of the Communist Party of the Soviet Union and the national government apparatus.*

Soviet communism is a form of ideological imperialism, advancing methodically and usually cautiously from day to day and, as Lord Trevelyan has pointed out, ready for withdrawals if the going becomes too tough. Inside the Soviet Union, after more than fifty years of government based on Marxism-Leninism, with secondary adaptations, it is still found necessary to preserve the police state. Not only that, but the Soviet Union has not been

---

* In 1968, at the time of the invasion of Czechoslovakia, the Politburo of the Soviet Communist Party consisted of eleven people, Messrs Brezhnev, Kirilenko and Suslov representing the Party Secretariat, and Messrs Kosygin, Mazurov and Polyansky the Council of Ministers. Of the rest, Mr Podgorny was President of the Praesidium of the Supreme Soviet (ie Head of State) and the remainder had functional or geographical attributions representing for instance trade unions or geographical soviets. There is no suggestion that this arrangement is unreasonable; it simply illustrates the interlocking interests between the state and an explicit ideological party.

able to afford real relaxation in the European neighbourhood. Hungarian freedom had to be crushed in 1956; so, even more significantly, had the Czechoslovak experiment in 'free communism' in 1968. If this experiment had been allowed to prevail, there could have been a threat not simply to the defence cordon round the Soviet Union but to the whole police system itself. Because of the necessity to defend the system, 1968 joined 1830 and 1848 in the list of tragic landmarks in the history of freedom.

A conscious effort is made to efface by silence the memory of 1968. This cannot finally succeed, and a haunting memory resurfaced in 1972. But since in the two countries most concerned no expression of the views of any doubters is permitted, silence can be very potent.

It has been necessary to go through this analysis because acquaintance with both history and organization has a very direct bearing on policy and its execution. 1967–68 was the year of the rush for détente. Everybody longs for a natural Europe in which there is no artificial barrier between East and West. In these two years this longing burst its bounds. Not only did NATO pledge itself to détente, but sundry European governments had channels and methods they wished to try out. The cause was naturally popular, and diplomacy with its knowledge in depth had the unenviable task of forwarding the purpose while discouraging illusions. For détente must be of the head and heart, and it is no use pretending that social democracy as practised in the West and communism as practised in the Soviet Union are united in their approach to human and political fundamentals.

I am conscious at this point that I have talked a little glibly about 'freedom'. The term 'free world' was a good one while it lasted. But it included a number of passengers without tickets. Since then Western democracies have lost some of their confidence in themselves; they ask themselves whether they are really headed in the right direction. Have not communist countries 'solved' such social questions as unemployment and universal education? (Admittedly the Nazis had made similar claims.) Against this these countries have stunted intellectual (as opposed to technical) growth, slowed up the creation of wealth and, in the case of the Soviet Union, devoted an immense economic and industrial effort to the production of arms, an effort whose magnitude and purpose the common man in the Soviet Union is not allowed to question.

In the end this argument comes down to a profession of faith. I will express mine in the words of Sir Isaiah Berlin:

'The doctrine that accumulations of power can never be too great, provided that they are rationally controlled and used, ignores the central reason for pursuing liberty in the first place – that all paternal governments, however benevolent, cautious, disinterested and rational, have tended, in the end, to treat the majority of men as minors or as being too often incurably foolish or irresponsible; or else as maturing so slowly as not to justify their liberation at any clearly foreseeable date (which in practice, means at no definite time at all). This is a policy which degrades men and seems to me to rest on no rational or scientific foundation but, on the contrary, on a profoundly mistaken view of the deepest human needs.'[5]

Is there then nothing to be done? And am I basically anti-Russian? The answer to the first is that of course much has been done and much must and will be done. Partial control of nuclear tests and the Berlin Agreement of 1971 mean progress, even if the Berlin Agreement lets West Germans go to East Germany without giving East Germans any general licence to go to West Germany. But the Czechoslovak tragedy broke the 1967–68 détente euphoria and put the search on the right basis – a search for common interests where they can be found, and not for meetings of minds which will have to travel far before they really meet. Progress will be slow, above all because of the habit of secrecy in communist countries. It is fantastic to imagine what could happen in disarmament if the present popular disposition in the United States and Britain could be matched in communist countries. I have no doubt that public opinion here would insist on total openness about nuclear matters if others would do the same. Let us hope that such a day may yet come.

On my attitude to Russia, the late Kingsley Martin spoke

[5] Sir Isaiah Berlin, Four Essays on Liberty, 1969 ed., p. lxii.

once in the *New Statesman* about: 'Russophobe Foreign Office officials like Sir Paul Gore-Booth'. Kingsley and Dorothy Woodman were affectionate personal friends. Dorothy regarded me as Jekyll and Hyde; Kingsley spent a cosy Christmas with us in Delhi in 1963 when he was not well enough to continue his Indian travels. I was able to experience his habit of getting something brilliantly wrong for the hell of it.

Nobody could be 'Russophobe' – nobody, that is, who has read anything of Russian literature, studied Russian drama or had even a little contact with Russians unconstrained by political fear. I have indeed liked and respected many Soviet colleagues and their wives with their strong attachments to family ties. But I do share the distress of all those in my generation who would have liked to know these wonderful, richly endowed people better. And like millions of others I do not want a system, which has imprisoned the peoples of Russia and debarred them from spontaneous intercourse with the rest of the world, to be imposed on others with the connivance of innocent persons who do not understand or do not care to face the deeper things which that system represents.

Envoi Extraordinaire

I entered the Diplomatic Service two years after the Statute of Westminster formalizing the independence of the self-governing British Dominions, and left it four years before British membership of the European Community.

I do not think that in 1933 anyone could have prophesied events this way. In 1933, despite the advent of Hitler to power, people still felt in their bones that, after the slaughter of the First World War, there could not possibly be a second round. But as Nazi aggression mounted in Europe and Japanese aggression in China moved ahead in parallel, the awful realization dawned, hesitantly and by no means unanimously, that it might happen after all. Then, deep down, came further anxieties that whereas in the First World War the Asian flank had been protected by Japan, there must be real doubt whether, if a conflict came, the Empire or Commonwealth could be protected by the British

Navy and Air Force in the circumstances of the neutral America of the thirties and a hostile Japan.

But before this was put to the test, the British of my generation and their fathers went through an experience which, as students of our national history, we had never expected. We had read about danger and deliverance from the Spanish Armada and from invasion by Napoleon; in 1940 all of a sudden we did it again, and that year joined 1588 and 1805 as great dates in our national history. We must not bore our successors with it all and the old man has had to refrain from telling his son and grandson; but let them remember with quiet respect the magnitude of what we did.

We never had, in our history, so high a level of military leadership in all the forces as we developed by the end of World War II, and we have never had so high a level of national organization for a common purpose. Whatever anyone may say of the then social and economic system, it set a standard which will always bear study and, in many aspects, imitation.

As can hardly help happening, the succeeding years, while in terms of social progress dynamic and impressive, were in terms of external policy disappointing. Above all things, it took us and others a long time to understand the economic forces which condemned us to more than two decades of struggle against pressure on the national balance of payments. Meantime the nation proceeded on the task of withdrawal from Empire. In less than twenty years we accomplished it, not easily or tidily, but on the whole with good sense and skill. It is my view, unrealizable of course, that we should leave the Empire alone for a while. We live in a Tudor age, not a Victorian one. We understand violence, struggles between ideas, and the world of agents, counter-agents and double-agents. We promote exploration (of the mind this time, the earth having been discovered); we live with splendid music and lively theatre. On the other hand we do not feel the rush of that kind of enterprise which made Robin Cruikshank entitle his book on the Victorian age *Roaring Century*; we do not accept that a prodigious self-restraint can also impart, in some other direction, an equally prodigious outburst of energy.

We forget the patient hours spent by serious people dispensing justice under palm and pine and take refuge in deploring the social callousness of the Victorian economy and scoffing at funny Victorian clothes. It will be better to remember that, as empires have been measured, ours was as just and temperate as any. And let us not talk of a 'Lost Empire'; that is a piece of 'unthink' which implies that, if only we had been cleverer, Australia would still have been governed from London.

The change that was on its way did not come about through neglect of Commonwealth on the part of British governments. It was, rather, that Commonwealth countries as they neared and reached independence naturally wanted to explore political and economic contacts with third countries, contacts thought at least superflous and sometimes dangerous by the former administrators. Regional co-operation had its attractions and there was an urgent need for sources of finance and productive power which Britain could no longer provide. None the less the idea of Commonwealth persisted. Countries, formerly British dependent territories, showed a regular eagerness to become members. A quite unfounded routine reproach addressed to British Governments is that they forced models of Westminster on people for whom these models were unsuited. In fact countries emerging into independence from British rule would have been deeply insulted had they been offered anything else – or less.

If the Commonwealth was one centre of our post-Second World War pattern, the special relationship with the United States was another. This is a subject invariably clothed in immense difficulty by popular writers at the time of American presidential elections. It is, in fact, very simple. One part of the special relationship, the dynamic interlocking of war effort with its close-knit personal friendships, inevitably faded away after the Second World War, not necessarily to the advantage of the world or the two countries themselves. The other half, reaffirmed by President Nixon, and including the ability to talk naturally at cultural, practical and governmental levels is, in so far as anything can be, eternal unless, of course, either party loses its democratic institutions.

Our third centre was Europe. But in 1950 Europe was third in comparison with the other two in order of British interest and preference. The idea of united Europe was, after so many centuries of divided Europe, scarcely credible and not necessarily attractive. In any case immediately post-war British Governments, including that of Winston Churchill, had, it seemed, too much on their hands to take on experimental Europe as well.

History, however, is not British history, and the years 1945 to 1952 were the years of American ascendancy. The policy, resources and diplomacy of the United States were used to put back on its feet as much of the world as could be reached. The Americans could not save Hungary or Czechoslovakia for freedom of choice, nor bring Chiang Kai-shek to reason, though they were able to bring him to safety. The American achievement was outstanding and will survive all misrepresentations. From 1952, however, the touch of Eisenhower and Dulles did not have the skill and instinct of Truman, Marshall and Acheson, and the Russian hydrogen bomb and sputnik of the 1950s showed that world power was not to be exclusively American. But the world went on expecting great things of the United States, and if I had been the devil, 'going to and fro in the world,' seeking to harm the United States, I would have assassinated President John Fitzgerald Kennedy. I would have done so not on any claim that he was the best president the United States ever had, but because he was the president the newly developing world wanted America to have, and that was almost equally important.

Whether Kennedy could have 'solved' Vietnam we shall never know. President Johnson, for all his underestimated merits, could not, and we had in the 1960s the sad spectacle of the exuberant nation of the late forties temporarily losing confidence in itself. American intellectual liberalism, hitherto an important influence for enlightenment, finding itself cumulatively oppressed by the iniquities of Senator Joseph McCarthy, the magnitude of internal problems hitherto skated over and the hopelessness of Vietnam, appeared from outside to become rancorous and, on external affairs, oddly naïve in its diagnosis of world affairs and with alarming tendencies towards a non-defined neo-

isolationism. Since that time President Nixon has broken new
ground with the Communist empires, with results which have
altered the world balance of forces. At the beginning of 1973
the President, by hard bargaining, had achieved an agreement on
Vietnam of a kind which many Americans had considered out of
reach and much of the world came to the conclusion, hitherto
shirked by many, that South Vietnam at least had a case.

As democratic countries wrestled with new economic and social
problems, Marxism-Leninism, while showing itself a formidable machine for the accretion, maintenance and expansion of
power, approached its autumn as a satisfactory system of government. In the Soviet Union it has shown notable organizational strengths, particularly in the system for the maintenance of
the communist leadership in power. But Marxism-Leninism as
now interpreted and practised has shown marked rigidities in its
relations with human beings which induce increasing restlessness.
It remains a hate-system. There have to be imperialists, Zionists,
saboteurs, bourgeois – all of them people to be crushed, if
necessary by force. But as the Christian persecutors of heretics
ultimately found, man will not live like this for ever.

Moreover, the implied equation, 'power = good, money = bad,'
is a false one as both Lenin and Khruschev perceived, The
acquisition of money or power (one of them does not necessarily
mean the other) corresponds to instincts in many human beings;
both forces corrupt, money if unlimited, power if unrestrained.
But some controlled power is needed to administer anything
from a tribe to a world and some controlled reward for the use of
money as opposed to its confiscation increases wealth and welfare.
To maintain the Russian Marxist-Leninist structure as now
understood requires a police state. The result is subdued questioning or evasion in Eastern Europe and the rather sudden emergence
of Alexander Solzhenitsyn as the most important Russian of our
time, a position from which he cannot now be dethroned.
Perhaps Prague spring ushered in Moscow autumn in a city
described by a writer in the magazine *Foreign Affairs* as a 'declining
ideological capital'.

Meantime the power structure will not change quickly, and

because of this the relationship between the United States and the Soviet Union exhibits an interesting ambivalence of sentiment. The mutual doubts and antagonisms remain and yet it clearly feels exciting to be half of a top league of two, and the two countries have an instinct that in these terms they can talk to each other as no other two countries can. This being so, those who are of an ultra-left persuasion are naturally in search of new movement. One obvious direction is Maoism with its promise of continuing revolution but also carrying within it the seed of ultimate standstill. Hence the attraction of anarchy or at least of total destruction of all existing systems and institutions. Thus Marcuse rejects any idea that existing systems and institutions have any virtues at all, and Rudi Dutschke and others speak of the 'imposition of socialist poverty' as a desperate and indeed logical consequence of the overthrow of existing systems.[6] This presents a very gloomy prescription for developing countries and for countries dependent on international trade.

The events and forces described so briefly above were perceptible as the new Labour Foreign Secretary, Mr Michael Stewart, took office in 1965. One asks oneself whether the Foreign Office had any basic doctrine with which to cope on behalf of Britain with the emerging world pattern. On this I have two pieces of evidence. The first is a note jotted down in March 1966. It says simply: 'Learning to become a second-rank power.' This seems trite now. It was not trite then. The idea reappeared four years later in the Duncan Report with Britain described as 'a major power of the second order'. On my last day in office in January 1969, a radio interviewer suggested to me that Britain had come 'all the way down'. Rather tiredly I insisted that this was exactly what we had not done. The object of policy had to be to ensure that a great nation could stop half-way down and establish itself as a second-level power with real tasks to perform and obligations to fulfil.

Another note, scribbled, I think, in preparation for a talk with the Duncan Committee, reads: 'Keeping the nation's nerve.'

[6] On the theory of 'the worse, the better,' referred to by Solzhenitsyn in *August 1914*, p.150.

This phrase evokes very vividly the memory of how, at that time, disturbed public emotion sometimes took almost hysterical form over Vietnam, over Nigeria and Biafra, over security, over student power. With this was coupled Parliamentary and public convulsion about Aden, the Falkland Islands and General de Gaulle. There was a real task for some institution thinking in world terms to keep cool and to devise and execute within the limits of knowledge, money and power, progressive but realistic policies to advance long-term interests rather than to satisfy immediate emotions. There is no great glamour about this. But we tried to do it, and not without success.

There was a double difficulty. The first was the explosive nature of the late sixties, a period in which all sorts of frightening truths were on our thresholds. You can take some at random. We would soon be able to lunch in London and breakfast in New York. The whole of civilized living might soon be changed by the simple truth that human sexual intercourse would no longer be fraught with what used to be called 'consequences'. Yet by the end of the century the population of the world, already bearing hard on its resources, would have increased by another fifty per cent.

Simultaneously with a growing realization of these truths, we passed, on the narrower professional field, through a bad time with the media of information. Fierce competition within the press and between the press and broadcasting had bad effects on quality, particularly in the handling of external affairs. The growth in attraction of television led to emphasis on photographic rather than genuine values, and this constantly distorted the news and its meaning. Below this surface lay more technical problems which were neither understood by the public nor solved. One, out of the control of the media, was the impossibility of a correspondent posted in a dictatorship or communist country reporting totally frankly and being allowed to stay there indefinitely. This meant that reporting tended to be more critical of our friends and ourselves than of people who wished us less well. It is also not generally understood that, while the object of a newspaper may indeed be to inform and entertain us and to preserve our liberties, its object will also be to sell more newspapers. This will influence the selection and treatment of its material, and its indignations, such as those about the necessary degree of confidentiality in government proceedings, will not always be purely righteous or objective.

During the Nigerian civil war, a statement was made by General Ojukwu which local British officials and the correspondent concerned knew to be wrong. It was reported and broadcast without comment and had a disquieting effect on people at home. The explanation given was that General Ojukwu was an important person, so what he said must be reported. With all respect, this explanation stated the problem but did not solve it.

The relationship between the Foreign Office and the BBC is naturally one of sensitivity, given the Foreign Office's sensitivity about external relations and the BBC's about its independence. I was immensely grateful therefore to Sir Hugh Greene and Mr Charles Curran for much co-operation in getting the mutual relationship on to a basis where we could talk very frankly to each other without treading on toes. But I left the problem with the feeling that its subtleties are even now not fully understood. The problem is not one of the relationship between two bodies, but the far more difficult one of the relationship between a public corporation in an exposed semi-monopoly position and the national interest.

I do not want to widen this analysis into a review of the Corporation as a whole, except to say that technically and aesthetically it probably produces the best television in the world, and I strongly oppose any idea that it should be split up, since it profits immensely from economy of size. Nor can one take too much issue with what is called 'creative' (though it is often destructive) art, since you have to choose among what people at any time will actually create. Impartiality is a fragile and precious thing and what one can do is, by virtue of a quarter of a century's assiduous listening, to detect that all important element, the impersonal, collective subconscious of an organization which does not have an editorial policy. The sub-conscious of the BBC in my time as Permanent Under-Secretary was hard on the Americans, benefit of the doubt (at least until 1968) to the Soviet Union, unenthusiastic about Europe and the Concorde project, lenient to demonstrators, hard on the police and so on. This meant a tendency in the treatment of external policy vis-à-vis the British public to operate slightly but consistently to the disadvantage of the policy of the government in power. I have much sympathy with what Lord George-Brown says on this point to the effect that too jealous an upholding of the BBC's independence, which is immensely important, can cause rejection of information, comment and advice from people, eg government officials, who really do know quite a lot about a situation, as this is their profession. This can be very harmful. I doubt whether anyone in government can or ought to 'induce' (Lord George-Brown's word) the BBC to reconsider this line; in good American the BBC does not induce easy. But I can only insist that it is a real problem and not a capricious gripe, and that it argues for a somewhat more conscious editorial control in the Corporation over what is said and how it is said when the country as a whole is involved.*

Having said this much in criticism, I should like here to repeat my previous public offer of a private Oscar to the Radio 4 programme *From Our Own Correspondent*. In this programme, as opposed to a minute and a half's dramatic news, a correspondent gives you five minutes of perspective on what is really happening. I must also pay tribute to individuals in the media who did outstanding work towards the wider understanding of world affairs, like Christopher Serpell for his authoritative work as diplomatic correspondent of the BBC, a most important and necessary office, and Peter Jenkins of *The Guardian*, for his thoughtful columns in that paper which went beneath the surface of the news. But by and large, diplomatic correspondents did not have a good time.

The effects of modern conditions on the basic principles of

---

* If anyone thinks I am overstating the fragility of impartiality, I suggest a small exercise. First read a small news item saying: 'At the Gasbourne Electric Power Station, ten men have come out on strike.' Then re-read, after inserting before 'come' the small word 'already'.

diplomacy has been less radical than is often thought, if only because those principles consist of listening intelligently, reporting honestly and using personal relationship to promote mutual understanding, and they remain the same as ever. There are differences of function, notably the vast increase in commercial diplomacy. In method a very obvious development is the far greater participation, due to rapid air transport, by members of the government, i.e. politicians, in diplomatic contact and negotiation. This is to be welcomed particularly since countries with less highly developed civil service and diplomatic practices naturally find it congenial. But it can lead to dangerous illusions about friendships between political leaders across international boundaries. It is of course very welcome when two political leaders united in a major cause admire and understand each other, as did Churchill and Roosevelt in the early and middle stages of the Second World War. But a leading statesman is bound to place first the interest or presumed interest of his country and the policies requisite to maintain himself in power, and it is no use supposing that the best personal relationship in the world is going to upset this. Many political leaders felt and indeed maintained that they had the particular touch needed for 'dealing with' General de Gaulle; given the General's convictions and policies this was just not the case.

Friendships across international boundaries at the official level are perhaps less difficult to maintain, but anyone with experience knows that if there are strains between governments, the mutual relationship cannot escape some fall-out.

The new diplomacy involves far more than the old in the way of direct contact at the expert level between countries. Mixed delegations of diplomatic and home service officials have become the rule rather than the exception and afford a healthy opportunity for absorbing each other's talents. Particularly with British membership of the European Community, this practice will produce a breed of people who are neither exactly national nor international in outlook. As Europe gets accustomed to itself, a knowledge of a number of European languages will prove very valuable and, a point too radical for the conventional wisdom, the study of Latin will be highly practical and help-ful.

With the decline in the absolute and relative power of Britain, some very able members of the service have left it for other occupations. Some diminution of interest compared with past experience, a period of poor promotion prospects and of official remuneration lagging behind that in the private sector, not to mention family problems (notably over education), have promoted this trend. But recruiting continues excellent, and I do not foresee the British Diplomatic Service lacking talent, willingness or effi-ciency – or work to do. To do this work well, it will need to retain the essential, if in these days largely unspoken, concept of service.

If I had to project what may come out of this restless period of world history, I would start with my hope in the late sixties that we might be fighting the Thirty Years' War, national and ideological, of the seventeenth century all over again without actually fighting, and that in the end we would reach the Treaty of Westphalia without casualties. Given the differences which have developed in the communist community (not, by the way, 'socialist'), this could happen, and the politics of President Nixon have promoted this objective. I only hope that this forecast may not be upset by the evolution of Asia including the Middle East into a zone of traditional power-political struggle just at the moment when Western Europe seems to be emerging from it. One can only trust that those in power realize the danger, and that Soviet-Chinese rivalry which already involves India and Pakistan will not spread outside Asia as European rivalries once spread over most of the World. In any case the inconceivable horror of nuclear war may make such war impossible.

One wishes very much indeed that the United Nations could resume the kind of status and activity foreseen for it in 1945. Tribute is rightly paid to its development and aid programmes and the many international activities of the specialized agencies. But, in the end, an organization based on the Charter stands or falls by its political performance and, as long as national and (one must never leave this out) ideological differences remain as they are, progress will be desperately uphill. For that reason, the few successes, like peace-keeping in Cyprus, will remain immensely precious.

In the international economic field, immense concentrations of capital have become technologically necessary in a sense different from that conceived by Marx. This could lead to a greater degree of mutual economic and commercial comprehension between communist and mixed economy societies than some years ago seemed possible. But the gap in outlook on the fundamental liberties and duties of mankind will remain harder to fill, at least to the satisfaction of those who prefer their realities to be real.

If the political succession to the various fascisms, to Nazism and to contending communisms is to be in the line of democratic development and of an avoidance of both the ruthless and the bleak society, it will have to be consciously sought, and on the basis of a compassionate social democratic (no capitals, no hyphen) political philosophy. Under it, human freedom must be maintained and necessary redistributions of wealth must stop short of the point of destruction. Such an order cannot ignore either power or wealth, but must severely discipline both. And social democrats will have to realize, however reluctantly, that in their relations with communists, when it comes to human rights, they stand there not as allies or neutrals but as targets.

As we try to achieve and uphold a society of the kind I have sketched, we must not despise the sinister threat of 'decomposition.' We have to contend with exploitation by the greedy, the malign, the cynical and the jealous, some of whom may receive applause from outside, of the inborn tolerance of most British people combined with their insistence upon their right to see, hear and experience practically everything. We must accept that there are elements in our own society who are impatient of progress by argument and consent and are anxious to see the social democratic experiment fail. And the chief instrument is to pervert natural controversy into intransigent antagonisms within our society – between races, between generations and between social groups.

All this is highly relevant to the success or otherwise of British external policy and diplomacy. For when a country cannot exercise power directly and when it is mature enough not to use its weakness for political blackmail, its diplomacy must in the end depend for its effectiveness on the standing and performance of the government it serves and the people it represents. Many individuals round the world look to Britain not for the exercise of power but as a country of a certain experience and wisdom which ought to move into the future with a stable political instinct and method. For this reason we cannot afford constant industrial strife, productive lethargy or the temptations of moral neutrality. A society in which the immense preponderance of people from the Queen downwards are employees cannot afford the old-fashioned indulgence of class warfare. This indulgence is largely rejected by the young, but is unconsciously assisted by those who classify our society in terms which consolidate antagonistic personal attitudes. If weakening and divisive tendencies persist, including a flaccid intellectual anti-patriotism, those who work hard and intelligently for the wider community, and there are many of them, will eventually give up.

Amid these immense world political, economic, and technological forces and their structures, how is the individual going to fare? This is the be-all and end-all of prophecy and of course I do not know. But I can offer from a remote personal past a small word of cheer. As an undergraduate on a Balliol Players tour of the west of England, I was one chilly summer morning lying in the open in my sleeping-bag trying to think of reasons for not getting out of it. A delightful Welshman, Oscar Hughes, walked up to me looking blue and shivery. Rather ponderously I said, 'Oscar, I see you are face to face with the grim, stark realities.' Oscar had an art of pronouncing with a twinkle. 'Pretty tough on the grim, stark realities,' he replied.

Perhaps this is the spirit in which the individual has to face his major responsibilities as well as his minor troubles. Maybe the grim, stark realities do pay some attention to individuals who refuse to be imposed upon.

I am sometimes asked 'But what do you think you yourself "achieved"?' I do not know the answer to this either. But I do recall a choice anecdote by that wonderful historian of the Southern

Confederacy in the American Civil War, the late Dr Douglas Southall Freeman. Talking with one of the last survivors of the lost cause, a private soldier of the Army of Virginia, Dr Freeman asked what he thought of it all now. The soldier replied simply: 'I ain't ashamed of nuthin' I done.'

Having failed to pass the Harold Nicolson test of diplomacy, I know I should not pass this one either. But it is not a bad ideal.

Index